WITHDRAWN

CHINA'S TECHNO-WARRIORS

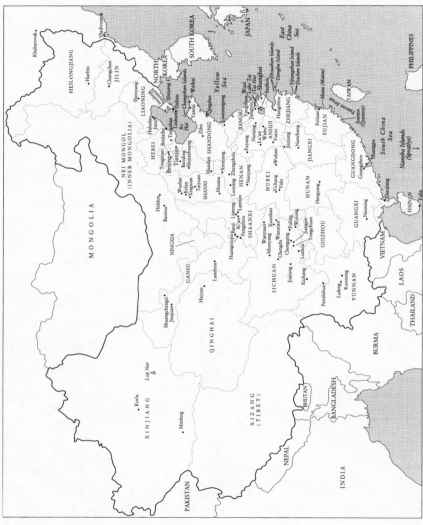

People's Republic of China with Major Military Industry Sites. From *China's Strategic Seapower: The Politics of Force Modernization in the Nuclear Age*, John Wilson Lewis and Xue Litai, Stanford University Press, 1994.

CHINA'S

TECHNO-WARRIORS

NATIONAL SECURITY *and*
STRATEGIC COMPETITION *from the*
NUCLEAR *to the* INFORMATION AGE

Evan A. Feigenbaum

STANFORD UNIVERSITY PRESS
STANFORD, CALIFORNIA 2003

Stanford University Press
Stanford, California

© 2003 by the Board of Trustees of the
Leland Stanford Junior University

Printed in the United States of America
On acid-free, archival-quality paper

Library of Congress Cataloging-in-Publication Data

Feigenbaum, Evan A., 1969-
  China's techno-warriors : national security and strategic competition
from the nuclear to the information age / Evan A. Feigenbaum.
      p. cm.
Includes bibliographical references and index.
  ISBN 0-8047-4601-X (alk. paper)
  1. China—Military policy. 2. National security—China. 3.
Technology—China. I. Title: National security and strategic
competition from the nuclear to the information age. II. Title.
    UA835 .F44 2003
    355'.033051—dc21

                                                    2002004727

Sections of chapter 2 were previously published in an article in *The China Quarterly*, Number 158,
June 1999; sections of chapters 4, 5, and 7 were previously published in *International Security*,
Volume 24, Number 1, Summer 1999.

Designed by James P. Brommer
Typeset by ICC in 11/14 Garamond and Helvetica Black

Original Printing 2003

Last figure below indicates year of this printing:
12   11   10   09   08   07   06   05   04   03

For my parents and teachers:

Alan and Arlene Feigenbaum,
    who pointed the way.

John Wilson Lewis and Michel Oksenberg,
    who led me there with grace and boundless
    confidence in what I could achieve.

CONTENTS

14 PAGES OF PHOTOGRAPHS FOLLOW PAGE 68

FIGURES, TABLES, AND PHOTOGRAPHS

14 PAGES OF PHOTOGRAPHS FOLLOW PAGE 68

ATM	asynchronous transfer mode
B-ISDN	Broadband Integrated Services Digital Network
CAD	computer aided design
CAM	computer aided manufacture
CAS	Chinese Academy of Sciences
CAX	computer aided exercise
CC	CCP Central Committee
CCP	Chinese Communist Party
CIMS	computer integrated manufacturing system
CMC	CCP Central Military Commission
COSTIND	Commission of Science, Technology, and Industry for National Defense
CPSU	Communist Party of the Soviet Union
CPV	Chinese People's Volunteers
CSC	CCP Central Special Commission
DF	Dongfeng (code name for China's ICBM)
EDFA	erbium-doped fiber optic amplifier
ELG	Electronics Leading Group
EU	European Union
FBI	U.S. Federal Bureau of Investigation
FYP	Five-Year Plan
Gb/s	gigabits per second
GDP	gross domestic product
GLD	PLA General Logistics Department
GMD	Guomindang
GO	General Office
GPD	PLA General Political Department
GPS	global positioning system
GSD	PLA General Staff Department
HTGR	high temperature gas-cooled nuclear reactor
IAE	CAS Institute of Atomic Energy
ICBM	intercontinental ballistic missile

ICT   CAS Institute of Computing Technology
IRBM   intermediate-range ballistic missile
JL   Julang (code name for China's first SLBM)
JPL   Jet Propulsion Laboratory (California Institute
            of Technology)
LG   Leading Group
LSI   large-scale integration
MB   megabyte
Mb/s   megabits per second
MEI   Ministry of the Electronics Industry
MIPS   million instructions per second
MIT   Massachusetts Institute of Technology
MND   Ministry of National Defense
MOST   Ministry of Science and Technology (post-1998 SSTC)
MPP   massively parallel processor
MPT   Ministry of Posts and Telecommunications
NASA   U.S. National Aeronautics and Space Administration
NCIC   863 National Center for Intelligent Computing
NDIC   National Defense Industrial Commission
NDIO   National Defense Industries Office
NDSTC   National Defense Science and Technology Commission
NPC   National People's Congress
OEM   original equipment manufacturer
PLA   People's Liberation Army
PRC   People's Republic of China
PWR   pressurized water nuclear reactor
R&D   research and development
RMB   renminbi (Chinese currency, measured in "yuan")
S&T   science and technology
SAR   synthetic aperture radar
SDH   synchronous digital hierarchy
SDI   Strategic Defense Initiative (U.S. anti-ballistic
            missile program)
SLBM   submarine-launched ballistic missile
SMP   symmetrical multiprocessor
SPC   State Planning Commission
SSBN   nuclear-powered ballistic missile submarine
SSTC   State Science and Technology Commission
STC   COSTIND Science and Technology Committee
STLG   Science and Technology Leading Group

STM	synchronous transport mode
TT&C	telemetry, tracking, and control (for missiles and satellites)
UK	United Kingdom
U.S.	United States
USSR	Union of Soviet Socialist Republics
VLF	very low frequency
VLSI	very large scale integration
VSAT	very small aperture terminal
WDM	wave-length-division multiplexer
WTO	World Trade Organization

I began working on this book as a graduate student at Stanford University in the mid-1990s. Living at the epicenter of Silicon Valley from 1991 to 1997, the core years of the go-go 1990s, I watched from a ringside seat as a technological transformation—the rise of the Internet economy—matured, evolved and, in some areas, began to sputter. Technology did not yet occupy the central place in U.S.-China relations that it has taken on in the years since I left Palo Alto. By the end of the 1990s, allegations of nuclear espionage and illegal technology transfers by U.S. companies, the Cox Committee report of the U.S. Congress, China's accelerating military modernization and swelling defense budgets, and the contentious domestic politics of both countries had catapulted technology issues front and center in U.S.-China relations. Still, even in the mid-1990s, technology already seemed to me to enliven some of the most compelling issues in the study of contemporary China.

Narrowly construed, this book tells a discrete story about patterns in China's development of strategic technology from 1949 to the present. But the book has a much larger purpose, as do I—to begin to pick apart some of the ties that bind together several of the biggest issues in contemporary Chinese public policy and U.S.-China relations. The two primary objects of my interest—technology and the role of the Chinese military—touch many of the contradictions that have been inherent to the Chinese Communist state since its founding, as well as patterns shaping China's emergence onto the global stage as a major power.

Consider, for example, that technology wedges across foreign and domestic policy, national security and economics, the role of government and its relationship to an emerging private sector, and the push-and-pull between raw power politics and cautiously reasoned public governance. The Chinese military itself is an extraordinarily ecumenical institution. It anchors China's national defense, but also stretches across the Chinese system, playing an important, if sometimes ambiguous, role in politics, industrial development, diplomacy, and society.

On the surface, then, this book appears to tell a story about contemporary China's development of high technology. But it also seeks to trace the interconnections among several threads that have made and sustained the Chinese state since 1949: warfare, diplomacy, economics, ideology, bureaucracy, management, politics, and the role of leaders in shaping public governance.

I readily admit that the book has taken too long to complete. Thus, it is something of a relief to at last have the chance to thank those who have shaped my ideas. I take the greatest possible pleasure in doing so, and express my deepest gratitude to them all for their advice, support, and friendship.

My research for the book benefited enormously from access to two unique Chinese primary sources: a collection of memoirs written by the designers and program administrators of nearly all of China's major weapons systems—strategic and conventional, ground, naval, air—as well as the electronic, space, and computer infrastructure requisite to the development and deployment of such weapons; and my very intense conversations over nearly eight years, from 1993 to 2001, with a large number of Chinese military officers, industrialists, scientists, engineers, politicians, and entrepreneurs. These individuals are spread across China—in places as far afield as Inner Mongolia, Shaanxi, Jiangxi, Sichuan, Hubei, Gansu, Shanghai, and Beijing. I have met them on field trips to China, in the United States, and elsewhere. We have debated. Sometimes, we have agreed. Often, we have disagreed, sometimes very strenuously. But even when we agree on little else, these Chinese specialists have deeply influenced my understanding of how those who have played the major role in forging China's ongoing technological transformation think about their work, achievements, and failures, and the world at large. They have had a profound influence on the overall framework within which I understand and analyze Chinese politics.

I first became interested in China in Mrs. Devens's eighth grade social studies class. It has been a long journey since, shaped by remarkable and generous individuals. Above all, I thank my two teachers of Chinese politics, John Wilson Lewis and Michel Oksenberg. John continues to teach me about China, but his more important lessons have been about friendship and the need to always follow through on the courage of our convictions. John once wrote me: "Be experimental, be eclectic, and be bold! Don't be apologetic, and don't let current fads govern your scholarship!" His example continues to mold not only my scholarship, but all aspects of my life and work. I only hope someday to live up to his example. The world lost Mike Oksenberg to cancer just as I put the finishing touches on this book. I miss him desperately, as do so many others whose lives he touched.

Yet I know Mike would have been proud of this work that he helped to shape. He was my very toughest critic, but he also set the standard. Mike was the first person who believed deeply in me as a professional. On my first day of college, he boldly enrolled me in his doctoral seminar in Chinese politics. For a teenager transitioning into the university environment, it was an extraordinary opportunity to be surrounded by graduate students who had decided to make a career out of Chinese studies. Simply put, John and Mike have inspired me, and led me to my current career through their example. I cannot adequately express what I owe them, but have dedicated this book to them for their inspiration and many kindnesses (as well as those of Jackie Lewis and Lois Oksenberg). Both men have changed my life in more ways than I can possibly relate.

I am grateful, too, to the other members of my Stanford doctoral committee: Condoleezza Rice, David Holloway, and Michael May. As my first teacher of comparative politics and first teaching supervisor, Condi Rice taught me that comparative and international politics must always be mutually reinforcing. Condi is the person I have continually run to in order to share my excitement when things are going right, as well as to seek advice and a sympathetic ear when things have seemed to be going very wrong. David Holloway is, quite simply, the model of the scholar I hope someday to become. Mike May kept me grounded, and asked the toughest questions I have ever encountered; above all, he brought the unique perspective of a nuclear physicist to my circle of doctoral advisors.

My colleagues at Harvard University's John F. Kennedy School of Government have shaped my work, my worldview, and many of my ideas about public policy. Above all, I single out Robert Blackwill, my mentor in the truest and best sense. Bob has taught me more about professionalism and how to get along in this world than has virtually anyone else who has come into my life. I owe Bob a great deal, and only hope he knows how very grateful I am for the extraordinary confidence he has repeatedly placed in me. Also at the Kennedy School, I must thank Graham Allison, Ashton Carter, Joseph Nye, Steven Miller, and John White, who have put their confidence in me and offered inspiration, guidance, and support.

I have been fortunate to learn from the wisdom of so many senior colleagues over the years. I single out Paul Godwin, David M. Lampton, Jonathan Pollack, Robert Ross, David Shambaugh, Ezra Vogel, and Xue Litai, who have taken the time to teach me about China, the promise of policy-informed research, and the past and future of our common endeavor in the study of contemporary China. For their friendship and guidance, I hope someday to repay David Bachman, Karl Eikenberry, Charles Wayne Hooper, and Roy Kamphausen. William Perry graciously sat down with me to check and embellish my account of his contacts with the Chinese in the early 1980s, just as he himself was settling back into university life. For comments on various portions of the manuscript, or for their unusually helpful comments at my public presentations of some of this material, I am grateful to John Frankenstein, Wendy Frieman, Merle Goldman, Houston Hawkins, Ellis Joffe, Nicholas Lardy, Barry Naughton, and the late Benjamin Schwartz. My friends have always kept me sane, grounded, and happy. They are too many to name, but for their impact on the development of this book, I wish especially to thank Jeremy Buchman, Daniel Drezner, Tracy Fitzsimmons, Frank Gavin, Paul Haenle, Kurt Hemr, Lorelei Kelly, and Amy Zegart.

For financial support, I thank the Center for International Security and Arms Control (now, Center for International Security and Cooperation) and the Center for East Asian Studies at Stanford University. Both centers provided dissertation and fieldwork support, and the former provided a home for four happy years. I am also grateful to the John M. Olin Institute for Strategic Studies and the Robert and Renée Belfer Center for Science and International Affairs at Harvard University. Both provided me with a home during my first professional years, and offered financial support. At Stanford University Press, Muriel Bell and Judith Hibbard shepherded the manuscript to publication and improved the book along the way.

I met the amazing Kim Foerster just as I was completing this book. Every day since has been filled with sheer joy, and our road ahead is more exciting still. The last word—unquestionably the most important—is reserved for my parents, Alan and Arlene Feigenbaum. Together with my two teachers of Chinese politics, I dedicate this book to them. And whether or not they know, they are the reason that I began it. I am a product of my parents. When I was seven or eight, my father inscribed a book of Civil War history with an exhortation to love history as he does in order to understand the past and, perhaps, make history myself in the future. My mother has been my greatest supporter, my confidante, my friend, and my rock. When all else fails, as well as when everything is smooth, it is my parents to whom I turn. I have no bigger fans. And they have no greater admirer than their son. They are truly my best friends. Mom and Dad: thank you most of all!

Cambridge, Massachusetts
June 4, 2001

Author's note: Shortly after I completed this book, I entered into a period of government service. The views expressed in this book are those of the author, not the U.S. Government.

A European friend, a scientist, asked me: "Your economy is still underdeveloped. How can you propose to undertake such a thing?" I told him: "We look at this from the standpoint of long-range development issues and national interests. It isn't a matter about which we can afford to be nearsighted." . . . If China hadn't had the atomic bomb, the hydrogen bomb, if we hadn't launched satellites, it couldn't be said that China is an influential great power. We wouldn't occupy our present international position. . . . China cannot afford to fall behind. China cannot afford *not* to be engaged in spite of the fact that we are poor. Because if you aren't engaged, if you don't develop in these areas, the gap will only become greater and it will become extremely difficult to catch up.

—DENG XIAOPING
October 24, 1988

Some Chinese-American scientists suggested . . . that China should focus on biotechnology. This is because America already has a tremendous lead in information technologies but since biotechnology is just getting off the ground, China would have an easier time becoming competitive. . . . When Premier Zhu Rongji went to the northeastern province of Jilin, the provincial leaders reported to him: "The Americans have so much! Soon the seeds will all belong to them. The seeds that our people improved for so many years become the property of the Americans just by the insertion of a gene!" . . . Zhu replied, "This is very important. The government is giving RMB 500 million to start transgenic plant work."

—CHEN ZHANGLIANG
Vice Chancellor and Professor of Biology, Beijing University
December 1999

Now, we confront a new situation of major power competition in high technology construction. . . . We need a strong sense of mission and urgency. We must have the kind of strategic vision that led to the development of nuclear bombs, missiles, and satellites.

—LI JINAI
Political Commissar, General Armaments Department
People's Liberation Army
June 28, 1999

chapter one

INTRODUCTION: NATIONAL SECURITY
AND STRATEGIC TECHNOLOGY IN CHINA

In the spring of 1987, the founding father of China's strategic missile program, Qian Xuesen, told colleagues that China must steel itself for a century of sustained "intellectual warfare." In the twenty-first century, Qian declared, national power, economic prosperity, military security, even social welfare, will require that a country be "in the lead in science and technology." If not, said Qian, "it will be difficult for [a country] to maintain its . . . international standing." Thus, national self-sufficiency in high technology might determine both the sustainability of China's development experiment and its place in the international balance of power.[1]

In the industrialized world, it is a commonplace to invoke sports metaphors to connect technology to national power and purpose. In 1961, President John F. Kennedy challenged Americans to mobilize for what was subsequently dubbed a "race" with the Soviet Union to the moon. Analysts of industrial policy in the European Union speak of "winners" and "losers" in the competition for state largesse. French bureaucrats steer government support toward industries and companies designated as France's national "champions." In China, however, it is military metaphors, not sports analogies, that are the convention. Science and technology are said to be "a kind of warfare." China's progress "on the technology front" is seen as intimately connected to the global strategic balance.

This use of military metaphors is not a linguistic peculiarity. It reflects the central role of the military in China's emergence as a modern state, especially in the period since the establishment of the People's Republic of China (PRC) in 1949. The military, its requirements, and the cadre of technical specialists who came to professional maturity under military patronage were the motive force behind China's development of high technology from 1949 well into the era of reform (1978–). China's most prominent and sophisticated technicians worked in military programs, under the patronage of the People's Liberation Army (PLA). Nearly all of the country's modern industrial sectors—from electronics to aerospace to space-age plastics and chemical synthetics—relied on military investment, the sponsorship of leading generals, and the commitment of China's senior political leaders to nurture an industrial base in support of national security.

Militaries often play this role in industrialization and state-building.[2] Even Silicon Valley—a region widely regarded as the archetype of private entrepreneurialism—owed much of its emergence as a technological powerhouse to a fortuitous combination of "plentiful sunshine, and even more plentiful government money" from military electronics contracts.[3]

Yet in China, it was not inevitable that the military should have come to play this role. Rather, China entered the nuclear age as a poor country, strapped for investment and facing challenges in nearly every facet of its economic and political life. Chinese missile engineers mastered inertial guidance even as Chinese peasants plowed their fields by draft animal and hoe, much as their ancestors had for three millennia. Imbued with revolutionary fervor, but confronting backwardness on nearly every front, China's Communist leaders committed themselves from the earliest days of the People's Republic to a broad-based modernization of their country. Inevitably, the military's powerful claim on a limited pool of resources, and its policy and technological priorities, became a subject of intense political controversy.

To sustain these priorities, key leaders of the PLA argued for more than simply new and better weapons; they fashioned a powerful set of ideas about the relationship between the state, technology, and national power in China. These leaders nurtured a novel set of management solutions to meet the challenges of implementing their ideas. Ultimately, a uniquely military approach to China's development became embedded in the ideologies of the country's political leadership, in policy choices about national security and economic development, and in the organizational solutions adopted to put these policies into practice.

Among leading politicians, technology became yoked to sweeping conceptions of national power and purpose; it became a strategic question touching China's very destiny as a great power. Out of the crucible of China's efforts to develop strategic weapons amid poverty and backwardness emerged a distinctive political ideology through which Chinese leaders came to link technological accomplishment directly to the country's position in the world and its relative prestige. Chinese policy came to emphasize self-reliance at all costs—an approach to technology that flowed directly from concerns about national security. The People's Republic has always supported purchases from abroad or the coproduction of technologies with foreigners, even during its periods of greatest international isolation. But the government has held freedom from external dependence as its absolute, consistent, and unwavering aim. Organizationally, this national security approach to technology depended on innovative management institutions that coupled top-down Stalinist-style mobilization to structures and incentives more akin to those in contemporary Silicon Valley, based on initiative, personal incentives, risk-taking, and networks of cooperation among experts.

This book tells the story of how and why the Chinese military came to play such a dominant role in China's economic development. It explores the powerful position occupied by the military and its technical advisors in economic and institutional debates, and details the programmatic and organizational solutions they advocated to shape China's overall political and economic trajectory.

But the primary purpose of the book is to explore and explain a paradox. This distinctly military approach to technology and development emerged during China's period of greatest external threat, from 1950 to 1969. Yet these ideologies, policy choices, and organizational solutions have continued to manifest themselves even as China has come to enjoy perhaps its most benign strategic environment in more than 160 years. In the 1980s and 1990s, military priorities became derivative of larger economic development choices. Still, policy makers continued to emphasize a distinctly mobilizational pattern of investments and ideas about technology, even though China's socialist political economy was simply eviscerated by change. China's remarkable post-1978 economic transformation is one of the most dramatic stories of policy reversal in the twentieth century. Despite this, the dominant strategies and institutions for high technology industrialization developed at China's moment of greatest external threat were carried over—even reinvigorated—at a time of peace and massive economic and social transformation. These ideologies, policies, practices, and organizational solutions persist to the present day.

This has not simply been the consequence of inertia and entrenched ideas. Rather, the persistence of these patterns in China's economic strategy, technology policy, and defense planning are the result of a complex interplay between domestic power politics and leaders' efforts to hedge against the fact of China's weakness. With a technology base that remains ten to twenty years behind international standards in so many areas that Chinese leaders consider to be "strategic," strategists must hedge against uncertainty in a world whose international politics could change radically at any time. Although there is no question that institutional inertia remains powerful and deeply entrenched in China's political economy, the sheer complexity of the relationship between national security, economic development, public policy, and political ideology in contemporary China remains striking.

In explaining these relationships, this book weaves together four stories. First, it examines Chinese views of technology over fifty remarkable years. Chinese leaders came to view technology as intrinsically strategic, and thus they defined, in large part, China's standing and power in the world by its technological prowess. When the United States threatened China with attack, Chairman Mao Zedong shelved his antipathy to the notion of weapons as a deciding factor in warfare: "If we are not to be bullied," he declared, "we cannot do without the bomb."[4] Likewise, Chinese leaders concluded that, since technology is linked to national power, they must break forever the shackles of dependence on foreigners. When the Soviet Union refused to assist China to develop an indigenous nuclear submarine fleet, Mao told Moscow's ambassador that China would spare no expense or effort, "even if it takes ten thousand years."[5]

These are perhaps the two most prominent themes in China's modern relationship to technology—technology as a matter of grand strategy and self-reliance as a strategy of technological development. Yet self-reliance, in particular, has contained built-in contradictions since China has been forced to *further* integrate with foreign partners to gain access to many of the technologies it has sought to indigenize. Indeed, it is this contradiction that defines much of China's recent struggle to modernize. Although Chinese technological and economic policies have long reflected a deep-seated nationalism, technological backwardness has repeatedly forced policy makers to compromise this principle. Particularly today, as China integrates into the global economy and the world trading system, its government must square a circle. To build a strong nation requires compromises that further integrate China into the very international system that crude variants of Chinese nationalism so distrust.

Second, this book explores the role of the military in Chinese life— political, economic, and social, not merely strategic. As the chapters that follow argue, those PLA visionaries who integrated national security with economic development sought, above all, to create an encompassing system—an organic development strategy that could both meet the PLA's weapons requirements and build the country's industrial base. But while this vision encompassed more than a concern with weapons, it was nonetheless a distinctly military vision and flowed directly from issues of national security and grand strategy. These visionaries had to confront opposition not just from civilian constituencies, but even from within the PLA.

In telling this story throughout the book I hope to enliven an old debate. In the traditional Chinese worldview, the military was relegated to the margins of political and economic life. Yet soldiers were integral to imperial politics in the last decades of dynastic decline. Throughout the ostensibly "republican" 1920s, warlords ravaged the political landscape. Armies led by a professional military man, Chiang Kai-shek, reunified the country, but only temporarily as it again broke apart during nearly two decades of foreign invasion, internal revolution, and civil war. When the Chinese Communist Party (CCP) won power in 1949, China had weathered some ninety years of nearly continuous armed conflict. Even China's industrial and organizational development reflected the military tenor of the times: the country's first modern industrial facilities were arsenals and its first Western-style organizations were restructured military units, such as Yuan Shikai's Beiyang Army. The military, in the words of historian Ralph Powell, was "the first aspect of Chinese society to reflect markedly the impact of Western civilization."[6] Imported ideas about development, Western science, modern technology, even Western industrial and organizational methods, came to provide the basis of political and professional legitimacy among Chinese military elites. Likewise, in the contemporary era, the PLA has been a key player in virtually every major political event since 1949.

However, its role—and that of its leaders—in Chinese politics and development planning, though obviously significant, has remained murky. This book seeks to elucidate the military's impact on national issues, not merely military and foreign-policy questions. Thus, our second major story is the role of the military as a political force and parochial interest group behind China's industrial and technological modernization.[7]

Third, the book explores the evolution of public management institutions in China, most notably the emergence of open and flexible conceptions of organization as an alternative to bureaucratic hierarchy. We are accustomed to thinking of the Maoist state, in particular, as either haphazardly decentralized, as in the Great Leap Forward and the Cultural Revolution, or else Stalinist in its centralized industrialization and regulation of its citizens' lives. The reality is more complex, particularly with respect to economic policy, where there always existed flexible alternatives that included a mix of incentives.[8] But in China's strategic weapons programs, led by PLA managers and their technical advisors, administrators created amid great secrecy a unique management structure that later became a national model.

This structure included comparatively flat hierarchies; extensive horizontal coordination across bureaucratic boundaries; competition; networking; the open exchange of information; peer review; standards-based performance metrics; encouragement of risk-taking behavior; and the political acceptance of failure. That this management arrangement has roots in weapons programs is so little recognized by Chinese officials today that they routinely promote its key features as a "major reform" of the Chinese system. In fact, public management in China—especially the emergence of open, flexible, network-based management methods—owes a considerable debt to the PLA's efforts to come to terms with the technological dimensions of China's national security. The story of how that management structure emerged and developed lies at the heart of the chapters that follow.

Fourth, the book explores the technological dimensions of the rise of Chinese power. For seven years after the Tiananmen Square tragedy of 1989, virtually all significant issues in U.S.-China relations became subordinate to American concern about China's denial of human rights and suppression of political dissent. It was not until after China's 1996 missile exercise in the Taiwan Strait that high technology issues came increasingly to replace human rights at the center of the contentious and often politicized debate about America's China policy. International discourse, too, has come increasingly to focus on the technological aspects of China's emergence onto the global stage: the effect of technological development on PLA force planning, on China's capacity to coerce Taiwan, on its role within the World Trade Organization (WTO), and on a variety of issues related to international trade and export control. Allegations concerning satellite exports and nuclear espionage, in particular, demonstrate the centrality of high technology to the debate about China's place in the world. This makes it more important than ever to explore links that may bind China's national technological and industrial policies to its approach to security and development.

This book also addresses a number of concomitant issues against the backdrop of China's national security and economic development debates. How has the understanding in China of the connection between technology and security changed as the past priority of militarized growth has given way to the rapid expansion of a commercial economy since the late 1970s? Who is responsible for making important technology decisions in China? Where and how has the PLA succeeded in dominating China's technology debate? How do Chinese leaders think about the relationship between technology and national power? Has political change affected their worldview? Can contact with international technical circles and exchange programs affect the Chinese approach to national high-tech strategy and investment? What does China's approach to technology mean for the rise of national power? Finally, what are the technological dimensions of the relationship between other countries—particularly the United States—and an emerging, more powerful China?

The structure of the book is straightforward. Chapter 2 surveys the legacy of China's militarization of the 1950s to 1970s. Early thinking about technology quickly became eclipsed by national security imperatives. How and why this happened, how various investment rationales derived from national security and development concerns interacted, and how militarization affected state investment, development policy, and management institutions during the period from 1950 to 1975 are all examined in this chapter.

Chapter 3 explores why China began to demilitarize its national priorities in the late 1970s and early 1980s. It probes this development on several fronts: the evolution of national security strategy and changes in defense policy; PLA demobilization; shifting domestic political currents; and the evolving role of science in development planning during these years.

Chapter 4 analyzes the impact of demilitarization on the PLA leaders and strategic weapons technicians who had long dominated China's high technology strategy. It also explores how renewed contact with the global economy and international networks of scientists and industrialists introduced new ideas into China's policy community. This gave Chinese specialists a new—and comparative—perspective based on their understanding of the ties between industry, science, the military, and the state in other countries. Ultimately, leading military-technical elites, not civilians, provided the initial push that made possible China's shift from narrowly weapons-focused innovation and investment strategies to more comprehensive approaches.

Chapter 5 turns to responses to changed political and economic conditions at home, as well as the introduction of influential new paradigms from abroad. In tracing an analytic history of China's experience with strategic technology, it reveals that military concerns have increasingly become derivative of the government's drive to build a more broadly based technological infrastructure. As this shift took place, at the head of the policy agenda emerged a top-priority critical technologies effort, established in 1986–87 and known as the 863 Plan, for the year (1986) and month (March) of its origin.

Chapter 6 explores the limits and boundaries of China's legacy of military developmentalism. First, it details the expansion of government technology programs, arguing that these have had a deeply self-limiting impact on China's technology base. Then, it investigates the continuing tensions between external dependence and Chinese ambition, especially as China accelerates its integration into the international economy and the global trading system associated with the WTO. Finally, it examines the intensely divisive domestic politics that began to emerge around important high technology sectors in China in the mid-1990s.

Chapter 7 concludes the book. It offers a caution to those who doubt the commitment of China's leaders to redress their country's weakness at all costs, or else belittle China's ability to make stunning technological breakthroughs against great odds. The history of military developmentalism in China should be sobering. With each periodic crisis that has arisen to expose Chinese weakness, China's leaders have time and again shown that their commitment to remedy that weakness is total. Yet this chapter also suggests that China's ambitious agenda for technology modernization will require a fundamental break with past legacies. State-centric, highly nationalistic approaches to technology indigenization are, in the end, deeply self-limiting. In China, the persistence of these approaches contrasts starkly with entrepreneurship and the globalization of technological knowledge. This makes the structural adjustment associated with China's entry into the WTO especially significant. Chapter 7 sets the four stories woven together throughout the book against a larger backdrop of technological change, the rise of Chinese power, contemporary international politics, and the future of U.S.-China relations.

Ultimately, to understand China's technological transformation—especially, the technological dimensions of its increasingly complex political-military and strategic agenda for the twenty-first century—it is necessary to appreciate the deep interconnections between China's strategic weapons programs and the elite that came of age within them; the evolution of its development strategy; the changes in its military doctrine; the dynamics of its domestic power politics; and the transfer of the "strategic" vision for high technology from the narrowly military side of the Chinese system to the foundations of the system itself. This book aims to contribute to our understanding of these interconnections and of their likely impact on China's development and its evolving role in the world.

part one

LEGACY

chapter two

MILITARIZATION AND ITS LEGACIES, 1950–1975

Military planners in nearly every country have influenced national strategies of investment and economic development. But in China during the first quarter century of Communist rule, the influence of the military was not confined to weapons, as is usual, but extended into the very heart of a vast debate about the nation's overall economic development priorities. Almost from the founding of the People's Republic in 1949, the PLA played a broadly developmental role in national economic and political life. An understanding of the origin, content, and evolution of that role remains important today for two reasons: it raises new questions about the impact of the military (as well as sectors and programs with military implications) on Chinese politics, industry, science, and education; it also highlights the historical basis for the enduring influence of generals, their technical advisors, and various national high technology programs on the course of China's overall economic trajectory.

As early as 1949, but particularly in the wake of the decision in January 1955 to acquire an indigenous nuclear deterrent, Chinese military scientists and their patrons among the PLA's ten marshals and leading generals began to offer their own preferred development policies for specific critical economic sectors. These proposals, which became a focus of intense political debate, were closely associated with strategic weapons elites and their PLA patrons. They emphasized high technology within the economy writ large and particularly stressed critical technologies planning by the central

13

government in Beijing. They also relied on crude conceptions of "spin-off" from military to civilian industries and "trickle-down" from critical technology sectors to the wider industrial base.

Most important, this military-associated approach directly integrated national security concerns with economic development priorities. It took China's relative standing on the international stage as a reference point for purely domestic economic policy choices. Critically, it depended on a strategic view of industrial policy and the role of national investment and government seed money. In this respect, the package of development ideas associated with the Mao-era strategic weapons programs took on many of the features that, in other contexts, have been termed "technonationalism." This is the notion that technology is fundamental to both national security and economic prosperity, that a nation's development policy must have explicit strategic underpinnings, and that technology must be indigenized at all costs and diffused system wide.

Thus, although strategic considerations shaped China's most important domestic industrial investments in the earliest years of the PRC, the rationales for choices in military industry became increasingly complex over the course of the Mao years (1949–76). By the early 1960s, just five years after the Politburo's January 1955 decision to acquire an indigenous nuclear deterrent, these efforts by some military constituencies had grown in scope and sophistication. These groups, now clustered around the nuclear weapons and delivery system programs, promoted a national investment strategy that openly sought to integrate national security concerns with purely domestic economic development goals. This strategy would lay the foundation for a series of important programmatic and investment choices that redirected scarce government resources away from certain critical sectors and toward others. And as a result, this strategy became the focus of intense opposition from competing military and civilian interests throughout the first four decades of the People's Republic. These leaders and their technical advisors split over the question of whether investment in "strategic" technology should be given priority. Their strategy, which favored investment in the most sophisticated technologies, was pitted against the notion that, in view of China's scarce resources, priority should be placed on more basic technologies and more broadly based strategies of economic development. In short, at issue was precisely where—and with what trade-offs— China should invest in its future technology base.

CHINESE TECHNONATIONALISM AND THE MAO-ERA
DEVELOPMENT DEBATE

The main policy alternatives of the Mao-era economic debate, which has received extensive treatment in the secondary literature, slighted agriculture in favor of industry, though in varying degrees, and each depended on a specific web of supporting interests and developmental assumptions.[1] Three alternatives were associated with civilian constituencies:

- A Soviet-style model of central planning focused on heavy industrial sectors, such as iron, steel, and petrochemicals. This approach sought to finance heavy industrialization via the extraction of surplus from China's rural masses. Agricultural development would then be financed through the reinvestment of industrial inputs generated by heavy industry.[2]
- An eclectic program, associated especially with the early 1960s and the ideas of Chen Yun, a leading Mao-era economic official. It mixed market with planned mechanisms and focused greater attention on light industries, agriculture, smaller units of production, and certain types of monetary incentives.[3]
- A "radical" or mass-based alternative premised on decentralization, local "self-reliance," the reproduction of complete systems in various areas, egalitarianism, and human initiative.[4]

From the mid-1950s forward, military leaders and their technical advisors stepped directly into this debate with an alternative strategy of their own. Initially, these leaders had little intrinsic interest in economic matters. But forward-thinking figures, such as Marshal Nie Rongzhen, soon reformulated their package of defense technology investments as a comprehensive strategy with implications that reached beyond defense.

As scholars of China's defense industrialization have long understood, military science became a favored sector that received top priority on talent and other resources. But Marshal Nie and his aides went a step further, and four decades later, it is clear that the influence of defense on China's economic and technological trajectory was not merely a by-product of the co-optation of China's best resources by defense work. It was also a matter of policy design. Strategic weapons programs, Nie and his circle argued in the 1950s and 1960s, should not simply reflect national security needs, but should also directly, explicitly, and comprehensively integrate security with core economic development concerns. These programs, Nie argued, could thus represent more than a pocket of excellence working to respond to pressing defense needs. In fact, they could lay the foundation of a truly systemic high technology industrial and science base that would promote China's overall industrial, scientific, and institutional development.

THE KOREAN WAR AND THE DIMENSIONS OF THE PROBLEM

Initially, this high-technology–oriented approach to development grew out of the PLA's strong interest in industrial modernization anchored in battlefield experience. As a variety of seminal studies of the Chinese military have demonstrated, the roots of the military's role in Chinese technology planning lay in the Korean War of 1950–53. In five major campaigns on the peninsula, the PLA paid perhaps the harshest and most immediate price for China's poverty in modern industry. Not surprisingly, the generals' rude introduction to advanced technology during the war thus became the breakpoint in the PLA's post-takeover shift toward Soviet-style emphases on hardware and mechanized tactics.

The strategic weaponeers' leap into China's comprehensive development debate, however, represented a radical departure for a military leader and his circle. For although China's experience in Korea led senior generals into debates about modernization in narrow defense contexts, the broader developmental concerns to which Nie Rongzhen gave voice were less clearly anchored in PLA traditions. Nie's more expansive approach can be traced to expensive delivery system programs that followed the Politburo's decision to acquire nuclear weapons. While the drive for nuclearization first began to involve the PLA in debates about economy and society broadly construed, follow-on programs to develop and deploy land- and sea-based delivery systems changed the stakes entirely.

Still, the Korean War was the decisive turning point in early thinking about technology, science, and advanced industry because it instantly shattered nearly all of the battlefield myths of a politically powerful military high command.[5] Terrain and geography made warfighting difficult and the conflict quickly developed into a "meat grinder" for Chinese forces, no less than for United Nations units. Although the Chinese People's Volunteers (CPV)[6] comprised some of the best divisions in the Communist army, within only seven months of China's entry into the war, by "June 1951, the CPV forces in Korea, largely as a result of General James Van Fleet's counteroffensive in May, had suffered an estimated 577,000 casualties, including 73,000 non-battle casualties, and had surrendered 16,500 prisoners of war. Moreover, they had suffered heavy losses of materiel and [according to U.S. intelligence estimates] were 'becoming increasingly dependent upon the USSR for logistic support.'"[7]

In a memoir published in 1990, General Hong Xuezhi, one of the founders of the PLA's post-1949 logistics system, recalls that the CPV's Fifth Campaign on the peninsula—a campaign designed primarily to stabilize Chinese positions near the 38th parallel—led to an overhaul of the logistics system because of the heavy casualties suffered by Chinese forces.[8] The logistics problem was sufficiently acute that the Central Military Commission (CMC), China's highest defense policy body, undertook to reorganize the entire logistics system for the war, creating a unified CPV Logistics Command under General Hong, which was placed in close coordination with PLA home forces in the Northeast China Military Region.[9]

In fact, the logistics problems confronting Hong's new command were intimately connected to larger deficiencies in PLA organization for warfare. Toward the end of the Chinese civil war, PLA forces, particularly those under the command of Lin Biao in northeast China, had become increasingly mechanized as the army adjusted to new forms of warfare by shelving the mobile guerrilla tactics of the anti-Japanese war. Chinese films from the period show mechanized PLA forces working in coordination with infantry units in massed ground attacks. In Korea, the challenges of mechanization proved much greater. On the battlefield, PLA light infantry proved no match for American heavy armor. Likewise, poorly coordinated and under-mechanized logistics and supply units were stretched to the breaking point as battle lines extended further down the peninsula toward the 38th parallel.

Although some of the logistics problems were apparently solved by the creation of Hong Xuezhi's reorganized command, the war revealed to Chinese military leaders a host of larger deficiencies and convinced them of the need for technological modernization virtually across the board. Thus, in the words of Alexander George, who interviewed Chinese prisoners of war for a RAND Corporation study, "drawing upon large quantities of Soviet military equipment and military advisers, the PLA commander in Korea [Peng Dehuai], began modernizing the PLA even while the war continued in a desultory but painful fashion on the bleak Korean terrain."[10]

"In general," John Wilson Lewis and Xue Litai note, "the trauma of the 1950–51 losses forced the PLA to rely ever more heavily on advanced technology and professionalism, even while its leaders clung to the language of fighting a people's war with a people's army. As part of the change, the PLA emphasized fixed defensive fortifications and brought in heavy weapons, including tanks and artillery. The Chinese equipped and trained an air force with 1,800 aircraft, including 1,000 jet fighters by mid-1952, in what the military historian William Whitson has called a process of 'modernization under fire.'"[11]

These trials had important and immediate effects on Chinese leaders: The war certainly drove them to a greater reliance on the Soviet Union for the transfer of defense technology, loans for industrial investment, the construction of new industrial facilities, and assistance in the development of an indigenous military industrial base. At the same time, doctrinal differences erupted full-force within the PLA, although the precise tenor and scale of the disputes remain difficult to gauge even five decades later. As early as 1952, Liu Bocheng, a hero of the civil war, began to deliver a series of now-famous lectures to division-level officers at the PLA's new Military Academy in Nanjing (Nanjing junshi xueyuan) that offered a theoretical rationale to undermine Mao's doctrine of "man over weapons." After the Korean armistice, the practical impact of American firepower combined with Liu's theoretical insights to establish what Lewis and Xue have termed a "new baseline of knowledge" for military professionals. The academy began to teach the "lessons" of Korea in the classroom and nurtured an entire generation of Chinese senior officers on the notions of "modern," mechanized, technologically oriented warfare that had emerged from the PLA's brutal encounter with American technology in Korea.[12]

Most important, Chinese leaders began to explore vigorously the utility of an indigenous strategic weapons capability. In 1949, the Chinese had largely assumed the Soviets would provide an umbrella of nuclear protection. For example, in July 1949, a full three months before Mao declared the establishment of the People's Republic from atop the gate at Beijing's Tiananmen Square, his second-in-command, Liu Shaoqi, on a secret visit to Moscow, requested a tour of Soviet nuclear facilities. Liu was refused by Stalin, who instead ordered that Liu's group be shown a film that purported to show a Soviet nuclear test.[13] In fact, the Soviets did not successfully test their first device until August, and the film was a fabrication. But Stalin's message was unmistakable: the Soviet Union can provide its allies with a nuclear umbrella; the American atomic monopoly has been broken.

By 1950, the Soviet nuclear umbrella was apparently an established fact. However, perhaps because of disagreements during the Korean War, the Chinese remained suspicious of Soviet willingness to guarantee China's security with the ultimate weapon.[14] As Lewis and Xue have argued, although "Mao welcomed [the Soviets'] protection . . . he believed, nonetheless, that the United States, which would not risk a nuclear confrontation over marginal territories such as Korea or Indochina, might well do so if it came to a showdown with [Chinese] forces. And should nuclear weapons be used, would the Soviet Union risk its national survival for its Chinese ally?"[15]

By 1954, then, the Chinese leadership had tentatively begun to discuss the need for an indigenous nuclear weapons capability. Numerous Chinese memoirists have told us that American nuclear threats during the Korean conflict were felt in Beijing as a form of blackmail. A 1952 report from Nie Rongzhen, then serving as chief of the general staff, to Premier Zhou Enlai suggested defense measures in response to the possibility of nuclear attack.[16] Bo Yibo, a leading economic planner, has noted that the first Taiwan Strait crisis two years later sharply escalated the immediate sense of external threat within the leadership, which led to the planners providing an increase in military expenditure for 1955.[17] The year 1954 also marked the first important step in China's development of a nuclear industry. Together with China's top economic planner, Li Fuchun, China's former commander in Korea, Peng Dehuai, proposed to the Politburo that China acquire with Soviet assistance its first nuclear reactor and cyclotron.[18] In this sense, Korea and the Strait crisis certainly held important lessons for China's leaders.

For Chairman Mao, the escalating sense of external threat, principally from the United States, must surely have been coupled with growing suspicion of his Soviet ally. This would deepen and grow, even as Mao ordered his subordinates to press the Soviets for expanded technological cooperation and aid. Meanwhile, individual PLA commanders, as Lewis and Xue poignantly note, had learned in Korea "firsthand the devastating might of modern arms and the high cost and probable military irrelevance of earlier revolutionary doctrines. Both the requirement for and the upper boundary on the modernization of the Chinese army were being created largely by the level of foreign technology: what was arrayed against them and what they could hope to obtain."[19]

These effects from the Korean War helped produce what became perhaps the three most important themes of China's early technological construction. First, the demand for ever-greater amounts of Soviet assistance led to the emergence of a symbiotic relationship between external dependence and indigenous development of advanced technology. The cleavage between high levels of reliance on Soviet assistance and even higher expectations for that assistance led Chinese leaders to rethink the place of technology development in their own indigenous allocation priorities.

Second, the doctrinal debate sparked by China's experience in the Korean War left space for the emergence of a military elite devoted to the acquisition of advanced technology. Because this elite was able to connect technology development to weaponization and thence to national security, its leaders and political patrons had greater room to maneuver within the Chinese political system than did similarly inclined civilian elites who also faced the ideological opposition of radicals to elite science, an opposition that remained nearly constant throughout the history of the Communist state. The evolution within the military system of genuine political space for science and technology not only served as an incubator for Chinese science; it insulated and protected the scientific enterprise, and the physical safety of scientists, during periods of domestic crisis. This lent much greater continuity to the work of military scientists and engineers than that enjoyed by their civilian counterparts. In this way, amid the topsy-turvy world of politics in the Mao years, military scientists and their patrons at the top of the PLA officer corps emerged as guardians of experimentation, the scientific method, and technological development.

Third, the dissatisfaction of China's leaders with the level of Soviet assistance and their consequent decision to acquire indigenous strategic weapons systems produced a constituency within the top political leadership that was supportive of the PLA's ideas for the development of advanced technology. As government resources grew increasingly strapped through several economic crises, the emergence of this constituency gave military scientists and engineers a voice in national political debates and enabled them to win a continuing increase in the share of national wealth. This allowed the elite's patrons in the PLA to link the development of military industry to larger debates about national development strategy. Military technologies thus became a matter of development policy, not merely national security planning. These three themes, which flowed directly from the lessons of China's Korean War experience, largely define the history of China's military industrial development.

THE MILITARY AND THE MODERNIZING VISION: LIU BOCHENG, NIE RONGZHEN, PENG DEHUAI

The difficult experience in Korea clearly convinced most Chinese commanders of the need for broad-based military modernizing.[20] Many Chinese sources credit the commander of Chinese forces in Korea, Peng Dehuai, with being the catalyst for systematizing this sentiment within the PLA.[21] But it was in fact Marshal Liu Bocheng who, in his lectures at the military academy in Nanjing, gave both doctrinal and spiritual expression to the modernizing current in the post-Liberation Chinese officer corps.

By the end of the 1950s, Marshal Liu's vision had laid the basis for two competing military concepts of technological modernization. The first emphasized raw military hardware; it grew out of Marshal Peng's initial struggle to modernize China's conventional forces. The other vision, which came to have a much broader, truly national and developmental scope, emerged several years later from the strategic weapons and auxiliary technology programs led by Marshal Nie Rongzhen. Both of these modernization agendas came to compete, not just with each other but with a number of alternatives articulated by civilian economic planners.

Liu Bocheng and the Modernizing Impulse

Marshal Liu's role was seminal. He was an important revolutionary hero.[22] As commander of the Second Field Army during the last stages of the Chinese Civil War, Liu played a major role in capturing southwest China. But what contributed most to his reputation was that he, together with Marshal Chen Yi, led the PLA to victory in the Huaihai campaign, the decisive pre-Liberation battles in which PLA forces crossed the Yangzi River and pushed southward to the Guomindang capital at Nanjing and then on to Shanghai. Liu had also played an influential role in the CCP in the 1930s, and had lost an eye, apparently in his exploits on the battlefield, a source of both admiring nicknames and much general respect within the ranks.

After 1949, Liu was assigned to oversee the training of a successor generation of officers at the new military academy in Nanjing.[23] While the evidence reveals Liu welcomed his new assignment, he also intended to use it to come to terms with some of the contradictions between PLA doctrine and practical battlefield experience. The PLA leadership's original intention had been to return Liu to Beijing to serve as chief of the general staff. But Liu was nearly sixty and had tired of administrative work. "I have already served four times as chief of the general staff," he is reported to have said. "Let me go run a school."[24]

In Nanjing, Liu wrestled with the doctrinal implications of the effect of technology on warfare and of the CPV's encounter with a superior version of military technology in Korea. He began with a look at the Chinese military classics, including works by Sun Zi and other early Chinese strategic thinkers.[25] The real change in warfare, Liu argued, had come with the introduction of new forms of technology in the modern age. Chinese soldiers had long been acquainted with the importance of military technology, although Maoist doctrine explicitly stressed the human element. Western scholars tend to mock the notion of "man over weapons." In doing so, however, they fail to recognize the large element of contradiction in Mao's thinking. The "message Mao imparted to his inner circle," Lewis and Xue write, "and to those who built the nation's retaliatory forces was far different: whatever they have, we must have."[26] But it is easy in retrospect to dismiss what was in actuality the enormously stifling effect of Maoist doctrine on innovative thinking in the Chinese officer corps. When Liu gave his lectures in the early 1950s, Mao's military thought had not yet ascended to the biblical proportions it would assume in the 1960s. Nonetheless, Liu had to struggle against an incipient Maoist orthodoxy in attempting to turn the attention of younger officers to problems about which Maoist thought offered little but dismissive (albeit morale boosting) aphorisms.

Marshal Liu, by contrast, took the technology gaps in PLA force planning very seriously, both in doctrine and practice. He also connected the need for high technology to military professionalism. Wars in the modern age, he argued, cannot be fought without technology. And there is no such thing, he declared, as a "people's technology" or a technology of the masses. Technology, Liu told his students, has no class character. A proper proletarian army could win victory only with proper equipment and proper training. "Because modern war and modern technology are one and the same," he argued, it is critically important to have "high-quality personnel."[27]

To illustrate his point, Liu frequently offered a historical analogy that backhandedly undermined Maoist assumptions about the virtues both of numerical superiority and of commitment in the absence of professionalism. During the 1905 Russo-Japanese War, Liu told his students, the Tsar had pledged one trillion rubles to the purchase and construction of battleships, "but his marshals and generals knew nothing of science." Russian officers and enlisted men had received poor professional training and knew little about their equipment or military technology more generally. The Japanese, Liu concluded, had won the war because they *did* understand technology and science. Japanese commanders recognized, he contended, that commitment, numbers, even the mere possession of technology, in the absence of scientific knowledge and a professional understanding of technology, would prove meaningless on the battlefield.[28]

A solution to China's technological backwardness, he told colleagues, was to study those who had successfully attained advanced knowledge. Mao himself had argued that soldiers must blend theory with practice, including their own experience. But Liu believed that this extended further than the soldier's individual experience on the battlefield. The Chinese army must also study American methods of warfare, he argued.[29] The dispatch of a number of his students to the front lines in Korea not only reinforced this belief but, via their personal communications with him, gave him grist for personal reflection, as well as future lectures.

In 1951, Liu convened three conferences at the academy to study the lessons of the first year of the Korean War. The conferences coincided with the CPV's Fifth Campaign in Korea—precisely the campaign that Hong Xuezhi has told us inflicted so much physical damage on Chinese forces and led to a substantial rethinking of PLA priorities in technology and logistics. Debate apparently was intense, and later that year, students who may have been in attendance received a rude transition from theory to practice when Peng Dehuai requested the transfer of some forty-four academy students to the front lines and to headquarters command.[30] Liu's official biography notes dryly that this provided his students with "abundant warfighting experience" (*fengfu de zuozhan jingyan*). But the reality is that academy graduates received a trial by fire.

Liu had asked that these forty-four students return to the academy after the war to lecture on their experiences, but some, including officers who later became top leaders of the PLA, did not wait so long. Qin Jiwei, later

China's defense minister, wrote Liu from the battlefield, where he was serving with the Fifteenth Army of the CPV's Third Corps. Qin extensively analyzed the tactical situation, as well as experience in command, communications, and logistics, three areas that posed enormous problems for CPV commanders. Yang Dezhi, one of Liu's oldest colleagues, who would soon become Peng Dehuai's deputy commander in Korea and a future chief of the PLA general staff, sent Liu detailed descriptions of his attempts to coordinate infantry with artillery and tank maneuvers. "We've essentially overcome the unwillingness of many in the CPV to adjust their thinking to encompass special [more modern] armaments," Yang wrote. Many officers in fact complained that they had too little artillery. Liu took this as evidence of a lesson well learned. "If in the past anyone believed that their knowledge didn't accord with the actual situation in Korea," he said, "that problem has now been solved." The realities of the CPV's encounter with modern technology on Korea's battlefields provided "a treasure house of experience" with which to train future officers.[31]

By the middle of the 1950s, then, Liu and his protégés had begun to lay the foundations for a revision of conventional Maoist military doctrine. Their revision turned on three assumptions based on the CPV's Korean experience: any future conflict would employ "sophisticated" (*jianduan*) weaponry; such a conflict could easily spread to the Chinese homeland; and finally, the enemy in any such conflict would most likely possess superior weapons technology and armaments.[32]

PLA modernizers inclined to Liu's view may initially have believed that the transition to a force equipped with more modern armaments and doctrine would be gradual, and thus they expected that the Soviet nuclear umbrella could buy them time. Yet a series of external events between 1953 and 1955 lent new urgency to the PLA's problems of military readjustment and force modernization. Changing perceptions of external threat fed domestic politics by pitting PLA modernizers—faced with the difficult and decidedly long-term task of changing the basic nature of the force—against civilian economic planners, who faced their own colossal challenge of domestic reconstruction. Given the scope and scale of China's domestic problems, the planners tended to favor an approach that would calibrate military budgets to assessments of China's immediate or near-term threat environment. But the PLA's challenge was long-term, as Peng's and Liu's initial steps had made clear. Even if the threats became more benign for a period, many senior commanders believed that time would be of the essence given how very far the PLA—and China's military industry—had yet to travel.

A short-term solution to China's predicament involved significantly increasing the acquisition of Soviet arms and technology and seeking Soviet assistance in the construction of an indigenous military industrial base. But by the end of the 1950s, the atmosphere in Sino-Soviet technological cooperation had begun to sour. And even before the break between the two Communist giants in 1960, the Chinese would express dissatisfaction with the pace and content of bilateral cooperation and exchange. Against the combined backdrop of an intensifying threat environment and the extraordinary, enduring challenge that many PLA leaders believed they faced, the disputes between the generals and Mao's leading economic planners became particularly urgent.

Nie, Peng, and the Planners: Three Visions

Although the PLA's difficult experience in Korea led nearly all senior generals into debates about modernization in the narrow context of defense, the emergence of a more broadly developmental view within the Chinese military can be traced to debates about expensive nuclear delivery systems, including land-based strategic missiles and nuclear submarines and their auxiliary equipment. While the Politburo's 1955 decision to acquire nuclear weapons began to involve the PLA in debates about economic development strategy, what followed changed the stakes entirely.[33]

The January 1955 decision, as Lewis and Xue have shown in their seminal histories of China's atomic bomb and strategic sea-power programs, would be followed in just three years by decisions to pursue vigorously a full range of land and sea-based delivery systems and thus all of the elements of a comprehensive strategic arsenal. These later decisions shattered the superpower precedent in the sense that they launched programs in nuclear weapons (1955), strategic missiles (1956), nuclear-powered submarines (1958), and submarine-launched ballistic missiles (1958) before the country even had the technical infrastructure to mine uranium. Chinese scientists, we have learned, could not offer a timetable for a rudimentary nuclear weapon until the fall of 1961. They would not have a bomb design of which they could be confident until 1963 and China would not explode its first nuclear device until October 1964.

All this brought advocates of intensive investment in strategic weapons into much larger arguments about China's spending and policy priorities during the first half of the 1960s.[34] The pursuit of a full complement of delivery systems in the absence of any overarching strategic concept for their employment engendered opposition from both military and civilian constituencies.[35]

In the wake of the Great Leap Forward (1958–60), retrenchment in state investment sharply intensified the bickering over national spending priorities. In 1961 and 1962, immediately following the end of the Great Leap, state economic planners implemented a sweeping program of budget and spending controls to deal with budget deficits that had swelled during 1958–60 and the excess demand and inflationary pressure that wracked the economy. Planners slashed central government investment from RMB 38.9 billion in 1960, the final year of the Great Leap, to just RMB 7.1 billion in 1962.[36]

In this atmosphere, with Soviet advisors withdrawn after the Sino-Soviet split of 1960, no working bomb design on the drawing board, and China's overall security environment improved over what it had been in the mid-to-late 1950s when China faced American nuclear threats, alternative constituencies within the Chinese government came to view all but the most rudimentary nuclear deterrent as wasteful excess.[37] The integration of security with development in China thus owed much to the need of its advocates to counter a broad-based military and civilian coalition almost immediately after the decision in 1956 to begin a strategic missile program.[38]

This opposition to the preference for strategic weapons between 1956 and 1962 was aggregated into two broad political constituencies, one civilian, the other military. For many civilians, led by a skeptical coalition of central economic planners, ambitions for the construction of a basic technological infrastructure would unquestionably be jeopardized by the expense of R&D involved in complex strategic weapons technologies.[39] Bo Yibo spoke for this constituency when he noted that "although rapid defense construction would influence the rapid [development] of power plants, iron and steel, chemicals, petroleum, civilian machine building, and even light industries . . . , the [ultimate] effect was to make matters extremely difficult for industry as a whole." This became, Bo remembers, "the most acute issue" (*zui jianrui de yige wenti*) posed to Chairman Mao during the last half of the 1950s. The failure to resolve it decisively, he adds, led to the growth of military industries that, in his view, was "excessive" (*guoda*) and reflected "over-urgent demands" (*yaoqiu guoji*).[40]

At the same time, most of the Chinese military establishment argued that all but the most rudimentary nuclear deterrent diverted money from the pressing need to improve conventional weapons. Under Marshal Peng Dehuai, the high command spent much of the 1950s trying to cope with the vast gaps in Chinese readiness and technology revealed by the Korean War. Influenced by Soviet doctrine, these men recognized the sharp divergence between the army's guerrilla traditions and its need for modern weapons.[41] Thus united by a nearly universal sense that the PLA's guerrilla heritage had lost relevance in the face of enemy firepower, military leaders divided over the extent to which a rudimentary nuclear arsenal would prove sufficient as a strategic deterrent. This split would widen after Peng fell from power in a purge in 1959 and was replaced at the top of the military system by Marshal Lin Biao, and as his position as the leading voice for conventional-force modernization was taken by Marshal He Long and General Luo Ruiqing, the new chief of the PLA general staff.

The systematic reduction of the military's proportion of state investment sharpened the debate. By 1958, the military share had dropped to 18.5 percent of total state investment, a reduction of approximately 3.6 percent compared to 1955.[42] This alone might not have raised concerns within the PLA given the overall expansion of the economy during these years. But the expensive strategic weapons programs all went into start-up phase during this three-year period. The Great Leap Forward would then intervene by wreaking havoc on the economy. As a result of state planners' moves to curtail dramatically all aspects of central government investment, a broad-based conventional weapons constituency in the PLA sought in the summer of 1961 to scale-back strategic programs and renew the 1950s' focus on armor, artillery, and aircraft. This purely military debate over acquisitions during 1961 and 1962 thus reinforced the pressure civilian constituencies had begun to apply to the most complex strategic weapons programs in the mid- to late 1950s.

In this atmosphere, challenged from all sides, Marshal Nie formulated a response that linked weaponization directly to the broader goal of economic development that preoccupied China's political leadership.[43] He and his aides thus stepped beyond the issue of weapons and integrated security with the drive for truly national economic construction. They did so in three ways.

First, they sought to integrate the issue of economic competitiveness into their appeal by suggesting that the formulation of national technology policy, even if focused on civilian needs, must have strategic underpinnings. Second, they offered a rationale for the pursuit of the most advanced technologies even if the development of the country's low-tech infrastructure might languish as a result. Finally, they championed technological indigenization, suggesting pointedly that the central government must take the lead in the development of critical technologies since neither government at the provincial or municipal levels nor international partners were fully up to the task.

Ultimately, this provided the foundation for a Chinese variant of tech-nonational development ideology. Although the notion of industrial "spin-off" promised by Nie may have been simplistic, his argument was quite sophisticated in its claim that the implications of strategic weapons investments were much broader than either of his two sets of antagonists had recognized. Civilians, Nie averred, were wrong to view strategic weaponization as merely providing greater firepower than the conventional alternatives advocated by other military leaders. At the same time, Nie insisted, military elites were also wrong because investment in strategic weapons could help China escape the trap of future obsolescence in ways that were vital to the country's long-range strategic goals, both in economic development and national security. His programs, Nie asserted, were not simply a matter of improving battlefield weapons for the next war, but of the future direction of the country and its position on the global stage.

Virtually from the outset, Nie and his aides thus thought in comprehensive terms. Their program catered to a widespread sensitivity to status: sophisticated technology, the Chinese believed, is something that all great powers (*daguo*) must have. It also obeyed a political rationale at a time when China's declared strategic doctrines still dismissed the implications of the nuclear revolution.[44] At its most fundamental level, though, it addressed concerns about how to foster innovation and offered a means to establish, organize, and finance an advanced technology base.[45] "One question on our minds," Nie wrote, "was whether a country such as ours could meet internal demand by using existing technology to increase varieties and specifications." Once he concluded that it could, he shifted his attention to areas where the connection between military and civilian uses and effects was a matter of degree. For instance, "modern high-performance weapons, particularly guided missiles, atomic bombs, and advanced aircraft set very high quality standards for new materials." The production of metals, Nie wrote in his memoir, had increased in the 1950s, but slowly and with little attention to variety and specification, while the situation with synthetic materials was almost as bad. "China's output of plastics in 1958 was only 1 percent of that of the United States and 2.5 percent of that of Britain." Most Chinese varieties of plastics were outdated and many were virtually antiques. In this sense, Nie argued to China's leaders, it was clear that

> without a range of heat-resistant materials, high-energy fuels, special materials of different properties, precision alloys, semiconductors, rare metallic elements, artificial crystals, ultra-high-purity materials, rare gases, and other types of new materials, we would fail not only to solve the problems associated with the production of missiles, atomic bombs, and auxiliary installations, but [in our efforts to develop] electronic installations and components and precision meters and instruments for both military and civilian uses. At the time, I often said to the comrades with whom I worked: "fuel, rice, oil, salt, soy sauce, vinegar, and tea comprise a family's daily necessities and are called the 'seven basic items.' In my view, new materials, precision meters and instruments, and heavy equipment are to military industry and the high technology branches of science what these seven items are to the family."[46]

Here, Nie's argument was far more sophisticated than that offered by others in the PLA. Where they held that "only with the modernization of national defense will there be protection for the industrialization of the state,"[47] Nie moved beyond the question of a minimal deterrent role for strategic weapons by arguing that economic development could itself be fostered by military investment. This formulation provided the basis for a military-led Chinese technonationalism in that it successfully redefined military programs as being concerned not merely with strategic *weapons* but with strategic *technologies* of broader significance and scope. Such technologies impinged on industrial competitiveness, international standing, and economic power, not solely military strength. In the end, Nie's view won the day because he succeeded in thoroughly convincing Chairman Mao.

Mao presumably accepted Nie's arguments because they suited the crude, but politically significant, benchmarking process by which Mao weighed Chinese progress against that of potential strategic competitors.[48] And happily for Nie, just as he was forced to fight for his more complicated delivery system programs in mid-1961, a rude shock from an unexpected source—Japan—arrived to shake the Chairman's confidence and reinforce the persuasiveness of Nie's ideas.

In the spring and early summer, a highly classified report on Japanese technical development circulated through the senior ranks of China's party and military leadership. The report prompted important decisions about high technology development because it confronted all competing constituencies with the harsh reality of growing Japanese capability and persistent Chinese backwardness. The report quoted an internal Japanese government study that argued for greater attention to the connection between defense technology and overall national industrial competitiveness. Because state-of-the-art military science and technology had outpaced Japan's current technical strengths, the report argued, Tokyo had to take immediate steps to rectify the problem.[49]

The Chinese version of this report, whether accurate or not, caused a stir among the Politburo members who read it. Not only did it suggest that Japan might be planning a major technology investment drive, but it also suggested that Tokyo, like Beijing, routinely gauged national progress against international trends in state-of-the art technology.[50] This played directly into Nie's hands because the report arrived on the desks of most leading politicians just weeks before a major conference was to be held to debate the issue of strategic versus conventional force investments.

For Nie and his colleagues, both military and civilian, the stakes could not have been higher. "In the face of [post–Great Leap economic] difficulties," he wrote, opponents asked

> should we continue our scientific research, especially the high technology projects exemplified by the guided missile and atomic bomb efforts? A sharp controversy emerged around this question. Some argued that we should slow our efforts to develop sophisticated defense techniques because the difficulties were so many and so formidable. Some comrades actually proposed to end such high technology projects, arguing that the expense was too great and had impeded the development of other sectors of the national economy. They wanted us to work only on aircraft construction and conventional weaponry, not sophisticated weapons such as ballistic missiles and atomic bombs.[51]

Five days before the opening of the conference, held in the seaside resort of Beidaihe from July 18 to August 14, Mao weighed in with a sibylic pronouncement: Since "the level of China's industry and technology remains far behind that of Japan," China must adopt policies to close the distance.[52]

When Nie and his antagonists began to spar at Beidaihe five days later, they had already received this strong indication of where the Chairman stood. And as usual, Mao's will temporarily decided the question. Nie held fast to his position, which again won the day, but this time upon the basis of much broader rationales than had undergirded the straightforward national security debate over the decision to build an atomic bomb. "My attitude was clear throughout," Nie wrote. In preparing science and technology plans and in strategic weapons start-up efforts, "we had become keenly aware that the pursuit of guided missiles and the atomic bomb would advance us in many other areas of modern science and technology. Instead of discontinuing the projects, I therefore argued that we should . . . move ahead. That was my unshakable belief."[53]

Hard Choices

The conflict between three of the PLA's leading commanders—Nie Rongzhen, He Long, and Luo Ruiqing—was not merely one of agendas, but of differing visions for China's technology base and for its proper relationship to the military. To Marshal He Long, a distinguished old soldier, force modernization was almost exclusively a problem of battlefield readiness, not of economic and scientific development broadly construed. The difference between this and Nie's vision could hardly have been more vivid. Inevitably, the dispute would play out in elite political struggles, as well as in pivotal controversies over allocation and equipment planning among PLA administrators and technical experts throughout the nation's defense technology complex.

To illustrate this, we need look only to a conflict that raged between Nie's missileers and advocates of expanded aircraft production. In the summer of 1961, when the two main military industry constituencies clashed at Beidaihe, this was already among the oldest and most intense disputes in China's struggle for military industrial development. Long before 1956, the year of the decision to develop strategic missiles and of the establishment of a research and development academy to oversee the task—the so-called Fifth Academy—advocates for the aviation industry had already been urging an expanded political commitment to aircraft production.

China had made important progress with simple fighters and training aircraft during the first half of the 1950s. Yet many in the industry regarded the production of smaller aircraft as insufficient. They tried to persuade

Premier Zhou Enlai to devote increased attention to the manufacture of larger craft with greater take-off weights, in particular heavy bombers. Chinese sources routinely identify Peng Dehuai as the major impetus in high-level command circles behind this push.[54]

According to an important, officially sanctioned history of China's aviation industry edited by Duan Zijun, the parties to this dispute arrayed themselves along a continuum of three main policy alternatives.[55] The first focused entirely on missile systems; it advocated the rapid development and trial production of inertially guided ballistic missiles. The second, and more balanced view, supported the simultaneous development of missiles and aircraft. The third argued for a concentration on missiles during the next five years of defense industrial construction with a return to an emphasis on aircraft production during the 1960s.

In April 1956, Zhou convened a high-level meeting of generals and defense scientists to discuss the question. Qian Xuesen, who had been a protégé at Caltech of the rocket pioneer Theodore von Kármán, and Ren Xinmin, the University of Michigan–educated specialist who developed China's liquid rocket propellants, were among the scientists on a panel that ultimately chose the second option.[56] According to the Duan history, this ushered in an era of moderate cooperation between the two camps, and an aircraft factory was even assigned to the Fifth Academy when it was founded later that year. This plant attempted to assist academy designers in the fabrication of trial-series missiles. And jet propulsion and rocket engine development were listed side-by-side as key development projects in the Twelve Year Plan for Science and Technology Development, the party's 1956 policy blueprint for the period ahead.

But while the Duan history argues that the decision for "simultaneous development" resolved most differences between the two camps, the reality seems otherwise. As with all of China's strategic technology programs, political support proved crucial in the start-up phase, and in the period after 1959–60 bombers simply did not receive the all-critical political backing that the nation's leading politicians gave to Nie's strategic weapons programs.

As a result of the lower political priority, the level of resources allocated to heavy bomber programs, which were developed by the bureaucracy also in charge of conventional military aircraft, never approached that of the nuclear missile and strategic sea-power efforts led by Marshal Nie. Not

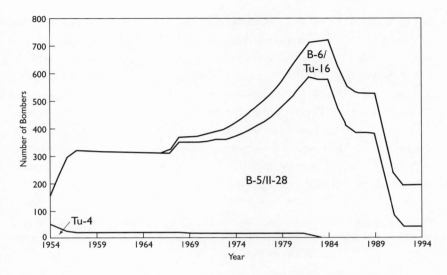

FIGURE 2.1   Chinese Bomber Inventory, 1954–1994.   SOURCE: Allen, Krumel, and Pollack (1995).

surprisingly, therefore, China had only a small inventory of bombers prior to the onset of the Cultural Revolution in 1966 (Figure 2.1). The gap in political commitment between missile and bomber programs during their crucial start-up phases becomes even clearer once we examine the politicians' half-hearted response to technical obstacles encountered in the bomber program during its first and second years. In this period, China's bomber engineers proved unable to smoothly absorb Soviet assistance.

With the aviation component of the First Five Year Plan completed ahead of schedule, China and the Soviet Union reached agreement on the transfer of technology originally developed for the Soviet Tu-16 bomber. The Duan history blames subsequent delays in the Chinese program on a change of construction venue during 1957.[57] This was exacerbated by China's late start in sophisticated metallurgy and by a continuing sense among prominent missileers that aircraft development should not be allowed to receive first priority.[58] In large measure, leading politicians appear to have concurred.

In the aviation industry's favor was the high degree of skepticism within key military and industrial constituencies that China could go it alone in strategic weapons development, particularly in the wake of the Sino-Soviet split, which came just nine months after the first test flight of a

Chinese-assembled Tu-16. Among Chinese strategic weaponeers, the nuclear scientist He Zuoxiu notes, guided missile fabrication was "considered superior to aircraft development for both offensive and defensive purposes because [missiles] have much higher Mach numbers than do airplanes. But [at this time] the Soviet Union had yet to launch its first satellite, a successful ICBM had not yet been developed, and there was no real consensus [in China] on whether missiles could become a realistic defense technology."[59] Moreover, "China was backward during this time" in science and advanced technology industries. Thus, for those in the aviation industry, as for Marshal Peng, the realistic—and immediate—challenges of air defense and offensive air power, particularly when coupled with China's poor scientific and technical infrastructure and perceived Soviet unwillingness to assist with the more complex missile programs, made the choice in favor of aircraft comparatively straightforward.

Qian Xuesen, however, took a dramatically different and more ambitious view. Throughout the missile/bomber debates of the next decade, he remained a decided proponent of missile systems. And although Chinese histories of the aviation industry generally argue that Qian supported simultaneous development at the meetings of April 1956 sponsored by Premier Zhou, he seems in reality to have preferred a higher priority for missile systems. Indeed, Qian advised Premier Zhou that R&D on aircraft and missiles were not the same. Thus while the Duan official history claims that broad technical similarities between jet and rocket propulsion eased collaboration between the two camps, especially as they dealt with similar problems, more recent accounts, such as that of He Zuoxiu, clearly suggest the reverse.

It now appears that Qian argued that any "similarity" between jet and rocket technologies actually made advancement of missile technology *more* imperative. Fabricating missiles, Qian told the leadership, need not be more difficult than fabricating aircraft with respect to parts and materials; the real challenge would lie in the development of inertial guidance.[60] However, guidance projects, Qian pointed out, could help China to develop a world-class optics industry. And he bet that the guidance problem could be solved within a "relatively short" time.

Qian also appears to have argued in 1956 that the problems involved in developing materials for missiles could be solved more easily than those confronting aircraft designers. "Missile materials need only be used once," he told the leadership, while "aircraft materials must be used again and again." Since aircraft materials were specific and required much experience to fabricate properly, a breakthrough in the development of missile materials would probably come sooner, he predicted. This could contribute to the development of aviation systems, whereas the development of aircraft materials would require longer lead-times and thus risked holding China back from what might otherwise be the rapid development of indigenously designed and fabricated trial series missiles.[61]

Qian Xuesen's arguments were reinforced, no doubt, by the essentially political rationale that guided China's first few rounds of national strategic technology programming. This is apparent when one considers that Nie's missile program was in deep technical trouble during the late 1950s and early 1960s, while the bomber program had made modest progress. Although initial return on investment favored bombers between 1956 and 1961, this ultimately was outweighed by political considerations and the nationalistic impulse for prestige. These tipped the balance in Nie's favor.

The fate of the bomber program therefore illustrates how a fast start could peter out in Maoist China in the absence of the intensive political commitment required to sustain mobilization and flexible institutional arrangements for the management of innovation. As with the early missile program, virtually all of the progress in China's heavy bomber program depended on Soviet aid. Moscow delivered a first set of technical data on the Tu-16 bomber in February 1959 and, by May, two prototype aircraft and a complete set of components to be assembled into a third plane. As a result, assembly was rapid, taking only sixty-seven days for final assembly between June 28 and September 3. This first Chinese-assembled bomber was flown on September 27 and then delivered to the PLA Air Force in December, just nine months before the mass withdrawal of Soviet technicians in August 1960.[62]

The easy and quick assembly of bombers from knock-down kits gave those who favored conventional weapons something to boast about in 1961. In contrast, Nie's continuing inability to deliver firm timetables put him at a rhetorical and practical disadvantage in the political fight over the agenda for national investment. No one could deny that nuclear weapons had changed the face of warfare; He Long himself admitted in October 1960 that "tomorrow's wars will make use of missiles and atomic bombs. . . . Without [such weapons] our losses could be tremendous."[63] Yet through the first nine months of 1961 and for more than a year after the withdrawal of Soviet technical assistance, Nie's lead time remained long and the army's short-term equipment needs continued to intensify. China's sense of danger escalated in the early 1960s as renewed threats from Taiwan along the southeast coast led more generals, such as Marshal Ye Jianying, to side with Nie's skeptics. Even five months after Nie's apparent victory at the Beidaihe conference, Ye asked rhetorically:

> If a war should come upon us in the next few years, what kind of weapons can we primarily rely on? . . . Here arises the problem of the relationship between conventional weapons and super weapons. . . . Though the power of atomic weapons is great, they can only attack the other party's centers in strategic air raids and destroy its economic potentialities. Afterwards they can only be used primarily according to their power, as [a] firing vanguard before an attack. To resolve the battle, to cut down the enemy's living strength, to capture positions, and to achieve victory, [China] will still rely upon the ground force, the army, and conventional weapons.[64]

Nie's agenda won at Beidaihe, then, because of the broad political commitment at the apex of the Chinese polity to the reasoning behind his strategic technology programs. Mao himself put the point plainly: "We should make up our minds to develop sophisticated technologies. We can't relax our efforts or discontinue [the strategic weapons projects]." Now confident of top-level political support, Nie summarized his key arguments in a report to Mao and the Central Committee. This was placed on the leadership's working agenda for the last part of the summer of 1961, and at last Nie offered a firm timetable: a working bomb design would be ready by the end of 1963.[65]

"What should we do now that we had decided to continue?" Nie asked.

> After much discussion, we decided that we should . . . give priority to key projects. Work on an over-extended front would strain all sectors. Specifically, we would ensure the priority of scientific research over production and of sophisticated weapons over conventional weapons. . . . Research in heavy equipment for the air, naval, and ground forces would be arranged in that order, *so long as it did not detract from the development of guided missiles, atomic bombs, and their auxiliary equipment.*[66]

Mindful of his opponents, Nie threw them the barest of bones and continued his attempt to win them over: "I asked the departments concerned to show consideration for our overall interests which were embodied in these [priority] arrangements. By way of analogy, I told them that this was somewhat akin to crossing a river. If everyone wished to cross a bridge of a certain width, they would have to queue up. If they all jammed their way onto it, no one would be able to pass."[67]

Despite a brief three-year suspension of the SSBN program from 1962 to 1965—an interruption that nevertheless allowed Nie to keep the development of the SSBN reactor on track—and despite reassessed national capabilities for air defense against conventional attack prompted by the downing of a U-2 spy plane in September 1962, conventional weapons programs remained of "secondary priority." This may perhaps have been because gaping holes in Chinese aircraft and other conventional weapons industries made strategic weapons the best option under difficult circumstances.[68] Nonetheless, Nie's use of high technology programs to tie security to development and competitiveness became the foundation of Chinese policy.

CHINESE TECHNONATIONALISM: A MILITARY DEVELOPMENT ALTERNATIVE

In practice, the military alternative that emerged from these debates comprised two essential components: a developmental doctrine, which I have termed Chinese "technonationalism," borrowing from the political economist Robert B. Reich; and an organizational style—based on networks, nonhierarchical management, and competition—that strategic weapons leaders promoted as the essential complement of the doctrine.[69]

Developmental Doctrine: A Chinese Technonationalism

The very notion of a technology-based "nationalism" assumes, first, that leaders make an explicit connection between technological accomplishment and the relative position of the state in the global order. Such a linkage, which can be traced back to the early mercantilists, found advocates in such diverse figures as Alexander Hamilton, Friedrich List, Thorstein Veblen, V. I. Lenin, Josef Stalin, and even Herbert Hoover. It came of age after World War II, in what historian Walter McDougall has termed "command technology." Alongside the four "war babies" of British radar, American atomic bombs, German ballistic missiles, and American computers grew "the institutionalization of technological change for state purposes, that is the state-funded and -managed R&D explosion of our time," and the linkage of that explosion to international competition and national purpose.[70]

For Chinese leaders, such as Marshal Nie, this came to encompass what Richard Samuels has termed a "technology and security ideology." There is no evidence that the Chinese directly borrowed this ideology from abroad, but there was an Asian precedent in the very successful Japanese development policy—about which Samuels and others such as Michael Green have written—which comprised three key elements that roughly paralleled the road the Chinese later trod: import-substituting indigenization—the identification and acquisition of foreign products and manufacturing/design processes in order to stimulate local development; diffusion—the distribution of this know-how throughout the economy; and the nurturing of a capacity to innovate and manufacture. In both nineteenth- and twentieth-century Japan, "technology, then, was a matter of national security, and the bundle of beliefs and practices that constitute this view can be called 'technonationalism.'"[71]

In the Chinese variant, indigenization and nurturing became critical aspects of national technology policy during the Mao years, but diffusion, though a key rhetorical element of the strategic weaponeers' argument, did not become a part of their substantive policy proposals with wide application until the introduction of new paradigms via renewed international exchange in the years after Mao's death in 1976.

"Indigenization" was the critical variable in Mao-era high technology policy. It refers to three principles covered by the Japanese term *kokusanka*—all of which have parallels in the Chinese case—an approach that Japanese leaders have consistently posited in a distinct order of priority: "first, domestic supply; secondly, if domestic supply is not possible, licenses using domestic manufacture and equipment; and thirdly, equipment with application beyond the project for which purchased. In accordance with these principles, in both military and civilian cases, it is not uncommon for each subsequent generation of Japanese product to depend less than its predecessor on foreign technology."[72] As a Japanese historian of technology has argued, "'self-reliance in technology does not mean autarky . . . [but rather] refers to the ability to absorb all needed technologies. . . . Self-reliance is attained not at a stroke but in stages.'"[73]

In China, the national R&D system lapsed into near autarky during the 1960s not by design but because of larger political events. As a result of the Sino-Soviet political and diplomatic divorce, in science and industry China was forced into "self-reliance" (*zili gengsheng*) far earlier than Chinese technology planners, both military and civilian, had anticipated. After less than a decade of dependence on licensing and aid from a foreign partner, Chinese R&D was essentially left to fend for itself. Yet, as we shall see below, the strategic weapons programs virtually alone received political guarantees from the party leadership in order to compensate.

The early Chinese Communist state also lacked Japan's commercial ambitions, thus yielding what might be called a technonationalism with Chinese characteristics. This can be summarized as follows:

- Technological development is intrinsically strategic (*zhuanlüe*); it has fundamental implications for the relative position of the state in the international balance of military and economic power.
- The central government must, for this reason, invest in critical technological sectors. Since the transition from research to application can often take a decade or longer, pressure to meet gross output targets will invariably prevent individual firms and provincial or local governments from bearing the risks of forward-looking R&D. The role of the central government will thus be crucial in critical technology sectors. This comprehensive developmental rationale should reinforce the center's preexisting interest in these sectors derived from military requirements.[74]
- The state should pursue import-substituting indigenization.[75]
- The central government must nurture an indigenous capacity to innovate.[76]
- Technology diffusion, at least as a long-term goal, should be made state policy, whether via military-to-civilian "spin-off" or civilian-to-military "spin-on."

Organizational Style: "Flexible" Mobilization

Parallel to the developmental doctrine of integrating security with economic modernization was a multifaceted organizational style that stood in stark contrast to much of the Chinese political economy during the first thirty years of Communist rule (1949–79). This organizational style, which became institutionalized in the management structure of Nie's programs, involved four key components: first, the devolution of decision-making power from bureaucrats and party cadres to scientists and specialists of the highest technical stature; second, the institutionalization of cross-ministerial

and cross-system collaboration as a corrective to the endemic compartmentalization that had long plagued the Chinese bureaucracy; third, the
introduction of flat, nonhierarchical organizational structures characterized
by high-low, central-local, and leadership-staff contact, coordination, and
decision making; and fourth, the application of a performance metric in
strategic weapons domains based on universal standardization and the
rigorous benchmarking of Chinese progress against international technical
developments.

In this way, despite the top-down, mobilizational character of the strategic weapons programs, the military S&T system left a comparatively flexible organizational legacy that continues to influence Chinese practice in
this area. Just twenty years ago, only the strategic weapons programs prac-
ticed genuinely sustained and collaborative R&D; in other sectors, political
repression dramatically impinged on collaborative work. Until the 1980s,
only military scientists enjoyed stable and comparatively unfettered access
to international publications and technical data. Nowhere else during the
Mao era was peer review so institutionalized and politicians so regularly
engaged with scientists and engineers over sustained periods on matters of
importance to China's future.

Ultimately, as we shall see in the four chapters of Part 2, this became the
backbone of the entire Chinese state-led high technology system because it
offered China's leaders four important legacies. First, it mirrored a variety
of successful, prevalent international patterns, common in the West and
Japan, in the organization of government-industry-science partnerships.
Second, it produced China's most impressive technological achievements
during the first forty years of the PRC. Third, it entailed a highly elitist and
professional model of organization that exalted the importance of scientists,
engineers, and technical personnel. Fourth and most important, it offered
a cooperative, open, network-based, and flexible alternative to the highly
bureaucratized, vertical, and compartmentalized organizational system that
characterized so many Chinese technology sectors.[77]

Who Decides?

The first of these key organizational institutions was the integration
of senior technical personnel into the administrative and programmatic
decision-making stratum. With a few exceptions, the inclusion of technical

personnel was not replicated in the civilian sector, where most managers of heavy industry were party bureaucrats, or in the conventional weapons and production side of the military industry system, where managers also tended to be party cadres or PLA men in uniform. This had especially perverse effects on China's conventional weapons sector, as Wendy Frieman has noted, where technically unsophisticated party cadres from production facilities who sought to influence major design and manufacturing decisions regularly confronted designers and technicians.[78] In top-priority strategic weapons programs, by contrast, technical personnel were integrated into virtually all phases of weapons design and production, as well as management, administration, and liaison with political leaders. Some of China's most famous scientists, such as the physicist Zhu Guangya, played purely an administrative role, serving as key links between industrial and scientific projects, politicians, and scientists.[79] They provided the requisite specialized knowledge for the management of mammoth scientific and technical undertakings, a characteristic feature of "project-style" management.[80] The integration of technicians into the senior ranks of administration helped to ensure that decision makers would make technically informed judgments that were sensitive to the professional concerns of staff and not merely react to the administrative problems associated with management and political control.

Nie Rongzhen's success in management stemmed in large part from the fact that he and his staff handpicked most nontechnical administrative cadres, both at the ministerial level and in academies and factories. This helped to ensure that technically sophisticated administrators, such as Liu Jie (a military commissar under Nie's pre-1949 North China Field Army) or Wang Zheng (the Red Army's leading pre-1949 administrator of communications technologies), would be in control at both levels.[81]

The case of Zhu Guangya illustrates how technical personnel were brought into positions of leadership. Li Jue, the director of the supersecret Ninth Bureau, which ran the nuclear weapons program, and the Ninth Academy—the code name for China's main nuclear weapons R&D facility, the Northwest Nuclear Weapons Research and Design Academy (Xibei he wuqi sheji yanjiusuo)—recruited Zhu into the academy's four-man Leading Group, a management committee charged with both administrative and political oversight. Chinese accounts make clear that this was no mere "paper" move.[82] Zhu's primary contributions were administrative and managerial. Beneath Li Jue and the Leading Group sat a trio of deputy directors of the academy, all senior scientists: Wang Ganchang, Peng Huanwu, and Guo Yonghuai. Lewis and Xue have noted that "a clear delineation between decision makers and staff becomes more justifiable only when we come to . . . a less renowned coterie of academy scientists."

Once work on the atomic bomb moved beyond theoretical calculations to design and trial manufacture, Li Jue eliminated a series of research sections in metal physics and automatic control in favor of four "high-level technological committees," all under the supervision of an "integrated technological commission." All of these decision-making committees were headed by leading figures in engineering or science, and three of the four were directed by eminent senior scientists. The first committee, in charge of overall design, worked jointly under Wu Jilin, a member of the academy Leading Group and a management cadre, and Long Wenguang, a senior engineer. Wang Ganchang and Chen Nengkuan led the second committee, charged with overseeing conventional bomb components. Guo Yonghuai and Cheng Kaijia led the third, which supervised weapons development experiments. Peng Huanwu and Zhu Guangya headed the fourth, which directed neutron ignition work. "These four committees," in the words of Lewis and Xue, "had direct access to higher officials in the academy and, with Li Jue's great authority . . . , to ministry leaders in Beijing."[83]

This arrangement also became the norm at the Tenth (radio electronics) and Fifth (missiles and space) Academies. For example, at the Fifth Academy, Qian Xuesen served as director in the early years; military technicians, such as Wang Zheng, became Qian's deputies.

Even of greater importance than the academies were the ministries, where too technical personnel commonly served as leaders. Qian Sanqiang, China's leading nuclear physicist, served as vice minister of the Second Ministry of Machine Building (nuclear industry), as did Wang Ganchang; Li Siguang, a top geologist, was minister of geology; and Wang Shiguang, an electronics pioneer, became a powerful official at the Fourth Ministry of Machine Building (electronics).[84]

Even at the factory level, where party bureaucrats tended to be most intrusive, Nie and his aides moved to give technical staff decision-making power. Sometimes, high-ranking ministry technicians spent long periods at plants solving technical problems. For instance, for much of 1963–64, Yuan Chenglong, a Second Ministry administrator, relocated from Beijing to work on technical problems at the Lanzhou Gaseous Diffusion Plant and the Nuclear Component Manufacturing Plant in remote Gansu Province. When technicians could not themselves serve as decision makers, Nie assigned military officers with long-standing personal links to himself or his closest comrades as administrative directors. At the Lanzhou plant, for example, administrators appear to have been chosen largely on the basis of connections forged decades earlier to Liu Bocheng and Song Renqiong, men with old and close and ties to Marshal Nie. Song Renqiong personally selected the plant's director, Wang Jiefu, whose relationship to Song and Liu dated to the 1940 Hundred Regiments Campaign against the Japanese, a military trial-by-fire that forged close bonds among the PLA men who commanded it.[85]

In all of these respects, the "mature" strategic weapons system became a protected world. Technicians of stature, not just cadres of technical bent, became bureaucrats and administrators. Administrators spent long periods in the laboratory or on the plant floor solving technical problems, not simply arranging administrative guidance from a bureaucratic perch in Beijing. This made management in the strategic weapons system very different from that in many civilian sectors. And ironically, it cleaved China's military industry into sharply divergent professional environments. The Nie group's unique decision-making structure lay at the heart of that cleavage, for the strategic programs not only integrated decision makers with staff, they also moved personnel back and forth across the two main tracks of the system—one technical (*jishu*), the other managerial (*guanli*).

This two-line management system reached its apogee in the institution of the chief designer (*zong shejishi*), which, by the mid-1960s had become the locus for technical decision making in the strategic weapons system. Despite the use of the same title—"chief designer"—in the conventional weapons industry, this institution operated quite differently there.

Marshal Nie's version of the designer system comprised one of two main decision-making tracks in strategic weapons R&D—the technical and the managerial. Strategic weaponeers commonly refer to this arrangement as a system premised on "two lines of command" (*liang tiao zhihuixian*). Along one line sat the technical decision makers, with the chief designer or chief engineer at the top, and a series of technical committees at lower levels. Along the other track, the administrative or managerial, sat officials of the relevant military industrial ministries, with an executive vice minister at the top and various administrative cadres below.

This system was the defining organizational feature of the technical side of the strategic weapons programs prior to the Cultural Revolution. Nie conferred substantive decision-making authority on all of his chief designers. Equally significant, he integrated technicians, such as Zhu Guangya, into the ranks of senior administrative decision makers along the *managerial* track. With technicians of stature securely in place in important managerial roles, Nie's aides built a purely administrative system consisting almost exclusively of three types of personnel: ranking technicians, such as Zhu; military cadres with strong technical credentials, such as Liu Huaqing and Chen Youming of the PLA navy; and specialized managerial cadres with strong professional relationships to technical personnel, such as Li Jue and a key official at the Second Ministry of Machine Building, Liu Jie.

Tu Shou'e, who served as chief designer of China's ICBM as well as shorter-range ballistic missiles, recalls that Nie's designer system suited China's self-reliant isolation in the years after the Sino-Soviet split of 1960.[86] This "mature" post-1962 designer system built upon an important trial foundation laid in 1961, which sprang directly from the early strategic missile program.

Initially, Tu has noted in a memoir, the leaders of the Fifth Academy established three tiers of designers for each major strategic missile system. For the design of the ICBM, which Tu himself would direct, the technical decision-making structure centered on a chief designer for the entire project (*xinghao zong shejishi*); an echelon of subsystems chief designers (*fen xitong shejishi*) just below, charged with design in areas such as guidance (*zhidao*), engines and propellants (*fadongji*), tracking and control networks (*cekong*), and telemetry (*yaoce*); and in the third tier, several component chief designers (*danxiang chanpin zhuguan shejishi*) in charge of the constituent parts making up each of the relevant subsystems.

Such a decision-making structure would have had little utility at the outset of the programs, Tu argues. Much of China's earliest strategic missilery was based on the use of technical documents acquired from the Soviets, including 10,151 volumes of technical material on the Soviet R-2 missile delivered to the Chinese in the second half of 1958.[87] This aid formed the foundation for China's initial long-range missile programs. With Chinese missile designers having been abandoned by their former Soviet mentors by the early 1960s, the Chinese decided to launch an indigenously designed DF-2 in 1962. The initial design was a disastrous failure. This, Tu recalls, was the proximate cause of the decision to establish an elaborate designer hierarchy.[88]

Nie's aides moved vigorously to reorganize the designer system in the wake of this first DF-2 failure. Their efforts reflected the struggle to solve the variety of problems confronting Chinese ICBM designers in the years 1961–64, which culminated in the successful test of a significantly redesigned DF-2. In November 1961, Qian Xuesen himself took charge of the design of a Chinese version—dubbed DF-3—of the U.S. Atlas and Soviet R-7 ICBMs. Despite his leadership, by 1963 technical setbacks forced Qian to cancel the program and shift attention to a much shorter-range version of the DF-3, a missile incapable of hitting the North American sites originally targeted.[89] Various Chinese ICBM series went through significant redesign during these years. This reinforced the weaponeers' commitment to the institution of the designer since it facilitated all of these various redesign and deployment projects.

In the chaos of the violent phase of the Cultural Revolution (1966–71), both lines of command—the technical and the managerial—fell rapidly off course. The former, in particular, came under severe pressure, with Huang Xuhua, the nuclear submarine chief designer, consigned for a time to pig farming after a summary "trial" by the military control committee at the Huludao shipyard. Along the managerial track, meanwhile, many of Nie's leading cadres were overthrown by battalions of Red Guards as well as discontented workers and staff. In general, then, the managerial track survived throughout the years of chaos; even so, its effectiveness and capacity to compensate for the collapse of the technical designer system were undercut by the seizure of administrative power by radicals opposed to technical-style decision making.

These few years of difficulty notwithstanding, the designer system—and its close connection with a managerial line populated by former technicians and technical cadres—produced important breakthroughs, as well as all of China's initial strategic weapons successes. This contrasts with the conventional weapons sphere, where "chief designers" operated in an organizational milieu reminiscent of civilian heavy industry. Wendy Frieman has noted, for example, that unlike the Soviet system, which produced Kalashnikov and Tupolev, the Chinese system insured that the conventional weapons chief designer would carry little authority in decision-making circles. Conventional weapons designers were denied autonomy, political access, and freedom from interference from enterprise managers and others.[90] They were even separated from regular access to their own advocates within planning circles and the PLA high command.[91] As in civilian industry, conventional weapons designers and factory managers functioned in a political milieu where leadership inspection tours and guidance were virtually the only occasion for contact with the top.

This was exacerbated by a de facto proprietary system through which the best minds in Chinese electronics and optics were routinely transferred to strategic weapons work. Antitank weapons can, of course, be made more sophisticated when based on wire guidance and advanced optical tracking. But China's leading optical physicists worked almost exclusively on inertial guidance for missiles and satellite attitude control, not on conventional weapons systems that might have aided in the guidance of ordnance. The only true deviations from this pattern involved conventional weapons developed under the strategic weapons rubric. These included the navy's basic attack submarine—a precursor to the nuclear-powered boat—and antiship cruise missiles, supervised by strategic weapons administrators and overseen by a chief designer, Liang Shoupan, who was also a major force in the development of engines and propellants for strategic missiles.

In stark contrast to the conventional weapons sector, in Nie's system strategic weapons chief designers met regularly with the premier and members of the Central Special Commission of the Chinese Communist Party (CSC) (Zhongyang zhuanwei), a coordinating committee, chaired by the premier, that reported directly to the Communist Party's inner circle, the Politburo.[92] No conventional weapons agency countervailed the CSC; thus conventional weapons chief designers had no vehicle for coordinating with top political leaders on technical matters. In practice, the CSC flattened hierarchy and institutionalized strategic weapons technicians' access to the top. This jibed neatly with the remarkable autonomy and decision-making power that they enjoyed under Nie's system.

Nie's system did not always work perfectly, however. Tension erupted between technicians and managers on both decision tracks, most notably in the period after the Great Leap Forward.[93] Marshal Nie himself has told us in a memoir that the Great Leap produced a "lack of respect for the objective laws governing research" even within the most elite of China's strategic weapons organs. Probably, this owed much to the mounting political pressure to deliver workable weapons designs at an early date, which was itself a response to the fever-pitch optimism of the Leap.[94]

Such problems eventually reinforced the Nie group's desire to clear the air within their system. For instance, in the winter of 1960, Nie initiated a survey of problems in Chinese science by investigating the effects of the Leap on the work of Qian Xuesen's Fifth Academy. Nie reasoned that if the atmosphere had deteriorated in this most elite of strategic weapons institutions, in Chinese science as a whole it must surely have become downright abysmal. Nie was shocked by what he found.[95] Qian's missile scientists "were able to spend less than half of their six working days each week on research, devoting much [of the remainder] of their workday to political study or manual labor with no connection to scientific research." Later, Nie undertook a survey of weapons-oriented organs of the Chinese Academy of Sciences (CAS); he found many of the same problems there.

Following these surveys, Nie issued a circular in the name of the State Council. It stipulated that five-sixths of his scientists' working time must be devoted to professional responsibilities. Nie also convened a series of high-level spleen-venting sessions—dubbed "by some comrades in our Party as a 'meeting of immortals'"—to clear the air between the scientists and the party apparat. At a meeting in Shanghai, and at a symposium in Beijing convened by the CAS, scientists bemoaned political interference and charged the bureaucrats with a "lack of clear understanding of the basic fundamentals of scientific research."

From this point forward, Nie and his aides moved decisively on two fronts. Within the realm of policy, they promulgated new guidelines for both groups: the Fourteen Articles on Scientific Work, which Deng Xiaoping, China's future paramount leader, would dub a "constitution for science" (*kexue xianfa*). These articles stipulated a new balance between research and politics. They explicitly recognized the dysfunctions of the Leap and made it clear that, from the leadership's standpoint, no matter what might be true of literature and the arts, the physical and engineering sciences had "no class character." Article 14, in particular, countered political interference in elite science and engineering by shifting leadership of priority R&D from local Communist Party committees to the party committees of the individual research institutes.

This dovetailed with Nie's second response to the damage caused by the Leap. Nie made a concerted, parallel effort to reinvigorate what had hith-erto been half-hearted attempts to move technicians into senior managerial positions. The evolution of the mature strategic weapons management sys-tem described above thereby accelerated as a *response* by Nie and his aides to the effects of the Great Leap. As a result of more vigorous efforts, the three-to-five man party leadership squads (*lingdao banzi*) that gained over-sight responsibility for strategic weapons under Article 14 consisted mainly of technical personnel, such as Zhu Guangya. At the institute level, moreover, virtually all committee members had either left technical roles for managerial duties, or else were cadres of technical orientation, such as Li Jue. At the ministerial level also party committees were soon led by tech-nicians, personally selected by Nie and his aides.

Cooperative Horizontalism

The second key organizational institution evolved from the strategic weaponeers' struggle to overcome the lack of collaboration across frag-mented vertical bureaucratic hierarchies, a counterpoint to the endemic verticalism of the Chinese system. Many scientific advisors strenuously complained that large-scale S&T undertakings simply crossed too many functional and disciplinary boundaries; the development of strategic weapons itself presupposed an extraordinarily complex interaction between science, industry, education, and other sectors. To manage this interaction, program leaders established an array of "research service centers" (*keyan fuwu jigou*) in such areas as information exchange, standards, instrumenta-tion, metering, chemical reagents, and library services. The work and facil-ities of these centers were made available to R&D organizations across the bureaucratic spectrum. Program leaders also moved to institutionalize hor-izontal channels of coordination in an array of small, but extraordinarily powerful, project "offices" (*bangongting*). These became especially valuable as command jurisdictions shifted repeatedly from one to another bureau-cratic organ—in the nuclear submarine program, for instance, from the navy to the shipbuilding ministry, to military R&D headquarters, and so on.[96] Irrespective of which command organ held authority over these projects, the vast coordinating authority granted these offices by the Polit-buro meant that technical staff could forcefully make use of their virtual proprietary rights to budgets, infrastructure, and personnel to overcome rivalry among organizations as well as to close the vertical gaps hindering the flow of communications and information.

These parallel efforts proved to be extraordinarily important. Functional diversity almost invariably translated into bureaucratic fragmentation, which dictated a need for horizontal coordinating and integrating structures. Within a single military industry, distinct bureaus maintained an array of horizontal coordinating ties into other bureaucratic systems outside the relevant ministry. Nie's aides established a group of administrative bureaus and academies that oversaw an expanding network of physicists, geologists, and radiochemists. These bureaus were responsible for research institutes and laboratories across the bureaucratic spectrum.

For example, under Nie's headquarters, the NDSTC, and a subordinate structure, the Second Ministry of Machine Building, Marshal Nie established the Ninth Bureau (*ju*), a functional section reporting to both the NDSTC and the Second Ministry in Beijing, which had vertical oversight of the Ninth Academy (*yuan*) as it conducted basic physics research and bomb design. But he also founded a Geological Bureau to take charge of uranium prospecting; a Mining and Metallurgy Bureau (Twelfth Bureau) to oversee mines and the management of uranium concentrates and uranium oxides; a Fuels Production Bureau take charge of uranium tetrafluoride, uranium hexafluoride, and plutonium facilities; a Construction Bureau to supervise factory construction and equipment installation; a Design Bureau to direct the design of nuclear power plants; an Equipment Manufacturing Bureau, created in 1961, to oversee instrumentation, metering, and equipment manufacture; a Sixth Bureau, created in 1957, to supervise transport, supply, and logistics; an Information Bureau (Eleventh Bureau) to handle the purchase, collection, indexing, and translation of technical books, reports, and materials from foreign countries; and a Security and Protection Bureau to supervise safety, health, and environmental protection, including special hospitals and the maintenance of health records on radiation levels. Nie also established a Finance Bureau, a Science and Technology Bureau, a Planning Bureau, and a Cadres Bureau.[97]

From this summary description of the wide variety of key Second Ministry bureaus in Beijing, it is possible to form a picture of how far flung and interconnected the strategic weapons system became. The Geological Bureau, for instance, maintained close ties to the Ministry of Geology, of which it had once been a part (it was known then as the Third Bureau). The Mining and Metallurgy Bureau had originally been the Third Department of the Ministry of Metallurgy, which together with the Ministry of the Chemical Industry had been formed largely at Nie's behest and continued to maintain close ties to his administrative network.[98] The Security and Protection Bureau ran its secret hospitals and radiation monitoring facilities in close coordination with the Ministry of Public Health. The Ministry of Posts and Telecommunications contributed to the satellite control network. Institutes of the CAS worked closely with Nie's bureaus on technical problems. So, too, did many research facilities based at major universities, all of which fell under the state educational bureaucracy.

This sort of horizontal coordination, as we have noted, diverged from the usual, rigidly vertical pattern of managerial organization in the PRC. The vertical pattern, which has been a major theme of the secondary literature on Chinese politics, would have assured, for instance, that bureaucrats in the Ministries of Public Health, Geology, and the PLA navy would have little institutionalized contact.[99] But in the pattern of organization applied to the strategic weapons programs, navy cadres overseeing work on submarine reactors were granted a substantial measure of routine and institutionalized contact with cadres in the Ministry of Geology charged with uranium prospecting, as well as with public health officials monitoring radiation exposure. This type of horizontalism evolved into a formal and institutionalized feature of the daily professional landscape.

These horizontal professional ties ultimately divided many bureaucratic hierarchies into separate domains, characterized by little professional and social overlap. Geological scientists in the strategic weapons program often had less bureaucratic and professional contact with fellows in the vertical geology hierarchy than with colleagues in strategic weapons work located in separate bureaucratic systems, such as reactor construction, fuels production, or missilery. What emerged as a result of this horizontalism were informal networks of shared professional identity and interest.

Flattening Hierarchy

Nie Rongzhen and other leaders of China's strategic weapons programs essentially swept away the conventional PRC organizational structure of an extraordinary number of administrative layers and rigid hierarchies.

In its place, they fashioned an array of institutionalized avenues of communication—such as the CSC—by which scientific and technical staff had direct and regular access to the country's most senior political leaders. With weapons scientists, engineers, and designers able to discuss directly with the country's most powerful politicians the technical feasibility of demands from above, as well as the resources that would be needed to fulfill those demands, a symbiotic connection between "demand pull" and "discovery push" was created.

To institutionalize contact between technical personnel and top political leaders, the leadership convened a regular series of leadership seminars. The very first seminar between top leaders and scientists and technicians, on the subject of uranium geology, and attended by Liu Jie, Li Siguang, and Premier Zhou, was in January 1955. This session was then repeated for Chairman Mao and the Politburo. It became the model that Nie strove to emulate, and thence to institutionalize.[100] Once institutionalized, it remained in place—with some exceptions between 1968 and 1970—throughout the entire Mao period.

In a typical seminar, held on June 25, 1971 in the run-up to the first test of what initially appeared to be a successful design of China's nuclear-powered submarine (SSBN), Nie arranged numerous sessions for technicians and the top political-military leadership. In a retrospective account written in 1988, Peng Shilu, co–chief designer of the nuclear submarine's power plant, recalls how Nie instructed him to attend this seminar in Beijing with Premier Zhou Enlai, Marshal Nie himself, Marshal Ye Jianying, and other senior political and military leaders.[101] As with all such sessions, this one covered a range of specific and detailed technical issues, in this case related to reactor performance and the feasibility of an early trial. It was at this meeting that the precise operational procedures for carrying out China's first nuclear submarine reactor test were settled; that is, not via guidelines issued from above by leading politicians, but through consultation and exchange between political and military leaders and technical specialists. In the case of the submarine reactor, Peng Shilu has told us, the premier recommended a go-slow approach premised on a four-phase test of the boat: at the pier, on the surface, submerged in shallow water, and finally submerged in deep water. When "abnormal phenomena" arose during the test, the premier again intervened to scale back ambitious plans and call for a "summing up" of experiences before further tests.[102]

From the perspective of the top political leadership, what Nie and his aides had established was a direct line downward to project technicians. This assured extraordinary political attention to specifically technical problems and enabled close and careful monitoring from above. But it also allowed technical staff to argue for more resources, including key material inputs that only high-level political intervention could guarantee.

Meetings to review performance and issue guidance are common in Chinese organizations. But they are often pro forma and serve the purely political purpose of transmitting instructions—a one-way flow. By contrast, seminars such as the one that Peng Shilu had with the top leadership were obviously substantive. Eventually, many high-priority civilian technical projects would attempt to copy this administrative arrangement. Sometimes, as with the Three Gorges Dam, the result was success, partly because large projects such as the dam are also intrinsically highly political and thereby command the attention of the top leadership.[103] More often, however, these efforts failed because of a lack of interest among senior political leaders and/or the inability of the project to institutionalize contacts with the most powerful leaders of the country.

Nie's staff also resorted to other means to create institutionalized horizontal coordination that served to further flatten bureaucratic hierarchy. Project offices represented one such means and proved crucial to success precisely because the attention of top political leaders is time sensitive and, hence, unstable. Nie's project offices regularized leadership-technician contact by limiting the number of administrative levels separating technical staff in the design institutes from the top political-military leadership in the Politburo and the CMC. Indeed, the creation of project-specific offices with Politburo sanction to "steal" personnel, gather resources, and raid other bureaucratic systems (including civilian systems) allowed the offices to work their will on behalf of technical staff throughout the fragmented and slow-moving Chinese bureaucracy.

Marshal Nie first began to experiment with such offices in the late 1950s. Still, the routinized and institutionalized form that the offices later took was something that emerged over a period of years. In the nuclear submarine program, a high-level office was not created until February 1968, when the so-called 09 Office, or Lingjiuban, was established in response to dissatisfaction among top politicians in Beijing with the program's lack of progress as well as political interference from mid-levels and lower.[104] By 1968, Nie's aides had already garnered considerable experience from experimenting with such groups in the atomic bomb and strategic missile programs of the previous decade. These offices provided a model on which to draw. Accordingly, the Lingjiuban was given great coordinating authority across the horizontal gaps of the Chinese political system, allowing technical staff to leverage the powers institutionalized within the offices by the top leadership in order to overcome bureaucratic and other barriers to cross-system collaboration.

Chen Youming, the navy officer whom Nie designated to head the Lingjiuban, exercised his authority frequently in the late 1960s. During this period, the higher-level command structure of the submarine program shifted repeatedly, as mentioned earlier. Chen's office lent a degree of administrative stability to the submarine project, while providing a direct and institutionalized pipeline above the heads of rival command organs directly to the premier. Thus, irrespective of which command organ held authority over the project, the Lingjiuban was guaranteed access to Zhou Enlai and, through him, to Chairman Mao. From this position of institutional strength, Chen Youming could provide the project's technical staff with stable upward-downward links to the topmost political leadership. And he could control for the more egregious dysfunctions of rigid hierarchy when command and oversight for the project shifted repeatedly from agency to agency.

The court of final appeal for project technicians—indeed, the most important structure of all in the entire history of Chinese strategic weapons development—was the Central Special Commission of the Chinese Communist Party (CSC), created in November 1962 to institutionalize contact between top technicians and senior political leaders. This, too, represented an attempt to flatten hierarchy, while coping with jurisdictional bickering.[105] Ironically, the origin of the CSC lay not with Marshal Nie, but with his rival, General Luo Ruiqing.

As noted earlier, the struggles between Nie's circle and that grouped around Luo and Marshal He Long had led to a breakdown of political-technical and cross-agency coordination that Nie's aides considered the crucial, defining feature of their evolving managerial system. Here, Nie bears some responsibility, since his battles with Luo introduced political struggle, albeit over control of the policy agenda, into the military industrial complex.

In the early 1960s, after more than five years of jurisdictional bickering, the premier began to search for an institutionalized means to resolve this dispute.[106] His search ended with the formation of the CSC, which had actually been in gestation for some time.

In 1958, Chinese political leaders took the first of several successive steps to reorganize the defense industry. On October 16, 1958, they established the National Defense Science and Technology Commission (NDSTC) (Guofang kewei), under the command of Nie Rongzhen.[107] The creation of the NDSTC marked the first move in centralizing control over the strategic weapons programs, for the establishment of a high-level body reporting directly to the party's Central Military Commission (CMC) seemed a logical administrative step to ensure cooperation among organizations at the bottom. First and foremost, this was because the NDSTC spoke on behalf of the CMC, and was thus an organ of the Communist Party and not a governmental agency. As such, the NDSTC could lay nearly automatic claim to extensive proprietary rights throughout the Chinese bureaucracy.

This lent Nie's new commission the ability to mobilize resources and to command compliance virtually at will. The NDSTC merged two older bodies created by China's initial push for defense industrialization in the wake of the Korean War: the Aviation Industrial Commission of the Ministry of National Defense, founded in 1956 by merging other agencies and headed by Nie; and the Research and Development Office of the PLA general staff (Zongcan keyan chu), charged with conventional weapons development and headed by General Zhang Aiping, the PLA's deputy chief of staff in charge of equipment planning. From this point forward, General Zhang, who will figure prominently in subsequent chapters of this book, entered Marshal Nie's patronage network.[108] Finally, in April 1959, the triad of agencies that comprised the original NDSTC was completed when the PLA's so-called Fifth Bureau, an administrative department in charge of the oversight of a wide variety of missile research facilities, was folded into Nie's commission.[109]

The NDSTC gave Marshal Nie and his circle control over resources in three often irreconcilable bureaucratic systems: the PLA; the ministries and government agencies of the State Council; and the defense-related institutes and university departments under the control of the Chinese Academy of Sciences. Marshal Nie exercised his authority within the PLA as chairman of the NDSTC; he controlled State Council resources from his post as chairman of the State Science and Technology Commission (SSTC); and as chairman of China's Central Science and Technology Leading Group, in charge of preparing national policy guidelines, and vice premier in charge of science and technology, he commanded most of the resources of the CAS. Nie further solidified his control by appointing deputies and staff secretaries in all three systems who shared key elements of his vision. These included four NDSTC deputy directors—Generals Chen Geng, Zhang Aiping, Liu Yalou, and Wan Yi—who were among the PLA's most ardent post–Korean War modernizers.[110]

All of this gave Nie an important power base to push his agenda, and promote his personnel, with the political leadership. But in December 1959, one year after the formation of the NDSTC, the CMC established a parallel body, the National Defense Industrial Commission (NDIC) (Guofang gongwei), under the chairmanship of Marshal He Long. This decision flowed from several vexing problems in equipment procurement after the Korean War, and at least initially the leadership clearly hoped that the NDIC could work to resolve these problems, while aiding Nie's NDSTC in its broader mission to develop China's military technology base.

But the NDIC was born just as China entered the Three Hard Years (1960–63) after the failures of the Great Leap Forward. This heightened wrangling within the PLA over priorities as resources dried up and political competition to control the budgets and supplies that remained intensified. He Long and his ally, Luo Ruiqing, thereby gained a platform from which to assert their alternative vision of PLA modernization—one that stressed conventional weapons and, as happened at Beidaihe, contradicted much of Marshal Nie's agenda.

Perhaps because of this, the NDSTC–NDIC system failed to solve supply bottlenecks and in fact spawned a political logjam within military industry. The leadership's next solution only exacerbated the problem. In November 1961, the politicians established a third body, in addition to NDSTC and NDIC, the National Defense Industries Office (NDIO) (Guofang gongban), directed by Luo Ruiqing.[111] Here, Premier Zhou sought to create a genuinely coordinating body that could mediate between Nie's NDSTC and He Long's NDIC, while coordinating R&D with production needs for all Chinese weapons programs, strategic and conventional.[112] But as we have seen, General Luo owed some of his rise to power to He Long and the two men shared the view that conventional weapons needs, particularly those of the air force, were being slighted. By the time of the Beidaihe conference, then, it had become clear that although the NDIO was originally intended to act as a mediator, NDSTC leaders viewed it as a less-than-impartial arbiter. As resources became tighter in the wake of the Great Leap, Nie badly wanted some of the NDIC's research facilities placed under the authority of the NDSTC. But Luo's office was in a position to throw up administrative roadblocks to prevent this. For example, Luo's NDIO exercised formal oversight over the Second Ministry of Machine Building, the ministry in charge of the nuclear industry, and thus had a direct line of control over the reprocessing of uranium, the production of nuclear fuels, plant construction, and auxiliary industrial production.

In September 1962, China's most senior politicians moved to resolve the problem once and for all. After receiving a 1961 report prepared by three of Nie's aides—Zhang Aiping, Liu Jie, and Liu Xiyao—that described the poor coordination in the nuclear industry, Zhou began to doubt that China could meet Nie's atomic bomb test deadline of mid-to-late 1964.[113] Thus, the premier, together with Liu Shaoqi, requested that Luo Ruiqing suggest a solution to the coordination problems that the creation of the NDIO had failed to solve. Luo proposed the establishment of a new top-level coordinating body, chaired by the premier, and reporting directly to the Politburo. With the acquiescence of Marshals Nie and He Long and other key figures, the leadership created the CCP Central Special Commission on November 17, 1962. The CSC had fifteen original members, all from top military and industrial bureaucracies. In March 1965, the membership was expanded to twenty-two, and the CSC was given its formal name.

As the direct agent of the Politburo, the CSC had final and unquestioned authority over all Chinese strategic weapons programs, including auxiliary work in fuels, metals, electronics, and chemicals. Nie writes in his memoir that "after the formation of the Central Special Commission, every important test in the bomb and missile programs, every existing problem, was submitted to the commission for discussion and resolution."[114] This ultimately enhanced the administrative flatness of Nie's system because CSC meetings soon came to deal with explicitly technical matters. Scientists and engineers were invited to attend specially convened CSC sessions for the explicit purpose of discussing their concerns directly with leading politicians and ministers. This was done in joint sessions that brought the scientists, the politicians, and the ministers together in small, highly focused, entirely technical discussions.[115]

Benchmarking, Competition, and Standards-Based Performance Metrics

The fourth and final component of the Chinese organizational style in strategic weapons programs—the rigorous measurement of progress against international technical developments—was something military leaders promoted even during Communist China's deepest periods of isolation from international commerce, intellectual discourse, and technical contacts. The presence of technicians at the administrative core of the strategic weapons programs had a decisive effect on both institutional evolution and work styles because incessant benchmarking and a culture of experiment lent a cosmopolitan flavor to strategic weapons work that was noticeably absent from most other parts of the Chinese system. Elsewhere, demands from above, channeled downward through elaborate hierarchies, reinforced tendencies toward the routinization of already existing procedures.

Strategic weaponeers had three special advantages in this regard. First, they enjoyed comparatively open access to information from abroad, which even during the worst years of China's technical isolation enabled benchmarking against international developments. Both competing reactor designs for the nuclear submarine were based on foreign models, one West German, the other Soviet. Similar competition took place in the design of the submarine's hull, as well as in determining the method of plutonium separation to fuel a hydrogen bomb.[116] Second, their design institutes benefited from the large-scale information clearinghouse system, established by the leadership, which included bureaus, such as the nuclear program's Eleventh Bureau, devoted to the collection, indexing, translation, and abstraction of foreign technical materials. Finally, they alone, unlike all other sectors of Chinese industry, possessed the full support of the Politburo to step outside the isolation that was an obviously unnatural state in which to conduct scientific research, especially in light of the comparatively borderless nature of international science during the twentieth century.

Nie Rongzhen and his aides accomplished all this in the first instance through several bureaucratic measures designed to foster a climate of openness. For the atomic bomb program, as we have noted, they founded an

Information Bureau, which gathered and translated Western and Soviet technical materials. This clearinghouse proved crucial to China's initial success with nuclear weapons technology in 1964.[117] In turn, privileged access to technical literature from overseas contributed to the effectiveness of everyday work. For example, in the competition for the design of the reactor for China's nuclear submarine, engineers were invited by the project leadership to submit proposals. Ultimately, two primary alternatives emerged: one, submitted in 1965 by the nominally civilian Institute of Nuclear Technology of Beijing's Qinghua University, proposed a pressurized water reactor (PWR) of a type then under development by the West German firm Gesellschaft für Kernenergieverwertung in Schiffbau und Schiffahrt mbH (GKSS); the alternative, competing design sought to refit a Soviet reactor used on a nuclear icebreaker to the requirements of a smaller submarine.

It seems remarkable in retrospect that the Chinese knew so much about the GKSS system. Certainly, this testifies to the comparatively open access to technical information from the West in the 1960s. The GKSS system had initially been developed for a 15,000-ton ore carrier and research vessel, the *Otto Hahn*. Qinghua's marine reactor engineers were familiar with the technical specifications of the *Otto Hahn*'s power plant because they had read an array of West German publications about the ship as well as GKSS's own internal technical studies. Qinghua's main competitor in the reactor contest—Institute 194 (Reactor Engineering and Technology Institute) of the Second Ministry—submitted the winning design, developed by a team working under Peng Shilu. Like the Qinghua proposal, Peng's design also centered on the reengineering of a foreign model. Using extensive Soviet technical publications and data, Peng's team proposed to convert a type of reactor developed for the Soviet nuclear icebreaker *Lenin* to submarine use. According to a memoir by the Mao-era navy commander Xiao Jingguang, Chinese shipbuilding circles were acquainted with the *Lenin* because PLA generals and navy cadres had been able to form some broad impressions of the ship during technology transfer negotiations with the Soviet Union in 1957.[118]

The competition over the two rival designs, both developed almost exclusively from foreign data, proved intense. The discussion ranged across a series of purely technical issues: Was the GKSS system too slow and small? Could an icebreaker system be adapted to underwater use? Of course, since the debate touched institutional and political rivalries, those may have played a role in determining the winning design, as may have patronage and personality—Peng Shilu was an adopted son of Premier Zhou Enlai and the natural-born son of Peng Pai, a revolutionary hero martyred during the Communist march to power. Still, the technical debate over these two systems was genuine and focused almost exclusively on data gleaned from abroad, including Western sources in protected, sensitive, and strategic industrial sectors.[119]

Borrowing from abroad, which became common throughout the Chinese strategic weapons programs, reflected a receptive and comparative style of work: "Which system is best?" "What are our capabilities?" This style was all the more important since by 1961, three years before China exploded its first atomic bomb and many more years before a viable SSBN design came off the drawing board, Chinese science had been forced into near isolation by the withdrawal of Soviet technicians. In a sense, China's strategic weapons community became utterly dependent on the capacity of Marshal Nie and his staff to guarantee access to overseas data and publications. Without the opportunity to travel abroad, to network and attend conferences, or to peruse the work of foreign colleagues, isolation would have been crippling were it not for the openness built into the strategic weapons system. This made scientific and technical work in China highly unusual, if not unique. Even Soviet weapons physicists, at the height of the Cold War, had been hosted at the British nuclear weapons laboratory at Harwell; the scientific leader of Stalin's nuclear weapons program, Igor Kurchatov, delivered a well-received lecture on controlled fusion at Harwell and dined with Nikita Khrushchev and Britain's political elite at 10 Downing Street.[120] For Chinese scientists, such a prospect would simply have been unimaginable during these years. Above all, then, it was the politicians' commitment to strategic weapons, and Nie's ability to institutionalize access to data, that sustained scientific endeavor during the darkest days of Chinese seclusion after 1960.

A culture of experiment also contributed to China's strategic weapons programs in the years after the Sino-Soviet split. For example, the SLBM chief designer, Huang Weilu, tested boat survivability in the event of ejection failure by repeatedly taking a team after midnight to the bridge over the Yangzi River in Nanjing to drop dummy missiles at different angles, evaluating damage to the missile, as well as extrapolating from that damage to estimate likely (consequent) damage to boat and crew.[121] Sometimes, experimentation implied a hands-on melding of theoretical design with mundane fact checking. When the SSBN chief designer, Huang Xuhua, and his staff had difficulty calculating the overall weight and center of gravity of the boat, Huang dispatched his engineers to the factory floor, measuring piece-by-piece the weights and gravity centers of each individual boat component. This recalls famous anecdotes from the history of American science and technology development—for example, NASA's piece-by-piece analysis of the components of a crippled Apollo 13. In this sense, it reflects the degree to which the "culture" of science compensates for some of the dysfunctions of a particular political and institutional climate.

THE MILITARY IMPACT: THE WEAPONS PROGRAMS AND THE TECHNOLOGY BASE

The decisive influence of the strategic military-technical alternative in shaping Chinese science, technology, industry, institution building, and development policy can perhaps best be appreciated by examining its role in three areas: personnel arrangements for scientists and technicians; the development of China's modern technical infrastructure; and the evolution of technical education and laboratory work in universities, the Chinese Academy of Sciences, and, of course, military facilities.

The Military and China's Technical Communities

The Chinese Communists began to assemble a national science system almost immediately after the founding of the PRC in October 1949. "In the early post-Liberation period," notes Marshal Nie Rongzhen, who would in effect take over the administration of Chinese science in 1958, when he was appointed chairman of both the national defense and civilian science and technology commissions, China's scientific infrastructure rested on a foundation of just "forty research institutes, engaging some 650 people who studied both natural and social sciences. In November 1949, when the Chinese Academy of Sciences was established [through the merger of] the former National Research Institute and the National Academy in Beiping, there were just . . . 200 research workers" in its core staff.[122]

Part of the problem for China's earliest nuclear weapons administrators, then, was that China lacked the basic scientific and technical infrastructure, and especially the personnel, to pursue advanced weapons technologies. The United States had launched the crash Manhattan Project during World War II with a large scientific staff of leading American and expatriate specialists in nuclear and detonation physics, radiochemistry, and mechanical engineering. In the Soviet Union, the Stalinist regime had successfully pursued its own crash program directly on the heels of V-J day because Kurchatov, Khariton, Landau, Flerov, and an assortment of other scientists associated with Ioffe's physiotechnical institute near Leningrad had been working in relevant research fields for more than two decades.[123] At the time of the January 1955 decision to develop nuclear weapons, by contrast, China possessed no institute akin to Ioffe's, and Chinese physics in the early 1950s had focused primarily on the problem of assembling laboratory infrastructure and research programs at major universities and in the CAS.

Having missed the revolution during what Hans Bethe has termed the "happy Thirties" in nuclear physics,[124] Chinese physics was, in a very real sense, carried into the quantum age in the 1940s–50s by the small core of physicists trained abroad by the pioneers of the quantum revolution. Nearly all of these men ultimately became pivotal players in the Chinese nuclear weapons program, hardly surprising in light of the strategic importance of their research and the opportunities it presented to "do" science in a fashion that largely freed them from political interference.

The pioneers of China's military nuclear program included virtually all of the major figures at China's leading physics departments during the 1950s—at Beijing and Qinghua Universities—as well as the small group of men who had established China's main physics infrastructure in the CAS.[125] Their undisputed leader was the nuclear physicist Qian Sanqiang, who trained in Paris with the Joliot-Curies, where he researched the tripartite fission of uranium and, together with his wife, He Zehui, won the Parville Prize. Their ranks also included Wang Ganchang, who worked on radioactivity and bubble chambers in Berlin with Lise Meitner; and Peng Huanwu, Max Born's first Chinese student at Edinburgh, who studied cosmic rays.

Outside physics, and especially in engineering, the pioneering influence of the men who later led China's strategic weapons development proved equally important. The leading figures, trained abroad, included several of those we have already mentioned. The aerospace engineer Qian Xuesen, who not only trained at Caltech but held an endowed professorship—the Goddard chair—there, led the Chinese missile program. Ren Xinmin, who studied at the University of Michigan and then moved to a university engineering laboratory in Buffalo, broke ground in liquid propellants for Chinese missiles and in satellite communications. Tu Shou'e, who studied at MIT and also worked in Buffalo, at Curtis Aircraft, became the chief designer of China's ICBM. Liang Shoupan, another graduate of MIT, became chief designer of China's cruise missiles and its foremost expert on missile engines. Because China's strategic weapons pioneers were also its scientific and technical pioneers, it was perhaps inevitable that they should have been recruited into military work.

The staff of the CAS was also top-heavy with scientists working in the strategic weapons programs. In the early years of the academy, leading posts were usually occupied by eminent scientists, such as Qian Sanqiang. Strategic weaponeers have traditionally comprised a large proportion of CAS academicians; the nuclear weapons design academy (the Ninth Academy) alone has accounted for twenty-one academicians, a high proportion when one considers that the CAS generally has only around 200 academicians in its membership. These include the founding pioneers of the discipline of nuclear physics in China, including the pioneers of basic research on cosmic rays (Peng Huanwu), bubble chambers (Wang Ganchang), particle and high-energy work, and other fields: Zhu Guangya, Cheng Kaijia, Deng Jiaxian, Guo Yonghuai, Yu Min, and Zhou Guangzhao.[126] This extraordinary proportion of strategic weaponeers within the ranks of CAS personnel becomes even higher when one adds academicians from other defense R&D academies and institutes, including Qian Xuesen, missile and satellite engineers such as Yang Jiachi and Chen Fangyun, and electronics and radar pioneers such as Luo Peilin.

In addition to the CAS members affiliated with research institutions throughout China, many of the main bureaus at the CAS headquarters in Beijing have also been thoroughly dominated by strategic weaponeers and military scientists. According to Gu Yu, in the 1960s half of the personnel under the New Technologies Bureau of the Academy (code-named the 04 Bureau), which Gu once headed, worked exclusively on strategic weapons–oriented projects. This totaled more than 30,000 individuals, of whom at least 10,000 were researchers and technicians.[127] This special bureau at the CAS headquarters had been established largely at the behest of Marshal Nie, as part of his search for institutionalized means to facilitate coordination between the military and the CAS and thus "to ensure that research institutes under the academy would coordinate more closely with military departments in the development of [strategic] weapons."[128] Zhang Jingfu, a vice president and key political leader of the CAS, acted as the main liaison official with the defense industrial system and Marshal Nie and his aides at the NDSTC. Coordination became close and remains so to this day. For instance, in 1956, during the start-up of the nuclear and land-based missile programs, the CAS convened a high-level meeting at Beijing's Xijiao Hotel attended by more than 200 scientists and technicians, plus approximately ten Soviet advisors, to discuss the academy's role in military industrial development. Considering that the CAS had a staff of just 200 six-and-a-half years earlier in mid-1949, it becomes clear how large a commitment to military industry is implied by the participation of 200 of its personnel at the 1956 session.[129] In short, throughout the 1950s and early 1960s, scientists connected with the military predominated at the CAS and in turn the CAS played a pivotal role in the development of all the main strategic weapons programs, particularly the nuclear and satellite programs.

This intimate relationship has left a significant legacy. Key figures in military technology and weapons design in the 1950s and 1960s went on to occupy leading positions in the CAS in later years. Wang Daheng (missile and satellite optics) and Shi Changxu (supersonic and cast multiholed turbo-prop aircraft metallurgy) successively became directors of the interdisciplinary Department of Technical Sciences—essentially the academy's high technology planning department—during the 1980s and 1990s. This department is heavily populated by former strategic weaponeers; its deputy directors have included China's most famous military supercomputer designer, the late Ci Yungui, and Chen Fangyun, China's leading radioelectronics engineer, who played a major role in missile and satellite tracking. Zhou Guangzhao, academy president from 1987 to 1997, formerly led the academy's Department of Mathematics and Physics. Zhou performed the final design check for the atomic bomb and was a key leader of that program under his mentor, Peng Huanwu, who led its theoretical division.

In addition to key leaders of departments and bureaus at the CAS headquarters, many famed CAS institute directors throughout the country, including Wang Daheng at the Optical and Precision Machinery Institute in Changchun, and Shi Changxu at the Institute of Metals in Shenyang, held administrative appointments in nominally CAS-based units that in practice (with respect to large parts of their work) fell under the supervision of key military technology Leading Groups, coordinating headquarters, and thus the administrative apparatus of the various high-priority weapons programs.

During the Mao era, three out of four chairmen of the China Association for Science and Technology (CAST) (Zhongguo kexue jishu xiehui)—a bridge between the government, professional societies, and scientists—were technical leaders of the strategic weapons programs: Li Siguang, the geologist, who gave Mao and the Politburo their initial seminar in uranium geology and reactor physics; Qian Xuesen of the missile programs; and Zhu Guangya, who, as we have noted, played a major administrative role in the nuclear weapons program and served as a key link between administrators and scientists. Only the Beijing University physicist Zhou Peiyuan played no role in weapons development.[130]

Marshal Nie and his staff moved quickly to build a network around these core scientists who had returned from an overseas training. At the outset of the nuclear program, for example, the leadership undertook to transfer a large number of technical personnel out of civilian R&D into military organizations and units. This began in August 1955, eight months after the atomic bomb decision, when the CCP Organization Department removed some seventy civilian electrical engineers, including Luo Peilin, into military industry. The truly crucial decision, Nie reveals in his memoir, was subsequently taken at a meeting of civilian bureaucrats from the education, machine building, chemical, and railways industries in June 1956. With the support of Premier Zhou Enlai, the leadership immediately transferred some 380 dispersed technical personnel into strategic weapons work, effectively "stealing" them from the civilian sector at a time when China's base of advanced research personnel was comparatively small.[131]

This powerful demonstration of the preeminence of the military in work assignments soon became institutionalized in procedures for job assignments for college graduates and personnel with technical training.

Once scientists and technical specialists entered the world of strategic weapons work during the Mao years, they effectively left the civilian sphere for a secretive bureaucratic realm controlled by the PLA. That they remained active in the CAS and in universities, and indeed that they often occupied leading positions in these ostensibly civilian institutions, reveals how deeply the military had penetrated society.

The Military and China's Technical Infrastructure

The influence military scientists and engineers exerted on the development of China's human infrastructure for high-level science and engineering was matched only by the impact of the strategic weapons programs on the development of a material and physical infrastructure for research, experiment, education, and "hands-on" laboratory training. The impact of strategic weapons on national science budgets, for example, is beyond dispute: after the decision in January 1955 to build nuclear weapons, "funds for science rose from about U.S.$15 million in 1955 to about U.S.$100 million in 1956; the Chinese Academy of Sciences received three times as much money in 1957 as it had received in 1953, with a large fraction going to purchase scientific literature from the West."[132]

The strategic weapons programs monopolized many of the best and most advanced research and laboratory facilities during the Mao years. This was in large part because the weapons programs were responsible for the construction of the facilities in the first place. Nie Rongzhen's administrative circle created China's most advanced (and often its first) wind tunnels, testing pools, blast facilities, and shock wave simulation chambers.[133] Laboratory facilities in critical areas, such as the development of chemical reagents, were often vastly inadequate until military administrators stepped in.

Even in civilian institutions, advanced research centers were built specifically for the strategic weapons programs. Major university laboratories, such as Jiaotong University's hydrodynamic wave tank, owed much of their funding to the nuclear submarine and other strategic weapons programs. And Qinghua University, as we have discussed, was a key site of weapons reactor design, submitting one of the two competing designs for the nuclear submarine power plant. Qinghua's Institute of Nuclear Energy Technology also played a major role in the bomb-grade plutonium separation program, while Zhejiang University in Hangzhou made important contributions in the field of optical physics for missiles and satellites.

The incorporation of a large part of China's elite university system into strategic weapons work reflects the power of the enterprise, but also the importance of the system-wide effort to advance science and technology in an atmosphere of scarce resources. Marshal Nie, for instance, spoke often of the division of scientific labor into five main "front armies" (*fangmianjun*), only one of which was essentially military: China's defense R&D institutes, such as the Ninth Academy or the Fifth Academy. The other four "armies," Nie declared, proved to be indispensable to the development of strategic weapons. Many projects were farmed out to the institutes and laboratories in these four, essentially "civilian," systems: the laboratories of the CAS, industrial departments, colleges and universities under China's education bureaucracy, and local research organizations. As noted, university scientists made special contributions, especially in reactor research and in optical physics. "We particularly stressed," Nie has written, "that civilian research organizations must aid the research of their military counterparts in sophisticated weapons work, exemplified in the guided missile and atomic bomb" programs.[134]

Precision industrial sectors, including metallurgy, chemical engineering, electronics, and so on, have especially strong traditions of military dominance. Indeed, China's metallurgy and chemical industries were initially organized largely around military programs and the heavy industries that served them. Marshal Nie himself played a critical role in arranging the bureaucratic command system for the sector. Likewise, China's telecommunications industry, though a (mostly) civilian sector from the early 1950s on, made important contributions to the strategic weapons programs.[135]

The Military in China's Technical Education

Not surprisingly, especially given the relative stability of strategic weapons work compared to the repeated political assaults on civilian science in successive ideological remolding movements of the 1950s and 1960s, the military and its technical programs have also exerted a powerful influence on the course of scientific education and training in China.

Paralleling China's vast military education network, including the Harbin College of Military Engineering and an array of specialized ground, naval, air, and defense industry technical institutes, as discussed earlier the military also controlled much of the high-level research performed by laboratories at civilian institutions during the Mao years.[136] As in the United States, where prestigious civilian academic institutions, such as MIT, Stanford, and

Caltech have performed vast amounts of military research, much of the core research for the strategic weapons programs was performed not in military institutes, such as the laboratories attached to the Fifth, Seventh, Ninth, and Tenth Academies, but in university laboratories, such as those at Qinghua University and the Dalian Institute of Technology.

As a result, the strategic weapons programs successfully created many of China's most important scientific education and training arrangements, with military influence manifest as a result at both the top (postdoctoral education and training) and bottom (undergraduate job assignment) of China's educational ladder in science and engineering. In the assignment of younger technical talent, many of the best and brightest in science and engineering were siphoned off in the 1950s and 1960s by Nie Rongzhen and his program administrators. After their college years, many Chinese scientists then received the equivalent of their doctoral or postdoctoral training in Nie's strategic weapons mentoring arrangements. An example from the atomic bomb program perhaps illustrates this point best. When a team under the Purdue-trained physicist Deng Jiaxian performed the final calculations in the run-up to the October 1964 test, its members averaged just twenty-three years of age. In effect, the bomb program provided these individuals with doctoral or postdoctoral training, and even today the Ninth Academy and other weapons-technical institutes continue to grant Ph.D. degrees, to award research fellowships, and to hold seminars, symposia, and national conferences. The Mao years were, of course, a time of widespread persecution of intellectuals, including scientists and engineers. The military provided the only continuous outlet during Mao's rule for training by leading scientists with state-of-the-art equipment and in modern laboratories and research facilities. Until the post-Mao reform era, the only consistently stable environment for scientific research and engineering in China existed in the high-priority facilities attached to the strategic weapons programs.

Marshal Nie endeavored to institutionalize technical training via formalized mentoring arrangements in all the major strategic weapons programs. This had the practical effect of transferring junior personnel from civilian or conventional weapons industry into strategic weapons–oriented apprenticeships under senior scientists (*daoshi*), such as Qian Xuesen, Wang Ganchang, Peng Huanwu, and Deng Jiaxian. The typical arrangement placed up to eight junior assistants under the supervision of a senior researcher. Zhou Guangzhao received early patronage from Peng Huanwu in such an arrangement, and a future director of the defense industrial commission, Nie Rongzhen's son-in-law, the (now-retired) optical engineer Lieutenant General Ding Henggao, appears to have worked under Wang Daheng at the CAS Optical and Precision Machinery Institute in Changchun.

The Nie leadership also transferred many Chinese students, both at home and in Soviet institutions, into technical subjects with military implications. One centerpiece of Sino-Soviet educational collaboration in the 1950s was an agreement that sent fifty Chinese engineers to the Moscow Aviation Institute for training in missile-related subjects. Nie also encouraged civilian universities to found departments of electrical engineering and radio electronics, fields he believed to be China's weakest links. Many contemporary electrical engineering departments in China trace their origins to this military push in the late 1950s.[137]

Taken together, this adds up to an important legacy of military development in China. First, the period from 1950 to 1975 yielded a unique template of managerial institutions. The survival of a comparatively flexible system for managing innovation amidst the stifling atmosphere that prevailed elsewhere in the Chinese system offered evidence that institutions could be fashioned in the Chinese context in which risk would be rewarded and eclecticism valued and encouraged from above. Second, the strategic foundations of so much of China's Mao-era economic policy became institutionalized as a developmental doctrine. By 1975, China's debate about the optimal road to economic modernization had become intrinsically linked to broader questions of national security and national power. The remainder of this book tackles the legacies of this era of military developmentalism. As we shall see, the power of its ideas, coupled with the survival of the strategic weapons elite through the chaos of the Cultural Revolution, made this doctrine and its organizational complement an important legacy for China's leaders as they moved to refocus the country's goals on national economic growth.

Marshal Nie Rongzhen (center), with missile pioneer Qian Xuesen (front row, third from left), visiting ground zero on the second anniversary of China's first nuclear test, October 1966.

Top, Chairman Mao Zedong (center)
at a military industrial plant.

Bottom, Marshal Liu Bocheng (saluting),
doctrinal innovator, at the Harbin College
of Military Engineering.

Above, Marshal He Long (applauding), advocate of conventional weapons modernization, at the Harbin College of Military Engineering.

Left, Gen. Luo Ruiqing (second from right), advocate of conventional weapons modernization.

Right, China's
post-Mao leader,
Deng Xiaoping.

Bottom, Marshal
Ye Jianying (center)
at an aircraft factory
in July 1972.

Top, Gen. Hong Xuezhi (at left, shaking hands), pioneer of China's post–Korean War logistics system, in 1988.

Bottom, Gen. Liu Huaqing (fourth from left), strategic weapons administrator, naval modernizer, and executive vice chairman of the Central Military Commission, in 1989.

Top, President Jiang Zemin talks with missile pioneer Qian Xuesen in 1989.
At far left is Lt. Gen. Ding Henggao, director of the Commission of
Science, Technology, and Industry for National Defense (COSTIND).

Bottom, Tu Shou'e (third from right), chief designer of China's
intercontinental ballistic missiles (ICBM).

Top, Liang Shoupan (second from right in front row), missile pioneer and chief designer of China's antiship cruise missiles.

Bottom, Huang Weilu (right), chief designer of China's solid-propelled submarine-launched ballistic missiles (SLBM).

Top, Nuclear weapons administrator and physicist
Zhu Guangya (center), with Marshal Nie Rongzhen (left).

Bottom, Ren Xinmin (left), chief designer of China's
liquid propellant rocket engines, and chief engineer
of China's communication satellite programs.

China's missile and space pioneers share a laugh: Liang Shoupan, cruise missile chief designer (second from left), Cai Jintao, missile guidance pioneer (third from left), Tu Shou'e, ICBM chief designer (fourth from left), Sun Jiadong, remote sensing satellite chief designer (fifth from left), Yang Jiachi, flight control expert (seventh from left).

Top, Huang Xuhua (second from right), chief
designer of China's nuclear-powered ballistic
missile submarine (SSBN).

Bottom, Peng Shilu (left) and Zhao Renkai (right),
co–chief designers of the nuclear reactor for China's
nuclear-powered ballistic missile submarine.

Top, Chen Youming, naval officer and director of the nuclear submarine project office, the Lingjiuban.

Bottom, Zhang Jingfu, longtime liaison between China's strategic weapons programs and the Chinese Academy of Sciences.

Right, Wang Daheng, optical physicist and pioneer of the 863 program.

Bottom, Ci Yungui (second from left), computer scientist and chief designer of the Yinhe supercomputer.

Top, Wang Ganchang (left), nuclear physicist and pioneer of the 863 program.

Bottom, Chen Fangyun (left), radioelectronics expert and pioneer of the 863 program.

Above, Yang Jiachi (second from left), flight control engineer and pioneer of the 863 program.

Right, Zou Jiahua (right), director of the State Planning Commission, and COSTIND deputy director Lt. Gen. Huai Guomo, an advocate of integrating military and civilian industry (center, in uniform).

part two

CHANGE

chapter three

CHANGING COURSE, 1975–1986

Militarization promoted China's rapid development of a high technology base, yet it also severely skewed investment priorities in high technology and precision industry throughout the Mao years. Above all, it saddled the Chinese economy with a mixed legacy of advanced technical competence in several highly specialized industries coupled with rank technical ineptitude in some of the most basic—yet essential—areas of industrial development.

This contradiction became the main target of reformers, who sought to shift high-tech industrial policy in new directions beginning in the late 1970s. As discussed in Chapter 2, during the 1950s and 1960s the agenda associated with Marshal Nie Rongzhen and his circle largely survived challenges from constituencies favoring either civilian priorities or conventional weapons. This reflected the political dexterity of the marshal and his aides. But it also spoke to the degree to which a vision of technology linked to national power could capture the imagination of China's top political elite, particularly Chairman Mao. Inevitably, Marshal Nie's vision became linked to China's precarious strategic position during the Cold War. Once that position changed and the strategic environment became more benign, reform-oriented leaders summarily dispensed with many of the policies that had emerged during the period of high external threat to China's national security.

As reform gathered momentum in the 1980s, the evolution of Chinese strategic technology policy became increasingly complex, touching wide-ranging debates about the relationship of defense and development, technology and modernization, and the military and politics. For the strategic weapons elite, the mere fact that they had survived the Cultural Revolution meant that even as the mass movement had devastated China's already limited cadre of technical specialists, strategic weaponeers had remained (mostly) protected from the political whirlwind. Elitism and intellectuals had been among the central targets of Maoism during the Cultural Revolution. However, it was the most elite among China's intellectuals—the scientists and technicians in the strategic weapons industry—who escaped from the worst of Maoism largely unscathed. Isolated by secrecy and the remote physical location of their work, as well the protective intervention of China's political leadership, the strategic weapons community found itself virtually the only effective technical cadre left in China when the violence at last petered out in the late 1960s and early 1970s.

This did not, however, mean that Nie's agenda for strategic technology could survive intact and wholly unaltered. As early as 1975, the support for strategic weapons as the basis for an integrated national high technology strategy began to erode and in its stead arose a changed political consensus about state investment priorities in high technology.

The new political consensus was premised, first, on China's improved strategic position and, second, on a creeping sense within the country's top political-military leadership that the Nie strategy had bought China a minimum strategic deterrent, but little else. To skeptics, the spin-off it generated had failed to produce the sweeping modernization of advanced industry that Nie so confidently predicted when fending off the opposition at the Beidaihe conference in 1961. The rise of this new, more skeptical political consensus thus led to a series of important changes in China's national security strategy, economic development policy, and investment priorities.

The five chapters of Part 2 consider these shifts in light of several questions: How did changes in priorities after 1975 affect the strategic weaponeers, their goals and policy approaches? What methods did the elite adopt to preserve their political influence amid the collapse of consensus on the Nie technology strategy? What programmatic solutions did they devise to meld past experience to present circumstances, both political and technical? And what have been the consequences of this for China's political economy and the strategic military balance in East Asia?

THE NEW ERA BEGINS

The shift in China's defense technology policy began with the sweeping change in the country's strategic environment in the 1970s, which itself resulted largely from the actions of China's leaders. Chairman Mao and his colleagues fundamentally redirected their foreign policy away from comparatively equal hostility toward the two superpowers to a decisive lean toward the United States. This culminated in the visit of U.S. President Richard M. Nixon to China in 1972.[1]

In the years after Nixon's visit, a struggle for political succession in China also produced a new domestic economic agenda. Together, these twin trends—one, external and related to national security, the other domestic and derived primarily from a struggle over economic policy—altered the underlying rationales for strategic technology planning as well as military force investments. By 1986, they had rendered completely anachronistic the strategy that Marshal Nie had formulated, promoted, and helped to enshrine as national policy during the first two decades of Communist rule.

The curtain rose on these changes just before Mao's death in 1976. In the early 1970s, political fallout from the violence of the Cultural Revolution (1966–71) and its aftermath (1971–76) bankrupted the most critical elements of the Maoist political and economic paradigm. The Cultural Revolution brought China to the brink of anarchy: fighting erupted on the streets of major cities, industry collapsed, and intellectual life ground to a halt. In 1969, border clashes with the Soviet Union nearly thrust the country into war. By 1978, moreover, ideology was largely spent as a political force, and the country's veteran revolutionary leadership, wracked by the upheavals of the mass movement, sought to remove those officials who had come to power after the purges of the late 1960s and early 1970s.

Political veterans argued that removing parvenu officials who had "risen by helicopters" would restore a semblance of stability to Chinese political life and resurrect a political constituency that could set the country back onto the path of sustained economic modernization.

Deng Xiaoping, a former general secretary of the party, was the outstanding figure among these veteran leaders. He was a first-generation revolutionary and had served as a Red Army political commissar during the civil war. Moreover, he had assiduously maintained an extensive network of personal ties to the senior cadres in China's three key centers of power: the

Communist Party, the PLA, and the government apparatus under the State Council.

In 1977, after twice being purged by radicals, Deng made his final, triumphal return to power. Within just two years, he quickly pushed aside Mao's nominal successor, Hua Guofeng, a provincial bureaucrat outmatched by Deng's long experience in national politics. With Hua marginalized, Deng steadied the country for a renewed drive toward accelerated economic growth and in the process he moved rapidly to remake virtually every aspect of China's economic and social framework. He also worked to forge a national consensus for a dramatic shift in the pattern of military involvement in Chinese life. By 1981, the first stage of Deng's demilitarization program was largely complete. The changes Deng introduced to China's military and defense economy during his first years in power sharply altered China's domestic and foreign policy priorities in ways that have resonated for more than twenty years.

DENG'S OBJECTIVE: A STRATEGIC POLICY REVERSAL

Deng Xiaoping's primary objective was to reverse the Maoist emphasis on military and capital-intensive industries. In their place, he favored a program of investment and new incentives to promote civilian construction, mainly in light industry and consumer-oriented sectors. Deng believed that China's investment strategy merited a complete reassessment because of failures of the Mao period. At the same time, he contended that it was China's increasingly secure national security environment that permitted this shift.

Even though Deng sought to demilitarize the Chinese economy, he was as intent as Mao had been on insuring national security above all else. China, he maintained, had been forced to develop a massive military economy in the 1950s and 1960s to protect itself from both superpowers. With the United States, then both the United States and the Soviet Union, arrayed against it, the PRC had fought several wars and otherwise faced a relentless struggle to survive. But after rapprochement with the United States and Japan in the early 1970s, China had cleared away two potential threats while checking Soviet pressure through new strategic partnerships. By the time he came into supreme power in 1978, Deng felt sufficiently confident to predict publicly twenty to fifty years of comparative security after nearly thirty years of unremitting peril to the Communist state.

To succeed in far-reaching demilitarization and a Chinese variant of defense conversion—the transformation of military resources to civil ends—Deng needed to win over entrenched Mao-era military and industrial elites. From the start, this represented a formidable obstacle. For the planners in particular, what Deng proposed was initially deeply unpopular. It not only ran counter to their enshrined values of the entire Mao period, but seemed to imply a diminished role for China's powerful military and industrial elite. But even as China demilitarized, Deng actually undertook to enhance the role of science and technology in national development. He extended and broadened the government's commitment to science in the economy, and invited leading scientists to think about how their work could be applied to civilian uses.

In summary, Deng's new agenda encompassed three fundamental changes: First, it shifted investment strategy from capital intensive to light industries; second, it promoted large-scale demilitarization of industry; and finally, it broadened the role of technology in economic policy.

All three of these shifts had a dramatic effect on how the pioneers of China's strategic technology projects worked, researched, and politicked. Within a few years of Deng's rise to power, Nie's strategic weaponeers faced an uncertain future. Although Deng had adopted Nie's faith in high technology, he deliberately did so in ways that effectively destroyed the political foundations of the strategic weaponeers' dominance of China's national S&T policy.

PHASE I, 1975: DENG HINTS AT FUTURE CHANGE

Deng Xiaoping carefully and painstakingly built a political consensus to sustain this shift in policy. The origin of his thinking on the relationships between national security and development strategy probably dates to the early 1960s. But the transformation of China according to his vision began in earnest only when he had won widespread support for downsizing the military in the face of the new, more benign strategic environment. Deng proceeded in several, highly deliberate phases—the first in 1975 when he began to promote change within the PLA, the rest after 1978 when he focused on the planners and on further rounds of change within the armed forces.

Deng's achievement was considerable, for these were extraordinarily powerful elites whose authority and influence rested on the bedrock of the Mao-era system. Deng's charisma—and his network of political connections—ultimately proved decisive. The consensus that eventually emerged can only be understood, therefore, in terms of Deng Xiaoping himself.

With the experience of the Cultural Revolution behind them, many Chinese leaders believed that the time had arrived for a significant change in economic policy. Deng's achievement was to bring to the challenge the unique political distinction of having supported the very military industry elite whose agenda he now sought to overturn. In the 1950s, Deng had been of considerable assistance to Nie's programs. He attended the January 1955 Politburo meeting on indigenous nuclear weapons development, and made regular visits to strategic weapons facilities thereafter to offer assistance and inspect progress during the 1950s and 1960s.[2] After 1974, Deng had even joined a reinvigorated Central Special Commission, where he worked intensively with Premier Zhou Enlai and Marshals Ye Jianying and Nie Rongzhen to prime the post–Cultural Revolution strategic weapons complex for tests of the SSBN and the SLBM and their eventual deployment. Deng was also a veteran revolutionary whose stature in the PLA remained high. He had once served as Marshal Liu Bocheng's political commissar, and the relationships he cultivated in that post and throughout the pre-Liberation period stood him in good stead when he began his drive for supreme power at the end of the 1970s.

The Military Shift: Demilitarizing the Economy, Downsizing the PLA

In the mid-1970s, Deng Xiaoping returned to full-time military work as executive vice chairman of the CMC. He was warmly welcomed "home" to the PLA by his former comrades. "You, too, are a veteran marshal," Marshal Ye Jianying told him at a party held in 1977 to celebrate Ye's eightieth birthday. "In fact, you are the leader of our marshals."[3] Using connections such as these, around 1975 Deng began to sell senior military commanders and the technology elite on his ideas for fundamentally reshaping policy. In several speeches to high-ranking commanders and commissars, Deng left little doubt that despite his extensive ties to the PLA, he believed its role in China's economy to have become disproportionately large. In these early talks, Deng gave a hint of things to come, while offering a new line of attack on Nie's strategy for high technology investment.

In 1975, with Chairman Mao and Premier Zhou Enlai gravely ill, Deng was recalled to military duty to serve a brief tour as chief of the PLA general staff. Almost immediately, he began a frontal assault on the integrated approach to national security and economic development articulated by Marshal Nie at Beidaihe in 1961. Deng's decision to do so seems to have been anchored in the disturbing conclusions he reached during his short tour at the general staff. In a speech to regimental officers on January 25, 1975, Deng attacked the idea that military priorities could continue to remain at the top of China's development agenda. He bluntly informed his audience that the PLA had become bloated, inefficient, and "not combat worthy" (*daqi zhan lai jiu buxing*).[4]

Deng argued that military readiness and modernization would best be served through consolidation, force reduction, and reorganization. "Our army has fine traditions," he told the officers, "[but] the army was thrown into chaos" during the period in power of Lin Biao and other Cultural Revolution era PLA "radicals." "Now," he said, "many fine traditions have been discarded and the army is bloated. The number of men in the ranks has greatly increased and the military proportion of the state budget is larger than before, with much of that money being used merely to feed and clothe the troops. . . . An excessively large and inefficient army is not combat worthy." Deng concluded: "I think that the overwhelming majority of comrades in the army are dissatisfied with this state of affairs. . . . Thus, comrade Mao Zedong has called for the consolidation of the armed forces. The size of the army must be reduced. We must deal with the problem of overstaffing and restore the fine traditions [of before]."[5]

No doubt, Deng was emboldened to take this approach by China's significantly changed strategic environment. In view of the rapprochement with the United States and Japan, Deng could feel relatively confident in 1975 that a reduction in the proportion of S&T and industrial investment tied directly to PLA priorities would not jeopardize China's security.

The Technical Shift: Expanding the Role of Science and Technology

Even as Deng worked to reform the military and China's defense economy, he cushioned the blow by proposing an enhanced role for high technology in the overall economy. Deng's new emphasis on S&T reflected his own policy inclinations, of course, but it also flowed from the conclusions other top leaders—including Mao himself—had reached as a result of renewed contact with respected overseas Chinese scientists.

Shortly after President Nixon's 1972 visit, a Chinese-born American Nobel laureate in physics, Chen-ning Yang, paid a visit to his homeland. In a meeting with Mao, Yang urged the Chairman to rethink the Cultural Revolution era denunciation of science as "bourgeois" and suggested to Mao that China could pay much greater attention to the application of science and engineering to problems of development.[6]

With the Cultural Revolution slowing down, Mao was inclined to listen. His support offered political cover to reformers such as Deng Xiaoping; thus, even as he worked to build a PLA constituency for reform, Deng also began to talk about a broadened role for scientists and engineers. Throughout 1975, Deng gave a parallel round of talks to scientists that attempted to redefine the role of S&T in Chinese society while bucking up the spirits of an intellectual elite devastated by the Cultural Revolution.

Deng's first step was to support unambiguously professionalism and a scientific ethos, despite the radicals' denunciation of science as "elitist." In the context of the time, with the succession to Mao still unsettled, this was a significant departure from prevailing policy. With anti-intellectual radicals still prominent in the Politburo, Deng's talks were heady stuff to establishment scientists and engineers who looked to political leaders for policy signals. Indeed, the reshaping of policy that Deng proposed was ideologically anathema, even to a post–Cultural Revolution political leadership who, with Mao's apparent support, seemed increasingly set upon rejecting the mobilizational strategies of the past.

Deng made clear during these years that scientists must again be valued. He began with an attack on untrained administrative cadres, a none-too-subtle form of praise for Marshal Nie's efforts during the 1950s and 1960s to integrate decision makers with staff. "As to people who neither 'know the ropes' (*bu dongxing*) nor are enthusiastic (*bu rexin*) and who have a factional mentality," Deng rhetorically asked a 1975 conference of CAS leaders, "why do we continue to let them remain on the leadership squads" (*lingdao banzi*) overseeing scientific work?[7] Since the integration of technicians into party leadership committees had been a central feature of strategic weapons management, Deng's 1975 speeches were an important step toward renewing the political legitimacy of science and its leading practitioners.

PHASE 2, DECEMBER 1977: PLA PROCUREMENT PRIORITIES SHIFT TO CONVENTIONAL WEAPONS

Some of these trends, particularly the renewed acceptance of elitism, clearly favored Marshal Nie's managerial innovations.[8] But at the same time, other shifts of policy severely undercut Nie's programmatic priorities associated with the strategic weapons elite. Months before Deng rid himself of the hapless Hua Guofeng, the PLA high command delivered a decisive first shock to the strategic weapons system. At this moment, fourteen months after Mao's death, Deng's grasp on power looked increasingly firm, and although Deng was in the midst of a power struggle with Hua Guofeng, we can clearly detect his hand behind the more important changes introduced by the CMC during this period.

In December 1977, the CMC and the State Council jointly promulgated a decision to make conventional weapons the main focus (*yi changgui wuqi wei zhu*) in the development of equipment for the armed forces. While demanding that the strategic weapons system fulfill the final stages of its three main assignments of the 1960s and 1970s—the Three Grasps (*san zhua*) of a fully operational and deployable ICBM, an SLBM, and an operational communications satellite—the CMC forthrightly pointed to a new dominant trend in China's post-Mao procurement regime. CMC leaders made clear that their intention was to reverse once and for all Nie's—and Mao's—emphasis on strategic weapons in favor of a program closer to that advocated by Luo Ruiqing from 1961 to 1965.

Like Deng, the CMC reversed Nie's programmatic priorities but appropriated his managerial template, lending its explicit support to Deng's efforts to reform management and extend Nie's old system of chief designers for major weapons programs.

This demonstrates the paradox that confronted strategic weaponeers during these years. Their raison d'être—strategic weapons—lost ground in state priorities and procurement decisions. Their managerial innovations, however, emerged as a national model. The programmatic change that undercut their power base began with the CMC decision on weapons acquisition. This was the culmination of a coalition-building movement started in

April 1977, when a reconfigured leadership was set into place at a revived and reinvigorated post-Mao CSC. This reconstituted, post-1977 CSC included the four top leaders of China, Hua Guofeng, who served as director, and the three veterans who ranked just behind him in the Politburo: Ye Jianying, Deng Xiaoping, and Li Xiannian, all of whom served as CSC deputy directors.[9] The CSC had always promoted strategic weapons; it had been created in the first place for precisely this purpose. Now, however, the political leadership adopted a new tack: Deng and Ye deployed the authority of the CMC to call for the fulfillment of the Three Grasps; yet even as they did so, the high command simultaneously directed that procurement must "emphasize the shift (*zhongdian zhuanxiang*) toward solving [problems in] conventional weapons and equipment by quickening the pace of R&D on new types of conventional systems."[10]

In the first stage, this new PLA force modernization program assigned priority to upgrading equipment for the ground forces. Not coincidentally, these forces, particularly infantry, armor, and artillery, were the only PLA units that lacked a substantive connection to the strategic weapons programs in their heyday. In this sense, above all, a shift of procurement in favor of the ground forces represented the broadest possible change of policy from the era when nuclear weapons and their delivery systems had dominated the PLA's acquisition regime.

The motivation for this change is obvious: the ground forces were among the very weakest links in PLA modernization during the preceding decades. In 1979, just two years after the decision to revamp procurement, China's brief border war with Vietnam amply demonstrated the scale and scope of the problems confronting China's ground forces. Conventional ordnance performed extremely poorly in combat. Logistics were appalling, with commanders in some cases waving flags at each other during action as signals equipment malfunctioned or broke down entirely.

Deng and Ye's main concerns during these early years of the new procurement regime included antitank weapons (*fan tanke wuqi*), ground-launched air defense weapons (*fangkong wuqi*), artillery ("suppression") weapons (*yazhi wuqi*), such as large-caliber cannons and rocket launchers, and tanks and armored vehicles (*tanke he zhuangjia cheliang*).[11] The R&D system in these areas was a world apart from the network of sophisticated laboratories, factories, and mines that had produced China's finest achievements in weapons modernization for Marshal Nie. China's best technicians worked on strategic weapons, not conventional systems. Moreover, its conventional weapons R&D network had developed along a bureaucratic track that was entirely disconnected from Nie's industrial system and resources.

Rather, the ordnance system had grown up around the so-called Fifth Ministry of Machine Building, which had had primary responsibility for ordnance industries during the Mao years, as well as conventional weapons–related sections of the Fourth (Electronics) and Sixth (Shipbuilding) Ministries, all with little connection to strategic weapons project groups, such as the Lingjiuban, or even to their own ministry leaders— Wang Zheng (Fourth Ministry), Liu Huaqing, another Nie aide (Sixth Ministry), and others.

In practice, this had led both to a gaping bureaucratic cleavage within the ministries and within the defense industry more broadly, as well as to two distinct design systems. In the navy, for example, a compartmentalized career track had emerged for those, such as Chen Youming, whose primary reporting and oversight relationships were to Marshal Nie and his leading groups and project offices, not to the navy headquarters. With conventional weapons now favored, the navy, like the ground forces, came in for scrutiny. While emphasizing the modernization of PLA ground forces, the CMC also decided in 1977 to speed up the "improvement of first-generation naval vessels" (*gaijin diyi dai jianchuan*), especially antiship missiles and torpedoes.[12] In November 1977, in the run-up to the December meeting that announced the new policy, the CMC had designated a Leading Group under Zheng Hantao to clear the way for the modernization of five types of craft: nuclear submarines armed with torpedoes (*yulei he qianting*) (the platform associated with the Three Grasps' SLBM); destroyers (*quzhujian*); conventional (diesel-propulsion) submarines armed with medium-yield torpedoes (*zhongxing yulei qianting*); speedboats armed with large-yield missiles (*daxing daodan kuaiting*); and antisubmarine (escort) frigates (*fanqian huweijian*). In 1981, a senior navy leader, Fan Muhan, took over the directorship of this Leading Group.[13]

Neither was the air force ignored, as the CMC's shift was comprehensive. Here the CMC chose to develop first a medium-altitude, high-speed fighter (*zhonggao kongsu jianjiji*), the favored platform of Nie's rivals. Leadership for this project fell mainly to a restored NDIO. In the early 1980s, the commission had expanded its plans for the air force and selected no less than four types of aircraft for development: the J-7II fighter, the

J-8 daytime fighter, the J-8 all-weather fighter, and the Q-5 long-range fighter.[14]

The Political Significance of the New Procurement Regime

Taken as a whole, the program promulgated by the CMC in December 1977 constituted a stinging reversal of victories that Nie had, in effect, won in 1965 with the purge of Luo Ruiqing. The new procurement regime amounted to a wholesale return to the agenda that Luo and He Long had advocated in opposition to Nie's strategic weapons programs. Indeed, the new emphasis must have stung strategic weaponeers all the more because it reflected the fact that the CCP leadership was now committed to closing the very gaps in ground and air preparation that had so troubled General Luo in the 1960s. These gaps had never been filled because priority had shifted to Nie's strategic weapons efforts, but also because conventional weapons facilities degenerated into a factional battleground during the Cultural Revolution. When Luo's agenda first reemerged as war planners began to weigh their options to counter a Soviet force buildup during the late 1960s and 1970s, the PLA discovered just how much it had allowed these conventional weapons capabilities to atrophy. During an emergency mobilization in 1969, planners had discovered that the PLA lacked much of the conventional capability required to defend Chinese territory against a Soviet invasion.[15]

Thus, the challenge that Deng and the CMC now posed to China's conventional weapons industries was staggering. Concerned with the buildup of Soviet forces, the CMC decided to shift resources to conventional weapons, but given the politics that had long plagued procurement decisions, Deng faced the daunting problem of assembling a coalition for such a sweeping change. The evidence remains incomplete, but it appears that Deng did so by gaining at least partial acquiescence from the strategic weaponeers, particularly Nie's longtime aide Zhang Aiping, who was brought into the decision-making process. That Deng felt obliged to win over Zhang suggests just how bad the situation had become for China's conventional forces in the mid-1970s.

Aside from co-opting Zhang, Deng Xiaoping endeavored to assemble his coalition in the months leading up to the December 1977 CMC meetings by bringing together several other old antagonists—Luo Ruiqing,

Hong Xuezhi, Wang Zhen, and Yang Yong—at two meetings in October and November 1977 to discuss PLA readiness.[16] While the presence of the rehabilitated Luo might seem significant in light of the group's decision to refocus the agenda toward his priorities of the 1960s, Luo would be dead within a year. Thus, his backing was clearly less important than Deng's own shift in this direction.

By December, this initial leadership coalition had been significantly expanded to include several key generals. Zhang Aiping secured Deng's support for a final push to fulfill the Three Grasps. Thereafter, however, procurement priorities shifted almost entirely to conventional weapons.

The year 1977 thereby marked a watershed. First, the CMC decision reversed in essence the outcome of the 1961 Beidaihe conference. Second, it returned China to a program closer to that advocated by Peng Dehuai in the late 1950s. Third, it adopted many of the procurement preferences espoused by Luo Ruiqing since the 1960s. And finally, it overturned a nearly twenty-year commitment to strategic weapons–based force modernization.

To be sure, the transition to this new procurement regime was gradual. The strategic weapons system managed initially to sustain comparatively intensive work on the ICBM program (deployed in August 1981) and on the SLBM (successfully tested in the summer of 1982). But the changes introduced in 1977 nonetheless presaged a more encompassing reversal of the broadly developmental emphases that had sustained the strategic weapons programs.[17] And although the CMC's decision in 1977 dealt strictly with R&D for weapons, it foreshadowed a much broader collapse of political support for Nie's strategy for high-tech development.

Microelectronics and the Emergence of Debate

This twofold shift—to conventional weapons in PLA force planning, and to demilitarization in national science and technology policy—did not merely undermine the weaponeers' agenda; it threatened their political and professional viability. This would be exacerbated over the next several years by the retirement of key patrons, the emergence of bureaucratic rivals in both military and civilian R&D, and, as the pace of technological change quickened, the ossification of China's system of technological innovation.

The CMC decision clearly posed a challenge to Nie's weaponeers: How could old approaches to technology be reframed to fit the leadership's new priorities? Specifically, the strategic weapons elite was forced to consider readjusting its own thinking lest it risk losing control of the military technology agenda to conventional weapons specialists. This laid the ground for a sweeping reassessment of the role of advanced technology in China. By 1989, scientists and technicians who had played prominent roles in strategic weapons programs were arguing forcefully that the entire concept of sophisticated (*jianduan*) technology had to be readjusted to conform to the realities of a world where the differences between strategic technology and conventional military and commercial technology had significantly narrowed.

For two decades, sophisticated technology had been a synonym in China for nuclear weapons and their delivery platforms, satellite technologies, and auxiliary systems. The apparent loss of control over the technology agenda in 1977 led strategic weaponeers to consider whether the concept of sophisticated technology could now be broadened to encompass component and process technologies with applications to conventional weapons.

To answer affirmatively required that prominent weaponeers, such as Qian Xuesen, essentially reverse many of their long-standing arguments about technology development. This was difficult indeed for technicians who had produced China's only real high technology achievements of global stature since the establishment of the Communist state in 1949. Now, technical specialists such as Qian Xuesen would have to argue that, for example, advanced jet propulsion technology deserved pride of place. Others, who had argued against ground and surface naval technologies in the 1960s, would also need to abandon their cherished convictions.

This was made especially difficult for many strategic weaponeers because of the rank hostility that had arisen during the Mao era between the air force and aircraft engineers, on the one hand, and the missileers under Nie's command, on the other. Beginning with the missile/bomber debates of 1956, up through Luo Ruiqing's 1964 dictum of "air force equipment as the point of breakthrough" (*yi kongjun zhuangbei wei tupokou*),[18] Nie's strategic weapons elite had invested enormous political capital in the notion that conventional weapons projects were insufficiently "sophisticated" to merit wholehearted support at the political apex. Accordingly, as they broadened their thinking about technology after 1977, strategic weaponeers floated a trial balloon that would justify their own dominance of conventional weapons R&D, and in the bargain would involve replacing many of the engineers who had toiled—often in obscurity—to develop these systems in the past. This strategy was premised on a call for special attention to microelectronics, a field that all Chinese technicians understood to be associated with Nie's programs.

Strategic weaponeers contended that microelectronics were essential to modern conventional, not simply strategic, weapons. For example, Zhang Aiping, Nie's heir as the weaponeers' patron in the high command, pressed the CMC leadership to place special emphasis on circuitry and other areas, "emphatically declaring that China's defense modernization essentially involves mechanization, automation, and [especially] electronicization" (*dianzihua*).[19]

Zhang quickly won supporters to his side. Yu Qiuli, a former PLA logistics chief who later became a top economic planner, proclaimed: "Electronics technology is by far the most important point of emphasis in the development of weapons and equipment."[20] The elevation of electronics became particularly significant because it provided a technical and political bridge between strategic and conventional weapons R&D. Weaknesses in electronics had also hindered the development of strategic weapons. Consequently, by moving electronics to the forefront, Nie's circle could gain leverage over conventional weapons R&D in the wake of the 1977 shift, and at the same time they could draw the CMC's attention to the very area that had hindered their own work on strategic weapons in the past.

The importance strategists attached to electronics must be understood against the background of technological development in the PRC. Although strategic weapons work constituted a relatively small component of the total activity of the Chinese electronics industry, it had consumed the attention of top industry leaders, such as Wang Zheng, and its most elite institutes and factories. During the Cultural Revolution, when the electronics industry virtually collapsed, Wang Zheng had appealed to the CMC to protect the sector. As one Chinese history points out, "the fact that sophisticated military technology . . . had been held back by the low level of the electronics industry became clear to more and more people" in the years after the Cultural Revolution.[21]

In the end, Zhang Aiping's argument for electronics carried the day, but with mixed consequences for the strategic weapons elite itself. In 1977, at the precise moment it decided to promote conventional weapons, the

CMC also endorsed the development of electronics and laid out targets for a number of projects. These included conventional weapons systems, such as radar. But the CMC also paid attention to three areas long dominated by the strategic weapons elite: communications (*tongxin*), command (*zhihui*), and reconnaissance (*zhencha*); missile and satellite measurement and control (*cekong*); and the development of a supercomputer capable of performing 100 million operations per second.[22] The first had long been a preserve of the strategic weapons industry because of the concentration on satellites as a means of communication and reconnaissance. The second, measurement and control, had also been a strategic weapons preserve because Nie's top-priority programs depended heavily on telemetry, optics, and the ability to calculate angles and axes for missile trajectories and accelerations. In fact, by the late 1970s, most of the leading figures in Chinese telemetry and optics, such as Wang Daheng, Chen Fangyun, and Yang Jiachi, had spent virtually their entire careers working in Nie Rongzhen's administrative domain under the leadership of the NDSTC and strategic weapons project groups that reported to the CSC.[23] The third area, supercomputing, was clearly in the strategic weapons domain because for its first twenty years, the Chinese computer industry had functioned virtually as a branch of Nie's programs. The leading lights of early Chinese computing, such as Ci Yungui, worked and came of age under the exclusive purview of the NDSTC.

Strategic Weaponeers Fight for Command: The Yinhe Supercomputer

A leading figure in China's early computer industry, Chen Liwei, has noted in a memoir that the various Chinese-designed computers of the 1960s to 1980s were used mainly in the strategic weapons programs. These computers, Chen writes, were utilized in "atomic and hydrogen bomb tests, the launch of man-made satellites, the launch of ICBMs to the southern Pacific Ocean, the underwater launch of SLBMs, and in meeting the tracking and other testing needs of communications satellite launches."[24]

The history of China's 100-million-operations-per-second supercomputer, the Yinhe or "Galaxy," illustrates how computing and strategic weapons developed in tandem and under the same administrative roof. Indeed, computing provides an especially good example of how strategic weaponeers after 1977 sought to leverage their leading position in electronics into the dominance of projects, including conventional weapons, with broader applications and implications.

Since computing was so closely related to strategic weapons, the NDSTC had long been assigned responsibility for most large projects in this field. But with the change in PLA procurement and some important national development priorities in 1977, the Yinhe project became a test of whether the weaponeers could remain in charge. In 1977, the NDSTC submitted a report on the Yinhe to the senior Communist Party leadership. But with all political trends favoring conventional weapons technicians or those who had worked on civilian projects, "there were five other organizations that hoped to develop such a supercomputer."[25] These were the Fourth Ministry, which had become increasingly involved in nonstrategic weapons projects as well as strictly commercial industry; the CAS; and the technology bureaus of the Shanghai municipal government, the Jiangsu provincial government, and the Heilongjiang provincial government. Deng Xiaoping himself "instructed Fang Yi [the vice premier in charge of science and technology] to work out a solution."[26]

After hearing Fang Yi's report in March 1978, Deng awarded the project to groups reporting to the NDSTC, proclaiming that the supercomputer should be a military, not civilian, undertaking. Deng also placed strategic weaponeers in the lead by designating the Computer Research Institute of the Changsha Engineering Academy (Changsha gongxue yuan, Jisuanji yanjiusuo)—an institution long associated with the NDSTC—as the lead research agency for the project.[27] Having won control, the NDSTC appointed a key strategic weaponeer, Ci Yungui, as chief designer of the Yinhe, Li Zhuang, the deputy director of the NDSTC's S&T department, as coordinator of management, and Zhang Zhenhuan, a deputy to Zhang Aiping at the NDSTC, as overall supervisor. "Now that the project is yours," Deng told Zhang Aiping, "you had best be sure to get it done."[28]

In their hard-won supercomputer project, strategic weaponeers enjoyed an opportunity to promote their managerial institutions, such as horizontal coordination, as a national model. In a 1989 memoir, Ci Yungui recalls that a variety of research organizations, both military and civilian, were brought into the Yinhe project by the NDSTC leadership. These included the Ninth Academy and Institute 701 of the Second Academy (inertial guidance) of the missile ministry. But on the strategic weapons model, the

NDSTC also included civilian institutions, such as Fudan University, Hunan Teachers College, Hunan University, and Wuhan University.[29] For strategic weaponeers who hoped to influence the course of conventional weapons R&D, the Yinhe provided a high-profile opportunity to turn anew to organizational solutions lifted directly out of past experience. This brand of horizontal cooperation between bureaucratically unlinked units offered a useful means to pursue projects with conventional weapons constituencies and civilian groups. Here, then, the NDSTC explored a "strategic weapons" managerial solution to a new, post-1977 technology problem. In December 1983, a prototype Yinhe passed state muster.[30]

PHASE 3: DENG SETS HIS PRIORITIES AT THE THIRD PLENUM

In 1977 the legacy of the Cultural Revolution dominated politics in China. Paradoxically, even as the Cultural Revolution radicals had attacked and repudiated all technical specialists, they unwittingly legitimated the strategic weaponeers' work style. Despite the violence seething around them, the weaponeers had made progress in key programs, most notably in the hydrogen bomb and long-range missiles. Now, in 1977, the post–Cultural Revolution party leadership faced a crisis of legitimacy, a damaged industrial economy, and a stalled development program. For this reason, the legacy of success amid chaos in the strategic weapons programs offered Deng's reform coalition a model useful in delegitimating the Maoist political economy. The strategic weaponeers were elite technicians. For Deng, this contrasted starkly with Red Guard and worker teams. Management in Nie's model was flexible, open, and network based. Here, too, the contrast with both haphazard Maoist decentralization and Soviet-style hierarchy was unmistakable.

As Deng moved to win support for his development strategy, then, he and his colleagues held up the weaponeers' faith in experimentation, cooperation, and flexibility as an example of something "new"—an alternative to the Maoist model. Strategic weapons, Deng suggested, were among the greatest legacies of the Mao era. And yet although Mao's support and protection had been critical, whatever had been achieved in strategic weapons programs owed much to a managerial style antithetical to Mao's own ideological notions of organization. Moreover, sheer havoc in nearly every corner of Chinese society save the strategic weapons industry demonstrated not just that the Cultural Revolution had been a disaster, but that the forces that had contributed to it, including the haphazard development strategy of the mid-to-late 1960s, should be rejected as a model for China's future.[31]

Deng's alternative, a sweeping reversal of many aspects of the previous thirty years of Chinese development strategy, came to life in decisions made at the Third Plenum of the Eleventh CCP Central Committee, held in Beijing in December 1978. For military industry, the policy adopted there had three key ingredients: civilian economic construction would henceforth have primacy; society would be demilitarized; and science and technology, consistent with Marxist theory, would be elevated to the status of "productive forces" (*shengchanli*), thus repudiating the radical notion of the Cultural Revolution that they have a class character.

Wielding this theoretical justification, Deng argued that S&T should not merely be stabilized or confined to discrete areas of society or sectors of the economy, but expanded to encompass—and thereby contribute to—all aspects of national economic construction.

"The Task Before Us"

Deng's crusade to reverse the core developmental policies of the preceding decade in large part sprang from the need to win back the allegiance of a populace disillusioned by the excesses of the Cultural Revolution. Although Deng began the march to restore the legitimacy of the party-state even before the Third Plenum, the plenum itself proved pivotal because it created a momentum that hastened the state's abandonment of Maoist policies.

At the plenum, Deng proclaimed the victory of "practice" (*shijian*) over ideology, blasting the political dynamic that had fed factionalism and the breakdown of intraparty discipline during the preceding decade. He promised to rehabilitate disgraced cadres by "righting every wrong" (*you cuo bi jiao*),[32] declared a need for new management and economic policies, and proclaimed the victory of his own approach. Deng's confidence was staggering: "The issue of political line," he declared at a work conference to prepare for the plenum, "has been settled" (*zhengzhi luxian yijing jiejue le*).[33]

By 1980, Deng Xiaoping had effectively consolidated his political position and the main thrust, if not all of the specifics, of his political line had been adopted by a powerful reform coalition within the party. Now, Deng

told his colleagues, the political basis had been laid for a new look at specific problems and challenges concerning policy. At a meeting of party and
nonparty representatives on New Year's Day 1980, Deng set out his proposed policy agenda for the next twenty years. On January 16, at a larger
meeting of senior cadres called by the CCP Central Committee, he expanded on these general themes. This second speech, "The Present Situation and the Tasks Before Us" (*Muqian de xingshi he renwu*), was one of
Deng's most important early statements of policy.[34] Like Mao's speeches of
the middle 1950s, it laid out a scheme that would dramatically affect broad
priorities as well as routine policies.

In this speech, Deng drew heavily from the thinking of the late premier,
Zhou Enlai. Near the end of his life, Zhou had begun to promote the idea
of Four Modernizations (*si hua*) in agriculture, industry, S&T, and national
defense as the blueprint for China's future development.[35] Implicit in this
formulation was the suggestion that political struggle had barred the way to
progress in all four areas. As Zhou lay gravely ill in a Beijing cancer ward,
Deng was tapped to lead the way. Once Zhou and Mao had passed from
the scene, and with his power at last consolidated after yet another brief
purge, China's new paramount leader made clear that his own version of
the Four Modernizations mirrored Zhou's commitment to banishing political struggle from the drive to modernize. Everything, Deng declared in his
"Situation and Tasks" speech, must be subordinated to a single goal. "In a
nutshell," he said, "the Four Modernizations add up to a single thing:
economic construction" (*si ge xiandaihua, jizhong qilai jiang jiu shi jingji
jianshe*).[36] And that single, unitary, and unquestioned purpose meant that
Deng could also resolve another important contradiction from the Mao era:
A military industrial base, he proclaimed, could never facilitate an encompassing national economic base. To Deng, Nie Rongzhen had been wrong.

In fact, Deng would ultimately come to accept at least some parts of
Nie's argument about the strategic implications of high technology development. But he would decisively reject the marshal's view of how military
R&D could boost broad-based civilian economic construction. Although
Nie Rongzhen had never argued that development of military industry
alone would result in a national high-tech base, he was convinced that
strategic military technology ought to be funded for the sake of development, not merely for the purpose of national security. It was with this fundamental point that Deng disagreed. Deng held that defense construction

and military work "could not proceed except on a sound economic foundation" (*mei you yiding de jingji jichu bu xing*).[37] Moreover, S&T, which had been the near-exclusive preserve of the military industry system for twenty-five years, should now primarily serve national economic construction. Deng agreed that Nie's military science system was most impressive and efficient. But, he added, spin-off was an especially inefficient model of technological development given China's post–Cultural Revolution challenges.[38] Since science and technology were to be "the key to the Four Modernizations,"[39] the scope and reach of technology within Chinese society must be expanded accordingly. Ultimately, as we shall see in subsequent chapters, this led to a vast civilianization of Chinese science and technology policy, as well as greater competition between bureaucracies and rival elites.

In sum, under Deng's leadership, economic construction was to be primary. Furthermore, there could be little question of PLA opposition to this new policy. During a 1981 exercise in north China, Deng told senior commanders: Of course China must improve the military's weapons and equipment while speeding up the modernization of national defense; but the PLA must also recognize that such progress can be made only "on the foundation of continuous, national (*guomin*) economic development" (*zai guomin jingji buduan fazhan de jichu shang*).[40] Henceforth, said Deng, China must "use the civilian to nurture the military" (*yimin yang jun*).[41]

Military Elders Assess the Shift: The Forging of Consensus

Inevitably, Deng's new strategy raised problems of political dynamics and coalition building. This was particularly true in light of opposition in the PLA to earlier moves toward civilian construction. Much as he had sold the shift from strategic to conventional weapons within the PLA, Deng assiduously engaged in coalition building with the PLA for this broader transformation of national development priorities.

In 1955–56, PLA commanders had resorted to high drama to oppose economic planners' attempt to readjust expenditures. Leading marshals, such as Ye Jianying, had taken to the rostrum at plenary sessions of the National People's Congress and the party to belittle "some people" who falsely believed that China's external environment permitted such a step. Likewise, in 1976–77, PLA leaders had fought Hua Guofeng's halting effort to readjust national investment.[42] Hua failed because he had neither the stature nor the political capacity to win the acceptance of so basic a change in priorities. Deng Xiaoping, however, was one of the army's own—in Ye Jianying's words, "the leader of our marshals"—and this gave him political leverage that Hua had lacked. Deng built consensus for the new political line, first, by co-opting the surviving marshals, including Ye Jianying. To them, he argued that the nation remained in domestic crisis but its external situation had significantly improved. This offered an opportunity that must be seized, the upshot of which was that national security would in the end be enhanced by the changes he was proposing. Many commentators have noted that the modernization of national defense has traditionally been listed last among the Four Modernizations. Defense, they have thus argued, thereby came to occupy the lowest priority in the hierarchy of state concerns after 1978. Yet it is important to remember that Deng successfully built a broad consensus for the rearrangement of national priorities. Discussions with Chinese interviewees reveal that, by 1981, PLA leaders understood clearly just how far China had fallen behind the West and the Soviet Union in the development of advanced technology. For the first time, PLA leaders began to connect the state of the national infrastructure to ambitious, long-range plans for weapons development—in effect, reversing the old spin-off model by suggesting that weapons modernization would instead be more efficiently served by putting modernization of the national infrastructure in the lead.

When observers rank national defense last among the Four Modernizations, then, they conflate a shift in emphasis with a decline in status and priority. We need not assume that Deng and his colleagues intended national defense to rank last in state priorities, nor that the military willingly accepted a loss of status. Rather, insofar as PLA leaders began to consider that national security would be reinforced if the national technology base forged ahead, commanders may simply have concluded that military modernization would fail absent a restructuring of national industrial policy. According to this formulation, military modernization was simply being delayed, not falling in priority. And the military itself could aid this process, as well as enhance the PLA's prospects for modernization, by supporting Deng's new line: the reach and scope of advanced technology would thereby expand. In the long term, this would accelerate defense modernization. With the problem posed in this way, it seems no surprise that Ye Jianying, who had so forcefully challenged and belittled the planners in 1955–56, played a decisive role in winning support for Deng's new line during 1978 to 1982.

Peace and Security: The Key to the Reform Consensus

"Everything," Deng asserted, "depends on us doing our work well" (*yiqie jueding yu women ziji de shiqing gan de hao bu hao*). Even China's position in world affairs will "depend on the scale of our economic achievements."[43] The Maoist development program, Deng averred, had created "improportions" or "imbalances" (*mei you anpai hao gezhong bili guanxi*). He declared in his "Situation and Tasks" speech: During the Mao years, China failed to balance development in agriculture and industry, light and heavy industry. At least by implication, this argument about proportions suggested that the military-civilian relationship had also become unbalanced.

Readjustment (*tiaozheng*), Deng warned, could not be accomplished quickly.[44] However, only one thing, he said, could stand in the way of China's new line: a world war—an "all-out war" (*dada*)—or a military conflict that directly threatened China. But Deng believed such a war was unlikely, and over the course of the 1980s he repeatedly raised his assessment of the length of this predicted period of peace. By the middle of the 1980s, it had reached as high as fifty years: a half century of free rein for full-scale economic construction.[45]

In addition to his answers to the problems of legitimacy and "imbalance," then, the relative stability of the global situation comprised another pillar supporting Deng's strategic edifice. Not only was a realignment of national development priorities long overdue, he argued, but the comparative stability of China's external environment lent immediacy to the task at hand. China had not enjoyed such stability for a century-and-a-half. Thus, the opportunities presented by the moment must be seized and turned to China's advantage. Of course, Deng cautioned, "it is difficult to predict what will happen internationally. . . . [But] we really need a peaceful environment" at this moment. For this reason, he declared, the basic thrust of China's diplomacy must be to guarantee "a peaceful environment for the realization of the Four Modernizations."[46]

In the end, even the all-important goal of reunification with Taiwan became caught up with Deng's optimistic assessment of the global situation.

In his "Situation and Tasks" speech, Deng had signaled his clear intent to reunite the motherland as a matter of national purpose.[47] But although China did not renounce the right to use force as an instrument of reunification, the thrust of Deng's approach during the 1980s was on constructive steps such as postal exchanges, communications, and transport contacts, as well as a "one country, two systems" (*yiguo liangzhi*) formula as a basis for achieving reunification peacefully. Deng's optimism owed much to his own skillful diplomacy. Building on the Nixon visit of 1972, Deng vigorously pursued normalization with the United States. In 1979, just one year before the "Situation and Tasks" speech, he visited the United States to normalize diplomatic relations with the Carter administration. Following normalization, American investment began to flow to China. In 1980, a U.S. Department of Defense delegation arrived to discuss technology cooperation and military exchange.[48]

Thus Deng moved forcefully to stabilize and guarantee a benign international environment through active diplomacy to strengthen and regularize contacts with the United States and Japan. He also vigorously deployed these alignments to oppose Soviet "hegemonism" (*baquanzhuyi*) in Asia and thereby check new pressures on China's northeast and Mongolian frontiers.

PHASE 4: SHIFTS IN RESOURCE ALLOCATION

The problems military industry faced during the 1980s were very much derivative of the budget crisis that resulted from Deng's policy of reform and realignment. For the strategic weapons elite, this problem became more acute in the years after the 1982 SLBM test. Most notably, the development and acceleration of a program of defense "conversion" reflected the decline in the allocation of resources to defense in real terms throughout the 1980s. This clearly affected the strategic weaponeers, not just the ordnance and lower-end sectors at the heart of the defense conversion program. For although strategic weapons elites intensified their activity in the run-up to the 1982 SLBM test, military expenditure, at least adjusted for inflation and devaluation, decreased during the 1980s. Finance Minister Wang Bingqian announced only a small cut in defense expenditure for 1980. Yet as the decade wore on, defense allocations, which rose steadily in nominal terms, were sharply curtailed even for many strategic weapons facilities once price and other adjustments are factored in. Hardest hit were individual enterprises in the conventional weapons sector, many of which were ordered to raise funds for basic operating expenses on their own.

Declining Real-Term Military Expenditure

Chinese defense budget figures have always been exceedingly murky. A considerable portion of military spending is not contained in the official defense budget of the central government. This missing component includes research and development, of course, but also the militia, which is paid for in large part off provincial government budgets, military enterprises, and the People's Armed Police. John Lewis, Hua Di, and Xue Litai have noted, for example, that "the State Council allocates funds to military industries for dual civilian-military use through the regular state plan, but in the form of unspecified block grants to the Central Military Commission for all military purposes except research and development on new weapons. These allocated funds are not considered part of the defense budget."[49] Richard Bitzinger adds that although we know the official "topline" figure for military expenditure (Table 3.1), and therefore can compute the official defense budget as a percentage of government spending and of GDP (Table 3.1; Figure 3.1), and although we have a rough breakdown of official defense expenditures, the "defense budget" is much narrower in scope than actual military expenditure.[50] One of the major themes in research on Chinese defense expenditure has been to decide which expenditures with military implications are not included in the official topline figure, and then, using scattered data, to estimate the size of those expenditures. This process has yielded an extraordinarily wide range of estimates (Figure 3.2).

TABLE 3.1
Official Chinese Defense Budget, 1986–1994

Year	RMB (billions)	USD (billions)	% of GDP
1986	20.1	5.83	2.6
1987	21	5.64	2.5
1988	21.8	5.78	1.9
1989	25.2	6.69	1.9
1990	29	6.06	2.0
1991	32.5	6.21	2.0
1992	37	6.76	2.0
1993	42.5	7.45	1.5
1994	52	6.10	1.5

SOURCE: Bitzinger and Lin (1994).

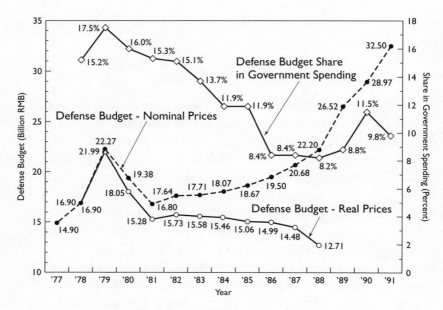

FIGURE 3.1   Chinese Defense Budget in Nominal and Real Prices and Share of Government Spending, 1977–1991.   SOURCE: Folta (1992).

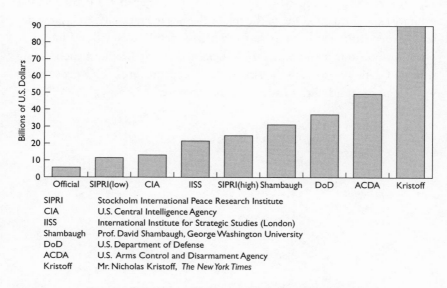

SIPRI	Stockholm International Peace Research Institute	
CIA	U.S. Central Intelligence Agency	
IISS	International Institute for Strategic Studies (London)	
Shambaugh	Prof. David Shambaugh, George Washington University	
DoD	U.S. Department of Defense	
ACDA	U.S. Arms Control and Disarmament Agency	
Kristoff	Mr. Nicholas Kristoff, *The New York Times*	

FIGURE 3.2   Range of Estimates of Chinese Defense Expenditures, ca. 1994.   SOURCE: Bitzinger and Lin (1994).

In spite of this type of hidden defense spending, however, the trend in the 1980s cannot be seen as heading in any direction but downward. This is especially true when one examines the gap in nominal and real prices (Figure 3.1) and when figures—official or unofficial—are adjusted for inflation and currency devaluations (Figure 3.3). Moreover, although nominal expenditures increased, especially between 1986 and 1994, official defense expenditure as a percentage of total GDP declined after 1978 and declined precipitously from the high tide of so-called Third Line construction in the Chinese interior in the mid-to-late 1960s.[51] According to one account that seeks to reconcile a variety of estimates, this share dropped from as high as 17.5 percent in 1979 to 8.2 percent in 1988 (Figure 3.1).[52] Another account calculates the defense share of total central government expenditure as declining from approximately 16 percent in 1980 to 9.6 percent in 1994.[53]

Even for the strategic weapons programs, therefore, financial constraints during the first part of the 1980s were severe. Two analysts, writing in 1994 after budgets at last went back up, suggested that China may spend as little as 3 to 5 percent of its total military budget on nuclear weapons, a figure of approximately U.S.$1 to U.S.$1.5 billion assuming annual total defense expenditures of around U.S.$30 billion.[54] Given the reduced status of nuclear weapons and their delivery systems during the 1980s, this proportion of strategic weapons in the military budget was, no doubt, lower in the years between the SLBM test of 1982 and the overall post-1990 budget increases.

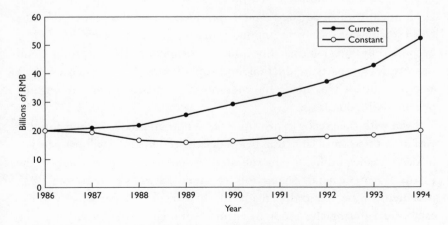

FIGURE 3.3   Official Chinese Defense Budget, Current and Constant, 1986–1994.   SOURCE: Bitzinger and Lin (1994).

Hard-Hit Defense Industry Enterprises

Ironically, in spite of the renewed attention to conventional weapons modernization, the CMC's December 1977 decision to shift the PLA procurement regime did not necessarily produce improved conditions for conventional weapons suppliers. Indeed, the 1977 shift of acquisition emphasis was accompanied by a larger transformation of the PLA's proposed package of conventional weapons priorities. During the early 1980s, ground force systems received highest priority, then from the mid-1980s onward naval and air force technologies took their place as highest priority. For this reason, manufacturers of ground force equipment became increasingly hard-pressed for PLA orders and defense investment capital. Particularly for the large ordnance operation deep in China's interior, reduced priority in procurement, redundancy in production, and underutilized industrial capacity vitiated any benefit from the shift to an emphasis on conventional weapons modernization.

These facilities were, in some sense, the physical expression of the unfortunate legacy of the 1960s. The Third Line policy of mobilization noted above had sought to re-create relatively complete industrial systems in various parts of the country, especially the interior, and thereby ensure military survivability through redundancy.[55] This primarily strategic rationale paralleled the decentralizing tendencies of Maoist economics.[56] But when planning and investment controls were recentralized at the end of the high tide of the Cultural Revolution, the policy served only to saddle the central government with an outsized military production complex burdened by the worst features of socialist economic planning. Most of these factories had become fully integrated facilities during this period: R&D, product and process design, parts production, and supply were all integrated within a single facility.[57] This made for widespread inefficiencies and intensified problems of redundancy.

Even with the greater expenditures and new emphasis on conventional weapons, therefore, a large number of defense production facilities were left in deep financial difficulty by the drop in state procurements during the 1980s. When General Zhang Aiping proposed in 1983 that total PLA procurement be reduced,[58] many of these facilities, particularly those established during the 1960s to ensure redundancy, discovered that the equipment they manufactured—ordnance, tanks, older naval surface combatants, and others—was no longer in demand. By 1985, the tension between surplus capacity and deflated demand had evolved into a spirited debate over sheer enterprise survival and worker welfare. Low—or canceled—orders meant that "redundant" enterprises needed to turn their attention to alternative markets, such as the consumer market, merely to survive. But this proved no simpler than market transition in any other socialist context. And as Chinese military industry enterprises groped their way toward a defense conversion strategy, greater demands were placed on the central government to replace expenditure on equipment for the PLA with subsidies, welfare allotments, and out-and-out enterprise bailouts.

Beijing found itself hard-pressed during the 1980s to provide these subsidies. First, the central government had hoped to use this money for other purposes. Second, military enterprises were almost universally "central" enterprises (*zhongyang qiye*), administered directly by ministries and ministry-level organs in Beijing. This had cut them off from contacts with local economies and governments virtually from their establishment. Such enterprises tended, also, to be very traditional socialist-type work units, with schools and kindergartens, hospitals, employee housing blocks, and a variety of other facilities that enterprises provided to their workers on the back of a state that had, until that time, been willing to provide subsidies for worker welfare. Finally, as the 1980s wore on, the central authorities grew increasingly impatient with the slow pace of the defense industry transition. At last, in the 1990s, the state would slash subsidies to defense enterprises. But initially, at least, Beijing sought to compensate by granting preferential commercial conditions, such as special licenses, tax deferments, and priority bank loans to these enterprises. For instance, in the face of competitive pressures from civilian motor vehicle manufacturers, a group of specially selected munitions plants were guaranteed a major government contract for transport vehicles for the oil fields of Xinjiang. Likewise, non-competitive mining contracts in gold and nonferrous metals were awarded to mineral metallurgy plants in the nuclear industry. According to a government analyst in the Budget and Planning Department in charge of PLA equipment, the total value of these contracts approached RMB 2.8 billion in 1996.[59]

Problems of Defense Conversion

The strategic and development policy shifts initiated by Deng Xiaoping began to affect military industry and associated elites almost immediately after the Third Plenum. And yet the nature of that change was at first un-certain, and later became still more muddied by conflicting signals from the leadership. For example, at the Third Session of the Fifth National People's Congress in August 1980, Vice Premier Yao Yilin called for the transfer of the "productive capacity and technical forces of the heavy and defense industries" to the consumer and civilian side of the economy. Then, on the very same day, Finance Minister Wang Bingqian announced an increase in defense expenditure during 1979 and a plan to cut the official military budget for 1980 by only RMB 2.94 billion.[60]

This apparent contradiction reflected a temporary increase of China's military budget to cope with the brief 1979 invasion of Vietnam. Moreover, it was an action with precedent: In 1955, the year after the first Taiwan Strait crisis, Bo Yibo and other planners had agreed to a temporary emergency in-crease of funding for the PLA. Indeed, Chinese leaders have consistently proved willing to increase military expenditures in the wake, or face, of crises.

Yet, Deng left little doubt at the Third Plenum about the overall direc-tion of the new policy line. In this sense, Yao Yilin's statement more accu-rately reflected leadership strategy, for in the years after the plenum Deng publicly declared his intention to transfer as much as two-thirds of the mil-itary industry's workforce to primarily civilian activity.[61]

This did not mean that China was abandoning its commitment to a massive overhaul of the PLA's creaking weaponry. As noted earlier, the PLA's modernization ambitions more than reflected the challenge it faced, even if implementing the CMC's plan to overhaul conventional ground, naval, and airborne weaponry proved difficult. Still, the trends for the de-fense industry reflected a shift of strategy as to how to achieve the specific operational objectives associated with the CMC's 1997 shift in procurement strategy. In 1982, Deng set out a sixteen-character guiding principle for large-scale reorganization of the defense industry. This had four compo-nents: integrating military and civilian production in each plant (*junmin jiehe*); mindfulness of latent military requirements as the focus of the sector shifted to the civilian side (*pingzhan jiehe*); priority on the maintenance of military capability during the transformation (*junpin youxian*); and using a modernized, civilian economy to foster military development over the long term (*yimin yangjun*).[62]

At a meeting of the CMC in November 1984, Deng directed that all industry, even within the military system, should henceforth concentrate on civilian products (*dali fazhan minpin shengchan*).[63] The rationale for this change mirrored the larger goals of the Deng era readjustment.[64] In addition, as this readjustment unfolded, it was accompanied by a shift in regional emphasis from interior provinces back to the densely populated coast.

Above all, then, civilianization left only the most vital parts of the military industry and science systems still engaged in purely defense-related work. Military industrial output, especially in low-end fields such as ordnance and diesel shipbuilding, was no longer needed on the same scale as before 1978. Any unit in a position to produce for the market was told to stand on its own. But the renewed attention to the coastal regions left many of these facilities—which were disproportionately located in the interior—without markets for their new, civilian products.

Most of the resulting problems—and there were many—were manifested at the lower end of the military industrial system. As part of his determination to promote science, Deng Xiaoping had ambitious, if vague, plans for the elite system that had once been primarily the bailiwick of Nie Rongzhen. However, Deng's program of civilianization had an uneven impact on military industry, which exacerbated the professional and political cleavages that had long separated strategic from conventional weapons elites. The hardest hit were redundant conventional industrial and ordnance plants—manufacturers of engines, parts, simple meters, and similar products—that now confronted underutilized capacity. This was a direct result of fewer PLA purchase orders and reduced subsidies. The outcome was widespread underemployment of much of China's defense industrial workforce.

Initially, the defense industry leadership reasoned that this excess capacity could simply be turned to the manufacture of light industrial and consumer products. But this proved naïve, not merely because many military plants lacked market data and skills, but also because the change in state priorities had radically transformed both the playing field and the stakes for defense industrial enterprises.

One Chinese account periodizes this transformation of the defense industry during the 1980s into three stages: A stage of "looking for rice to put in the wok" (*zhao mi xia guo jieduan*) (summer 1978 to autumn 1983); a second stage of enterprise initiative (*zhudong kaifa jieduan*) (autumn 1983 to summer 1986); and a third of "thoroughgoing development" (*shenru fazhan jieduan*) (summer 1986 and after).[65] During the first phase, declining state procurement expenditures led to a search for "rice"—income—wherever available. Later, civilian goods production became a matter of serving national economic construction in a planned way, not merely of finding "rice to eat" (*bushi weile zhao fan chi, shi yao yi guomin jingji jianshe fuwu*).[66] Eventually, many military enterprises realized that they must break out of the "small world" (*xiao tiandi*) of military production and move to develop commercially viable products in a longer-range, more calculated, and rational fashion.[67]

Another Chinese account suggests just how chaotic this process became for many enterprises. It divides the decade of the 1980s into three periods of "spontaneous production"—haphazard production—of civilian products (*zifa shengchan jieduan*) (1979–82); a second phase of enterprise initiative (*zhudong kaifa jieduan*) (1982/83–1986); and a third of efforts to "integrate with the national economy and stride forward" in a more coherent fashion (*tong guomin jingji fazhan ronghe qilai, maixiang shenru fazhan jieduan*) (1986 and after).[68]

All Chinese accounts concur that the period from the Third Plenum forward was characterized by initial chaos in the defense industry, followed by a settling. The change over time can probably be explained by levels of leadership interest in the problems of the defense industry's transition to the new policy environment. Once the leadership learned just how naïve it had been, it became far more vigorous in its effort to prevent "spontaneous" conversions of military industry plants, while promoting a planned and guided transition. In an interview in late 1995, the head of China's national defense conversion Leading Group in Beijing periodized state interest into stages of halting, high, and then low concern.[69] Between the second and third phases, he explained, the state moved decisively to plan for a more directed transition.

As part of this transition, in July 1986 all military industry ministries and leading organs were placed under the dual leadership (*shuangzhong lingdao*) of the State Council and the CMC. This step proved crucial, one Chinese analyst, Sun Zhenhuan, has suggested, because it formally integrated most military industry facilities into the civilian bureaucratic world. In theory, at least, this facilitated their integration into the larger civilian economy.[70]

Chinese accounts commonly argue that defense "conversion" (*junzhuanmin*) into civilian market niches was the direct result of these changes. Yet the story is made considerably more complex by rejiggered figures and the removal of these figures from their proper context. Chinese data suggest tremendous movement in the ratio of civilian to military production in the total output of defense enterprises during this period. One account that places this ratio at 8 percent to 92 percent in 1979 documents the shift to an extraordinary 80 percent to 20 percent by the end of 1994.[71] Yet Chinese government sources readily concede that the gross value of military output remained mostly constant over the same period. Even as civilian output grew, then, there appears to have been an increase in the total activity of Chinese defense enterprises, nearly all of it on the civilian side.

Of course, this indicates nothing about a decline in military output per se. But it does suggest a puzzle: military output in most defense enterprises remained flat, but total output from defense enterprises expanded during this initial period of reaction to Deng's shift of policy. The solution to the puzzle lies in three parallel processes.[72] First, considerable intersectoral rebalancing within military industry took place during these years. Thus, even as some sectors, such as ordnance, became thoroughly civilianized during the 1980s, others, such as aviation, expanded both military and civilian output to meet increased demand by both military and commercial customers.

Second, some military industries, such as aerospace, moved to diversify their work into new fields, such as commercial space launch, in order to raise capital. This does not imply, of course, that the profits from launching satellites were automatically plowed back into the coffers of China's missile builders. Some profits, no doubt, did contribute to the modernization of China's strategic missile force and the development of better, more accurate nuclear weapons. This was the conclusion of a special select committee of the U.S. Congress, the Cox Committee, in 1998. But at least some of this income appears to have been devoted to welfare. Few defense industry leaders, moreover, particularly in industries such as ordnance, preferred to concentrate on their PLA contract requirements and weapons production quotas. Commercial products proved far more profitable, a particularly poignant fact at a time when enterprise welfare was coming under increasing pressure. The "one factory, two systems" scheme that underlay the *junmin jiehe* program became ever more problematic as managers resisted their military-imposed production quotas. One manager complained that he had to "expend 50 percent of our efforts to produce barely 5 percent of our output [military products]."[73] Others contrasted the marginal payments they received for their military output with the profitable market prices for commercial goods.[74]

Third and finally, then, Chinese strategic weapons leaders became increasingly convinced during the 1980s that dual use process and component technologies, such as fiber optics and mineral metallurgy, had considerable commercial value.[75] For example, the nuclear industry, one of China's few producers of stable isotopes and radioisotopes, sought to capitalize commercially on the expertise of its research staff. The potential demand for its products was obvious: some 2,000 units across 30 provincial-level administrative divisions employ nuclear isotopes and radioisotopes in their agricultural, industrial, and medical work. In the 1980s and 1990s, the industry shifted much of its work away from nuclear weapons to reactor construction for the Chinese power grid, but it also promoted nuclear medicine, agricultural irradiation, and production of irradiated industrial goods and foodstuffs.[76]

PHASE 5: THE CMC FORMALIZES AND INSTITUTIONALIZES THE SHIFT

PLA Demobilization

A logical step in the demilitarization of economic development strategy was the out-and-out reduction of the PLA. In 1985, after nearly seven years of demilitarization following the Third Plenum, the CMC at last ordered a reduction in the overall size of the PLA. In an official declaration, the CMC judged the probability of conflict to be extremely low in the short to medium term.[77]

The 1985 demobilization was the eighth, and by far the most significant, since 1950.[78] An army that Deng had disparagingly condemned as "bloated" ten years earlier now saw its ranks reduced by almost one-third as it was transformed from a Maoist force suitable for waging a People's War into a smaller, better equipped military more appropriate to the new strategic conditions.

Deng himself took a leading role at the CMC meetings, held in Beijing from May 23 to June 6, 1985, that decided on the demobilization. In line with his position that strategy must adapt to changed conditions in the external environment and that economic construction would be the key to China's future, the ranks of the PLA, he maintained, should be shrunk to ensure a smaller, more efficient, and more combat-ready force. This would entail abandonment of preparations for "an early war, an all-out war, a nuclear war" (*zaoda, dada, da he zhanzheng*). According to a Chinese military history of the period:

> The guiding ideology of the strategic shift set new and higher requirements for the military work of the [PLA]. . . . [First, the army] should correctly handle the relationship between military construction and national economic construction; military construction should serve national economic construction. [Second, it should] correctly handle the relationship between current military construction and long-term military construction; current military construction should serve long-term military construction. [Third, it should] correctly handle the relationship between general (*yiban*) construction and capital (*jiben*) construction; general construction should serve capital construction.[79]

Organizational changes accompanied this decision to demobilize one million soldiers, including an administrative readjustment that shrank the number of China's regional military commands from eleven to seven.[80] On June 8, 1985 the CCP Politburo, the CMC, and the State Council jointly proclaimed that in the "new historical era" defense construction and force modernization must be built upon—and serve—national economic construction.[81] This was both a formal and institutionalized expression of Deng's new developmental line for the PLA.

Institutional Consolidation: The Designer System Is Restored

For the strategic weaponeers, these changes in procurement regime and declining budgets for a smaller PLA made it imperative to consolidate their political strength. This natural defensive reaction by a once-privileged elite manifested itself on two levels—one, institutional, the other, bureaucratic and political.

Institutionally, the leaders of the strategic weapons elite, such as Zhang Aiping and senior scientists, moved forcefully to restore some of the most important managerial solutions of the past by reconstituting the post-1977 strategic weapons system in the image of Nie's original programs of the 1950s and 1960s. Among their first steps was the restoration of the marshal's original system of chief designers, which had mostly fallen by the wayside during the Cultural Revolution when it was condemned as elitist by radicals and Red Guards.

As noted in Chapter 2, this system had emerged in the long-range missile program and then rapidly found its way into all of Marshal Nie's strategic

weapons projects. In October 1977, three months after the CMC decision
to shift the procurement regime to conventional weapons, strategic weaponeers, in anticipation of a final push toward deployment of the SLBM,
acted decisively to restore the designer-based decision-making system to its
former preeminence. Once again, then, the missile and space programs
moved into the vanguard of a transformative change in China's industrial
and technology management system.

The NDSTC and the Seventh Ministry, responsible for missile and
space programs, formally appointed chief designers for the three main programs in this sphere: Tu Shou'e for the ICBM, Huang Weilu for the SLBM,
and Ren Xinmin for communication satellites.[82] As noted in Chapter 2, the
collapse of the designer system during the late 1960s proved disastrous,
especially when coupled with the promotion of radicals and nontechnical
cadres into leading positions along the managerial track. This had resulted
in the politicization of both technical and administrative decision making,
running directly counter to Nie's intention in setting up the institution of
the chief designer.

The restoration of the chief designer system in 1977 was followed by the
formation from May to July 1979 of two new Leading Groups charged with
the certification of strategic and conventional weapons. These two functioned, in effect, to assure quality control. Zhang Aiping took charge of
both groups, first placing the office of the conventional weapons group in
the headquarters of the general staff, then awarding the NDSTC oversight
of the new strategic weapons certification Leading Group.[83] In 1982, both
groups were moved under the oversight of an integrated military industry
headquarters, the Commission of Science, Technology, and Industry for
National Defense (COSTIND).

The restoration of the chief designer system, as well as the creation of
quality control and certification organs with centralized authority, flowed
from the desire to reinvigorate a technical style of decision making and to
accelerate the development of key strategic weapons systems left over from
the pre-Cultural Revolution period, particularly the first test of a long-range
missile to the southern Pacific Ocean. This test was successfully conducted
under the supervision of the Seventh Ministry in May 1980.[84]

By 1981, chief designers had reemerged as the key technical decision
makers in most major military R&D projects. Thus, the strategic
weaponeers' effort to renew old institutions became a national managerial

model. In a memoir published in 1989, Tu Shou'e, the ICBM chief designer, explained why the lessons of the 1960s continued to have such force, relevance, and appeal. Most important, according to Tu, during the 1960s strategic weaponeers paid close attention to the technical relationships among interdependent design questions, such as range and payload specification, and the need to resist vertical bureaucratic boundaries by keeping system designers in close touch with component designers and technicians.[85] These features retained their attraction as the CMC sought to accelerate the deployment of key systems after 1977.

Bureaucratic Consolidation: The Creation of COSTIND

If their restoration of the designer system was the strategic weaponeers' first step in institutional consolidation, their next move, five years later, in 1982, was to consolidate their political position within the defense industry. Bolstering their political position would provide especially useful support within the bureaucracy as strategic weapons institutes and factories sought to adapt to the post-1977 shift to a conventional-weapons-oriented procurement regime by "escaping" into new lines of work.

COSTIND, the new, integrated defense industry commission, for the first time brought the NDSTC and the NDIO under the same administrative roof. But because so many strategic weaponeers had survived the Cultural Revolution while their NDIO antagonists had not, they dominated the new headquarters even though the focus of military R&D had shifted toward the NDIO's old charge of conventional weapons.[86] The strategic weaponeers' dominance of COSTIND can also be explained by leadership politics: Nie Rongzhen and Zhang Aiping had survived the Cultural Revolution and both remained active in 1982. He Long had died in 1969, and Luo Ruiqing in 1978. When COSTIND was established in 1982, both Nie and Zhang moved to place their protégés—and in Nie's case, his relatives too—into positions of leadership.

Although Zhou Enlai, Ye Jianying, and Deng Xiaoping had begun to stabilize the military industry system during the early 1970s, they had proved unable to resolve residual antagonisms and conflicts of interest within the system. The post–Third Plenum reform coalition was thus particularly concerned about stabilizing, streamlining, and rationalizing military industry in preparation for large-scale demilitarization. This was the essential impetus for merging former bureaucratic antagonists into COSTIND, a single, unified military industry headquarters for both defense R&D and industry.[87] As noted above, the new commission subsumed what remained of Marshal Nie's NDSTC as well as the NDIO, which had been Luo Ruiqing's power base; it also included the Science and Technology Planning Department of the PLA general staff. With strategic weaponeers in positions of comparative political strength, the move largely eliminated most residual contention between the NDSTC and its rivals.

The original COSTIND was not large. It had a staff of just several hundred, but its administrative purview encompassed the entire strategic weapons R&D system, as well as production and planning for both strategic and conventional weapons. COSTIND was also charged with coordination between weapons designers and the ministries that oversaw China's weapons production facilities.

With such a broad portfolio, the early COSTIND was a powerful agency, despite its small staff. In its mature form, reached in the 1990s, it exercised its authority through a tight administrative structure consisting of headquarters, logistics, and political departments; a science and technology department; a foreign affairs bureau charged with overseeing defense technology imports and exports and international coordination; and smaller project offices (Figure 3.4). COSTIND personnel referred to its structure as "five departments, one bureau, one office" (*wu bu, yi ju, yi ting*), and, after a manned spaceflight office was added in 1992, as all of the above plus "one project office" (*yi ban*).

Since COSTIND amalgamated a civilian industrial organ under the State Council (the NDIO), with two military organs under the CMC (the NDSTC and the S&T department of the general staff), it was placed under the dual leadership (*shuangzhong lingdao*) of both the CMC and the State Council. In practice, COSTIND continued to function primarily as an agent of the PLA; nearly all its personnel wore uniforms and held ranks, and it was regarded as a PLA "headquarters" (*silingbu*), albeit one with less power than other PLA headquarters, such as the general staff. But the State Council connection built explicit bureaucratic coordination into the system by reinforcing ties between COSTIND, on the one hand, and the industrial ministries and production facilities under civilian leadership, on the other.

The merger of former antagonists was eased considerably by the common challenge confronting the two systems—NDSTC and NDIO—and their

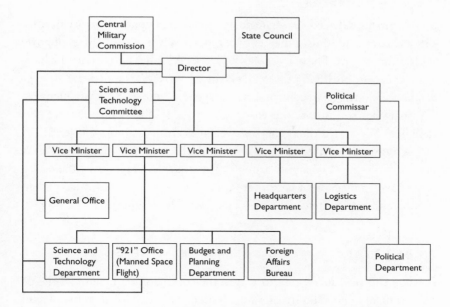

FIGURE 3.4   Organization of COSTIND, ca. 1993–1997.   SOURCE: Interviews.

leading elites. Changes throughout the military, such as demilitarization, had rendered the two bureaucratic systems' main interest largely one and the same: to fight for defense industrial and technical investments at a time of crisis. Clearly, the Deng coalition hoped that overlapping tasks and interdependencies between R&D and production might lead a unified headquarters to develop a corporate interest, thereby minimizing any former differences.

This made COSTIND quite different from the CSC, which had been created in the 1960s for precisely the same purpose of reconciling contending interests. Where the CSC had been a grand bargain, an attempt by politicians to create a structure to mediate among contending bureaucracies, COSTIND represented an effort to end contention by vertically integrating the antagonists under a single roof. By unifying China's military industrial system and then setting it in competition with other military headquarters for a smaller, more selective pool of resources at a time of shrinking budgets, the Deng coalition hoped to mute, if not eliminate altogether, the bureaucratic and elite contention that had plagued the system in the past.

In hindsight, the creation of COSTIND was neither a classic case of pure vertical integration nor a merger of roughly equal power centers. Rather, its establishment reflected the strategic weapons elite's political victory over traditional rivals and, thus, a merger of comparatively unequal centers of power within the system. The active roles played by Marshal Nie, General Zhang, and others, in bolstering COSTIND in its early years aided the strategic weaponeers' struggle to control this new agency. By 1986–87, Ding Henggao, Marshal Nie's son-in-law, was ensconced as COSTIND's director and Nie's daughter, Nie Li, led the agency's powerful electronics group. Clever Beijing wags commonly referred to the defense industry and its leading organ as the *Nie jia jun*—the "Nie family army."[88] For strategic weaponeers, the victory must have seemed sweet after more than two decades of bureaucratic contention and intermittent power struggles with the NDIO elite.

PHASE 6: THE WEAPONEERS SEEK A MEANS OF ESCAPE

Despite this bureaucratic victory atop the commanding heights of the defense industry, the main thrust of the initial post-Mao decade remained unchanged: conventional weapons were receiving greater emphasis than ever before. Moreover, strategic weaponeers who looked to their colleagues in COSTIND for leadership still faced the reality of rapid system-wide demilitarization. Even as they fought battles over procurement and leadership, then, some strategic weaponeers began to seek a means of escape from purely military related work.

At the same time that he stressed demilitarization, Deng himself provided one such route when he proposed a broadened role for science, engineering, and technology in Chinese society. Out of this emerged an expanded role for China's strategic weapons elite. Even as the Deng coalition cut the procurement budget and promoted defense conversion, it established new means for those who had worked on strategic weapons to reinvigorate their role in the development of strategic industries.

The 1978 National Science Conference: Deng Rethinks the Role of Science

In 1978, the government convened a National Science Conference to reevaluate the role of science and formulate a new political line. Such a meeting had an important precedent. In a 1956 speech on intellectual life, Premier Zhou Enlai had urged scientists to work cooperatively with the party in the interest of China's overall national development. Now, Deng's coalition adopted a similar approach. Like Zhou, they rallied scientists and engineers to the cause of national construction.[89] Scientists' goals, they argued, should mirror those of the party, namely to leave the political struggles of the Cultural Revolution behind and proceed into a new era. Both sides—the party and China's community of scientists and engineers—should work together to build a powerful, modern, and prosperous China.

Deng had mulled this issue and tested the waters in speeches throughout 1977. By the time of the 1978 National Science Conference, he had reached several important decisions. First, scientists as administrators, not party cadres, should have overall responsibility for the work of research institutes (*suozhang fuzizhi*). Party oversight would remain in the event that problems emerged, but primary leadership would henceforth belong to scientists, not to the party cadre.[90]

This was a step of historic proportions, one that Marshal Nie had first urged upon the leadership in the 1961 Fourteen Articles on Scientific Work. Deng told the National Science Conference that "party committees should give both power and responsibility (*you quan you fu*) to professionals occupying administrative posts, whether or not they are members of the party, and in a manner that reflects their functions [and positions]."[91] In this way, the party would "respect knowledge and [professional] talent."[92] "We must create within the party an atmosphere that allows us to . . . oppose the false notion that intellectual work is not worthy of respect. Whether or not work is mental or manual, it is [still] labor. People engaged in mental work are also laborers. In the future, it will become harder to distinguish between these two forms of work."[93]

Once he had bestowed political legitimacy on China's scientists, Deng launched into a broader explication of the role of science and technology in a developing economy. Deng himself took overall political charge of work in science and education.[94] His involvement extended to honoring a once scorned community. At the 1978 conference, he both "thanked" and "saluted" the leaders of Chinese military and civilian S&T. At the outset of his remarks to the conference, he introduced a theme that he would elaborate in his speeches across the 1980s: "Science and technology," Deng told the assembled delegates,

> are the key to the Four Modernizations. . . . Without modern science and technology it will become impossible to construct modern agriculture, industry, or

defense industry. Without the rapid development of science and technology it will become impossible to build the national economy. The party Central Committee decided to call this conference to mobilize the entire party and country to emphasize science, decide on a program, praise advanced units and individuals, and consider measures for the promotion of science and technology.[95]

Science, Deng concluded, is to be a primary force in future development planning.

Since Chairman Mao himself had approved the Fourteen Articles on Scientific Work,[96] Deng built on this approach by moving in two directions. He laid a theoretical foundation for the recognition of science in the economy and society; then, he revived and promoted a new administrative framework for science policy. Following Marxist theory, Deng claimed, science and technology should be recognized as "productive forces." Marx, Deng said, had understood this. The radicals—and, by implication, Deng's own opponents—did not. "Modern science and technology," he declared, "are in the midst of a great revolution."

> Modern science paves the road to improvements in production technology. It determines the direction of these improvements. Many new instruments and technical processes first emerged in the laboratory. A series of new industries, including high-polymer [chemical] synthesis, atomic energy, computers, semiconductors, space [technology], and lasers were all founded on the basis of newly emerging sciences. Of course, both now and in the future, there will be many theories for which there appears to be no practical use. But history has proved that once a breakthrough in theoretical work is achieved, sooner or later, significant progress in production and technology follows in its wake. . . . On what have advances in the productive forces and labor productivity depended? Mainly, they have depended on the power of science, the power of technology.[97]

Legitimating and Extending Scientific Methodology

Deng's decisions had the practical effect of extending political legitimacy to scientific approaches to problem solving. This resonated with changes elsewhere in post–Third Plenum China, particularly within the community of reform economists surrounding Premier Zhao Ziyang and other technically oriented personnel. The rise of scientific methods of analysis and decision making in post-Mao China traces its origin to this period, and is reflected in experiments to apply forecasting techniques, quantitative social science methodologies, cybernetic theories of decision, and system dynamics models to economic planning.

These experiments were undergirded by the strenuous efforts of senior reformers in Deng's political coalition "to provide alternative economic projections to those [of] the planning bureaucracy."[98] Out of this grew the so-called *China Toward the Year 2000* project, whose title aped the American *Global 2000 Report to the President*. A copy of the latter had been given to Chinese S&T policy makers during the winter of 1980–81 by the executive vice president of the Rockefeller Brothers Fund, Russell Phillips, and then to a visiting delegation of rural economic reformers by U.S. Secretary of Agriculture Robert Berglund.[99]

Much of the initiative for the *China 2000* project came from officials who had once worked for Marshal Nie Rongzhen, particularly when he had simultaneously headed the State Science and Technology Commission and the CAS. At least two leaders of the *China 2000* project had strong connections with strategic weapons work: Zhang Jingfu had been a senior CAS official working directly on strategic weapons projects in the 1950s before moving to Nie's SSTC office in the period before the Cultural Revolution; Song Jian was deputy chief designer of China's SLBM under Huang Weilu, and had been in charge of designing the missile's guidance system, while also helping to pioneer cybernetics in China in the 1960s.[100]

In July 1981, these reform-minded scientists invited Gerald O. Barney, the director of the American *Global 2000* study, to visit China.[101] Their discussions with Barney centered on rural development, particularly on issues dealing with population and food. But Barney's visit emboldened reformers in a wide variety of sectors to promote scientific methods of forecasting and economic analysis in policy making. As the political scientist Carol Lee Hamrin has written,

> When asked what China should do [Barney] recommended that China make better use of human resources, address the problem of soil erosion . . . and do a study of China in the year 2000. These suggestions had big reverberations even before Barney left China. He was told at the end of his visit that the [SSTC] would be proposing that it begin a China 2000 study. . . . By the fall of 1981, the State Council had approved the study.[102]

The State Council appointed Ma Hong, soon to become president of the Chinese Academy of Social Sciences, as the key project coordinator.

While *China 2000* was a work of social science, not of technology, and proposed no specific program or organizational system, it was nonetheless critical to China's early S&T reforms. It represented the first application of cybernetic theories and scientific methods to policy analysis outside the natural sciences and the strategic weapons programs.

Almost at a stroke, the *China 2000* project reinforced the legitimacy of the larger concept of "scientific decision making" in China, which had two important effects: it focused the leadership's attention on an array of non-military technologies and issues, and it brought home the lesson that enhanced contact with foreign specialists who had themselves wrestled with these problems would aid China's transition. In this respect, Barney's visit was by no means an isolated example of international contact and exchange. As we have seen, during the Mao years the strategic weapons programs had been virtually the only sector guaranteed a steady supply of overseas publications and technical materials. Now, *China 2000* built upon this legacy to facilitate the growing availability of such materials to other experts, particularly social scientists.[103]

The original *China 2000* study shifted into high gear by the summer of 1982 as its compilers solicited reports and forecasts from hundreds of state agencies. Although it employed Western social science methods to systematize and analyze the data it gathered, its presentation of alternative best-and-worst-case scenarios suggested some of the older traditions described in Chapter 2. Hamrin has described *China 2000* as representing "pioneering" policy analysis; the social science methodologies it employed were indeed revolutionary.[104] But scientific decision making had been a staple feature of the CSC and the programs within its purview long before 1978. For instance, Zhou Enlai routinely convened technical seminars to discuss best-and-worst-case scenarios concerning the weapons testing schedule. And it was Song Jian who in 1979 "initiated the first long-term forecasts in the population field," even as he was completing the inertial guidance design for the 1982 SLBM test.[105]

By the middle of the decade, scientific decision making was being widely promoted throughout China.[106] Ma Hong initiated a second *China 2000* study, again soliciting reports from hundreds of government departments. COSTIND, too, actively participated in the project. In February 1986, COSTIND submitted its report, "China's Defense Science and Technology in 2000," to Ma Hong's office. Over 2,000 people in COSTIND's domain, including 100 senior specialists, contributed to the study.[107]

In this way, *China 2000* set a tone that would become useful to strategic weaponeers in formulating concrete programs that would carry their influence and managerial institutions beyond military S&T. It also symbolized the extent to which renewed international exchange had begun to change the way Chinese scientists and engineers thought about their country's place in the world and how best to attack scientific problems.

In responding to the challenge of the broad, systemic changes wrought by Deng Xiaoping's reforms, the strategic weaponeers drew upon their time-tested ideas about technology and their well-honed notions of management. For them, the scientific decision making advocated by *China 2000* was hardly new; they had always tried to be "scientific." Accordingly, as they navigated the new era of reform—that is, as they sought to adapt to a new policy environment—they took in hand their old charts, so to speak. The story of that voyage forms the subject of the next chapter.

chapter four

THE STRATEGIC WEAPONS ELITE
CONFRONTS CHANGE, 1975–1986

For twenty years, from 1955 to 1975, China's strategic weapons programs depended on two pillars of support: the politicians' commitment to strategic weapons development, and the political position of crucial patrons such as Nie Rongzhen. As we have seen, the weaponeers always occupied a tenuous position, even at the height of their power during the Mao era. Their failure to institutionalize their power base—their dependence on Mao Zedong's whims, Zhou Enlai's capacity to broker deals on their behalf, and Nie's standing in military politics—left leading members of the elite politically vulnerable. With the shifts of the late 1970s and early 1980s, strategic weaponeers faced a newly precarious future. They could fade into obscurity as strategic weapons modernization lost relevance in the PLA's procurement regime, or they could redirect their efforts to conventional weapons R&D, as some microelectronics specialists had sought to do. But the results had been mixed, at best. As a longer-range alternative, therefore, some leading specialists began to seek to expand outward from narrowly demarcated weapons development projects to technology projects of broader scope.

This chapter examines how Marshal Nie's heirs first wrestled with these choices as they confronted the political and technical consequences of Deng's reforms. Politically, it is clear that whatever defensive measures they had taken to consolidate their power base, key specialists in China's strategic weapons programs also understood that they (and COSTIND) would probably never play the powerful role they had in past decades—dominating China's priority, national high technology agenda. The shift to broader, system-wide economic development had empowered civilian technology elites who now sought greater influence over the state's agenda after three decades of military dominance. Meanwhile, the new emphasis on conventional weapons had moved the locus of weapons decision making much closer to its end users. This increased the importance of what the Chinese term "equipment" (*shebei*), which fell under the purview of uniformed service headquarters, at the expense of "technology" (*jishu*), which had become the formally mandated preserve of China's defense-technical elite. Not surprisingly, this change favored uniformed elites in the PLA's general staff, navy, and air force at the expense of once-influential weapons scientists.

China's defense R&D community also began to confront mounting evidence during these years that its Mao-era technical system had ossified. From the mid-1960s onward, a dramatic shift in the industrialized world reversed prevalent thinking about the relationship between military and civilian sectors in spurring innovation. Where military innovation seemed firmly in the lead in the period after World War II, by the late 1970s–80s, largely as a result of the microelectronics revolution in semiconductors and integrated circuits, the flow of innovation appeared to have changed direction (Table 4.1).

The post-1960s Silicon Valley model reshaped innovation relationships in the West. China, however, missed this change almost entirely. Its technological infrastructure was a good fifteen years behind that of the West. Moreover, the initial stirrings of this revolution in innovation coincided with the violent phase of China's Cultural Revolution (1966–71) and initial period of recovery (1971–77). Nineteen years behind the United States in the development of an atomic bomb, Chinese technicians could not confront fundamental issues of innovation until tasks from the 1950s and 1960s—the Three Grasps—were completed.

By the late 1970s, with some of these major tasks still unrealized, information about this sea change in innovation began to seep into China. An externally induced crisis of confidence thereby began to compel Chinese defense technicians to reassess their approach. The proximate cause of this self-reflection was the renewal of international S&T exchange at the end of the 1970s. Foreign visitors offered new ideas about the role of high technology in society and economy. Nie's weaponeers became the pivotal point of

TABLE 4.1
Flow of Technological Innovations

Period I (1945–mid-1960s)	Military Technology	Civilian Application
	Bombing radar systems	All-weather civil air transports
	Tactical field radios	Police, safety, rescue communications
	Fire control computers	Industrial process control systems
	Infrared sensors	Geological mapping
	Radar magnetrons	Microwave ovens
	Satellite systems	Communications satellites

Period II (mid-1960s–present)	Civilian Technology	Military Application
	Integrated circuits	Command and control systems
	Space-based sensors	Military intelligence
	LSI, VLSI	Cruise missile guidance
	Fiber optics	Missile guidance
	Electro-optical devices	Intelligence sensors
	Lasers	Target designation, range measurement
	Artificial intelligence	Smart weapons

SOURCE: Adapted from Samuels (1994). Copyright © 1994 Cornell University Press.

contact for these new approaches because they had dominated most high-end R&D and precision industry since the late 1950s. Buffeted by these pressures, some of the most prominent of Nie's heirs would begin to lay the groundwork for a more aggressive strategy.

POLITICAL AND BUREAUCRATIC PRESSURES

In the last chapter, we saw how acquisitions within the military system shifted toward conventional force modernization at precisely the moment the Deng coalition demilitarized national resource allocation. Strategic weaponeers thus lost one pillar of their influence. Their attempt thereafter to leverage their dominance of component sectors, such as microelectronics, into influence over the conventional weapons R&D agenda mostly failed. Then, at nearly the same time, the weaponeers lost the second pillar of their influence.

The Elders Begin to Retire

In the early to mid-1980s, the senior political and military patrons upon whom China's strategic weapons elite had depended for two decades began to retire in rapid order. By 1986, Mao Zedong and Zhou Enlai had been dead for a decade, Marshal Nie had retired, and Zhang Aiping was near retirement. Meanwhile, the CMC decision to give priority in procurement to conventional weapons was nine years old. The systematic policy of demilitarization initiated by Deng Xiaoping in 1978 had been underway for eight years, and it appeared thoroughly irreversible. In this context—and for the first time since 1955—leading members of the strategic weapons elite found themselves confronting rival elites and alternative technology agendas without strong military and political patrons.

Such retirements were inevitable. As early as 1978, Deng had begun to urge veteran cadres into semi-retirement by shifting them to advisory commissions and honorary positions in what he called the "second line" of party leadership.[1] The impact of this on the weaponeers' political patrons was not immediate because they ranked among the most prominent revolutionaries in the party. Some leaders at the apex, such as Nie and Zhang, were initially exempted from the new retirement norm in order to preserve continuity and stability at the core of the CCP.[2] As the party's leading theoretical journal *Hongqi* (Red Flag) put it in a 1982 editorial: "We need a few dozen veteran cadres with international reputations who are capable of careful and long-term planning, who maintain a comprehensive view of the situation, and who are still in good health. [We need them to remain] in positions at the core of leadership in the Party and government, to help stay the course."[3]

The exemption of these senior leaders was a short-term political bargain struck at the apex of the polity by the ten or fifteen top CCP veterans, including Deng. Thus, any attempt by the weaponeers to rely on these senior patrons for continued influence seemed a poor strategy at the time. Against the backdrop of demilitarization and the new PLA procurement regime, this raised important questions about the sheer survival of the strategic weapons elite. What would happen if the eldest scientists failed to promote junior specialists in their forties and fifties into positions of high leadership? Without its military and political patrons, what would be the prospects of the elite surviving if it failed to institutionalize its power base, while moving away from reliance on generals, politicians, and top-level cadres?

China's strategic weaponeers had less than a decade to begin formalizing and diversifying the sources of their influence on development planning and technology policy. Their challenge was compounded by the

comparatively weak position of the most important source of their bureaucratic power, COSTIND. As described in the preceding chapter, the formation of COSTIND in 1982 gave Nie's heirs uncontested control of the
military industrial system. But the dominance of that special, often secretive, system became far less important in the 1980s in the overall calculus of
Chinese military politics. When Nie had headed the NDSTC in the 1950s
and 1960s, he served concurrently as a vice chairman of the Central Military
Commission and, during a period of Lin Biao's absence in the early 1960s,
shared daily operational responsibility for the PLA with Marshal He Long.
In the mid-1980s, by contrast, COSTIND's director, Ding Henggao, was
not even a member of the CMC, and Ding was forced increasingly to fight
for influence over technology decisions within and beyond the military system. Some of Ding's bureaucratic rivals, on the other hand, especially senior
generals in the PLA general staff, were key leaders in the CMC. For the
strategic weapons community, then, the logic of diversification into other
than exclusively military activities became obvious as the 1980s wore on.

Weakness Among Second-Generation Elites

The core political problem facing the strategic weapons elite during these
years was that with its last line of patrons—Zhang Aiping, Liu Huaqing,
and several others—well into their seventies, the leaders of the next generation, such as Ding Henggao, would be unlikely to rise to leading positions
in Chinese military politics. As COSTIND grew weaker vis-à-vis other military headquarters, such as the general staff, the position of its leading administrators, who lacked prestige in the PLA, also grew weaker. Himself a
former chief of the PLA general staff, Marshal Nie had compensated for his
own bureaucratic weakness in the early years of the strategic weapons drive
by circumventing formal procedures and talking directly to veteran colleagues, including Chairman Mao, Premier Zhou, and others. If general
staff cadres attacked the NDSTC in the early 1960s, no matter. As a first
generation revolutionary, Nie's prestige and power base were, in some ways,
independent of the bureaucracy he controlled.

These informal ties mediated nearly all political-military leadership
patterns among the PRC's first generation of PLA commanders. But by the
late 1970s, China had become much more bureaucratic, and PLA career
patterns increasingly were stratified. A military technician, such as Ding
Henggao, could almost certainly never emerge as a chief of the general staff.

He could only hope to be the director of a specialized headquarters, such as COSTIND, with a narrow professional and functional mandate.

Therefore, unlike the first generation of strategic weapons leaders, such as Nie, as well as the second generation, such as Zhang Aiping and Liu Huaqing, the third generation, such as Ding, found that their influence was *not* independent of their bureaucratic domain. Rather, the formal posts they held were the major source of their influence. Without COSTIND, Ding would have had little power at all, even though he was Nie's son-in-law. And yet as noted in Chapter 3, COSTIND was hardly a powerful base on which to build a political-military consensus for specific, highly contentious, technology investments. The most prominent members of this third generation—Ding Henggao, Shen Rongjun, Nie Li, Wang Shouyun, Qian Shaojun, and others—could never hope to match their predecessors' political prestige.[4] They were technicians, not warfighters. They required a bureaucratic power base, and possessed only a weak one. And unlike Nie Rongzhen, Zhang Aiping, and Liu Huaqing, they had few informal sources of influence. Thus, the primary power base of the third generation derived from personal relationships with increasingly elderly patrons. Ding was Nie's son-in-law. Nie Li was Ding's wife, and Nie's daughter. Wang Shouyun had been the personal secretary of Qian Xuesen. These ties sustained the elite for a time. But they could not possibly substitute for the political weight that a Nie, a Zhang, a Liu, and others in the first generation carried with leading politicians, such as Deng Xiaoping.

The Military Debate and Pressure from the General Staff

This comparative political and bureaucratic weakness was manifest in both the military and civilian spheres.[5] On the military side, the General Staff Department (GSD) emerged during the first half of the 1980s as both the operational center of the PLA and a claimant on functions and resources long concentrated in the hands of other headquarters. This revived institutional rivalries dating back to the late 1950s and also demonstrated the extent of the strategic weaponeers' dilemma.

As the PLA evolved during the first thirty years of the PRC, individual headquarters departments came to resemble fiefdoms: autonomous bureaucratic systems, each headed by a powerful officer, that jealously guarded their power, privileges, and patronage. Marshal Nie dominated military R&D. Marshal He Long, together with General Luo Ruiqing, directed much of China's conventional weapons development. Marshal Luo Ronghuan briefly built a network of political cadres before his death in 1963. General Hong Xuezhi built a network in logistics. This comparatively balanced system was eventually upset by several purges from 1959 to 1971, particularly during 1965–69 when Lin Biao's allies, mostly from his pre-1949 Fourth Field Army, won control over vast swaths of the PLA once led by those who had been purged.

During Marshal Ye Jianying's political restoration of the 1970s, directed by a small committee called the Administrative Meeting (*bangong huiyi*) that acted as the agent of the CMC, much of the old system of balance was restored.[6] Members of Nie's network reasserted control over defense industry and R&D. Other veteran PLA officers associated with Marshals Ye, Chen Yi, and Liu Bocheng, as well as General Su Yu, moved into key slots in operations. These included two veteran commanders, Yang Dezhi and Qin Jiwei, who remained prominent through most of the 1980s, as well as Hong Xuezhi, who returned to the CMC and his old logistics fief, where he restored many members of his network to power in the PLA General Logistics Department (GLD).

For this reason, the Central Military Commission—the top policy-making body in the Chinese military—came to function in the 1980s much as it had during the 1950s—as an arena in which the heads of the main constituent systems of the PLA bargained, thrashed out problems, and sought consensus amid fragmented responsibility.[7]

When COSTIND was formed in 1982, strategic weapons leaders at last won the political contest for power in the military industry system. But the PLA's post-1977 procurement agenda blurred the lines between science and engineering and research and production. While the strategic weaponeers succeeded in eliminating rivals, such as the NDIO, control of the military industry bureaucracy without a broader power base was a weak foundation upon which to influence long-term policy. By the mid-1980s, COSTIND had become one of four main PLA headquarters departments, the so-called *si da zongbu* or "four big headquarters" (Figure 4.1).[8] But the political ground had already begun to shift almost as soon as the third generation of strategic weapons leaders consolidated their position within COSTIND.

The Deng coalition's decision to slash PLA budgets, to reduce the importance of military industry in overall national development planning, and to civilianize military industry saddled COSTIND leaders with much of

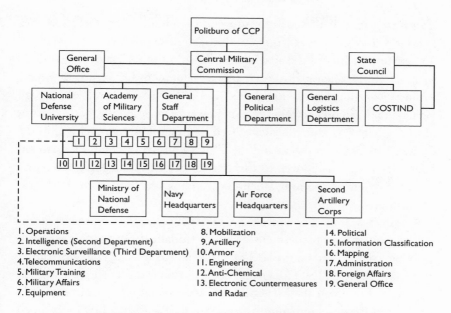

1. Operations
2. Intelligence (Second Department)
3. Electronic Surveillance (Third Department)
4. Telecommunications
5. Military Training
6. Military Affairs
7. Equipment

8. Mobilization
9. Artillery
10. Armor
11. Engineering
12. Anti-Chemical
13. Electronic Countermeasures and Radar

14. Political
15. Information Classification
16. Mapping
17. Administration
18. Foreign Affairs
19. General Office

FIGURE 4.1   China's Military System and General Staff, ca. 1982–1997.
SOURCES: Zhang Aiping (1994), Han Huaizhi and Tan Jingqiao (1989),
and interviews.

China's most inefficient industrial facilities. Furthermore, Nie's heirs achieved control just as conventional weapons industries were ordered to "convert." This burdened leading strategic weaponeers, such as Ding Henggao, with responsibility for administering a huge, inefficient, and stagnant industrial system.

The political consequences of the 1977 shift in procurement thereby compounded this challenge to COSTIND's new leaders. It moved acquisition decision making much closer to the end user on the battlefield. The general staff had been shut out of many key procurement decisions during the Mao era. This was partly because Nie's rival, Luo Ruiqing, was chief of the general staff during the key period of the early 1960s when procurement debates raged most intensely, and strategic weapons—controlled by the NDSTC, not the general staff—won the day. The GSD had played only a minor role in strategic weapons R&D. For example, officers in the GSD's Third Department (Electronic Surveillance) worked closely with CAS scientists in the 1950s on computer systems for the strategic weapons program.[9] But this was an exception to a larger bureaucratic rule, and the

Third Department played little substantive role in most R&D for Nie's programs. Instead, it was largely confined to reconnaissance and monitoring operations. Indeed the general staff lost most of its input into strategic weapons R&D when its Research and Development Office, led by Zhang Aiping, was transferred into Nie's new NDSTC in 1958.[10] Although General Luo and others would remain powerful voices in the R&D debates of the early 1960s, these debates played out on a personal level within the Central Special Commission and the CMC. The General Staff Department had little institutional power to affect investments in strategic weapons and auxiliary systems. Moreover, when Luo Ruiqing was purged, the GSD was left with even less influence.

The 1977 shift back to conventional weapons gave the GSD an opportunity to reenter the procurement debate.[11] Initially, from 1977 to the mid-1980s, it tried to secure a place for itself in R&D. General staff cadres pleaded with COSTIND for greater coordination across headquarters, so as to keep end users on the battlefield and their representatives in the GSD involved in the development of weapons. By 1986–87, the GSD was much more insistent, and some GSD leaders appear to have argued that COSTIND should be eliminated altogether.

General staff leaders argued to the CMC that COSTIND's control over military technology marginalized end users by keeping them at arm's length during crucial phases in the development of weapons. In fact, COSTIND depended heavily on precisely the kind of horizontal coordination that Nie had set in place as a management model in the 1950s. COSTIND created code-numbered bureaus (*ju*) under its Science and Technology Department (Keji bu), each charged with cross-headquarters liaison in specific functional areas applied to weapons (Figure 4.2). Each COSTIND bureau coordinated with two structures. One bureau coordinated with air force headquarters and the GSD's air force bureau in planning the service's equipment needs. Another bureau worked with the navy and the GSD naval bureau. Still another coordinated with ground force planners, and so on.

This system functioned according to the principles of "coordination" (*xietiao*) developed between Nie Rongzhen's NDSTC and the navy during the years before Chen Youming's submarine office—the Lingjiuban—was founded in 1969. But during the first half of the 1980s, many general staff, navy, and air force officers began to question their secondary status in the

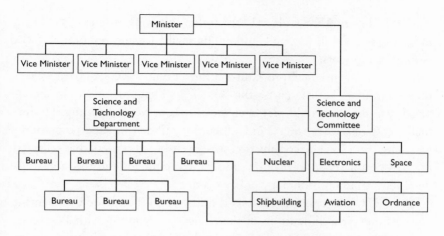

FIGURE 4.2   COSTIND Science and Technology Department, 1980s–1990s.
SOURCE: Interviews.

process. Some asked what would happen in the event of interheadquarters conflict over the direction of conventional weapons investments and priorities. They contended that end users ought to be given greater influence over procurement decisions, especially as high-level science and basic research—the backbone of the autonomy of strategic weapons programs—were increasingly supplanted by "mere" engineering.

The 1977 procurement shift significantly buttressed these arguments for greater attention to the needs of end users. As an alternative to Nie's old system of coordination, some general staff officers favored a more decentralized system of decision making that involved, among other things, drawing a distinction between "technology," which would be assigned to a weaker COSTIND, and "equipment," which would be primarily their responsibility as end users.

The Civilianization of Technology Development and the Rise of the SSTC

This forceful challenge within the military to the strategic weapons elite was echoed by an assault on broad national S&T policy making, for even as COSTIND and Nie's heirs beat back attacks from the general staff, the Politburo decided to revive the civilian State Science and Technology Commission (SSTC). This had been a weak Mao-era bureaucracy that had succumbed during the Cultural Revolution. Now, as early as 1977, Deng moved to reestablish it as an autonomous, civilian supervisor of high technology investments.[12]

But while the original, pre–Cultural Revolution SSTC had been weaker than its military counterpart—the NDSTC—Deng made certain the revived commission would play a vigorous role in S&T planning. He formally reestablished the SSTC in October 1977 under the supervision of his close ally Fang Yi. The commission was given broad powers that reflected the new emphasis on science in national development and the large-scale demilitarization of technology policy making.[13]

The SSTC was assigned two broad missions: to illuminate the scientific and technological dimensions of the choices confronting China's leaders, and to raise China's S&T standards. In the Chinese bureaucratic system, which is organized as a matrix, the new commission also established a professional relationship with the science and technology bureaus that exist in nearly every production ministry and unit nationwide.[14] The SSTC thereby usurped the role of advising leaders on major technology choices and investments that had usually fallen to the NDSTC and military scientists in previous decades. And the SSTC's authority was premised on its capacity to expand its role in factories and industrial units. To enhance its authority, the commission sought to marry S&T to economic planning, which also led it to encroach on an area long monopolized by the State Planning Commission (SPC). The SSTC lacked a formal role in production and had little money to allocate to the conversion of research into industrial techniques, dealing as it did primarily in knowledge rather than material resources. Yet its importance grew as Deng increasingly emphasized science and demilitarization over the course of the 1980s.

Over time, then, the SSTC became the leading bureaucracy formulating national policy guidelines and setting national priorities in S&T. In this way, during the first half of the 1980s control over the agenda in both the military and the civilian spheres shifted away from COSTIND and the strategic weapons elite, setting the stage for intensified competition over investments in technology and industry.

In April 1984, a drafting committee of the State Council issued a report on what it termed a "revolution" (*geming*) in new technologies. The report identified several sectors as critical to China's development, including information technology, space, aviation, and nuclear technologies. All these, which had long been dominated by strategic weaponeers, were now to be developed according to the concept of "dual use" (*liangyong*).[15] The committee argued that although "new" technologies in these areas had implications for defense, their greatest utility lay with their potential civilian applications. Thus, the standard for judging all future projects should be their potential for dual use and their specific contributions to overall national economic construction.[16]

This reflected a fundamental change in the underlying assumptions of technology policy. For the first time, the leadership believed that technological achievements should be judged according to the ease with which they could be commercialized and industrialized. The new line also had political implications; some Chinese analysts suggested that the military R&D system had failed the national economy because it had been insufficiently "conducive to the commercialization and industrialization of high-tech achievements." Similarly, it had not been "conducive to [the promotion of] technical progress in traditional industry or the fostering of S&T personnel."[17]

This conclusion certainly ran directly counter to the main thrust of Marshal Nie's assertions throughout the 1950s and 1960s. The second and third generations of strategic weapons leaders counterattacked by publishing an array of heroic histories of the strategic weapons programs that invoked their legacy as a precedent for the future. Yet it was precisely here that the strategic weaponeers were most vulnerable: the political leadership seemed convinced that the legacy of their programs had become much less relevant to China's future.

In 1986, a White Paper (*baipishu*) issued by the SSTC enshrined the revisionist argument as the official policy of the Chinese government: "S&T work must turn toward (*mianxiang*) the national economy. . . . Scientific personnel must devote themselves to the great cause of socialist modernization and construction, and to economic construction in particular."[18] By 1989, this call would be supplemented by extending the defense conversion program from conventional weapons factories into the research academies that had been the backbone of Nie's strategic weapons system. A State Council "Outline on Medium and Long-Term Science and Technology Development (1990–2000–2020)" called for the implementation of all "necessary steps to remove existing institutional barriers to facilitate the transfer process."[19]

In sum, by 1986, strategic weaponeers, their bureaucratic perch in COSTIND, and the major weapons academies that supported their R&D

agenda faced an uncertain future. COSTIND's own role seemed likely to shrink as the general staff and the SSTC intensified their campaign to dominate both military and civilian technology planning.

A TECHNICAL AND PROGRAMMATIC CRISIS OF CONFIDENCE

These political challenges left Nie's heirs floundering after just nine years (1977–86) of PLA procurement reform and change in the national technology bureaucracy. This purely political quandary was compounded by a sense among leading Chinese scientists that the national R&D system had failed to keep pace with technological change.

The R&D System Stalls

The basis of the weapons elite's search for new models was a creeping sense that China's R&D system had ossified even in areas where the foundations appeared strong. While S&T planners could point with pride to China's technological successes—areas that had been intimately connected to the privileged strategic weapons program, including space and materials science—they could not ignore China's major weaknesses, particularly energy technology and transportation.[20]

By the late 1970s strategic weaponeers had begun to reach a consensus that a broadened focus would be necessary both to sustain themselves politically and to strengthen Chinese S&T as it attempted to keep pace with global innovation. This consensus required a plea for greater state attention to science, which the political leadership promised at the 1978 National Science Conference. But the rapidity of the substitution cycle for military equipment drove home how difficult it would be for Chinese scientists to keep pace with global trends. As Zhang Aiping argued in 1983, "modern science and technology change at an extremely rapid pace, and the cycle within which newer military equipment must be substituted for old models is becoming increasingly short. The present struggle between the two superpowers is, at base, a competition in science and technology. Future wars will not only be contests of manpower, materials, and expenditures, but of science and technology [as well]."[21]

To many in the strategic weapons community, this problem would likely be exacerbated by the collapse of defense S&T, as China's external environment became increasingly stable and national strategy shifted toward economic development. Strictly military problems therefore came to reinforce the growing recognition that technology had become increasingly dual- and multi-use in nature. The strategic weaponeers' initial response to defense cuts was to argue for a policy reversal and new expenditures. But within a few years, many had come to a different view. On the one hand, force modernization amid shrinking budgets implied a need for greater attention to the fundamentals of defense-related S&T. The solution to the problem of developing next-generation military equipment, as Zhang Aiping argued in 1983, would be to involve S&T in new weapons work and "in all its branches, including basic theory and technical sciences, as well as [to emphasize] applied technology and [systems] engineering."[22] Yet given the growing interdependence of defense technology and commercial innovation, strategic weaponeers soon took the position that China's national R&D system, not its defense-technical system, was the real issue at stake.

As strategic weapons leaders came to see this problem, endemic stagnation in R&D during the Mao years meant that only the strategic weapons system had created organizational and management institutions conducive to rapid and sustained technical progress at (roughly) international standards. Most nonmilitary R&D was fragmented, vertical, and compartmentalized. Only strategic weapons administrators had built cross-system collaborative structures, integrated decision makers and staff, promoted competition in design, and institutionalized peer review.

Foreign Influence, New Approaches

As was also true of their colleagues throughout Chinese S&T, then, the strategic weapons community engaged in turbulent self-reflection during this period. The debates that emerged became especially urgent because of what the strategic weaponeers learned through renewed international exchange.[23] The opportunity to participate in international symposia, to travel abroad, and to host overseas colleagues in China had an immense effect. It demonstrated that China's technical infrastructure had fallen far behind global standards and that the simple spin-off conception underlying Mao-era strategic technology policy had become anachronistic.

The first steps in the reassessment of Chinese technological capabilities took place among scientists and engineers after a number of Sino-American and Sino-European S&T agreements led to working-level exchanges.[24] In the late 1970s, for example, the U.S. National Academy of Sciences sponsored a series of delegations to China that initiated U.S.-China exchanges. Many of these groups met with key strategic weaponeers, including one who would later propose the 863 program to Deng Xiaoping: the nuclear physicist Wang Ganchang. Wang's interlocutors, an American nuclear physics delegation, arrived in China in the late spring of 1979. The delegation, led by Allan Bromley of Yale, who later became science advisor to President George H. W. Bush, comprised both theorists and experimentalists and included some of the most prominent physicists in the United States.

These various delegations proved crucial to the Chinese by providing benchmarks against which to assess relative progress and by introducing them to the evolution of Western technical ideas.[25] The American nuclear physicists' two main interlocutors at the leadership level were both prominent strategic weaponeers: Qian Sanqiang, the group's official host, and Wang himself, then director of the Institute of Atomic Energy in Beijing.[26] Members of the U.S. delegation remarked in a report after the trip on the openness of the Chinese, who were forthcoming not simply with general information about the state of Chinese research but also frank about the manifold weaknesses of (and their consequent frustrations with) the Chinese R&D system. Wang was particularly adamant that he wanted technical criticism of his research program, not merely of his institute's equipment.[27] As Bromley wrote:

> Clearly the Chinese scientists recognize that they must increase their interactions with the international scientific community manifold if they are to achieve their stated goals. . . . The delegation members normally split up into smaller groups to tour teaching and research laboratories and facilities, and in several instances, at the specific request of those in charge, reconvened following these visits for discussions of our impressions and suggestions. Although each group asked very seriously for our criticisms of their work and plans, we felt it prudent, given the vastness of our general ignorance of things Chinese, to limit our comments in these sessions to specific responses to scientific or technical questions or to general recommendations in which the entire delegation concurred.[28]

The Chinese also pressed during these years for membership in international scientific federations, participation at conferences, and increased exchanges and visits. Qian and Wang pushed the Americans in the nuclear delegation particularly hard on the issue of formal PRC membership in the International Union of Pure and Applied Physics.[29] Wang Chunying, one of Wang Ganchang's deputy directors at the Institute of Atomic Energy (IAE), visited Yale in July 1978 with eight senior associates, some months before Bromley's visit to China. Later, the IAE would attempt to construct a virtual replica of the Wright accelerator that Bromley directed. Likewise, Yang Jiachi, an important figure in the development of flight control technologies for China's missiles and space satellites, became active in the International Federation of Automatic Control and served as vice chairman of the Executive Bureau of the International Astronautics Federation.[30]

Plugged back into the world of international science, Chinese professionals rejoined what the political scientist Peter Haas has termed "epistemic communities"—cross-national networks of experts who derive from these connections both political benefits and new knowledge.[31] Epistemic communities are important, Haas has argued, because they can help governments identify their interests on complex technical issues by framing problems for debate and enhancing the coordination of international policy. But exposure to new ideas transmitted through these networks can also change the way a national elite formulates problems within its own country.

In addition to arranging meetings with "purely" scientific groups, such as Bromley's, weapons program managers began a parallel round of talks with foreign defense-technology innovators. These grew out of the normalization of military-to-military exchanges, and ultimately proved to be important because as strictly military exchanges they automatically excluded non-weapons scientists. Hence, strategic weaponeers were the main point of contact with foreign administrative innovators who had themselves wrestled with new patterns and modes of innovation.

Perhaps the most important of these sessions were held with William Perry, the U.S. undersecretary of defense for research and engineering (1977–81), a pioneer of "smart" weapons and "stealth" systems in private industry and government, and a future U.S. secretary of defense.[32] Perry's meetings in China grew out of concern over the Soviet military buildup in the Far East during the 1970s. For the Carter administration, this strategic concern reinforced diplomatic and economic considerations by offering a compelling rationale for defense and security cooperation with China. Perry's exchanges would have a broad and enduring impact within China itself. His comments about technology—some casual and

offhanded—powerfully resonated with a Chinese military R&D community that had begun to struggle with problems of innovation long before
Perry visited Beijing. As with Bromley, Perry's hosts were prominent strategic weaponeers, including two officers who had been among the three to
five leading administrators of the Mao-era strategic weapons programs:
General Zhang Aiping, who worked with Perry during his time in Beijing,
and General Liu Huaqing, who traveled with the delegation and carried on
more informal discussions during site visits and inspections.

In the summer of 1980, China's defense minister, Geng Biao, arrived in
Washington on a visit that initiated military-to-military contacts between
the two countries. The main topic on the Chinese agenda was the acquisition of U.S. defense technology and the development of a wide-ranging defense technology relationship. Defense Secretary Harold Brown designated
Perry, who directed U.S. weapons research, as Geng's primary interlocutor
in Washington. On a purely social level, the two sides apparently got on
well, laying a firm foundation for future cooperation; Perry even secured
the presidential box at the Kennedy Center for the Performing Arts for an
evening of American entertainment.

On the issue of technology—the business at hand—the meetings were
more restrained. The Americans focused heavily on questions of interoperability affecting PLA requests for more sophisticated American defense technologies. Before Geng Biao left Washington he insisted that the
Americans make a reciprocal visit to China to get a close view of China's
military technology, and offer suggestions for a broad-based PLA modernization agenda. Geng may have wished to convince the Americans to re-
consider several more contentious areas of technology transfer by giving a
high-level U.S. delegation a closer look at the procurement system into
which the PLA hoped to absorb the technology.

For the reciprocal visit, Brown again designated Perry to lead the
American delegation. In the weeks that followed Geng Biao's return to
Beijing, Perry (on behalf of the Department of Defense), assisted by representatives from other U.S. agencies on an interagency committee formed to
prepare for the trip, developed a long list of sites that they hoped to visit
while in China. High on the list, Perry recalls, were supercomputing institutes, ICBM facilities, and missile test bases. When he presented the list to
the Chinese ambassador in Washington, the ambassador's jaw dropped.
"But even *I* could not hope for permission to visit such facilities!" he told

Perry.[33] In the event, Perry got much of what he wanted, as Beijing consented to visits to the main facilities on the Americans' list. Perry also recalls that American specialists were accorded a fair degree of access to individual Chinese scientists and defense engineers. The Americans brought an array of their own technical experts, together with two lieutenant generals decked out in uniform for much of the trip.[34]

Perry concluded his visit by bluntly informing the Chinese that the most expansive among their ambitions were unrealistic. In a 1998 account, the American journalist James Mann argued on the basis of American documents that the defense technical cooperation that resulted was, in the main, far broader than many of the American protagonists recalled two decades later. Perry did insist, however, that a full spectrum of defense technology cooperation would prove unfeasible so long as China's low technical level persisted in areas identified for collaboration by Beijing. The rank backwardness of China's R&D system exacerbated interoperability problems. Thus, while the United States might agree to grant several defense technology licenses, Perry nonetheless appended a private alternative to China's ambitious plan for technology transfers.

Perry privately suggested, in addition to the sale of certain weapons, a longer-range, less military-specific, more broad-based program of technology cooperation across a spectrum of areas. "If I were Chinese," Perry remembers having told Zhang and Liu in these off-the-record sessions, "I simply wouldn't go about doing it your way. Your real need is to build a national technology infrastructure which, if you do it right, may give you some dual-use potential." A purely military technology base, Perry added, would simply be too narrow a foundation upon which to modernize China's industry, much less to overhaul its backward conventional armed forces.[35]

Interviews and Chinese sources reveal that Perry's visit, supplemented by private contacts he had with Zhang, Liu, and others after leaving government, sharply altered the perspective of leading strategic weaponeers as they debated high-tech issues. First, the Perry meetings—as well as other contacts with foreign defense technology officials—introduced Chinese strategic weapons technicians to the wholesale movement away from complete "systems" toward subsystem-level components (microelectronics and information technologies), and from hardware toward software-based "processes." From both shifts—systems to components, and hardware to software—the Chinese took away one extraordinarily important lesson: system-level improvements had become increasingly incremental; thus component and software improvements bulked larger in American and European approaches to force modernization.

In the West, however, these improvements had come about primarily through innovation in the civilian computing and electronics industries. As Perry and other foreign visitors told their hosts, the relationship between defense and more comprehensive "national" industries had become increasingly complex since the mid-1960s. In the United States in particular, this had been associated with the growth of start-up companies, which sometimes relied on government contracts, but in any event always had strong entrepreneurial tendencies.

Although many Chinese engineers were certainly aware of the increasingly entrepreneurial bent of the electronics industry in the United States, given the scope of China's backwardness and the scarcity of available resources, key leaders of the strategic weapons community now made a deliberate choice to promote change through continued reliance on state planning and target setting. Indeed, despite all the talk of entrepreneurialism in U.S. industry, the Chinese were reinforced in this view by their reading of the paradoxical evidence that at least some U.S. elites continued to regard state-directed strategic technology programming as important. The Reagan Strategic Defense Initiative (SDI) became the main piece of evidence in support of this argument. By 1985–86, many weaponeers had come to view SDI as proof that state-directed S&T planning remained necessary wherever R&D was risky and when comparatively long lead times were needed to take research to application, commercial viability, and deployment.

Thus, despite Chinese politicians' insistence that defense conversion was the main issue confronting military R&D in the 1980s, prominent strategic weaponeers chose to direct their attention elsewhere. For them, the key issue was not "conversion," but the much more fundamental relationship between technology and organizational culture. They reasoned that even if one accepted the need for conversion—to foster and diffuse multiple-use technical knowledge—vastly different organizational cultures between weapons- and nonweapons-oriented R&D sectors would inevitably make coordination and absorption difficult.[36]

To this extent they questioned the notion that diffusion was simply a matter of reorientation and political will. The real problem seemed altogether different: if technologies could not be easily transferred irrespective of their multiple-use nature, the gap between civilian and military organizational cultures could be bridged only through the creation of institutions conducive to the diffusion of multiple-use technology. To many, however, what might make this possible was a comprehensive diversification of the strategic weapons elite itself.

On some level, the notion that the solution lay in diversification beyond weapons research and movement out of weapons institutes and bureaucracies reflected a political calculation; this elite, after all, was attempting to cope with civilianization and the shift of the military procurement agenda. But it also reflected fairly straightforward managerial reasoning: since the Mao-era strategic weapons programs had developed the framework of cross-system nonhierarchical coordination that Deng now promoted as a national model, the best way to solve the "cultural" problem would be for strategic weaponeers themselves to penetrate the civilian world of technology. If the right kinds of institutions were created to manage cross-system coordination, so much the better. Collaboration between strategic weaponeers still in the defense technology system and their (former) colleagues now primarily in civilian work could ease the transfer of technology while helping to build a cooperative managerial infrastructure better able to promote multiple-use, "new era" high technology.

Coming to Terms with New Ideas

This conclusion that it was necessary for some weaponeers to leave the military research and development system was reached only with difficulty. How Zhang Aiping came to terms with this change between 1983 and 1986 illuminates the path strategic weaponeers took to break out of the dilemma they faced: abandoning calls for increased military expenditure in favor of a comparatively innovative reformulation of their own role in technology planning.

In a famous 1983 essay, Zhang launched a ringing defense of military expenditure in general and strategic weapons in particular. He argued forcefully for a continuing emphasis on military R&D, narrowly construed. Here, echoing many of Marshal Nie's arguments from the 1950s, Zhang insisted that the spin-off model of technology development remained valid and relevant. Civilian development, including conversion, was important, Zhang admitted, but the real opportunities for technological breakthroughs remained in military work. As the economy develops and as S&T flourishes under the reform, funding for national defense should actually increase, not decrease as trends seem to indicate. "First-rate scientific and technical personnel, as well as newer scientific and technical results, will be shifted to military industry to promote the development of defense modernization."[37]

By 1986, Zhang had grown sober. He told a June conference of military S&T leaders dominated by strategic weapons personnel: "The purpose of our meeting is to examine how to achieve a strategic shift (*zhanlüe zhuanbian*) in military technology work, as well as how to perform that shift well." "What is a strategic shift?" Zhang asked rhetorically. He answered with an almost verbatim restatement of Deng Xiaoping's view of the matter:

> It is a shift from our past preparation for an early war, an all-out war, and a nuclear war, to today's period of comparative peace and long-term respite from war. It also means that from now on, the military S&T front must [shift its attention] to national economic construction. It must be the main focus of its strength. We must continue to develop new weapons systems. Their number will be smaller, but quality must remain high. [In short], we must shift from the single task of developing and producing weapons to the performance of two tasks.[38]

This sobering statement contains several important concepts that would come to guide Chinese technological development in the years ahead: developing multiple roles for military scientists; finding dual (and multiple) uses of high technology; building a military technical base on the foundation of a national base, rather than the other way around; and finally, distinguishing the diversification of S&T from mere industrial "conversion."

From "Sophisticated" to "High" Technology

An important manifestation of the strategic weaponeers' changing emphasis was a change in the way their leaders talked about technology and its effects. For example, Qian Xuesen began in the mid-1980s to make speeches calling for a new paradigm, but one that retained an abiding faith that core features of Nie's past approach could help China deal with fundamental changes in technology and industry.

By 1989, Qian worriedly told interviewers that the new term "high technology" (*gao jishu*), which had come to replace the euphemism long used for strategic weapons—"sophisticated technology" (*jianduan jishu*)—failed to capture the strategic rationales that, he believed, remained valid for China's future. Joined by scientists from the nuclear and missile programs, Qian began to speak of the need for a more strategic definition of high technology.

In the past, when we worked on the atomic and hydrogen bombs, we referred to the technology that we used as "sophisticated technology." Now, we call it high technology, and this includes a great many things. What we used to refer to as "sophisticated" technologies are those that play a crucial role in our country's socialist construction [i.e., strategic technologies]. We could also say that from now—at the end of the twentieth century—through the first part of the twenty-first century, we must make strenuous efforts to master this technology. So I think that we need to renew the notion of "sophisticated technology." But the question is to decide which types of technologies belong in the category of sophisticated technologies, and *this is a decision for the state*.[39]

As in the strategic weapons programs, Qian appears to suggest, the state needs to define strategic needs for technology development but in accordance with the changed constraints and needs of the new era. Thus,

with respect to both civilian and military technology, I would include "intelligent robots" as a sophisticated technology. In the 1930s–40s, when computers first came into existence, not many people appreciated their utility. Many even thought that their development would prove meaningless. Now, it is clear that this was absurd. Many tasks cannot even be carried out without computers. But today's computers are often clumsy since they depend on human commands. If you tell it to do something, it will; if you tell it not to do something, it won't. From a human perspective, a computer is basically an inferior "person." But if a machine had an [independent] ability and intelligence, including the ability to handle situations that transcend the specifics of its instructions by handling these independently, this would be the basis for an intelligent robot. Computers have changed society tremendously. And one can imagine how an intelligent robot would influence the future. No country with technological strength can afford to ignore this and there is thus a good deal of global competition in this research. The United States has done much. Japan is forging ahead. The countries of Western Europe are cooperating, making an effort to catch up. Even the Soviet Union is expending great effort. So we too should include intelligent robots as a sophisticated technology, whether from a military or civilian angle.[40]

THE FOUNDATIONS OF A NEW APPROACH

Focal Points and New Emphases

General Liu Huaqing, Perry's traveling host, gave voice to this thinking in a series of interviews during the first half of the 1990s. In the face of so many competing spending priorities, Liu said, strict limits on R&D funds precluded an all-out effort, such as the Mao-era nuclear weapons program. But this did not eliminate the need for mobilization; rather, it required a new approach to mobilization: a concentration of funds and a choice of specific focal points so that government monies would not fall through cracks in the system or be squandered. "Especially since we have entered the age of high technology," Liu observed, "the development of military S&T has become extremely difficult and highly interconnected. As a consequence, we must make full use of the socialist system's advantage of being able to concentrate resources for major undertakings, engage in coordinated national-scale planning, mobilize and direct all relevant forces, and engage in a coordinated struggle to overcome scientific and technical bottlenecks."[41]

Liu directly invoked the precedent of the strategic weapons management system. "In the 1950s and 1960s, when China's industrial and S&T base were extremely weak, one of the most important ways we were able to post major achievements was [by making] full use of centralized and unified leadership." Thus, "in terms of macro–policy making and management, we need a unified program, unified command, and unified implementation." And contrary to the dominant administrative trend in the Chinese system, "we must overcome undesirable tendencies toward decentralization."[42]

This new argument for state programming complemented an economic argument: the market could not fully sustain investment in advanced technology, making state investment imperative. According to this view, the development of technology was burdened by endemic market failures that had led to public R&D investment even in highly developed capitalist economies.[43] Given notoriously long R&D cycles, laboratories and industry must absorb high costs over long periods before the fruits of their work become commercially viable. State support for key projects was therefore necessary even if R&D became marketized. In the absence of state support, research institutes and high-tech enterprises would have little incentive to make investments that were unlikely to yield a quick return.

On two different bases, then, strategic weaponeers rearticulated a focal-point concept. In part, this was a reflexive fallback on targeted S&T strategies of the past. Yet it occurred primarily because leading weaponeers came to believe that the government must finance and set technology agendas in areas critical to the state. Key strategic weaponeers argued that state investment must come from the central government specifically, not from the provinces and local governments: despite decentralizing tendencies in Chinese science and industry, the burden of investment must fall on Beijing because provincial, local, and enterprise-level authorities had few incentives to finance R&D projects unlikely to yield almost immediate commercial returns. Moreover, only the central government possessed the all-critical ability to mobilize a community of high-quality scientists and technicians.

Big Pushes

On one level, this type of "big push" concept had become anachronistic in China by the mid-1980s. Such pushes were associated with the Great Leap Forward and, in military circles, with largely unproductive military industry investments in the deep interior during the 1960s. But strategic weaponeers had attached a unique institutional model to the big push that enhanced the benefits of committing vast resources and ensuring smooth top-down guidance. In their final form, the strategic weapons programs were not merely showcases of the regime's achievements. They were also evidence of the success of intermediate management institutions that the programs' PLA patrons had attached to the push and persuaded China's senior political leaders to endorse and guarantee.

Essentially, these institutions depended on tacit acceptance by leading politicians of a unique organizational style: the top political leadership should engage with experts directly and in great detail on technical, not merely policy, issues, and regularly, not merely on an ad hoc basis; they should guarantee the primacy of technical solutions; they should facilitate the institutionalization of routines making technical assessment and continuing leadership-expert contact possible; and, finally, they should commit resources to the targets specified by the experts. These commitments thereby presupposed leadership engagement, not merely a willingness to provide resources, and attempted to check political interference by working to ensure that such contact would be based on explicitly technical assumptions.

Like their former colleagues among the strategic weapons technical cadre, administrators such as Liu Huaqing had taken from their experience a commitment to parallel managerial legacies that had enduring relevance even as resources shifted. This involved, first, the commitment of top leaders to targeted strategies. But these could be sustained only by specific types of institutional and political guarantees. As the locus of Chinese technical innovation began to devolve to local and nonstate agents in the reform era, then, former weaponeers retained faith in the guided development of strategic technologies by the center.

By itself, this might not have been sufficient to carry along a targeted plan led by the central government. But the weaponeers moved forcefully to ensure that they would be the elite charged by the political leadership with carrying out the task. The elite buttressed its senior patrons, now well into their seventies, through the creation of powerful advisory structures that institutionalized their influence. Meanwhile, a younger generation of strategic weaponeers in their fifties mobilized, and still younger weaponeers in their thirties and forties fanned out across nonmilitary administrative systems. These strategies for coping with political and technical change ultimately produced a new era of strategic technology investments. These programs—and their initial impact on China's technology base, military posture, and political economy—are the subject of the next chapter.

chapter five

"OLD" SOLUTIONS TO NEW PROBLEMS, 1986–1992

For China's elite military planners and defense technical specialists, the debates sparked by Deng's reforms reached their climax in March 1986. Four of the most prominent strategic weapons elders finally formulated a response to the arguments of the first half of the 1980s. On March 3, 1986, the space program's most prominent optical physicist, Wang Daheng, joined three colleagues—the nuclear physicist Wang Ganchang, the radio electronics engineer Chen Fangyun, and the electrical engineer Yang Jiachi—to approach paramount leader Deng Xiaoping with a proposed response to the "new technological revolution."[1] Together, the four traded on their collective status and standing with the political leadership, circumvented "routine" bureaucratic channels, and took their case directly to Deng on an essentially personal basis.

These men ranked among the small core of Chinese strategic weapons pioneers of the years of glory under Mao Zedong. Wang Daheng, Wang Ganchang, and Chen Fangyun were virtually the founding fathers of China's optical physics, nuclear physics, and radio electronics, respectively. Yang Jiachi is routinely hailed in histories of the missile and space industries as one of a handful of "chiefs"—a special term of respect—of China's astronautics.[2] As such, these men possessed a degree of prestige and credibility with Deng and others in the Politburo that only strategic weaponeers could leverage into a high-priority, well-funded R&D program on the strategic weapons organizational model. In particular, by virtue of that status, they had a special connection to Deng, who had been present at the Politburo's first technical briefing on nuclear weapons in 1955 and was involved with strategic weapons scientists in various ways thereafter. Their personal appeal to China's paramount leader was thus part of the strategic weapons elite's response to the remaking of the PLA procurement agenda and the civilianization of the nation's S&T agenda as well as to technological change, shifts in the strategic balance, and the increasingly important role of economic competition as a basis of state power.[3]

Deng's response to the scientists' proposal was immediate. Two days after receiving it, he scribbled on his copy of the report, "Action must be taken on this now; it cannot be put off!" (*cishi yi su zuo jueduan; bu ke tuiyan*).[4] Within months the Politburo approved the plan and by 1988 it had become China's premier industrial R&D program, insulated from sustained opposition because of Deng's personal imprimatur. Indeed, within just nine months of their March 1986 letter, an elaborate system of decision-making structures and expert task forces had been established, led and directed by high-level political figures. Even after Deng's death in 1997, the 863 Plan, as the program came to be known, for the year (1986) and month (March) of its origin, continued to carry the weight of his personal endorsement.

The program adapted the core principles of China's technonationalism to new strategic and technical challenges. In some cases, programmatic and planning documents lifted near-verbatim quotations from Marshal Nie's old directives for strategic weapons and technology development. The 863 Plan borrowed Nie's notion that the central state, in close partnership with some of the country's most renowned scientists and engineers, must bear the burden of funding and otherwise promoting technologies of unusual strategic value. It sought to preserve a critical role in policy and technology planning for individual strategic weaponeers. And, finally, it aimed to train a new generation of technicians, much as Nie's strategic weapons mentoring arrangements had done in a strictly military context.

Externally, the 863 program and its successors have aimed at enhancing China's position in the hierarchy of great powers. Almost precisely like the strategic weapons programs of decades past, it has offered ideological, developmental, and organizational solutions to China's most pressing problems of technological and economic backwardness. Domestically, the 863 Plan and other "new era" (*xin shidai*) strategic technology programs initially sought to preserve the influence of one elite, sometimes at the expense of rivals, and to refashion the role of the state in technological innovation; these are, of course, political programs. Institutionally, the drafters of the 863 Plan clearly hoped to loosen the grip of compartmentalized management styles as well as hierarchical, Soviet methods of policy planning and implementation.

ELITE DIVERSIFICATION AS "GREASE" TO RENEWED DOMINANCE

The emergence of the 863 Plan and other post-Mao strategic technology programs owed much to the weaponeers' success in spreading from the military science and industrial complex to other important bureaucratic systems. Prominent strategic weaponeers succeeded so well that by the mid-1980s they sat at the top of nearly every office in the Chinese government concerned with science and technology policy. When the Wang group's proposal became institutionalized in the 863 Plan, all major interagency leading committees were, as a result, dominated by program alumni.

These men and women, who shared a strategic vision of national high-tech programming, were bound by a common professional heritage, an extensive network of personal and career ties, and a deep commitment to the managerial practices first tested in the large-scale military programs of the 1950s and 1960s. Such connections reveal much about why strategic weaponeers fashioned 863 in an image they knew and valued: it eased coordination among agencies that had long been rivals. Particularly on the issue of how to apportion budgets, informal social and professional connections controlled much of the contention that normally characterizes the Chinese appropriations process.[5] They also provided a rapid, wholly informal communications channel that allowed leaders of relevant agencies to circumvent the maddeningly incremental process of interagency coordination and decision making in China.[6] Powerful interagency liaison groups that normally serve to reconcile contending interests could instead be leveraged by their members on behalf of a shared agenda.[7]

The State Science and Technology Commission

Song Jian. The most prominent example of this type of lateral professional movement is the thirty year career of Song Jian, deputy chief designer of China's SLBM, who became head of the SSTC in 1985, a state councilor two years later, and vice chairman of the Chinese People's Political Consultative Congress—a high-level political advisory group—after his retirement in 1998.[8] Song was able to exert enormous influence on technology agendas and administration from his perch at the SSTC. He chaired a commission that dispensed as much as 40 percent of China's national R&D budget, much of which targeted S&T guidance plans, such as the 863 Plan, a National Basic Research Plan, a technology commercialization plan (the Torch Plan), and a rural technology development plan (the Spark Plan).[9]

Song Jian's appointment to chair the SSTC in 1985 revived the strategic weaponeers' leadership of the commission just as S&T policy became increasingly civilianized in the first decade of Deng's paramountcy. During the 1950s–60s, Nie Rongzhen himself had served concurrently as director of both the SSTC and the military NDSTC. But when Song took up the leadership of the civilian commission in 1984, the NDSTC's successor in weapons oversight—COSTIND—was in the midst of repelling bureaucratic and political competition from the military. Whereas the NDSTC had easily dominated its civilian sister in the past, Song's appointment to lead the civilian body reflected the degree to which strategic weaponeers with the "right" technical background, managerial skills, and political patronage could successfully penetrate bureaucratic domains rivals regarded as being legitimately "theirs."

This was certainly true of the SSTC in the mid-1980s. Unlike their counterparts in military science and engineering, most civilian specialists had been continually buffeted, attacked, and sometimes ruined by the political upheavals of the Mao years. In the emerging technocracy of the Deng years, then, many civilian technical elites saw a unique opportunity to at last leverage expertise into political and administrative power.

And yet the fluidity of career patterns among Nie's weapons engineers allowed them to move laterally across bureaucratic hierarchies, flouting the rigid career patterns that had developed within these hierarchies over thirty years. A more powerful civilian SSTC rose to power during the early 1980s on the watch of Deng's close political ally Fang Yi. Thus, when Song Jian took over the commission in 1984, a former missile guidance engineer who was among China's most prominent strategic weaponeers inherited a more powerful civilian agency whose new importance was severely eroding COSTIND's influence over national R&D planning.

Song had been singled out early in his career for high-level patronage. One of his mentors was the father of the Chinese missile program, Qian Xuesen. As a Chinese journalist, Gu Mainan, has told it, Qian and Song had not yet met when the Fifth Academy was founded in 1956, but Qian was "aware of Song's achievements." Indeed, "when someone praised his own achievements in the field of cybernetics, [Qian] would say with sincerity, 'Not at all. The present authority on cybernetics is not me but Song Jian.'" [10]

After returning to China in 1960 from doctoral studies in the Soviet Union, Song was assigned to the Second Subacademy (under Qian's Fifth Academy), where he pioneered the indigenously designed inertial guidance systems crucial to missiles, flight control, and targeting. By the time the PLA began to deploy China's own first-generation indigenously produced strategic missiles, Song Jian was already a legend within the strategic weapons community.

Qian Xuesen's patronage was critical to the advancement of Song's career, for his access to the highest stratum of political-military leaders was unparalleled among scientists. Song Jian himself has acknowledged as much, telling the reporter Gu Mainan a story about how Qian came to recommend him to be the Chinese representative at the third congress of the International Federation of Automation Control. Song remembered that, in Gu's words, "China had recommended only one paper for presentation at the conference, an entry personally selected by scientific elders such as Qian Xuesen. . . . At the [time of the] meeting, Song Jian was then thirty-one years old—the youngest scientist to read a paper before the more than 1,000 scientists in attendance." [11] At the very height of the Cold War, Gu relates, even American scientists offered congratulations to the young Song Jian.

After his appointment to lead the SSTC in 1985, Song rapidly became the most prominent player in Chinese science and technology policy, a role he retained through most of the 1990s. Coming at a high tide of demilitarization, that one of their own was selected to head the civilian commission was undoubtedly a boon to strategic weaponeers in promoting their solutions to China's new technological challenges. Song could lend a sympathetic ear to the elite's problems; moreover, he was among the most prominent scientists in the 1980s to advocate precisely the type of "strategic" investments that Nie had urged on the politicians during the Mao years. Since

Song had spent his pre-SSTC career as a prominent technician in Nie's strategic weapons institutions, his chairmanship of the SSTC lent the strategic weaponeers a voice—and a potential advocate—at the highest levels of technology planning, budgeting, and policy implementation on the civilian side of the Chinese system.

Li Xu'e. After 1988, the handful of Song Jian's deputies at the SSTC included another prominent strategic weaponeer, Li Xu'e. Like Song, Li was a missileer whose lateral movement from warhead and general design configuration to an SSTC deputy directorship reflected broader processes of lateral movement by the strategic weapons elite. During the late 1980s, Li served as Song Jian's principal deputy at the SSTC. He was deputy chairman of the commission's Standing Committee and, in all likelihood, held the parallel position within the commission's Communist Party cell. With Li in the SSTC deputy's slot, former strategic weaponeers thus held the first and second-ranking posts at the civilian S&T commission in the critical start-up years of the 863 Plan.

Li had joined the CCP in 1955, and lacked Song Jian's wide-ranging technical credentials. Indeed, some Chinese missileers regard Li as a scientist skillful in politics who owed much of his rise to patronage and connections rather than the kind of technical accomplishment that sustained the careers of other prominent weaponeers, such as Wang Ganchang and Song Jian.[12]

In the early 1980s, however, Li served in a prominent technical role as chief engineer of the design team under Huang Weilu and Song Jian charged with developing the SLBM warhead for the JL-1, China's first indigenously designed and produced SLBM. Most of Li's contributions appear to have revolved around the configuration of the missile, including readjustments to accommodate new warhead designs. But like Song, before joining the SSTC Li had spent his career affiliated with missile-related leading organizations and institutes, particularly the missile ministry's First Subacademy, where he was in charge of general configuration and rocket engines.

After graduating from the aerospace engineering faculty of Qinghua University in 1952, Li served during the critical design years of 1962–71 as deputy director of Institute 14 (warheads) of the First Academy. He later served as director of the academy, and as vice minister and chief engineer of the Seventh Ministry. Li received a state prize in 1985 for his contributions to the missile program. In 1980, Li, Wu Mingchang, and Song Jian (the principal deputy chief designer) were appointed the three deputy chief designers of the SLBM under Huang Weilu.[13]

The Chinese Academy of Sciences

Zhou Guangzhao. Zhou Guangzhao, Song's counterpart at the Chinese Academy of Sciences after 1987 and another prominent strategic weaponeer, also moved laterally from the weapons system to the leadership level at a new bureaucratic domain.[14] With the SSTC, the CAS, and COSTIND as the three main agencies responsible for setting and implementing agendas, this was important to coalition building and interbureaucratic coordination. By 1987, after all, all three agencies were headed by prominent former strategic weaponeers: Ding Henggao (COSTIND), Song Jian (SSTC), and Zhou Guangzhao (CAS).

Like Song, Zhou was among the most prominent of the younger scientists in Marshal Nie's programs. As a junior physicist in the initial atomic bomb project, he had been charged with checking all calculations in preparation for the first nuclear weapons test of October 1964. Zhou's supervisors included his mentor, Peng Huanwu, who headed the bomb project's theoretical division. But he may also have worked under Zhu Guangya and Wang Ganchang during this period.

Like many Chinese nuclear physicists, Zhou began his career at Qinghua University, where he first met Peng Huanwu, then a leader of the university's physics faculty. After graduating in 1951, Zhou moved to Beijing University to complete graduate work, and thence to the Joint Institute for Nuclear Research in Dubna from 1957 to 1960, when Wang Ganchang served as deputy director. Zhou's connection to Wang Ganchang had especially important implications for the formulation of the 863 Plan since Wang was one of the four weaponeers who proposed the plan to Deng. The CAS, under Zhou Guangzhao's leadership, played a critical role in the early phases of 863 planning, design, and implementation.

After returning to China from Dubna in 1960, Zhou joined the Ninth Academy. Later, he moved laterally to become an administrator in the CAS system, running the CAS Institute of Theoretical Physics, then serving as director of the CAS mathematics and physics department, and finally as vice president of the academy and vice chair of the China Physics Society. In 1987, Zhou was appointed president of the academy.

Like many other strategic weaponeers, including Song Jian in the field of cybernetics, Zhou was a pioneer in developing the scientific disciplines in post-revolutionary China. He has consistently been among the leaders of Chinese physics, putting forward a theory of spiral amplitude of particles and contributing an array of associated mathematical models. This supplements his more obvious contributions to Chinese detonation physics, radiation hydrodynamics, and computing. In 1964, the year of the first atomic bomb test, Zhou, along with several colleagues from the nuclear weapons program, was the co-winner of the first Chinese state prize for the natural sciences.

Ultimately, Zhou's strategic weapons experience seems to have been formative, for he never lost sight of the strategic agenda for high technology first articulated by Nie Rongzhen when Zhou was a graduate student. In a 1990 interview, when he was the CAS president, Zhou framed his own priorities—as well as those of the CAS—in an almost-verbatim restatement of the main points of the 863 program.[15]

The State Planning Commission

Zou Jiahua. Not all military industrialists imbued with the strategic weapons vision had worked directly under Nie. Although conventional weapons constituencies had resisted the weaponeers' more developmental ideas in favor of a narrowly military-focused vision, some military industrialists had adopted elements of the strategic weapons vision in their own work. One such man was Zou Jiahua, who had spent his career in the development of conventional weapons, but, once he rose to political prominence, became an eloquent voice for many of the technonational ideas and flexible managerial practices associated with the strategic programs.[16]

Zou was unique among Chinese military industrial leaders in his intimate ties to the strategic weapons community, even though he was never truly a part of its world. In 1982 Zou departed from a career in conventional weapons administration and enterprise management when he became an aide to Zhang Aiping at the NDSTC. Zou was appointed Zhang's deputy director, and thus although he had spent the previous five years as deputy director of the strategic weaponeers' onetime bureaucratic nemesis, the NDIO, when he arrived on the scene Marshal Nie's heirs were in full control of the Chinese military industrial system.

In this way, Zou came to be a deputy director of the NDSTC at the precise moment that these two longtime bureaucratic antagonists, the NDSTC and the NDIO, prepared to merge into a new, integrated COSTIND. By helping to lay the groundwork for the merger, Zou Jiahua was instrumental in planning R&D organization under the new regime.

Zou also possessed a purely personal tie to Marshal Nie and the strategic weapons programs. He was the son-in-law of Marshal Ye Jianying, a close Nie ally who had played a decisive role in the work of the Central Special Commission between 1971 and 1975. Thus Zou had watched—and forged connections to key strategic weaponeers—as his father-in-law worked with Nie and Premier Zhou Enlai to purge the military system of Lin Biao's residual influence and then restore disgraced strategic weapons technicians to their posts. Between 1971 and 1977 it was Marshal Ye, as the most senior leader of the PLA and head of its key decision-making body, the CMC "Administrative Meeting," who provided the most critical political support to the strategic weapons programs. Marshal Ye granted them the highest priority in China's immediate post-Cultural Revolution procurement regime, convening more than twenty sessions of the Central Special Commission, a pace that exceeded that even during the heyday of the strategic weapons effort in the early 1960s.[17]

Zou could therefore play a significant part in support of certain ideas closely linked to Nie's technonational vision because, after a brief stint as minister of the ordnance industry, he moved laterally out of the military industry system to become director of the State Planning Commission (SPC)—at that time the most important resource-allocating body in the entire Chinese bureaucracy.[18] Together with the SSTC and COSTIND, Zou's SPC played a critical role in deciding investment priorities, policies, and the scope and direction of resource allocations.

Gan Ziyu. The man who most closely supported Zou in this task was also particularly close to Marshal Nie and his inner circle: the senior vice minister of the SPC for science and technology as well as military industry, Gan Ziyu.[19] In the 1980s, the SPC headed by Zou and Gan managed virtually all cross-agency coordination preceding the evaluation and decision process for major national projects. Bureaucratically, the SPC exercised this role through several functional departments and bureaus under the day-to-day control of its vice ministers. And as noted, both science and technology and military investments were overseen for more than a decade by the vice minister in charge of two SPC departments (*si*)—one, in charge of S&T, the other in charge of military industry, both coordinating closely through the leadership of the same vice minister.

Gan Ziyu, who served in this crucial vice ministerial position throughout most of the 1980s, was an electrical engineer who had once been Marshal Nie's personal aide and secretary. He began his career by assisting the marshal in science planning at Nie's SSTC office from 1956 to 1958. Then, Gan became involved with military science through personal service to the marshal, and finally he transferred into planning and administration under the SPC bureaucracy in 1975—his first major promotion to a significant national bureaucratic post.

By 1978, Gan had become an SPC vice minister and was in charge of SPC interagency coordination with the SSTC, NDSTC, NDIO, and later COSTIND—in short, all of the key Chinese military industry and science bureaucracies. Gan also had considerable oversight for technology transfer policy as director of the State Council working group on imports and exports.

Sheng Shuren. A third crucial figure at the SPC during the 1980s was Sheng Shuren, who was also a vice minister of the commission.[20] Like Gan Ziyu, Sheng had forged a complex career, typical of ambitious officials with high-level patronage. Over time, he had moved in and out of various systems, aided by formal training as an economist with special expertise in financial management.

When Sheng Shuren entered the SPC in 1988, he had served in both the strategic and conventional weapons bureaucracies, and at the State Council office and State Economic Commission, where he had headed the General Office (*bangongting*), in charge of document flow and interagency coordination. Yet Sheng's key professional distinction was as a weapons program manager—and administrative cadre—having spent the first 28 years of his career as a financial planner for defense technology investments. At age twenty-three, Sheng had joined the Second Ministry, in charge of nuclear development. He then remained in defense work until the age of fifty-one, when he at last left the Third Ministry (aircraft) for his new job at the State Council.

This combination of Zou, Gan, and Sheng in crucial roles at the State Planning Commission—with Zou overseeing the agency, Gan heading its S&T and military industrial departments, and Sheng leading its financial planning—was of considerable potential benefit to military industry. For example, both Zou Jiahua and Gan Ziyu are widely acknowledged in China to have been major supporters of the defense conversion program. This aided much of the conventional weapons sector at a moment when the government flirted with cutting many of these facilities loose from the apron strings of the state.

For strategic weaponeers in particular, the SPC's job of arranging resources to sustain high-level policy initiatives made the presence of Zou, Gan, and Sheng especially significant as key weaponeers sought to sell the 863 program to the political and bureaucratic elite. COSTIND, the SSTC, and the CAS, like all public agencies in China, formulated their own five-year and annual plans within the constraints set out by the SPC. This commission was the crucial "strong sister" in any effort to create a national program.

Consider, for example, the case of China's national surface physics laboratory. In 1992, Fudan University in Shanghai—led by a president who had worked in the strategic weapons programs, the nuclear physicist Yang Fujia—was authorized to establish a national "keypoint" laboratory for surface physics (*biaomian wuli*) and semiconductor development for the electronics industry.[21] The SPC, the main agency in charge of authorizing national investments in this area, not only made the decision to fund the laboratory, it also authorized the choice of Fudan and gave the State Education Commission the go-ahead to inspect and certify the new facility. Likewise, for 863 and similar projects, the influence of the SPC—and influence over the SPC's decision-making process—was critical. For as in the case of the surface physics lab, without the SPC's authorization, neither the Education Commission (in charge of Fudan University), nor the SSTC and the CAS (in charge of science planning), nor Fudan itself could have proceeded with the facility.[22]

Formal Fragmentation, Informal Coordination

The case of the Fudan surface physics laboratory illustrates in stark relief why the leadership of all agencies concerned with a particular problem can affect policy agendas and allocation plans. As mentioned earlier, by 1986 strategic weaponeers, together with others who had worked on auxiliary aspects of the programs under the leadership of the PLA, held the top posts of every key industrial, science, and planning bureaucracy in China, as well as one level down the hierarchy. These included the SSTC, COSTIND, the SPC, the CAS, and others. The common professional backgrounds of these men, and the close personal relationships of some of them—for instance, Marshal Nie's son-in-law (Ding Henggao) with his former assistant (Gan Ziyu)—had important implications for the politics associated with the promotion of the strategic weaponeers' development ideas and models of project management.

One of the key themes in academic writing on Chinese politics is the incremental nature of policy making in China.[23] In a sharply fragmented bureaucratic polity in which cross-agency coordination is essential but difficult, the strategic weaponeers consistently demonstrated a capacity to leave the military system to penetrate nearly all key agencies in the Chinese government concerned with large technology investments.

This introduced a wholly informal, personal channel of communication and coordination. As an American program administrator has remarked of such ties, "You go to the people you have known. You go the shortest distance necessary to get the information. I hate to ask a question and have the person wait to clear through twelve people before he can respond."[24] Likewise, in China, where insufficient information is a frequent cause of bureaucratic deadlock, the leadership of key agencies by long-standing colleagues and friends takes on manifestly political significance and can often determine who controls the agenda.[25]

The Institutionalization of Technical Influence

Nie's heirs further solidified their capacity to shape agendas during these years through the institutionalization of their technical influence in formal advisory groups that operated at a very high level within the bureaucracy. These gave strategic weaponeers direct, and almost unimpeded, access to political and military decision makers.

A prime example of this phenomenon was COSTIND's Science and Technology Committee (STC), a structure whose roles have since evolved on account of major changes to the defense technology bureaucracy since 1998, when COSTIND was split into a General Armaments Department under the PLA (for long-range planning of R&D, as well as weapons testing) and a new industrial commission (for production) under the civilian State Council, which oversees industrial sectors with military implications.

However, the arrangement that prevailed at the time sheds light on why, and how, the weaponeers could push a new strategic technology agenda into high gear during this period.

The STC was a highly autonomous body of leading military scientists and cadres of very high political and technical prestige. Its director, the physicist Zhu Guangya, held a bureaucratic rank equivalent to that of the COSTIND director, General Ding. Thus Zhu could circumvent his nominal boss by invoking rank to appeal to the commission's oversight bodies: the Central Military Commission and the State Council led by the premier. This meant that the STC was not a "regular" part of the defense industry bureaucracy; as noted in Chapter 4, "normal" oversight fell under COSTIND's much less powerful Science and Technology Department (*bu*). Zhu's committee (*wei*), subsumed area-specific planning groups whose leaders headed these systems nationally. Thus, Major General Qian Shaojun (a physicist and former commander of the nuclear test base at Lop Nur) exercised de facto oversight over the entire nuclear weapons R&D complex from his post as director of the nuclear group under Zhu's STC. It is not difficult to imagine how this became a basis for informal coordination among like-minded, and powerful, figures.

THE ELDERS APPROACH DENG

In leveraging their control of the policy agenda through their leadership of the key bureaucratic agencies (COSTIND, the SSTC, the CAS, and the SPC) as well as interagency Leading Groups, coordination groups, and working groups, the strategic weaponeers extended the reach and scope of both technonational ideas and military-style project management institutions. The 863 program is perhaps the most significant example of their success, although it was not the only place where these "old" institutions were revitalized and took on new importance.[26]

The 863 program had dramatic beginnings. It was premised on a single big idea: the extension of notions of technonational development to a new set of challenges in a radically transformed international environment. The scientists, engineers, administrators, and political decision makers who were present at the program's creation sought, first and foremost, to revitalize and then institutionalize ideas of Nie Rongzhen, Zhang Aiping, Liu Huaqing, and others, that had been central to the strategic weapons effort.

Pioneers and Legends

Wang Daheng. In 1986, Wang Daheng still served as the director of the Changchun Optical Machinery Institute of the CAS, a position he had held for two decades. The institute was crucial to strategic weapons since optics had been a major bottleneck as missile engineers sought to measure angles with high precision for tracking and inertial guidance systems. The Changchun institute had made particularly important breakthroughs for the SLBM program led by Huang Weilu, Song Jian, and Li Xu'e.[27]

Like many other strategic weaponeers, Wang had an unusually cosmopolitan career. He had studied physics in England and published in English language technical journals such as the *Proceedings of the Physical Society* (UK), before returning to China in 1948. Optics was a particularly underdeveloped area of Chinese physics, and his training immediately placed Wang at the forefront of Chinese scientists in his field.[28]

In 1951, just two years after the establishment of the Communist state, Wang convened the first of a major series of planning meetings for optical science on behalf of the newly reconstituted CAS. He worked closely with Soviet specialists to establish China's first facility for the manufacture of optical equipment, Plant 208.[29] Nie Rongzhen himself acknowledged Wang's importance to the development of Chinese strategic weapons, crediting him with leading metering and instrumentation development for the missile and nuclear weapons programs.[30] Wang was also instrumental in laying the foundations for optical remote sensing for Chinese satellites. In October 1960, he became chief engineer of Project 150, a major effort to upgrade telemetry, tracking, and control capabilities (TT&C) to meet the needs of a post-Soviet generation of indigenously developed strategic delivery vehicles.[31] Wang was also a key figure in Project 160, a program to upgrade TT&C for China's intermediate-range surface-to-surface ballistic missiles.

Wang Ganchang. Wang Ganchang was one of the three or four most senior physicists in the Chinese nuclear weapons program.[32] We have already encountered Wang in several previous chapters, including as host of Allan Bromley's delegation of American nuclear physicists at the IAE in the earliest years of renewed Sino-American scientific exchange. In 1986, when the 863 group submitted its proposal to Deng Xiaoping, Wang still served as the IAE's director, having succeeded two of China's most prominent physicists in this position: Zhao Zhongyao, a student of Robert Millikan's at

Caltech, and Qian Sanqiang, the scientific father of the Chinese nuclear weapons program.

In fact, Wang Ganchang had served in key managerial posts for the nuclear weapons program, not simply as a senior scientist. He did a stint as vice minister of the nuclear industry and, like his colleague Zhu Guangya, played both bureaucratic and technical roles in China's development of strategic weapons. In this sense, Wang was the living embodiment of at least two of Nie Rongzhen's managerial institutions—the integration of decision makers and staff, and the establishment of formalized mentoring arrangements. In the former category, Wang had marched up the managerial ladder from administrative deputy director of the Ninth Academy to vice minister at the Second Ministry in Beijing, and in the latter category, from 1956 to 1960, as the Chinese began their bomb project, Wang served as deputy director of the Joint Institute for Nuclear Research in Dubna, training the cadre of younger physicists who later supported the senior technicians in the development of the atomic bomb. Wang helped lead the Joint Institute when Zhou Guangzhao was a postdoctoral fellow there. As a technician, Wang also served as director of the bomb program's technological committee in charge of nonnuclear components; he later took charge of developing and testing the explosive assembly and initiator for the bomb.[33]

Wang Ganchang, too, was a cosmopolitan, much like Wang Daheng and so many of his other fellow weaponeers. Wang held a German Ph.D. and was one of the few Chinese nuclear physicists who had made a disciplinary contribution of stature: In 1942, Wang proposed a scheme to verify the hypothesized existence of the neutrino through the application of ^{7}BeK-capture, a test successfully performed by the American physicist J. S. Allen.[34] Wang also organized the construction of China's major cosmic rays experimental station in the southwestern province of Yunnan, and put forward new concepts for the restriction of nuclear fusion through laser inertia.

Chen Fangyun. The third of the four 863 scientists, Chen Fangyun, was one of the most pivotal technicians in the development of the TT&C network that controls Chinese missiles and satellites.[35] This was a pioneering contribution that proved as crucial as Wang Daheng's contributions in optics;[36] TT&C systems are used to monitor accelerations along a missile's axes, thereby enhancing the accuracy of inertial guidance calculations.[37]

Like the two Wangs, Chen Fangyun had significant international experience. After graduating from Qinghua University in physics in 1938, he spent the years 1945–48 in Britain working as a researcher in a Cossor radio electronics laboratory. After returning to China, Chen turned his career toward radioelectronics and digital pulsed circuitry.[38]

Chen is best known in China for his work in the space program. In May 1966 he and Wei Zhongquan coauthored the ground observation plan for the first Dongfanghong (East is Red) satellite.[39] He later served as chief designer of consolidated microwave measurement and control systems for China's earth-observation satellites.[40] In 1976, together with Shen Rongjun, later COSTIND vice minister in charge of strategic weapons, Chen was coleader of a technical group in China's leading TT&C research facility, the Luoyang Institute of Tracking and Telecommunications Technology in Henan Province, where they reported to the NDSTC.[41] So significant were Chen Fangyun's contributions to TT&C that official histories of China's defense technology enterprise routinely hail him as the founder of the network.

Yang Jiachi. The final member of the 863 scientists' group, Yang Jiachi, graduated from Shanghai's Jiaotong University in 1941 and received his doctorate in electrical engineering at Harvard University in 1947. After working in American computing groups, he returned to China in 1956 and continued to work in the general computing field before spending the best part of his career on missile and satellite TT&C.

Yang is best known in China for his contributions to the automatic control systems of Chinese missiles and satellites. Under the Seventh Ministry, he collaborated with another prominent weaponeer, Zhang Guofu of Institute 502 (which developed solid rocket propellants for the ICBM), to design a three-axis attitude control system for China's earth-observation satellites.[42] By 1986, when the scientists approached Deng, he had been a key figure in space science and satellite control work for more than twenty years.

Yang has also had a significant interest in the dual-use and civilian potential of the Chinese space industry. Here, he has studied the uses of space-age technologies for medicine, geology, electrical engineering, industrial instrumentation, thermal control, and vacuum systems.[43]

All four of these scientists were among the very small core of important Chinese scientific pioneers whose careers had been co-opted by the party, state, and PLA in the 1950s in the service of strategic weapons development. Having earned the respect of Deng Xiaoping and the Politburo, these strategic weaponeers were in a position to influence decisions about R&D at the very highest levels. When informal discussions among colleagues evolved into a concrete warning to the leadership about China's declining technological standing, it was these men who made the approach, and formulated a proposal, to the political elite.

The Anatomy of a Proposal

On March 3, 1986, Wang Daheng and his colleagues passed a letter directly to Deng Xiaoping's office that laid out the general background to what they termed the "new technological revolution" (*xin jishu geming*). To this, they appended a proposal for a large, new program of targeted investments in technologies of "strategic" significance to the state. The scientists titled their proposal "On Following the Development of High Technologies of Strategic Significance around the World" (*Guanyu genzong shijie zhanlüexing gao jishu fazhan*). As noted at the outset of this chapter, Deng's approval was forceful and immediate.

In their letter, the scientists proposed a carefully targeted attack on key deficiencies in the seven sectors they regarded as most crucial to China's long-range national security and economic competitiveness: automation, biotechnology, energy, information technology, lasers, new materials, and space technology. The scientists explicitly evoked China's past achievements in strategic weapons development, as well as the organizational model in which they had come of age in the 1950s–70s within the strategic weapons programs. Throughout their proposal, they sought to present to Deng an analysis of how high technology had altered the stakes of international competition.

The scientists' proposal had three sections, each presenting in sequence a set of interconnected arguments about technology, state power, international competition, and development. The first section explained that technological innovation in the industrialized world now depended on structural changes that China had yet to assimilate. China, it argued, risked being left behind since the dominant trends were themselves changing far faster than China could keep pace. Thus, the development of weapons technology was no longer sufficient to the challenge this "revolution" posed. This was especially true because China's strong foundation in aerospace and materials science had already begun to crumble in the face of the dizzying rate of technical change among the industrial powers.

The second section evoked the importance of technical talent, and of science itself, in the development of the national economy. High technology, it declared, must be the main battleground for China's long-range economic construction. The seven sectors on which the proposal urged the state to focus its attention would determine China's development prospects over the fifteen years from 1986 to 2000. At the same time, a route to high technology development that privileged military programs now seemed the wrong solution to the challenges confronting China. Civilian, dual use, and especially process and component technologies, the proposal contended, must become the focus of future work.[44]

The third and final section of the proposal urged a concentrated attack in these seven areas, involving targeted government investment and political mobilization. It invoked two metaphors that Nie had often used in the strategic weapons programs: a "concentration of forces" (*jizhong liliang*) and a "unified command" (*tongyi zhihui*).[45] Thus, the scientists staked out ground for a strategic weapons style "big push," but with the focus on a broader front than mere weapons engineering. They offered the leadership a strategic rationale for the development of national industries that drew on military metaphors. And they argued that the administrative dynamics of any such program should remain largely unchanged from those of Nie's day.

In sum, what the strategic weapons elite now urged, albeit amid constraints on resources and a less threatening international environment, was a concentration of state attention on technology sectors of strategic significance. The focus would be shifted, and program leaders would lack the nearly unlimited and unconditional proprietary privileges of the Mao era. But the programmatic requirements, and the institutional prerequisites, were clear.

The Evolution of Deng's Thinking

What the weaponeers proposed had special appeal to Deng because his own thinking had evolved in this direction since the late 1970s. The 863 proposal came at a time of widespread debate about the need to decentralize the S&T system. Premier Zhao Ziyang, Party General Secretary Hu Yaobang, and many others strongly supported decentralization. There is, to be sure, no evidence of direct opposition to the 863 Plan that might have erupted during the critical months leading up to the Politburo's approval of the program. But the discussion of the 863 Plan occurred when virtually all debate about S&T suggested that centralization and targeting were partially responsible for the backwardness of China's commercial technology base. In this light, Deng's active engagement in the start-up effort and initial years of the 863 program probably proved crucial. And this squares with what is known about the role of leadership in Chinese politics: although Deng's authority was less charismatic than Mao's, Chinese sources repeatedly stress that Deng considered 863 one of his pet projects. Such a role mirrors that of leading politicians in the strategic weapons program of the Mao era; Mao and Zhou often overruled opposition, particularly in the early 1960s. Indeed, in a scene reminiscent of the Central Secretariat meeting in 1955 at which Mao's Politburo took the decision build an atomic bomb, the Deng-led Politburo convened to approve the 863 program at the very highest level in October 1986.

By the middle of the 1980s, Deng himself had transposed many technonational ideas of the Mao era to the challenges of a new era focused on economic construction rather than external threats to the state. He stressed precisely the sort of symbiotic connection between indigenization and external cooperation that had characterized many Mao-era projects in weapons development.[46] Deng's abiding faith in the role technology could play in economic development had now become far more encompassing than was evident in his speeches to the 1978 National Science Conference.

Deng now concluded that science and technology were not merely a part of the productive forces; they were "the number one productive force" (*di yi shengchanli*).[47] His argument thoroughly—and finally—buried the Mao era radical critique of science as "elite." His declaration, he told foreign visitors, is a matter of "strategic" (*zhanlüe*) policy.[48]

The strategic weapons elite figured heavily in Deng's calculations, not just because of the 863 proposal but because Nie's programs offered Deng three useful precedents. First, they demonstrated a genuine capacity for high-level scientific and engineering achievement even in a poor China with a backward technological infrastructure. Second, such achievements had strategic implications touching China's status in the world and position relative to the other great powers. Third, they showed that China could indigenously produce breakthroughs when "demand pull"—manifest through targeted state guidance—and "discovery push" functioned smoothly.

In his talks and speeches in the mid to late 1980s, Deng now transposed these precedents to the new, less threatening era. He asked rhetorically in 1988, are we too ambitious? By way of reply, after telling an audience of physicists at Beijing's electron-positron collider about the American Strategic Defense Initiative and Europe's Eureka plan for high technology development, Deng offered to "tell a story" to his listeners. "The next century," he told them, "will be the century of high technology." Thus,

> many countries have implemented high technology development plans. . . . A European friend, a scientist, asked me: "Your economy is still underdeveloped. How can you propose to undertake such a thing?" I told him: We look at this from the standpoint of long-range development issues and national interests. It isn't a matter about which we can afford to be nearsighted. This was true in the past, remains true today, and will be true in the future. China must develop its own science and high technology. [We] must take our place in the world in these areas. From the 1960s, if China hadn't had the atomic bomb, the hydrogen bomb, if we hadn't launched satellites, it couldn't be said that China is an influential great power. We wouldn't occupy our present international position. This issue reflects a people's abilities. It symbolizes [whether] a people's and a country's development efforts are flourishing. As the world is now developing, science and high technology are moving at an extremely rapid pace. China cannot afford to fall behind. [We] must take our proper place. This is the significance [of the collider project]. . . . China cannot afford *not* to be engaged in spite of the fact that we are poor. Because if you aren't engaged, if you don't develop in these areas, the gap will only become greater and it will become extremely difficult to catch up. We are at present backward in some areas. But we are not backward in all areas.[49]

Here, and in other talks, Deng established an explicit connection between the strategic weapons programs of China's past and the high technology challenge facing the country as it sought to come to terms with its future in a new era of reform. In other speeches in 1988, Deng continued to articulate this comparison between strategic technology programs of the present and strategic weapons programs of the past. In two speeches in September and December 1988—first, to foreign visitors, then to a work group on price and investment policy—he repeated his refrain: "Did we not produce our own atomic and hydrogen bombs, satellites, and aviation technology?" he asked. "Is our electron-positron collider project not at the forefront internationally?"[50]

China, Deng told his colleagues, could hardly devote the full measure of its resources to high technology projects as it had in the strategic weapons programs. Nonetheless, he concluded, the strategic weapons programs, and their lessons, retained their force and relevance.

Deng surely sought to invoke the purely symbolic power of the comparison. Strategic weapons had given China a measure of prestige in the 1960s that belied the unlikelihood of their use. China's nuclear achievement was a metaphor for many things: scientific prowess and the taming of natural forces; military strength and historically unprecedented destructive power; national will yoked to the task of a technically complex achievement. Indeed it is useful to recall the famous story of Oppenheimer's Los Alamos scientists returning from the successful first test of their creation in the desert at Alamogordo in 1945, pumping their fists in the air and clasping their hands in triumph. For Chinese politicians, scientists, even for ordinary citizens, the strategic weapons achievement was all the greater because China—unlike the other nuclear powers—was both miserably poor and internationally weak when it began its nuclear weapons program. China exploded its first nuclear weapon in 1964 at a time when both the United States and the Soviet Union were hostile. For China's political leaders, in particular, the achievement thus symbolized all these things: prowess, prestige, power, and national will. But the mere possession of strategic weapons did not end either the struggle or the competition. The great industrial powers had already turned to information technologies and other new fields by the early 1970s, nearly a decade before China's weaponeers achieved success with their first SLBM.

No doubt, this drove Deng to draw direct parallels between the strategic technology programs of both past and present. In the late 1950s, the West and the Soviet Union seemed to be immeasurably ahead of China. Now, the same was true in many new technologies. The parallel to Nie's programs and the call for a national crusade had great political power in China. As Deng sought to galvanize his leading technical specialists for a march to the twenty-first century, no metaphor could possibly draw off a greater reservoir of purely symbolic power than the legacy of China's strategic weapons programs. Mao had said, "If we are not to be bullied we cannot do without the bomb." Similarly, Deng now argued with respect to the latest high technology, "China cannot afford *not* to be engaged." This evokes almost precisely Marshal Nie's arguments to China's strategic weapons skeptics between 1955 and 1965.

Deng may also have had a more concrete purpose in mind beyond exploiting the purely symbolic power of the comparison, namely to lay down a political rationale for very high levels of spending on esoteric technologies.

As political scientist Jonathan Pollack has noted, China lags behind other nations in so many areas of basic technology, including infrastructure and training, that analysts often wonder how and why it routinely sinks so much money and infrastructure into esoteric areas, such as gene splicing and complex new materials.[51]

The answer can again be found in the strategic weapons legacy, for Chinese leaders have never utilized conventional technical parameters to evaluate such investments. The mastery of broadband telecommunications and intelligent robotics carries prestige in the eyes of China's political leaders, akin to that which China acquired as a result of its strategic weapons achievements. And for all the Deng coalition's talk about Mao era "imbalances," it never rejected outright the notion of an imbalance in national investment.

Rather, Deng and his colleagues openly accepted the core tenets of Mao-era technonationalism, even as they rejected its primary orientation toward new and better weapons. Although Deng's coalition regarded the Great Leap Forward as ill considered and excessive, it accepted the notion that development need not be symmetric. Some regions of the country were permitted to "get rich first." Likewise, prestigious technology projects could contribute in certain sectors and places, and thus, over the long term, lead the way for the whole industrial system.

Here, Deng offered a political vision of technology no less encompassing than Marshal Nie's. Complex gene research could remain conceptually distinct from the construction of a stronger basic infrastructure in the biological sciences. China had always had showplace factories, institutes, and industries.

Deng and his lieutenants appear to have genuinely believed in the strategic weapons model. This did not imply that they were willing to re-create its conditions precisely, at least with respect to budgetary commitments. But they accepted in principle the fundamentals of the technonational idea. Although Deng would never accept Nie's arguments about military-to-civilian spin-off, he embraced wholeheartedly the marshal's larger point about how technology shaped the strategic dimensions of China's place in the global order.

Rationales and Assumptions

By lending his personal imprimatur to the scientists' proposal, Deng ensured that it would become China's premier industrial research and development plan. The 863 program enshrines in a single, top-priority program four main goals of the state. All focus on applied science, although some basic work receives funding under the plan. As the Wang group's rationales imply, 863 seeks above all to yoke technological achievements to strategic goals of the state. These no longer are limited to national security alone, but also extend to long-range economic competitiveness. Yet they have become increasingly inseparable, and the 863 Plan is premised on a partnership between political and technical elites.

The designers of the 863 Plan intended, first, that it should anchor the struggle to close the technology gap separating China from the international state of the art in the seven initial areas of focus under the program. The plan thus "aims at the high-tech industries of the late twentieth and early twenty-first centuries" and at "leading-edge fields."[52]

Second, 863 has a goal the Chinese view as "strategic": it directs seed money to projects that inevitably affect long-range industrial competitiveness and military strength. Unlike programs that seek to diffuse technologies to poor areas or to commercialize various gadgets, 863 concentrates on China's relative position in high-tech fields. Thus Zhu Lilan, the civilian chemist who oversaw daily management of the program before becoming China's minister of S&T in 1998, argues that "the [S&T] challenge for us today is one of system versus system and nation versus nation. We must respond to this historic transformation [through a strategy that] guarantees that the disparity with the developed countries in S&T and economic sectors will steadily shrink." Zhu calls for greater attention to tracking international standards and ensuring breakthroughs. China, she argues, must use 863 to "set the foundation for a closing of the gap across the board."[53]

Third, 863 aims to fashion a symbiotic connection between basic and applied work. Like the strategic weapons effort, 863 emphasizes applied R&D. But the former presupposed at least some basic research, particularly in engineering as applied to delivery systems. China runs the risk of developing a cadre of specialists who understand what a 1989 U.S. biotechnology delegation termed the "mechanics" of relevant fields "but not the underlying science or the road ahead."[54] Yet 863 allocates between 2 percent and 5 percent of its budget to basic research[55] to support exploration into such topics as Einstein's special relativity and space-time postulates; these, it is hoped, will contribute insights on the physics of high dynamic flight.[56] But, notes Zhu Lilan, the plan will only fund "basic research tasks closely related to the technological realization of strategic objectives."[57]

Finally, 863 seeks to fashion a symbiosis between science, engineering, and industrialization. It forces scientists and engineers to think about applied uses of technology when seeking grants and the longer-range significance of their proposals. The program also seeks to promote diffusion by opening to contract bids areas that include aids to production, such as computer integrated manufacturing systems (CIMS), comprised of computer aided design (CAD) and computer aided manufacture (CAM).

863 and State-Led S&T

The creation of a formal 863 system was inevitable given the leadership's enthusiasm for the plan and, in particular, Deng's personal commitment to it. In April 1986, just one month after Wang Daheng and his colleagues delivered their letter and received Deng's rapid response, COSTIND and the SSTC, with support from the State Council's Science and Technology Leading Group (STLG), jointly convened a three-week meeting of 124 leading Chinese technicians. The meeting sought to identify specific areas for development within the seven broad sectors proposed by Wang and his colleagues. The experts in attendance quickly divided into twelve smaller topic groups within each of the seven areas.

Between May and July, the STLG appointed a national task force of thirty representatives from a variety of agencies—mainly COSTIND, the SSTC, the SPC, and the CAS—to begin drafting the framework plan, and then to establish project-centered task forces of specialists. These project groups ultimately selected fifteen major topics, including computer integrated manufacturing systems (CIMS), computer aided design (CAD), and computer aided manufacture (CAM) in the automation field; fiber-optic telecommunications in the information technology field; and space-age composite and synthetic materials in the new materials field. The fifteen topic groups also set out specific guidelines, overall goals, and a handful of initial specific targets.

By August 1986, these groups had laid the groundwork for a third phase of administrative organization. The STLG invited sixty more leading scientists and engineers to comment on the plans for the fifteen selected topics. Once these suggestions had led to further revisions, the politicians reentered the 863 planning process. In October, an enlarged Politburo meeting under the chairmanship of CCP General Secretary Hu Yaobang approved the plan in principle. Within one month, the Party Central Committee and the State Council had jointly lent the program their formal stamp of approval on behalf of both the Chinese Communist Party and the Chinese government.[58]

The establishment of a formal 863 program, built around an elaborate bureaucratic architecture of procedures, subsequently passed through four distinct stages: first, a preparation phase in which the plan was announced and, beginning in 1987, codes and regulations drawn up for applications for support, high-level approval, and the disbursements of state funds; second, an application evaluation, review, and selection phase in which expert committees in the seven focal fields were appointed and subordinate task groups in charge of the fifteen selected topics established; third, a formal beginning phase in which the 863 program began to disburse state funds and oversight and inspection procedures were established; and finally, a start-up phase in which new topics were added, in an ongoing fashion, on the basis of the various expert groups' evaluation of work already performed.[59] All of these procedures soon became institutionalized in the 863 Plan's bureaucratic system, based explicitly and directly on the strategic weapons model.

The 863 program's allocation procedures are akin, in many respects, to contract R&D in the United States. Expert groups comprised of leaders in each focal area set state goals, invite bids, and then choose "winners" who receive funding to fulfill the contract. Separate subcommittees of specialists in each area peer review proposals and bids, which are then approved by panels selected by the top S&T bureaucracies.

Competitive bidding empowers these small groups of specialists because they have additional responsibility for monitoring performance and fulfillment of contracts. The 863 program's grants, both to individuals and corporate entities, have consistently been among the largest in China. In the first year of the program (1987), when S&T grants were smaller, biotechnology groups typically awarded four-year grants of RMB 500,000 to RMB 2 million or about U.S.$135,000 to U.S.$540,000 (at a contemporary exchange rate of RMB 3.71 to U.S.$1).[60] Although grants of this size are small by Western standards, biotechnology has a low funding threshold, and in 1987 these grants were considered large. Sometimes, scientists have found themselves playing politics: certain 863 expert groups have been accused of using the power of the purse to direct contracts to their associates, a phenomenon that intensified as competition for grants deepened.[61] Yet, despite the intrinsically political nature of the program and its connection to state goals, technical criteria appear to govern most funding decisions.

The 863 program is funded as a special budget item outside the normal allocation system for R&D. Usually, Chinese R&D funding follows one of three patterns. It can fall under regular S&T line items on ministerial or state enterprise budgets. Sometimes, block grants are allocated to these organizations. Finally, labs and enterprises can establish commercial ventures to raise money, with parent units providing the capital from budgets or via bank loans. This last arrangement compensates for undeveloped capital markets by shifting firm capital from the state sector, which follows the plan, to the commercial sector, where product mix is guided by the market.[62] But, of course, such decisions can run into the market-failure problem characteristic of long-range R&D. As we have noted, in the 863 system, by contrast, funds are allocated not through the bureaucratic system but to the 863 expert groups, which channel money downward on the basis of bid decisions. In the 1980s, this created a cross-system, extraministerial arrangement outside normal lines of competition and command in R&D, which lent salience to informal network coordination.

No reliable figures support an estimate of how much money is allocated to the 863 system as a whole. But as early as 1989, it comprised the largest source of research grants in China's biotechnology industry.[63] An official estimate from a leading figure in the program suggests that the central government spent approximately RMB 100.2 billion on direct block grants under the program between 1987 and 1999.[64] By industrialized world standards, this number seems small at first glance, constituting some U.S.$27 billion at 1987 rates of exchange, but closer to U.S.$12 billion at 2001 rates (RMB 8.276 = U.S.$1). But cross-institutional comparisons are enlightening, for even at the lowest number on this range—U.S.$12 billion—the figure seems significant when viewed comparatively. In 2001, for example, the entire annual budget of the Chinese Academy of Agricultural Sciences—China's most important institution of agricultural research, which was a focus under the biotechnology area of the 863 plan—was just U.S.$10 million.[65] Clearly, then, annual R&D spending in the billions of dollars under a single targeted program has had a significant impact on the priorities in China's research agenda, as well as the focus of its major institutes of technological research.

Although little information has been released about the absolute levels of funding granted under the 863 Plan, the relative priority assigned to various fields, other than space technology and laser technology (which are managed largely by defense planners), can be deduced from published funding

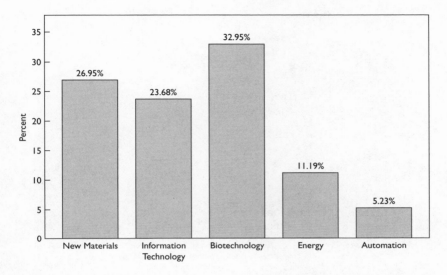

Figure 5.1   Allocation of 863 Funds to SSTC-Led Fields, 1988.   SOURCE: Shang Mu (1989).

ratios. For instance, in the five 863 fields managed by the civilian SSTC in 1988, the second year of the program, biotechnology was heavily favored (Figure 5.1).

The SSTC channeled funding downward to units under the regular ministerial system (Figure 5.2). In 1988, universities under the State Education Commission, for example, received 26 percent of funds distributed under the plan in the five "civilian" fields. Laboratories under the Ministry of Public Health—which probably received support exclusively in the biotechnology field—garnered 7.5 percent of the total annual 863 budget.

At the CAS Institute of Microbiology, China's premiere institute of microbiology, 863 funds accounted for 16 percent of R&D income in 1996, the second-largest category in the institute's budget and the largest domestic source of its funding—more than double the amount of R&D funding allocated by the CAS itself under its own academy program (Figure 5.3). This 16 percent figure is especially important because it primarily involves one major project—the development of genetically engineered pest-resistant cotton—and the institute is just one among five contractors on that project. Funding under the 863 Plan, therefore, can have a considerable impact on China's leading-edge research budget.

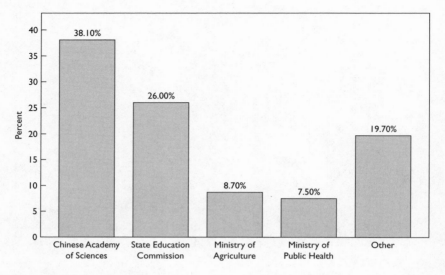

Figure 5.2   Allocation of 863 Funds by SSTC-Led Agencies, 1988.
SOURCE: Shang Mu (1989).

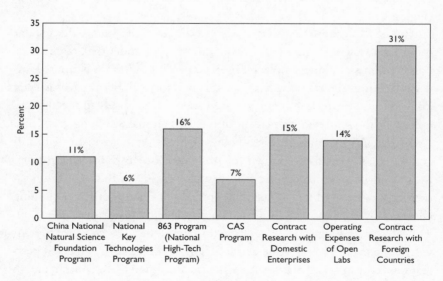

Figure 5.3   Constitution of R&D Funds, CAS Institute of Microbiology, 1996.
SOURCE: CAS Institute of Microbiology (2001).

Under this system, the 863 biotechnology management group channels monies downward to its various expert groups for distribution. These committees then direct the money to contractors selected for support under the program. Coordination is important, and often takes place cross-sectorally through a variety of agencies, with 863 groups working closely with the bureaucracies in project design, planning, and management. Coordination for China's manned space program, for example, was based largely in two sets of offices during the early years of the program, initiated in 1992—the so-called 921 Office of COSTIND, and the relevant 863 expert committees.[66]

Competition is also the norm in the 863 program. In one contract competition—the application of state-of-the-art CIMS automation techniques to industry—some 100 bidders were narrowed to about ten successful contractors, including Chengdu Aircraft, one of China's largest producers of airplanes.[67] In 1987, 500 biotechnology bids were narrowed to 100 contractors, distributed in a ratio of 40 percent for agriculture, 40 percent for medicine, and 20 percent for protein engineering.[68]

The expert topic groups that decide on targets and contractors report to managerial staffs in the seven main 863 fields. As noted, two of these fields—space technology and lasers—are dominated by military planners and bureaucracies; the other five—automation, biotechnology, energy, information technology, and new materials—have almost entirely civilian staffs.[69]

This does not imply that all work on space technology and lasers is weapons related; particularly in space technology, improvements in the design and production of both space vehicles and commercial aircraft are major goals of the program. Much of it is, however, including the development of synthetic aperture radar (SAR), a project discussed below. SAR has significant applications to commercial satellite work in such areas as hydrology and mapping. But it also is an important technology for the precision guidance of munitions, a major component of PLA force modernization, and a technology that has been developed in the United States with considerable attention to its weapons applications. The PLA also has become deeply interested in lasers—as used in ground-based weapons and electronic-pulse weapons that can blind enemy satellites—as part of its broader concern with information warfare.[70]

Neither does the location of five managerial groups under the civilian bureaucratic structure imply a lack of military interest in these fields.

Leading PLA technology planners, as we have noted, are deeply interested in information technology; for example, Chinese military specialists interviewed for this book discussed the evolution of a command, control, communications, and intelligence technologies project group within the defense R&D system.[71] And yet the strenuous—but unsuccessful—efforts of former defense industry elites to break into commercial telecommunications sectors also demonstrates that commercial goals remain paramount in most information technology spheres in China.

The key theme in the 863 Plan, therefore, is the creation of symbiotic technology systems rather than the development of dual-use hardware per se. The plan has, of course, influenced China's capacity to develop and deploy dual-use technology. But its strictly civilian targets and projects are of greater significance. Furthermore, the program's intended goals were quite encompassing—to create a high technology structure, to establish an implementation process, and thus to create a program that might raise all boats in the Chinese R&D system.

The 863 program's organizational influence has reshaped China's entire state-directed R&D system as technology planners system-wide assimilate key managerial elements of the program. This was precisely what the Wang group intended when it offered an alternative to the compartmentalized "ministerial-style" R&D system that predominated from the 1950s on. And as noted in earlier chapters, the problems of China's high technology development have long been managerial and political, rather than purely scientific.

Although China continues to lag behind international standards, its entire state-directed system of technological development is now set up on the basis of institutions that produced tangible results in earlier large-scale projects. By contrast, the "ministerial" systems that Wang's group wanted to remake were largely self-contained, encapsulated, and isolated from other parts of the R&D complex. Strategic weapons programs spanned the national system. Yet nonweapons (and even many conventional weapons) sectors and programs tended to recruit from their own schools, obtain equipment from their own factories, and assign virtually all phases of R&D to their own laboratories. The more powerful civilian ministerial systems, such as telecommunications and pharmaceuticals, were also notoriously noncooperative: monopolistic in their reluctance to share responsibility for work within their purview and engage in cooperative R&D with "outsiders."

Some military industrialists, then, clearly regarded "cooperative" R&D as a euphemism for monopoly breaking. The more important legacy of 863, however, has been to drastically reduce compartmentalized R&D. It spread institutions and practices once confined to the strategic weapons sphere throughout China's state-led civilian R&D complex. This is most obvious in the devolution of final decision-making authority on budgets and contracts to state-organized task forces of technicians.

"OLD" INSTITUTIONS, NEW PROGRAMS

This represented an extraordinary change in the power of technicians throughout the Chinese system, including in civilian sectors, where scientists and engineers never before possessed such authority. Its influence can perhaps best be seen in three areas: ways of making decisions, methods of coordination, and patterns of organizational design.

Who Decides?

The 863 Plan put great power in the hands of technocrats: control over the direction of state investment through selecting winners and losers in the competition for financial, contractual, and political largesse. This devolution on technical personnel of the power to dispense patronage and control the purse, as opposed to a role that is merely advisory, was an extraordinary departure from the practice of politics in post-1949 China. For instance, 863-related start-up ventures appear to possess the authority to circumvent normal contract and licensing provisions. This political development bears on issues of commercial competition, especially where foreign partners who can provide licenses and transfers are involved. In this way, technicians in 863 projects have gained previously unheard-of opportunities for patronage: they have the power to allocate state contracts involving large on-budget investment, the right to priority access to infrastructure and materials, and the authority to assist in expediting legal arrangements involving everything from approval of contracts and ventures to allocation of labor.

As earlier chapters have discussed, it was Marshal Nie Rongzhen and his aides who first institutionalized the notion of scientists as political and managerial, not merely technical, decision makers. In the 1980s, the institution was carried to its logical conclusion in the 863 Plan. A 1995 SSTC white paper described the phenomenon simply: "Implementation of the 863 plan requires compact organization and management, and nationwide coordination. A management and operational system was established based on trial and error. The core of the reform under the 863 plan is reform of the fund appropriation system and *expert participation in decision-making.*"[72]

Chinese sources invariably treat this development as tantamount to a revolution in nationally directed technology policy, especially since peer review has increasingly become the norm.[73] Numerous Chinese analysts have argued that the use of peer review in the 863 program reflected a "major reform" of the Chinese management system involving the "establishment of projects, subdivision of topics, designation of performing organizations, funding and the like."[74] But as we learned in Chapter 2, the institution is neither new nor revolutionary, for the integration of experts into decision making was the backbone of strategic weapons R&D, twenty years before the 863 scientists proposed their plan to Deng Xiaoping.

The Structure of Power

The history of the strategic weapons programs that led up to the 863 Plan also tends to disprove the widely held view of Chinese politics as "overbureaucratized": that the struggle among competing organizations yields not initiative and the decisive allocation of resources but mere incrementalism.[75] One reason strategic weaponeers proved so influential was that they and their patrons built links to the political elite. This enabled them to sell "nonroutine" programs and thus enshrine as a national model a structure of power that aims at cooperative, yet still authoritative, solutions to critical problems of industrial modernization. This power structure is not based on rigid commands from the top, nor does it depend primarily on the bottom-up bureaucratic bargaining that makes policy making in China so incremental. Rather, it blends cooperative with authoritative mechanisms. In its early phase, the 863 program depended heavily upon an informal network of connections among its founders to mediate the endemic formal constraints so common in Chinese politics.

Because of bureaucratic compartmentalization, the formulation and implementation of policy in China usually take place within bureaucracies and through bargaining among central formal agencies. In the early years of the 863 system, informal connections bridged this chasm of bureaucratic verticalism. By the early 1990s, this comparatively unstable informality had given way to a more controlled and institutionalized horizontalism. This was manifested in two 863 institutions: the diverse array of 863 expert groups vested with the power to set goals and allocate funds, and a variety of national research coordinating centers and information/standards clearinghouses that 863 designers modeled on strategic weapons precedents from the 1950s and 1960s. It should be recalled here that Marshal Nie had established horizontal "research service centers" in areas such as standards, computing, wind tunnels, shock waves, information sciences, and library services. In the earliest years of the 863 program, its designers urged the reproduction of these types of cross-system institutions to meet the new technical needs associated with their plan. There are currently eight such 863 "national research centers" in optoelectronics (information technology field), artificial intelligence and high-performance computing (information technology), genetic engineering of vaccines (biotechnology), computer-integrated manufacturing systems and experimental engineering (automation), intelligent robotics (automation), genetic engineering of pharmaceuticals (biotechnology), genetic engineering of biological products (biotechnology), artificial crystals (new materials), and photoelectric technology (lasers). These centers conduct research, integrate results from contracts awarded under the program, train personnel, organize national meetings, procure state-of-the-art supplies (particularly through overseas purchases), and promote standardization and the diffusion of knowledge through the establishment of "high-tech R&D basements."

The eight centers report directly to the relevant 863 expert groups. This relationship is facilitated by a considerable overlap of leading personnel. Thus the director of the 863 center for intelligent computing, Li Guojie, served concurrently as deputy director of the artificial intelligence group in the 863 information technology field.[76] In addition to reproducing an organizational style associated with weapons development projects, some of these centers—particularly the artificial crystals center—have the same R&D priorities that Marshal Nie articulated as early as 1958.[77] But the desire to shatter vertical boundaries lies at the heart of attempts to graft horizontal structures onto the 863 program. As the Chinese government has itself noted: "These research facilities created excellent conditions for the establishment of . . . bases for the country's high-tech research, staff training, exchanges and cooperation, unit technical tests and integration, [and] product development."[78] This is an almost verbatim restatement of Marshal Nie's intentions in the Mao era weapons programs.

Flattening Hierarchy

The combination of political commitment and the scientists' effectiveness at explaining technical requirements to politicians that sustained the strategic weapons programs during the Mao years would not have survived without institutionalized channels of access. The strategic weapons programs depended on "flat" organizations not just because socialist-type hierarchy is, it seems, endemically inefficient. Such organizations were also the essential prerequisite to success because they presupposed a symbiosis between political and technical will.

When strategic weapons alumni sought to build a national program for the post-Mao era, they paid special attention to this institution. On paper, the 863 Plan appears to have been built around comparatively rigid organizational layers: a high-level leading group, seven focal-field managerial groups, first-tier expert groups, and second-tier topic groups. In practice, however, communication across levels has been comparatively fluid: leading experts from the topic groups are required to engage with the recipients of 863 support. New topics are added and old ones adjusted via coordination across levels. Experts at all levels converge on the national research centers for the exchange of information and the planning of technology. Most important, China's leading politicians have been engaged in programmatic issues, and the top decision-making structure in the 863 program—the leading group—was vested from the beginning with limited proprietary rights to resources and infrastructure. The close involvement of state planners in the 863 program facilitates the exercise of these rights because 863 assumes "equal" engagement of experts with managers at all levels of planning, implementation, and oversight.

The 863 program's "hierarchy" is, for this reason, designed to divide expert labor among various groups for the evaluation of complex technologies. These various key technological priorities are broken down into constituent focal areas and then amalgamated in the formulation of programmatic goals. Communication across levels can be fluid because specialists deal less with different areas of responsibility than with different parts of the same problem. Administratively, this means that a telecommunications committee leads a fiber-optics committee, which in turn leads groups charged with broadband, nodes and switches, and so on. Although hierarchy is established for convenience, not command, it has not always worked perfectly. Nonetheless, it is viewed in China as a transformative reorganization of goal setting, implementation, and administrative oversight in policy making.

A Quick Illustration: Telecommunications

Information technology is one of the original seven fields in the 863 Plan. When the program was established, it was directed by a managerial group based in and exercising its authority through the SSTC headquarters. Various areas within information technology—for instance, optical electronics, information processing and automation, and so on—were overseen by topic groups that established, in turn, specialized project groups. Qian Zongjue, a senior information technology specialist and 863 group leader, has described how this structure came to operate by the early 1990s with respect to fiber-optic technology (Figure 5.4).[79] As the leader of the project group dealing with engineering a Chinese information superhighway, Qian Zongjue reported to a telecommunications topic group that worked within the priorities established by the managerial committee for information technology.

Qian notes, for example, that the 863 telecommunications leadership selected a number of specialized fiber-optic projects for the Eighth Five-Year Plan period (1991–95), including research on SDH fiber-optic communication technology and STM-1 (155 Mb/s) and STM-4 (622 Mb/s) systems. Other systems slated for investment included an STM-16 (2.488 Gb/s) optical communications network, wave-length-division multiplexers (WDMs), and erbium-doped fiber-optic amplifiers (EDFA). All of these projects were comparatively ambitious, requiring expert management, large investments, and intensive cross-bureaucratic, interagency coordination.

For each of these narrower topics—WDMs or EDFAs—a group of leading specialists was appointed which, in turn, selected contractors from among bidding firms and laboratories. Having made its selections, the expert group that had made the assignment then monitored contractor performance, undertaking periodic technical evaluations. Since competition for funds and contracts has been intense, however, these expert topic groups are in a position to exert considerable influence not just over programmatic decisions but over investment choices and indeed the fate of many applicants. Dominance of expert groups is essential to the control of contractor selection procedures under 863.

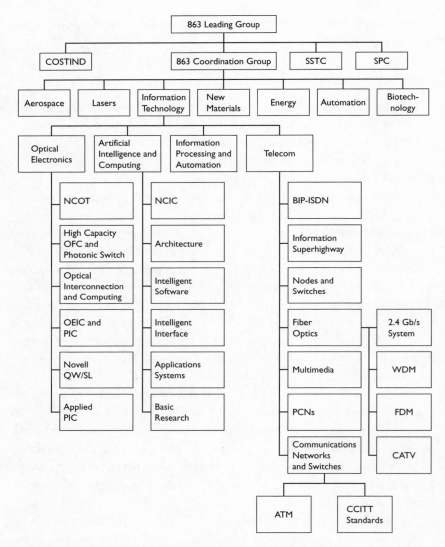

Figure 5.4   Organization of 863 Information Technology Field, ca. 1993–1997. SOURCE: Interviews.   NOTE: See Appendix 3 for details and clarification.

Implementation to Recipients

By the early 1990s, Nie's heirs controlled the 863 program's leading structures and influenced the development of topics and expert groups that defined the rules, routines, and institutions of the program.[80] As we have said, these were established according to models of management and organization derived directly from strategic weapons precedents.

In the implementation phase, the 863 plan and other state-led programs established according to the same model proceed through four stages: first, expert groups evaluate and recommend proposals; second, they or various topic subgroups formulate guidelines to dispense funds; third, they oversee a bidding process through which budgets are set and contractors chosen; and fourth, they evaluate progress and implementation of the plan.

For example, another national program established on the same model, the Key S&T Projects Plan, borrowed much of its framework from that of strategic weaponeers in the 1980s. Expert groups of up to ten members investigate projects proposed by institutes or the industrial departments of enterprises. This is followed by an evaluation in which a second committee of up to ten members scrutinizes the first group's recommendations for programmatic choices and areas that should be opened to contract bids. No members of the first committee are permitted to sit on the second.[81]

In both programs, in other words, expert committees held most of the power to approve (or disapprove) and evaluate projects. Thus experts were involved in setting and clarifying specific guidelines for competitive bidding on contracts. Under the automation field of the 863 program, a topic group on CIMS set a range of short, medium, and long-term goals in the late 1980s as follows: short—an experimental production line by 1992; medium—component technology for a demonstration line by 1995; and long—a completed demonstration line by the year 2000. These goals were then assigned to project groups on CAD, CAM, and so on.[82]

Expert groups in the 863 program also monitor the eight intersectoral research centers. There they assume a range of political functions. They do not merely make technical recommendations for plan guidance and revision, but offer recommendations on which contractor applications are to be selected for awards.

Chinese commentators have noted that the 863 leadership publicly adopted "selective and competitive" procedures for assigning tasks.[83] But 863 did more than this. It granted the expert committees out-and-out decision-making power over the ultimate allocation of blocks of financial support.

As the leadership developed 863 and other technology programs, senior cadres found that widespread and unchecked interference from the industrial departments bidding on contracts often hampered the selection of projects.[84] To compensate, they gave the expert groups direct power over the selection of sites and the awarding of contracts. This proved to be an extremely promising development for the Chinese R&D system because it introduced technical criteria to investment choices and policy decisions. But it also introduced a political dimension to an ostensibly technical process. Control of relevant expert groups could potentially help particular industrial groups and technical elites to protect or promote their agenda in a given area. The Chinese specialists commonly refer to these twin phenomena as *dapo fengsuo* ("blockade busting") and *hangye bilei* or *hangye baohu* (industrial or professional self-protection).

Once contract monies are allocated, 863 expert committees have the final function of carrying out periodic evaluations and progress inspections. The groups are expected to recommend future directions within current focal topics, as well as new areas in which to establish contractual relationships with industry or scientific facilities. One recipient of CIMS funding in the automation field, the massive aircraft factory in Chengdu, underwent twice-yearly inspections by experts from the CAD/CAM topic group. A special committee formed within the enterprise from among the top three to four engineering and management cadres conducted liaison with this group.

863 Projects

Initially, the main topics covered in each of the seven fields in the 863 Plan were divided into the following broad areas:

- *Automation*: computer integrated manufacturing systems (including CAD and CAM as applied to industrial automation), and intelligent robotics;
- *Biotechnology*: foodstuffs, medicine, and protein engineering;
- *Energy*: coal magnetic technology, and nuclear reactors;
- *Information technology*: optoelectronics and system integration, artificial intelligence and high-performance computing, information acquisition, processing and automation, telecommunications (including subgroups for nodes and switches, information superhighway issues, personal communication networks, fiber optics, multimedia, and broadband);
- *Lasers*: pulsed power, plasma technology, laser spectroscopy, and laser-based materials;
- *New materials*: optoelectronics and information technology–related materials, high-performance, anticorrosion and light structural materials, special function materials, high-temperature-resistant composite materials, and microstructure theory–based materials; and

- *Space technology*: carrier rockets, manned spaceflight, coordination with biotechnology groups on seed cultivation in space.

Each of these areas was managed through the first- and second-tier topic groups upon which the 863 structure was built (see Appendix 3). The 863 Plan's programmatic priorities were—and remain—extraordinarily ambitious. As Zhu Lilan has said, China is aiming for an indigenous capability to develop and deploy leading-edge technologies in several strategic areas, including radar, remote sensing, intelligent robotics, diamond film, as well as other highly competitive areas in biotechnology, nuclear reactor design, energy-storage materials (such as high-energy batteries), and industrial automation techniques.

Below are a few of the more significant projects funded under the 863 Plan.

Satellite-Based Synthetic Aperture Radar (xingzai hecheng kongji leida). The CAS Electronics Research Institute has been tasked under 863 to develop an indigenous synthetic aperture radar system that meets a variety of tightly controlled specifications, such as heat homing requirements of 22–55 degrees Celsius, discrimination of a 10 m × 10 m target, and observation capability at 50 kilometers.[85]

Synthetic aperture radar (SAR) provides extremely high resolution images in inclement weather, and at nighttime as well as in daylight.[86] Freed from time, climactic, and other conditions, the radar gives a unique view of a "target" at a much lower electromagnetic frequency than optical sensors. SAR is a dual-use technology with many applications to important civilian work in environmental monitoring and earth-resource mapping. It has provided terrain structural information to geologists for mineral exploration, oil spill boundaries on water to environmentalists, and sea state and ice hazard maps to navigators.[87]

SAR has also been useful in the precision guidance and targeting of munitions, a focus of PLA force modernization. The main military applications of SAR include all-weather day-and-night image sensing for reconnaissance, surveillance, and targeting; all-weather navigation and guidance; and expanded moving-target indication. Specifically, SAR has the ability to automatically detect ground-based moving targets even when motion causes the radar signature of the target to shift outside the normal ground return of a radar image. The U.S. Army has an SAR program on real-time automatic target recognition of multiple and simultaneous targets (STARLOS). The

U.S. Navy has aggressively pursued SAR technology to upgrade existing APS-137 radars on P-3 aircraft.

As the U.S. Sandia National Laboratory has noted, most civilian applications of SAR have "not been adequately explored because lower cost electronics are just beginning to make SAR technology economical for smaller scale users." However, like so many other Chinese strategic technology efforts with dual-use applications, it is difficult to analyze precisely why Chinese planners place so much emphasis on SAR. The PLA surely would gain greater capabilities for precision targeting from SAR. Yet the capabilities specified by the 863 program guidance might be only marginally superior to the uneven missile guidance capability that China currently possesses. Chinese missile engineers presumably would be able to achieve the 10 m × 10 m targeting capability specified in the 863 contract for SAR by using alternative guidance technologies. SAR will have a variety of commercial benefits for such activities as oil exploration in the South China Sea. But here, too, while SAR research is of "world standard," is "strategic," and reflects the latest and best international technology, it seems a costly choice in light of existing alternatives and challenges.

High-Temperature Gas-Cooled Nuclear Reactors (gaowen qileng dui). Under the direction of Wang Dazhong, who has served as president of Qinghua University and leads the nuclear energy program under 863, the prestigious Qinghua Institute of Reactor Technology was designated as the sole contractor in a project funded under the 863 Plan to develop indigenously designed and constructed high-temperature gas-cooled nuclear reactors (HTGR).[88] This is truly a cutting-edge technology that may put China into the forefront of innovation in nuclear engineering. HTGRs emit heat at about three times the rate of pressurized water reactors (PWR) and, as such, are considerably more efficient at generating electricity. HTGRs are also considered much more economical for the nuclear component of a power grid than either PWRs, graphite-moderated reactors, or boiling-water reactors.

As part of China's ambitious expansion of nuclear power for commercial electricity, therefore, in 1992 Qinghua was charged by the 863 energy managerial group to expand exploratory HTGR work begun in the 1970s. Past Chinese HTGR projects were limited almost exclusively to fuel fabrication, helium technology, and design methodologies. But under 863, Qinghua was asked to develop a wholly indigenous design of a 10 megawatt test reactor. Dubbed the HTR-10, the first test reactor under the project was ignited on December 21, 2000, at a site some 40 kilometers outside Beijing. The reactor was designed to serve as a test facility for further HTGR work; this is intended to contribute to China's national electricity grid.

Diamond Film (jingangshi bomo). Two institutions, Jilin University and the Beijing Artificial Crystals Research Institute, are joint contractors on an 863-funded effort to develop diamond film technology.[89] As diamond has the highest thermal conductivity of any material, it is an important thermal management solution for advanced electronic systems, such as chips, laser diode arrays, and microwave circuits, and the packaging of microelectronics on spacecraft. This ties the 863 diamond film effort to another 863-funded program—China's manned space project, the 921 Program, and its space capsule, the Shenzhou.

Diamond film is a futuristic crystalline material that can also potentially be used to develop microscopic machines, such as palm-sized space satellites. Because the diamond material rapidly dissipates heat from high-powered, densely packed, high-frequency circuits, it can facilitate advanced circuit configurations, while adding to the life span and reliability of microelectronic systems.[90]

Large-Scale Parallel and Distributed Computing, Symmetrical Multiprocessing (da guimo bingxing jisuan jishu). The 863 National Center for Intelligent Computing (NCIC) is the prime contractor in the develop of massively parallel processors (MPP) and symmetrical multiprocessors (SMP)—important high-performance supercomputing technologies with wide-ranging applications.[91] In 1993, the center established the Dawn Corporation (Shuguang gongsi) to market its Dawn I parallel computer, a symmetrical multiprocessor capable of running parallel advanced programming languages. Such processors allow large computing tasks to be distributed to parallel executions. The NCIC's 863 contract requirements included the development of machines capable of performing 10–12 floating-point operations per second, virtual systems, and list processing capability in standard programming languages such as Fortran, C, and C++. Much to the planners' satisfaction, indigenously designed SPC digital exchanges enjoyed a 30 percent domestic market share by 1998.[92]

The NCIC offers a window on the function and missions of the national 863 research centers. Established in March 1990, the NCIC is located administratively within the CAS Institute of Computing Technology (ICT), which provides organizational support. However, the NCIC is directly supervised by the intelligent computing expert group of the 863 program. Its first director was Li Guojie, a civilian computer scientist with a Ph.D. from Purdue University. Li worked as a postdoctoral associate at the Coordinated Science Laboratory of the University of Illinois before returning to China in 1987. A leading professor at the ICT, Li was appointed concurrently director of the NCIC and deputy director of the 863 intelligent computing expert group. This reflects the primary oversight relationship between 863 and the NCIC: most NCIC staff maintain an affiliation with the ICT, but work on 863-related projects.

Like the other "horizontal" coordinating centers, then, the NCIC is charged with several tasks. First, it plays the leading role in the development of advanced computer technology, especially in the areas of parallel and distributed computing. Second, it seeks to integrate the results of all computer research under the 863 Plan; the NCIC is thus empowered to select useful R&D results from 863-funded computing projects nationwide and then to synthesize these into commercially viable and internationally competitive computer systems and software products. Third, the NCIC leads China's national-level research on high-performance computers and intelligent computing systems. Fourth, it trains the leading specialists in China's next generation of computer scientists; it maintains postdoctoral and research programs, while carrying out international cooperation and academic exchanges. In 1996, the NCIC had twenty postdoctoral students, all working closely with its fifteen Ph.D.-level researchers and twenty M.S.-level staff. This mirrors the mentoring institutions that Marshal Nie Rongzhen pioneered within China's strategic weapons programs.

The NCIC promotes a key research role for younger scholars. Projects under the 863 Plan give many Chinese scientists and engineers an opportunity to work on the cutting-edge of international research, while coordinating with foreign colleagues. In this regard, the NCIC and the other national 863 centers seek to train a new generation of scientists through hands-on laboratory experience.[93] The NCIC regularly hosts leading computer scientists from abroad. It has established a "high-tech R&D basement" as required by the 863 Plan. This functions as a kind of information clearinghouse. Of course, the center also maintains some of China's best research facilities, including state-of-the-art computer workstations for use by authorized researchers from around the country.

Among all of these roles, the most crucial for the various 863 centers may well be integrating nationally generated results within their specific technical domains. In the case of the NCIC, this includes the integration of all computing projects funded by the 863 Plan. In the spirit of the strategic weapons design competitions, NCIC frequently holds contests to promote new hardware designs and software applications. In this sense, above all, NCIC is a truly national center—akin to Nie Rongzhen's national strategic weapons R&D centers—for high-level collaborative work across bureaucratic domains. It regularly hosts as many as 100 visiting scholars from institutes and universities around China, including Qinghua and Beijing Universities, CAS laboratories, and military scientific institutes.

Intelligent Robots (zhineng jiqiren). Five main 863 contractors (the CAS Institute of Automation in Shenyang, Institute 702 of China's state shipbuilding corporation, the CAS Institute of Acoustics, the Harbin Shipbuilding Engineering Academy, and Jiaotong University) have individually and collaboratively developed an underwater robot capable of operating at depths of 6,000 meters.[94] This project revives a partnership from the nuclear submarine program when Institute 702, which has among the largest testing pools in China, and Jiaotong University's Hydrodynamic Laboratory, whose experimental tanks were also used by Huang Xuhua, played a major role in SSBN hydrodynamic experiments.[95]

In 1997, the 863-sponsored robot successfully conducted explorations at depths of 6,000 meters, covering seabed landforms and multimetallic nodule abundances in the Pacific Ocean. In this area, the primary interest of the 863 planners seems to have been to facilitate developments in related areas, such as systems engineering, navigation and control technology, sensor technology, acoustics, and high-efficiency sources of energy.[96] Specific R&D requirements tasked by the 863 project committee for intelligent robotics have included design of the carrier system (*yunzai xitong*), sophisticated control systems, and acoustic systems.

Manned Spaceflight. China's manned space program, the 921 Project (*921 gongcheng*), is controversial; some Chinese scientists have condemned it as a nationalistic publicity stunt.[97] Yet spaceflight has tremendous resonance in China, much as President Kennedy's space challenge and the Apollo program did for Americans in the 1960s–70s. As journalist Craig Covault has argued, moreover, a workable manned space program could give China at least some leverage to seek inclusion in large projects associated with the international space station. Chinese leaders and technicians have discussed the creation of a small Chinese space station over the first two decades of the twenty-first century.[98] In both contexts—national and international—the launch of the Shenzhou manned space capsules has accelerated domestic discussion of ambitious concepts of manned spaceflight.

With 863 funding, together with direct allocations channeled in the late 1990s through COSTIND, China developed a craft, the Shenzhou, that combines features of the American Gemini vehicle, launched in 1964, with the Soviet Soyuz of the late 1960s. Shenzhou lacks the rendezvous, docking, and flight endurance capabilities of either of these craft, but China is ambitious in this area, and three versions of the Long March booster in operation in 1996 were already capable of handling the Shenzhou payload.[99]

The main contractor on the Shenzhou project is the Chinese Research Institute of Space Technology (Zhongguo hangtian jishu yanjiusuo), which directs a far-flung national effort on the strategic weapons model. It draws together a team of more than 1,000 technicians and specialists, including prominent figures under Marshal Nie. Like Chen Fangyun, the Shenzhou chief designer Qi Faren also worked on the Dongfanghong satellite under the command of Nie's NDSTC. Indeed, Qi came of age in Nie Rongzhen's organizational model; he was a key player in the development of important management institutions in the strategic weapons context. In April 1970, for example, Qi Faren, together with key missileers Qian Xuesen and Ren Xinmin, and Nie's onetime administrative aide in the strategic weapons programs, Yang Guoyu, worked closely with Premier Zhou Enlai to solve technical problems associated with the satellite.[100] As in all other areas in the 863 program, then, Qi designed Project 921's R&D structures according to the models and modes associated with this experience.

Computer Aided Automation (*jisuanji fuzhu zidonghua*). From the very outset of the 863 program, planners placed considerable stress on industrial automation. The program even has its own website on CIMS, with extensive information on programs, plans, and targets.[101]

An assortment of enterprises, including Chengdu Aircraft, have been granted support under this area of the plan. Laboratories and educational institutions are frequent contractors. These include Beijing's University of Aeronautics and Astronautics (Beijing hangkong hangtian daxue), as well as Zhejiang University, where Qian Sanqiang was once president.

The 863 CIMS program concentrates on electronic data interchange, CAD, CAM, computer aided exercises, and the integration of advanced automation techniques into product design and manufacture and industrial assembly lines. In accordance with 863 managerial techniques, CIMS goals in the year 2000 emphasized both indigenization and competition. For example, CIMS groups welcomed contractors to bid for 150–200 CIMS dissemination projects, and required that 50 percent of these use wholly indigenous software.

The CIMS area of 863 also encourages international cooperation as a basis for improvements in indigenous design capabilities. In November 1998, Spatial Technology, Inc. of Boulder, Colorado, a division of Dassault Systèmes S.A., and the world's leading developer of open-component three-dimensional modeling technology, announced the first commercially available application from China enabled with its trade-marked ACIS technology. ACIS is a solid modeling component that provides software developers with three-dimensional modeling technology to support CAD, CAM, and engineering applications. Such a system is of special application to original equipment manufacturers (OEM) in countries such as China. Accordingly, Spatial Technology developed its partnership and licensing arrangements with the 863/CIMS Design Automation Engineering Laboratory in Beijing, one of the program's national research centers.

This national 863 lab developed its own CAD/CAM software based on the ACIS system. This software is now used in several Chinese industries, including aviation, automotive manufacture, space systems, and electronics. The laboratory's product, Lonicera MDA, was developed as a native language application. It was the first locally supported and maintained ACIS-enabled application in China.[102]

Two-Line Hybrid Rice Technology (*liangxi fazhi jiaodao jishu*). Biotechnology groups under 863 have sought to alter the highly labor-intensive techniques used for cultivating rice in China. For example, Chinese farmers generally seed male and female rice parents separately at different times and in different beds. These rice parents are then transplanted to adjoining areas, carefully monitored for growth by observing the leaf count of the plants, with water and fertilizer adjusted accordingly. Later, growth hormones can be applied, and pollen is often transferred by hand through the use of a rope moved across the field.

With 863 support, five institutions attempted both individually and co-operatively to develop what Chinese biotechnologists term "two-line" hybrid techniques.[103] These avoid the necessity of increasing the proportion of male sterile plants by the tedious and time-consuming method of planting them in uniform populations adjacent to maintainer plants. The two-line method also seeks to avoid the selective harvest of the seeds formed on the male sterile plants. Contractors for this work have included the Hunan and Hubei Provincial Academies of Agricultural Sciences, the Jiangsu Provincial Agricultural Research Institute, Central China Agricultural University, and Zhongshan University.

China is deeply committed to this hybrid rice technique, despite skepticism voiced by some foreign specialists that its reliability is highly questionable given not only its dependence on the length of daylight but also its vulnerability to variations in ambient temperature—natural phenomena that cannot be controlled.[104] Nonetheless, from 1986 to 1997 the growing area for these hybrids reached 1.6 million acres. Its proponents claim accumulated yield for the same period to have been 1 billion kilograms.[105]

Genetically Engineered Treatments for Malignant Tumors and Other Diseases (exing zhongliu deng jibing de jiyin zhiliao jishu). The 863 Plan sponsors pilot production plants for some twenty genetically engineered drugs and vaccines. Chinese scientists have conducted extensive research on the genetic foundations of malignant tumors and other diseases, and are also active in cloning—for example, they cloned five goats with the gene for human Factor IX, a protein involved in blood coagulation.

In 1998, the vice minister of science and technology, Hui Yongzheng, claimed that 863 support had enabled China to produce the first interferon a-1b cloned from a human gene. Contractors in this area have included the Drug Research Institute of the Chinese Academy of Preventive Medicine, Shanghai's Tumor Research Institute, Fudan University, and the Basic Research Institute (Jichusuo) of the Chinese Academy of Medicine.[106]

Breeding Seeds in Space. As a final example, Chinese biologists have developed an aggressive program with 863 support to breed seeds in space aboard satellites, high-altitude balloons, and the Shenzhou space capsule.[107] In writing about this effort, Chinese scientists particularly like to stress that China is the only country to have developed such a program.

Under the direction of Liu Luxiang, director of the Space Technology Breeding Center of the Nuclear Energy Application Research Center of the

Chinese Academy of Agricultural Sciences, 863 researchers argue that the space environment allows for the breeding of high-yield crops that cannot be developed through ordinary breeding techniques on Earth. Thus, space breeding sends seeds into orbit in a recoverable spacecraft or aboard high-altitude balloons.

Chinese scientists premise this program on the belief that the high-vacuum, low-gravity, and strong-radiation environment of space leads to mutations in the seeds that, upon return to Earth, will lead to breed strains with higher quality and yield, and which may be resistant to disease. In this regard, they make three major claims: rice seeds returned from space have a 10 to 15 percent higher yield than comparable seeds bred on Earth; a tomato strain developed from space-mutated seeds, cultivated by the Agricultural Institute of Heilongjiang province, grew to as much as 800 grams; finally, bell peppers grown through this 863 supported program have shown yields 25 percent higher than comparable seeds on Earth, a 20 to 25 percent higher vitamin content, and growth weights up to 750 grams.

By the spring of 2000, biotechnology groups had used 863 support to launch over seventy varieties of crop seeds—including rice, cotton, oil, vegetables, and fruit—on eight recoverable spacecraft and five high-altitude balloons. In November 2000, the maiden flight of the Shenzhou carried tomato, watermelon, radish, green pepper, corn, barley, and wheat seeds, as well as different types of herbal medicine. By May 2000, China had planted nearly 405,000 hectares of rice fields with space seeds and 8,100 hectares of space vegetables. With 863 support, the government planned to add 243,000 hectares of rice fields devoted entirely to space seeds in 2000.

This has also led to the establishment of companies and agricultural partnerships. At the end of 1998 Dajiang Town in Shandong Province in eastern China and the Chinese Academy of Sciences established China's first "Space Vegetable Foundation." In January 2000, Changxing County, some 150 kilometers west of Shanghai in Zhejiang Province, announced the signing of a collaborative agreement with the China Aerospace Industry Corporation to build the largest space seed nursery in the world, occupying more than 4,000 hectares, with a total investment of RMB 30 million.

By the end of 1998, the 863 program had contracted for a total of 10,000 projects, including those described above.[108] Other areas supported by the plan have included experimental research into infrared adaptive optics, fiber-optic telecommunications, pest-resistant crops, airborne remote-sensing and real-time-transmission systems, and basic research into the physics of high dynamic flight as potentially applied to global positioning calculations. Appendix 3 outlines some more programmatic highlights of 863.

Yet as the next chapter discusses, strategic weapons–style institutions, and the entire notion of a nationalistic state-led approach to technology, began to founder in the 1990s. Despite the promise that Marshal Nie's heirs, politicians, scientific leaders, and even PLA generals saw in the 863 model, such programs often became deeply politicized.

"Planned" innovation based on targets set from the top has intrinsic limitations. It flies in the face of much of the recent history of technology. Chinese technical, political, and military leaders began to discover these limitations at precisely the moment that China accelerated its integration into the global economy and faced a renewed round of export control debates in the United States and other countries. The government's insistence on indigenization at all costs therefore became subject over the 1990s to many pressures, with important effects on the country's economic trajectory, military force planning, and technology acquisition strategy.

The next chapter rounds out the story of China's approach to strategic technology through the year 2000, detailing the politics and pressures associated with some of these limitations. The final chapter of the book will then critique some of the more enduring assumptions of the strategic weapons model. It sets China's entire experience with national security and strategic technology against the backdrop of international conflict, political economy, and domestic change in China since the death of Mao Zedong.

chapter six

THE COMPLEX LEGACY OF CHINESE
TECHNONATIONALISM, 1992–2000

In the spring of 1992, a second group of scientists, including three of those who had proposed the 863 Plan to Deng Xiaoping, made another approach to the Chinese leadership. At a meeting of CAS departments held in April 1992, Shi Changxu, a military metallurgist who had succeeded Wang Daheng as director of the CAS Department of Technical Sciences, proposed expanding the program, including enhanced attention to telecommunications and one new managerial area, ocean technology.[1] The group particularly emphasized large-scale engineering endeavors, such as the construction of particle accelerators and continuing work in Yang Jiachi's field of space technology. Finally, the scientists placed special emphasis on electronics, especially chip technology, computer software, and advanced broadband telecommunications networks.[2]

This second attempt to persuade China's political leaders to reinvigorate national strategic technology planning reflected just how crucial high technology had become in Chinese political calculations during the second half of the 1980s. Shi Changxu explicitly yoked high technology to state power and international standing when he pointedly discussed the importance of competition in high technology to the international rivalry among states. International relations, said Shi, is about competition between all the elements that comprise national power—political, military, industrial, and the rest (*biaoxian zai zonghe guoli de jingzheng*). But in that struggle, he added, the most important element is high technology.[3] Thus, much as Marshal

Nie had told the political leadership four decades earlier, technology above all else would determine China's national standing.

By 1992, five years into the 863 program, strategic technology planning was one of five pillars that supported China's twenty-first century technology agenda. The other four were:

- The acquisition of foreign systems through technology transfer in joint venture, licensing, and coproduction arrangements;
- Promotion of commercial initiative in scientific laboratories through market-driven, profit-oriented technology ventures—so-called "second stage" spin-offs (*di'er ci kaifa*) that allowed laboratories to earn money by selling products derived from their research. This introduction of material incentives was intimately connected to the revival of a patent system in 1985;
- Creation of a budding venture capital industry that would substitute for public finance by steering equity capital toward innovative technology start-ups; and
- Promotion of a greater role for industrial enterprises in R&D and fostering linkages (*lianheti*) between research laboratories and industrial enterprises.

Although strategic technology planning comprised just one of these five pillars, it nonetheless remained crucial. First, the 863 Plan and related programs represented perhaps the strongest connection between national security and economic development in China's policy debate. In addition, they remained a critical link between purely domestic economic policy and the international security concerns so central to Chinese decision makers.

Second, strategic technology planning was the largest source of direct central government finance for R&D in priority sectors, such as space, lasers, and supercomputing. Although the system of financing technology had gradually begun to include something closer to equity investment, direct public allocations remained enormously important. Public investment was funneled not through the intermediary agency of the ministry and state corporation budgets or via the major government banks, but through its own administrative system with unique procedures. National technology planning was thus caught up in a wide-ranging debate about the proper role of public, as opposed to risk and equity, finance in shaping national competitiveness.

Third, strategic planning concentrated on "applied" (*yingyong*) research and medium-term results. Strategic programs laid bare the main military, civilian, and dual-use technical goals of the state for the early twenty-first century, reflecting the key technological pressure points at which concrete investment choices met rhetorical bluster and wishful musing.

Finally, strategic technology planning continued to preoccupy China's most prominent scientists, engineers, and principal industrial cadres—men such as Shi Changxu. By 1992, a group of younger technicians in their thirties and forties, many with experience in entrepreneurial technology ventures abroad, had begun to influence Chinese R&D debates. But national programs still stood front and center on the agenda of China's older science and technology establishment, including major players at universities, national laboratories, and key industrial enterprises.

Despite the promise that Chinese scientists and politicians initially saw for the 863 Plan and similar programs, these programs became ever more problematic as the 1990s wore on. The 863 Plan, the strategic weapons management style, even the notion of a technology-based nationalism, foundered on some of the same imposing challenges that confronted China's political system.

This chapter concludes the story of how China adapted old ideas to new challenges by considering three such problems, all of which show the limits and boundaries of the technonational approach and the strategic weapons style in China. First, state-led technology development expanded during the 1990s, but although this appeared to bring some limited, albeit impressive, achievements, it did little to make and sustain the broader innovation that Chinese leaders had hoped to create. Industrial policy is a peculiar phenomenon, and in China the commitment to "manage" innovation through bureaucratic procedures, however flexible and creative, became increasingly self-limiting. Second, China's unwavering commitment to indigenization ran up against the reality of the country's continuing dependence on foreign technology transfers. Likewise, the nationalist ideologies that had sustained that commitment for five decades conflicted with the compromises to sovereignty and state power necessitated by China's integration into the global economy and the international trading system. Third, even when planners sought to build a competitive marketplace in high-tech industries by shattering old monopolies and encouraging new domestic entrants, administrative fiat too often determined the outcome of competition. Despite the commitment to technical solutions embedded in the 863 program and its offshoots, politics often continued to determine winners and losers.

THE EVOLVING ROLES OF STATE TECHNOLOGY PLANNING

By 1992, change in virtually every arena of China's technology system—state planning, technology transfer, factory-level R&D, and the first stirrings of risk finance—had led to a concerted effort to reshape the role of the state in policy development. The government promulgated a series of plans to guide technology that it hoped would provide market incentives to investors, manufacturers, and researchers, while spurring the diffusion of technology through targeted state assistance (Table 6.1).

Each of these new plans targeted different aspects of China's system of technology diffusion. But unlike the 863 Plan, the bulk of this new planning was geared either toward the popularization of technology in under-mechanized sectors, or else toward commercialization. The commitment to commercialize became the raison d'être of the so-called Torch Plan (*huoju jihua*), whose goals included the creation of local high-tech development zones and other commercial incentives.

In a 1991 essay, Song Jian provided a framework for understanding the interrelation among the various state-led programs then being set into place.[4] He argued that technology must not just be about meeting the state's strategic requirements; it must also meet the needs of industry and agriculture. As such, Song demarcated the strategic weapons/863 model from other models, while offering a rationale for moving beyond central government targeting toward experiments with localization. "Industrial development," Song declared, must have "one body and two wings": Large and medium-size enterprises represented the body; township and village enterprises comprised one wing, and high technology industries the other. "Having a body alone will not work, and naturally, only having two wings will not work either."[5] Thus, he divided Chinese S&T planning into a three-tiered hierarchy (*cengsi*): the first tier consisted of local development plans and programs to create a basic infrastructure, the second of nationally supported R&D programs, such as the 863 and the Torch Plans, and the third of basic scientific research. But the 863 and Torch Plans had critical differences from each other that reflected the special role of strategic technology programs and the increasing divergence between the strategic goals of the state and all other roles of technology.

TABLE 6.1
China's State-Led Science and Technology Guidance Plans

Plan	Orientation	Sample Activities
Key Technologies R&D Plan	Technologies of particular benefit to economic construction	Breeding of 200 new crop varieties to increase land yields
	Modernization of oil and gas technologies	Water conservation and soil improvement
	Reducing energy consumption	1–2m integrated circuits
		High-speed railway technologies
National Basic Research Priorities Plan	Basic science and engineering National data banks	Basic research in mathematics, biology, chemistry, physics, medical science, agronomy, computer science, materials science, mechanical engineering, space science, and resource and environmental science
Torch Plan	Industrialization of R&D	Local high-tech zones
	Commercialization of R&D	Managerial training
	Technology exports	International high-tech markets research
		Biotechnology, energy, electronics, and new materials
863 Plan	International-standard high technologies in eight strategic industries: automation, biotechnology, energy, information technology, lasers, new materials, ocean and marine technology, and space technology	Special research centers
		Fast-breeder nuclear reactors
		Manned spaceflight
		CAD/CAM automation
		Supercomputing
		Fiber-optic telecommunications
Spark Plan	Agricultural mechanization	Composite fertilizer
	Special fertilizers	Nonmetallic minerals
	Rural management	Textile and light industrial processing
		Building and construction materials
S&T Popularization Plan	Mobilization of technical personnel	Improved seed strains
	Promotion of technology and mechanization, especially in the countryside	Processing technologies for sideline products to potential users
		Pesticides
		New agricultural machinery and plastic film
		Film mulching

The First Tier: Experiments with Indirect Finance

In the mid-1980s, the government began to implement a number of guidance programs, such as the Spark Plan and Bumper Harvest Plan, that were intended to raise the level of technology in agriculture and local, small-scale industry. Beijing was particularly concerned to improve the low technical standards in poorer rural locales and townships, and to improve the diffusion of technology to small and medium-sized rural industrial enterprises. The Spark Plan disseminated technical tools, such as mechanized equipment, composite fertilizer, building materials, and nonmetallic mineral products to rural locales. It had some roots in the rural technology decentralization and popularization programs of the Cultural Revolution era. Indeed, the plan took its name from Mao's dictum that just "a single spark can start a prairie fire" (*xinghuo liaoyuan*).

By 1992, 85 percent of China's counties had received some form of Spark-related investment, equipment, or training.[6] The program represented an initial step by the state to move away from exclusively central-government mechanisms of financing technology toward the development of newer, market-based mechanisms. For example, Spark relied heavily on China's agricultural and industrial development banks to provide finance. Thus, unlike the strategic weapons/863 model, direct central government outlays comprised just 3 percent of Spark funds in 1992, in contrast to the 36 percent from state banks and 50 percent from rural development research institutes.[7] In 1991–92, the SSTC moved to bring Spark guidelines into compliance with the lending requirements of the World Bank, and by the end of 1992, 24 percent of Spark outlays were funded by the World Bank.[8] Where the strategic weapons model required direct, targeted central government finance, the limited role of the center in funding Spark reflected the degree to which responsibility for key aspects of technological transformation had begun to devolve to institutions dealing with rural development, including banks, research institutes, and quasi-state foundations established to alleviate poverty.

The Second Tier: Experimenting with Localization and Commercialization

In the second tier, the Torch Plan, like 863, required a significantly higher level of government investment and involvement. But Torch sought, nonetheless, to fulfill an alternative assortment of planning goals that revolved around, first, state-supported commercialization, industrialization, and high-tech transformation.[9] Thus, although Torch and 863 were intended to be mutually reinforcing, Torch, unlike 863, dealt with few of the broad strategic goals that have defined Chinese technonationalism since 1950.

At a forum in January 1991, the former strategic weaponeer then serving as SSTC deputy director, Li Xu'e, reminded his audience that Torch had been established on the basis of nongovernmental mechanisms. But, Li lamented, Torch planners appeared not to have gotten the message: "The Torch Plan Office did not do much to publicize my ideas, so today no one talks about [nongovernmental investment as key goal of the program]."[10]

Here, Li contended that the Torch experiment was foundering on a continuing tendency among Chinese technicians to rely on the state. Part of the problem was status. "Some people," said Li, "suppose that doing research is high level, but [developing technology products] is low level. . . . Getting people to change these notions is very difficult."

> I read on a notice board about a young sales manager in a Shenyang electric cable plant who looked to be slightly more than thirty years old. The plant had been losing money, but after she became sales manager, sales shot up to tens of millions of yuan within two to three years. People said it was all her doing. So who is the more capable person, she or a chief engineer? I feel you cannot say she is any less capable than a chief engineer. The Shenyang Electric Cable Plant is a large plant whose sales manager is slightly more than thirty years old and not necessarily a college graduate. But because of her sales work, the plant turned its losses into a huge profit. That's a great achievement, isn't it? Who is more qualified—the chief engineer or the sales person? I say that both are highly qualified. He develops new products, and she sells new products. Both are indispensable. My hope in saying this is that more projects will [be pursued] in both [areas].[11]

In this sense, Torch was an experiment in high technology not as a means to enhance China's strategic position, but rather as a way to promote commercial viability and (as in Li's Shenyang example) enterprise profitability. Unlike 863, which was largely a central government affair, Torch aimed at attracting foreign technology and investment at the local level, in this case in high technology development zones. By the end of 1994, China had established over 120 such zones, 52 of which had received state recognition and government financial support.[12] Such zones offer preferential tax and investment treatment as a spur to foreign technology transfer. And as Li Xu'e has argued, "it is high technology industries that we are supporting, not the processing of raw materials brought in from outside China to make high technology products. Torch projects are supposed to develop our technology or foreign technology. We can also develop technology that comes from abroad, making it succeed. But we cannot process high technology products from imported raw materials for foreigners."[13]

Further, Torch sought to upgrade infrastructure at the local level, not in priority national laboratories and enterprises. As Li Xu'e argued, it was intended that national-level projects should gradually be shifted toward local development zones.[14] Finally, then, Torch sought to pry undisciplined firms away from their grasping hold on the state's purse. Li once put this point bluntly, harshly criticizing a university that had tried to couple industrialization to research and training. "Just emphasize getting rich and making money," he told them. "That is all that is needed. If you make money, soon you will be able to improve the old professors' dormitories and improve conditions for running the school and doing scientific research. Isn't that better than coupling teaching and research? . . . You should find out which [technical] projects will make money, then start work on those projects as quickly as possible."[15]

The Third Tier: Basic Research

In Song Jian's third tier, the government continued in the 1990s to nurture at least some basic research. Under the Eighth Five-Year Plan (1991–95), Beijing pledged direct financial support to 20,000 research projects. It established an SSTC-supervised Basic Research Plan that treated seven branches of basic research: mathematics, physics, chemistry, mechanical engineering, astronomy, geography, and biology. The plan promised support to basic research with potential application to energy development, materials science, information and computer science, agronomy, the medical sciences, resource and environmental science, space science, and engineering.

The Basic Research Plan extended the institutions of peer review, and at the national level, through the National Natural Science Foundation of China (NNSFC) and the Chinese Academy of Sciences, it involved individual researchers in writing grant applications. By 1999 the NNSFC was funding 16 percent of the 20,000 grant applications it received annually, all of which were peer reviewed.[16]

Hybrid Institutions

All this demonstrates that at the local level in particular, strictly commercial pressures began in the 1990s to drive the creation of institutional hybrids. Such forms shifted resources from the plan to the market, while creating at least the potential for greater bottom-up innovation at universities and enterprises.

Initially, for parent units, such as Beijing University or state industrial firms, to create "spin-off" companies was not, in itself, innovative. As the political scientist Corinna-Barbara Francis has noted,

> the fact that Chinese spin-offs are usually established after or just at the point when the research and development on a particular product or technology is complete suggests they are a mechanism by which institutions commercialize an existing technology, and are not, at least initially, engaged in developing new technologies. The technology used [by such firms] is often complete from the perspective of basic research, requiring only the secondary stages of commercialization in order to develop marketable products. The Capital Computer Company (Hanjing Diannao) was established by a group of computer scientists from the Software Institute of CAS with the specific goal of commercializing a software and hardware system which had been developed over many years by institute researchers.[17]

One can conceive of how commercial pressure might sometimes lead firms to be increasingly innovative as they shift from meeting state planning targets to meeting market demand. For example, spin-off firms are an avenue of information for Chinese technology manufacturers because the success or failure of commercial ventures automatically provides data about consumer preferences and market trends.

Yet—again—the lingering attachment to state planning remains profound. Francis has noted, for example, that the "technologies that are commercialized through spin-offs are often developed by specifically funded government projects, many of which may last for years and involve large numbers of researchers."[18] As a result, the role of the market in connecting spin-offs to parent firms is particularly important for what it says about the evolution of capital allocation in China's technology industries. Parent units are simply vital to the formation of spin-offs; it is they, not the state technology investment budget, that provide capital. As Francis notes, "Spin-offs have been a critical mechanism for fostering entrepreneurial activity and transferring capital resources from the state sector to the commercial sector, a particularly important role given the underdeveloped state of China's capital markets."[19]

Most often, such transfers involve a single round of capital infusion from the parent unit. Then, since basic technology upon which a product will be developed has already been provided by the parent, capital is mostly used for product design, market research, and manufacturing, which in turn can bring further infusions of capital into the firm, but from commercial sales and successful marketing of products.

> China's market reforms have strengthened the incentives for and pressure on individuals and institutions to set up spin-offs. Government policies have allowed, and pressured through budget cuts, state entities to engage in commercial ventures in order to generate extra-budgetary revenue with which to maintain and improve the living and research conditions of their employees and their members. Universities and research institutions in particular have been encouraged to get involved in the computer and high tech business. The revenues generated by these commercial ventures are expected to alleviate fiscal pressure on the government. Spin-offs set up in this way not only pay taxes to the government, they also generate extra revenue for their parent unit and its employees which alleviates some of the state's fiscal responsibility. Within the computer and high technology sector, universities and scientific research institutes have been very active in setting up commercial ventures. According to one report, at least 600 high tech enterprises had been set up by colleges and universities in China by 1993.[20]

Infrastructure and State Planning

All of China's national planning experiments during the 1990s serve to show how very special was the strategic weapons/863 model in the overall calculus of how technology could—and should—meet state goals. After a tenth anniversary conference in 1996, Song Jian ordered several expert groups to supplement the original 863 targets with a so-called Super-863 (or "S-863") program (*chaoji 863 jihua*), designed to track global technology developments for a further ten years, from 2001 to 2010.[21] Submitted to the leadership in its final form in 1997, the Super-863 program aimed to build on the successes of the 863 experience, renewing and reinvigorating the politicians' commitment to the development of high technologies in the main focal areas under the program.

Yet there was a rub. For although 863 was—and remains—very special, the state retained a penchant throughout the 1990s for planning and large-scale, highly mobilizational infrastructure projects, all of which involved major capital construction and state targeting. The most notable such projects are probably the so-called Golden Projects, which have given spin-off firms the opportunity to market technology directly to these government programs.

The Golden Projects were initially conceived as a means to create a context for government-led construction of an information superhighway. And not surprisingly, a number of 863 expert groups became deeply involved in Golden Project planning. These included the information superhighway expert group under the 863 information technology field, the same group that oversees the NCIC.

Initially, government planners conceived of just three Golden Projects, but later expanded their horizon to include other areas of infrastructure (Table 6.2). The initial three projects were the Golden Bridge, which aimed to construct a sophisticated telecommunications network linking ministries and commissions of the State Council with 30 provinces and autonomous regions, 500 cities, 12,000 large and medium-sized enterprises, 100 leading business conglomerates, and keypoint industrial projects involving large-scale capital construction; the Golden Customs Project, which linked government departments of foreign trade administration, foreign exchange control, and customs services to foreign trade enterprises and state corporations (this, it was argued, would accelerate the efficient processing of customs statistics, tax rebates, cash settlements, the verification of customs licenses, and the issuance of certificates of national origin to import and export products); and the Golden Card Project, which supported the development of a noncash economy by creating a

TABLE 6.2
China's Initial Golden Projects

Project	Focus
Golden Bridge	Telecommunications network linking departments of the State Council with provinces and autonomous regions, 500 cities, 12,000 large and medium-size enterprises, 100 leading business groups, and national keypoint construction projects
Golden Card	Electronic financial network to replace cash transactions with checks, credit cards, and ATMs
Golden Customs	Electronic data and telecom linkages between state offices of foreign trade, foreign exchange control, customs supervision and surveillance, and statistical bureaus. Designed to modernize customs, trade tax rebates, and import-export licensing and verification
Golden Tax	Satellite network for the accounts-clearing system of the People's Bank of China, with an audit center in Beijing and connecting centers in 50 major cities. Includes 40 VSAT satellite stations, software systems, and nearly 800 regional and county-level value-added tax stations
Golden Sea	Information system yielding parametric data for macroeconomic policy making

sophisticated network linking banks and credit agencies in ten key coastal cities, such as Shanghai and Guangzhou.

At a National Work Conference for the Electronics Industry in 1995, two additional Golden Projects were introduced: a Golden Tax Project to provide a satellite network for the accounts clearing system of China's central bank; and a Golden Sea Project to give central government financial and economic bureaucracies parametric data in support of macroeconomic policy. Trial operation of the latter Golden Project began at the end of 1994.[22]

In the Golden Projects, as in the 863 Plan, the state drove policy with laboratories and firms following behind. The NCIC sought to provide a sophisticated domestic alternative to overseas computing technologies, and thus win a share of the state contracts awarded in connection with the Golden Projects. Likewise, specially formed companies on the spin-off model fought to market microchips developed in 863-supported laboratories. China's first-generation distributive array processor, with a rate of 1,320 MIPS, was developed in 1991 by information processing groups under 863's information technology field. An 863 system integration laboratory that had been established to develop super-high-speed and real-time signal processing managed to design and market super-high-speed FFT and DBF microchips. All such companies hold special rights to 863 innovations, and in February 2000, the government announced the establishment of sixteen "enterprise bases"—industrial conglomerates—tasked to commercialize 863 results in partnership with the contracting agents.[23]

All of this explains, at least in part, China's eagerness to follow the original 863 program with supplemental targets. But this has hazards, for China's real challenge is to break with such practices. The state has remained committed to important elements of a planned approach, which continues to drive much of China's technology agenda. By the fall of 1996, Chinese scientists proudly pointed to a total of 1,200 "achievements" of the 863 program, among which half were deemed to be of "international standard."[24]

BACKWARDNESS AND FOREIGN DEPENDENCE: TECHNONATIONALISM AND TECHNOLOGY TRANSFER

The almost reflexive commitment to state planning highlights the first theme of this chapter: China remains wedded in many ways to "planned" innovation from the top down. If this is intrinsically self-limiting, so too is the almost equally reflexive commitment to nationalism in technology policy.

Ultimately, the goal of strategic guidance plans such as 863 is to create an indigenous Chinese capability to innovate and manufacture. This is, in some sense, also true of plans that rely more heavily on nongovernmental and market mechanisms, such as Torch. But for all the government's effort, China remains utterly dependent on foreign technology transfers in many areas, exemplified both by arms purchases from Russia and by strenuous complaints about American export controls during the WTO negotiations. In fact, Beijing has always supported purchases from abroad or the coproduction of technologies with foreigners. This was true even under Mao, when a strong commitment to industrial modernization compelled China, with little technical infrastructure of its own, to acquire technology from abroad, particularly from the Soviet Union.[25]

The Communist victory, and the Sino-Soviet treaty of friendship of 1950, ruptured most of China's ties to its most important pre-1949 trading partners. To fulfill the leadership's ambitious goals, then, the government took steps that sharply politicized technology acquisition policy. This included a unique role for the state in compensating for a lack of traditional forms of international intercourse, as the central government began to pursue technology transfer as a matter of foreign policy.

In retrospect, it is easy to confuse China's Mao era expressions of "self-reliance" (*zili gengsheng*) and "independent development" (*duli zizhu*) with autarky. Yet autarky was never Beijing's intention. Rather, larger political events—a Sino-Soviet split arising from politics, nationalism, and clashing security concepts as well as from ideology—forced China's technology system into nearly complete "self-reliance" far earlier than most Mao-era technology planners had anticipated.

Zili gengsheng referred, first, to the relationship between the state and economic development, for in practice, "self-reliance" meant that China would acquire technologies imported from abroad while planning for a future, potentially far down the road, free from the shackles of external dependence. China needed an indigenous high technology R&D system. But it would have to follow a series of preliminary stages involving partnerships, licenses, coproduction arrangements, and direct foreign aid. Although the long-term goal of *zili gengsheng* was freedom from dependence, the initial

Chinese variant of technonationalism thus placed considerable emphasis on external assistance.

The Chinese government has, however, held freedom from external dependence as its absolute, consistent, and unwavering aim. In more recent decades, this technonational impulse clashes with China's growing integration into the global economy. And it contains inherent contradictions, since China must further integrate into international manufacturing, finance, and commerce in order to gain access to many of the technologies it seeks to indigenize.

It is this contradiction, as I argued in Chapter 1, that defines much of the PRC's struggle to modernize. China's technology and economic policies have long reflected a deep-seated nationalism, but technological backwardness has repeatedly forced policy makers to compromise this principle. To build a strong nation requires compromises that further integrate China into the very international system that crude variants of Chinese nationalism so distrust.

Not surprisingly, then, the issue of high technology has dominated much of China's foreign policy, both in defense and trade. In sectors related to national security, allegations of compromising transactions and thefts of proprietary American commercial and military technology plagued bilateral ties in 1998 and 1999. In the economic realm, even as China negotiated its entry into the WTO, technology bureaucrats defied trends in the global high-tech economy by announcing their intention to impose new restrictions on foreign investment in high-growth, high-profit technology industries. The November 1999 agreement on China's entry into the WTO committed the government to reverse these policies. But implementation and compliance remain important question marks. And the sheer persistence of such restrictions twenty years into China's economic internationalization is astonishing.

In the weeks leading up to the WTO agreement, China's powerful minister of the Information Industry, Wu Jichuan, reaffirmed a long-standing ban on foreign equity participation in both Internet service and content providers. This defied a world reshaped by venture finance and reinforced commitments to regulatory roadblocks in China's telecommunications industry at a time when Web-based communication and electronic commerce had mushroomed in China. Predictably, the restrictions became a major point of contention with the United States in talks on China's entry into the WTO. Chinese technology bureaucrats seem repeatedly to flirt with new programs of state subsidies, often incorporating new protections, including potential market share ceilings.

Despite its aspirations to become a global leader in technological innovation and manufacturing, then, many of Beijing's policies continue to defy accepted wisdom about the borderless world of technology and the utility of unfettered markets. Technology has radically transformed the Chinese economy. Yet in at least some top-priority areas, it seems to have had little impact on the state's *political* relationship to the marketplace.

In ways both large and small, technonational principles with roots in strategic weapons programs continue to manifest themselves in all aspects of China's technology transfer policy. In the software industry, for example, China has flirted with more strenuous government promotion of the Linux operating system as an alternative to Microsoft's Windows. Both Chinese and foreign analysts routinely suggest that part of the reason is that the more open Linux system will allow China to continue building a wholly indigenous software industry.[26] I noted another example in Chapter 5: China has expanded its manned space program in ways that even many Chinese scientists find wasteful. Yet the program's most vociferous supporters invoke technonational principles—sometimes coupled with a rejection of market principles—to make their case. "Because the space industry *resisted* market forces," claims one program supporter, it has become "'the only industry we can be proud of.' Strong government direction and support for technology development . . . is a necessity and the manned program is 'the right direction.'"[27]

Still, China continues to wrestle with the realities of external dependence. A Chinese Academy of Sciences report prepared at the end of 2000, "Two Kinds of Resources, Two Markets," argued that China's resource security strategies should place much heavier emphasis on international markets, including expanded imports of oil, food, and energy. Markets, the report argued, intersect with nationalism and security in complex ways. For example, the report predicted that enhanced reliance on international markets for resources would be less risky for China—a "market-making" large country—than for a smaller country; these risks could be decreased further by active involvement in the development and commercialization of international resources.[28]

Dramatic Shifts in Foreign Direct Investment

Clearly, there are important differences from classic Mao era technonationalism expressed in these ideas about China's ability to tolerate resource dependence. But, then, reform era economic change has, inevitably, invited change in technology transfer policies. Since 1978, Chinese technology planners have particularly stressed the kinds of software issues—know-how and training—that fell off the agenda in the 1960s. As a U.S. government survey noted in 1987,

> Modes of technology that offer more intimate interactions with foreign technical personnel have come to be preferred. A wide variety of instruments of transfer, including licensing, joint ventures, cooperative ventures, wholly foreign-owned ventures, compensation trade, and the use of consultants and the procurement of technical services are being used. Much emphasis is being placed on foreign provision of training in contract negotiations of Sino-foreign technology transfer. As a result of this change, a much greater proportion of the technology imported since the end of the 1970s has been "unembodied" technology, or pure know-how.[29]

Government spending on imports has also increased significantly. Even in the earliest years of the reform, the sixth Five-Year Plan (1981–85) allocated U.S.$9.7 billion to foreign technology imports, some 15 percent of plan investment funds. This facilitated over 1,300 technology import contracts with foreign firms.[30]

Perhaps the most important new trend in technology transfers is a widening of the circle of technology importers. Where technology acquisition decisions were once highly centralized in state planning agencies, the proliferation of firms and the diffusion of decision making to a wide variety of central and subcentral agents have broken the monopoly of the center.[31] Most government bureaucracies have had import-export agents since the earliest years of the People's Republic. But direct overseas investment by Chinese firms created alternative points of access in the 1990s to foreign ideas, experience, and technology. Local firms are today in a far stronger position than in the past to negotiate their own terms with potential foreign partners. Most can now negotiate of their own accord, without exclusive reliance on the intermediary agency of central foreign-trade corporations and ministry bureaucrats.

Technology acquisition through imports is thus intimately tied to improvements in China's creaking production system and physical infrastructure, including industrial plant and machinery. More recently, this effort runs in parallel to the modernization of China's commercial infrastructure in telecommunications, air traffic management, and electronic finance.

Continuities: A Reconfigured (but Recognizable) Technonationalism

Despite these dramatic changes, old ideas and behaviors persist. Indigenization remains the ultimate goal of economic integration with foreign partners; leaders in Beijing feign little interest in the liberal underpinnings of economic globalization. Rather, senior politicians often appear to take a mostly instrumental view of technology transfer and commercial cooperation. This was evidenced in the 1950s when Moscow offered advanced technology in return for implicit Chinese support for Soviet leadership of the Communist bloc. Today, this trade takes place in a market context. But Chinese transfer policy calls for acquisition at as low a cost as possible and with few long-term guarantees.

Moreover, China continues to stress the strategic underpinnings of technology and economic policy, even as it enjoys its most peaceful external environment in nearly a century and a half. Technonationalism remains important because the lessons of dependence from the 1950s still inform critical goals. Even where export controls have been liberalized, reliance on foreign imports can produce a subtle form of dependence: on parts, labor, and the supply of technical knowledge.

This is precisely the technonational rationale that once spurred China to indigenize even those technologies that the Soviet Union was willing to provide. Today, strategic technology planners argue that Chinese R&D will languish if advanced systems can only be acquired from abroad. By this logic, "reinventing the wheel" has enormous software benefits. Chinese engineers may be building a system that foreign producers already have; but if they did not, the planners argue, China's domestic knowledge base could not advance.[32] Even as the role of foreign acquisition has become more important in both defense and economic modernization, strictly political rationales have retained force even where freedom from dependence may have little economic justification in the short term.

Continuing Faith in Hardware, Growing Emphasis on Software

Above all, the dramatic changes in the Chinese economy of the past twenty years have not altered the extraordinary faith of policy makers and industrialists in the raw merits of hardware. Foreign business partners and industry analysts view this, at best, as naïve, at worst, as blind. Central government acquisition plans reveal a continuing belief that hardware purchases will somehow make China "modern." For instance, China's telecommunications bureaucracy has an ambitious shopping list of imported broadband and fiber-optic systems. But to acquire such technology is one thing; to develop the skills and know-how to understand and re-create these systems is quite another.

Recognition of this problem has led to an increasing emphasis on software. In the late 1980s, a Chinese manager visiting the 3M Corporation in Minneapolis made a dramatic realization. "If only we had one percent of what is here," a member of his delegation remarked of the 3M equipment, "we could change our entire province." But the manager was astounded less by the modern machinery than by 3M's methods. He recognized that technology acquisition involved more than technical sophistication.[33]

Current policies continue to reflect China's mixed history of technology acquisition. The continuing stress on hardware that foreign coproducers, licensees, and sellers find so discouraging follows trends from the height of Sino-Soviet cooperation. But the new government emphasis on software in the 1990s—which, in many cases, still differs sharply from the work of a "real" private sector since it continues to stress state targeting and narrowly construed goals—echoes a similar concern for indigenization and priority on software in military technologies from the 1960s.

A Continuing Role for the Center

Finally, the dramatic shift in the locus of decision making in recent decades has in no way displaced the central government from its pivotal position in technology acquisition. Rather, the nature of the center's role and the configuration of players have changed.

As noted above, as a result of recent reforms, the central ministries and foreign trade corporations have ceded ground to a myriad of players, including enterprises, local governments, and new trading corporations. This is one of the most significant departures from China's experience with technology transfer. But the center's planning of "strategic" technology acquisitions remains crucial in several respects. Only it can call upon a broad array of technical experts from the spectrum of disciplines, for only it has mobilized such individuals for more than forty years. And as Chinese technicians have argued in recent years, only the center can ignore the market considerations that often impede forward-looking R&D investment. It is one thing, state planners point out, for a wealthy American or Japanese corporation to invest in R&D with few near-term commercial applications in anticipation of long-term results. It is quite another for a Chinese company to make investments with little prospect of short-to-medium-term commercial gain. This is a kind of market failure. It will change with economic growth and encouragement, largely unknown in the past, of enterprise R&D.[34] Also, foreign partners will increasingly assume the role, formerly played by the central government, of cushioning the impact of change. But the center continues to be an important partner for China's technology industries. The center not only calls upon the services of a multitude of specialists, it also fosters a variety of new technology analyses and planning processes that mirror the pattern of government investment in many other countries. Even the United States has proposed several versions of a national technology strategy since the Eisenhower administration created a Presidential Science Advisory Committee (PSAC) in response to evidence from Sputnik "that American science was not all it was expected to be."[35] Most important, then, this is part of an intensifying debate in China about the proper place of public, as opposed to risk and equity, finance in fostering innovation. This debate is real. But the growing importance of outside agents in technology acquisition and planning does not mean that the center's former powerful role has evaporated.

THE POLITICAL DYNAMICS OF TECHNOLOGY COMPETITION

The third self-limiting aspect of China's commitment to a strategic and planned approach to technology during the 1990s was the continuing politicization of the enterprise. By design, strategic technology programs such as the 863 Plan institutionalized a cooperative approach to the development of new technologies. It is striking, therefore, that the expansion of one of China's highest growth and profit sectors—telecommunications—became so deeply scarred by political fiat and competition played according to nonmarket rules.

In recent years, a variety of excellent studies of the expansion of telecommunications in China have appeared. All demonstrate that a marketizing transition proved much harder than was initially hoped in a sector that underwent massive systemic change during the 1990s, including the smashing of monopoly conglomerates through the creation of rival equipment and service providers.

In brief, three points are essential to an understanding of broader technology policy trends in China in relation to technonational principles and the fate of strategic weapons style management institutions. First, the collaborative research and development model that defined strategic weapons development during the Mao years, and the 863 program more recently, contrast starkly with the compartmentalized organizational system that China's telecommunications elite brought into the 1990s. While the 863 program enshrined cooperative R&D as a national model, telecommunications became deeply politicized. Second, military industry elites were instrumental in the emergence of a new telecommunications agenda.[36] Third, the ostensibly "strategic" approach to technology that lies at the heart of so much Chinese technology policy remains a complex—and, often, burdensome—legacy. Even as market incentives and competition have appeared in key technology sectors, such as telecommunications, strains have remained because of a lingering attachment to a largely political approach to high technology development.

The resulting push and pull between old monopolists and new entrants in sectors such as telecommunications with high growth and profit potential, has revealed just how powerful politics remains in the development and deployment of technology in China. As China entered the 1990s, its telecommunications monopolist—the Ministry of Posts and Telecommunications (MPT)—retained an elaborate system of institutes and factories from which it sourced its own equipment and designs, performing little, if any, collaborative research with the Ministry of the Electronics Industry (MEI), the military, or others. This compartmentalization not only contrasted with the approach that the four 863 scientists sought to promote as a national model, it inevitably led to politicization. As its monopoly came under assault in the mid-1990s, the MPT sought to protect its position of strength. Telecommunications became a high government priority, and foreign partners entered the market. Thus, the financial stakes of this competition for all players rose considerably.

Cooperation, Compartmentalization, and Competition

Chinese histories of the telecommunications sector reveal that most of the historical exceptions to the encapsulation of R&D within the

MPT system lay in the strategic weapons sphere. This fact is often missed, since most Western studies of China's telecommunications industry ignore the sector's military roots.[37] The MPT had in fact provided considerable support to Marshal Nie's strategic weapons designers and administrators, especially in the development of radio telecommand equipment for missile and satellite launches.[38] By contrast, the bulk of the MPT's network of design and production units was highly encapsulated in organization and operation.

The MPT itself thus had two organizational models on which to draw as the government began to plan its future telecommunications agenda in the 1990s. But whatever debate the 863 Plan spawned over the merits of collaborative R&D and cooperation between ministries and units, telecommunications became caught in a cycle of bureaucratic competition and politicization that stood on its head the collaborative model the 863 scientists advocated.

The reason for this was, in the first instance, financial; the commercial stakes in China's telecommunications industry became enormous. Even a cursory glance at China's telecommunications ambitions during the Eighth Five-Year Plan (1991–95) reveals why. Plans for telecommunications during this period, which was concurrent with the development of a second round of 863 targets, were staggering. From 1991 to 1995, China invested some RMB 241.4 billion in fixed posts and telecommunications assets, twelve times the investment during the Seventh Five-Year Plan (1986–90). Newly built fiber optic cable trunk lines totaled 80,000 kilometers, toll telephones reached 800,000 circuits, the annual rate of increase in long-distance switching capacity reached 50.4 percent, and the switching capacity for local telephone circuits reached 42.7 percent. China's telecommunications sector also grew during the ten consecutive years of the Seventh and Eighth FYPs at even faster rates than the overall national economy.[39]

Fiber optics became one of the prime grounds for interunit and inter-ministry competition because the technologies involved were, in effect, competitive with the satellite communications technologies and services that had long been controlled by China's space industry, which as we have discussed evolved directly out of the strategic weapons effort. This provided a motive for space and electronics specialists both to resist the dominance of the MPT and to invade its bureaucratic territory.

For other Chinese industrial elites, meanwhile, the main motive to resist the MPT's near-monopoly of fiber optic and related technologies stemmed from heightened competition and the authorization of large-scale construction involving new fiber-optic lines. But the MPT had already constructed an extensive network of optical fiber lines, making many rival efforts redundant. The MPT's rivals in space, electronics, and other fields, could offer an alternative to optical fiber, such as applied satellite technologies.[40] And at the same time, the MPT initially found itself dependent on others for satellite transponders as it constructed its national telecommunications network.[41]

Before 1996, then, when the PLA established Great Wall Mobile, a service joint venture with the MPT, the ministry's competitors mostly shunned cooperation.[42] Instead, they adopted a strategy of monopoly breaking that politicized China's telecommunications industry over the course of the 1990s. For these elites, especially under the MEI, the preferred strategy was to invoke political connections to break down the dominance of the MPT, thereby obviating the need to cooperate.

This might well have introduced real competition to the telecommunications sector. But it became caught up in elite and bureaucratic parochialism, not in an impulse to market dynamism. Predictably, the MPT's response was to deploy—to considerable effect—virtually the entire repertoire of techniques of resistance and delay endemic to the Chinese bureaucracy. The MPT played this game well. Thus, by the end of 1997, competition had been created in China's telecom sector, but it had come into being mainly by administrative fiat from the senior political leadership in Beijing. The MPT remained dominant. Many foreign partners were dissatisfied with their contracts with the new entrants.

For China's leadership, the "solution" was to reintroduce a measure of collaboration to the sector—a strategic weapons managerial solution that proved wholly ineffective in this very different context. Cooperation, even amid deep competition, had worked well in strategic weapons domains during the Mao era because of a common sense of national purpose among all Chinese technicians, as well as an overriding sense of mission that the leadership had attached to its big push in these areas. Although the 863 Plan sought to spread these managerial solutions and a sense of national purpose to high technology industry at large, competition in telecommunications nonetheless remained deeply political. Leading groups and supercoordinating structures either became bargaining arenas or else committees in which the MPT and its rivals struggled over control of the agenda.

This shows clearly the limits and boundaries of the strategic weapons model in the nonweapons context. In the spring of 1996 the State Council formed an "informationization" leading group led by Zou Jiahua, the man most MPT leaders believed had played the pivotal role in challenging, and then breaking, their monopoly. The group included representatives of as many as eighteen agencies, including the MPT, the MEI, the SSTC, the SPC, the People's Bank of China, and the State Economic and Trade Commission.[43]

Reconciling so many bureaucratic interests and voices is precisely the role of such interagency leading groups. But in this case, the key members of the group, particularly the MPT and the MEI, were contestants in an industrial sector over which the group was empowered to lay down rules, guidelines, and governing regulations, including the formulation of development strategy, the organization and allocation of on-budget expenses to projects, and the setting of national standards. This group was also placed in charge of the initial Three Golden Projects.

Hangye Baohu and *Dapo Fengsuo*

Ultimately, telecommunications showcased the opposite of the strategic weapons/863 model, as established agencies resorted to a wide array of bureaucratic tactics to protect their niche. As mentioned in Chapter 5, the Chinese term these tactics *hangye baohu* or *hangye bilei*. Both phrases suggest self-help and resistance, as does the counterstrategy—*dapo fengsuo*—which can be loosely translated as "blockade busting." Both "self-protection" and "blockade busting" are deeply dependent on the mobilization of political ties. Thus unlike the 863 model, political links are employed not to facilitate, but to resist and obstruct.

Throughout the mid- to late 1990s, the MPT and the MEI found themselves competitors in a classic bureaucratic contest. Although both ministries were involved in 863 programming, the model clearly had little effect on the dynamics of their commercial competition. Both oversaw their own network of production and research facilities that sought to develop and manufacture fiber-optic equipment for telecommunications. But as we have noted, the MPT had long enjoyed a monopoly over the provision of telecommunications service; the only sectors outside its network were the military (whose telephone lines remained under the control of the PLA's telecommunications department), the railways, the public security forces, and the petroleum industry.

In the early 1990s, the provision of public telecommunications service became deeply competitive as China moved to expand its telecommunications infrastructure, laying local optical fiber networks, connecting these to MPT-controlled trunk lines, and expanding Internet, videoconferencing, and electronic mail services. To all players, the expansion of the market for service providers, as we have noted, held out the promise of large profits. Thus, the MEI and its partners in other ministries struggled to break down the MPT's de facto monopoly on the provision of telecommunications services to the government and consumers.

In 1993–94, the government permitted the establishment of two new market entrants: Liantong (United Telecommunications, or Unicom) and Jitong. Both new firms were backed by an array of bureaucracies, all seeking to muscle in on the MPT's domain. Jitong would soon become a primary contractor for the Golden Projects. Some of its backers had been involved in strategic weapons development, most notably the MEI's Institute 54 which, like the MPT, had helped to develop radio telecommand equipment for the space program.[44]

Almost immediately, the MPT began to engage in *hangye baohu* tactics in order to protect its monopoly.[45] From the start, this contest was clearly political. And both Chinese and foreign observers of Chinese telecommunications readily acknowledge that the intervention of Zou Jiahua—by then a vice premier—proved critical in enabling Liantong and Jitong to move into MPT-controlled markets. Zou himself praised both firms as monopoly breakers. At Liantong's licensing ceremony, he delivered an unusually blunt speech for a Chinese leader, making little effort to hide the political dynamics of the contest. Liantong, Zou declared, would "introduce competition" to Chinese telecommunications, and thus "break a monopoly."[46] But although both new entrants received plaudits and a good deal of foreign interest, including memorandums of understanding, initial investment, and legally approved joint venture partnerships, their performance proved to be disappointing.

This stemmed from several factors. First, the MPT's experience with relevant technologies and skills gave it the upper hand. Most important, however, the creation of competition served only to discipline and transform the MPT itself. A generational transition in the ministry's leadership led to a considerable reinvigoration of top-level management. This was followed, in turn, by several waves of reorganization, in which an autonomous regulatory body emerged, and in which eventually the old MPT system was divided into two distinct administrative structures in charge of telecommunications and postal services, respectively. Ultimately, the entire contest in telecommunications was circumscribed by the creation of a superministry—the Ministry of the Information Industry—that merged the MPT and the MEI into a single domain. But this new ministry was controlled at the top, and at important middle management levels, primarily by the old MPT elite.

The MPT's blocking tactics had shown that elite to be adept at buying time to build strength. When Liantong and Jitong were formed, the central government had given the MPT a regulatory role, since a truly autonomous regulatory structure had yet to be created. For Liantong and other new entrants, however, this rendered the regulator and their prime competitor one and the same. Of course, this played directly into the MPT's ability to deploy *hangye baohu* tactics.

The MPT at first simply denied Liantong access to its vast network. In 1997 the journalist Henny Sender explained that

> this meant [Liantong's] cellular-phone subscribers could only talk to each other. . . . It was only when faced with an ultimatum from the State Council in September 1996 that the MPT finally provided [Liantong] the access it needed. By this time, the ministry's own cellular networks had already established themselves. As a result, [Liantong] faces an uphill battle for market share. In Guangdong, for example, the MPT has 400,000 [subscribers], while [Liantong] has a paltry 15,000. It doesn't help that, in markets where both companies operate cellular services, the MPT has been aggressively lowering the rates it charges for handsets, to undercut the fledgling competitor.[47]

Liantong's primary problem was the explicitly political nature of its entry into the marketplace. China's entire competitive telecommunications market was born out of administrative fiat from Beijing, with Zou Jiahua as midwife. Liantong's early fate was "decided more by official fiat and political maneuvering than by skilled marketing."

> Because support for [Liantong] isn't universal among the members of the State Council and State Planning Commission, [it] must also play politics. And those politics often dictate actions which are completely irrational in economic terms. Thus, for example, [Liantong] slices its projects into small units to get around

the requirement that anything that costs more than US$30 million must get SPC approval. That means the projects on offer frequently make little economic or financial sense.[48]

Liantong "fractured the market." As an American observer noted, "eventually, for everything to become seamless you will need complicated intracompany agreements." No shareholder committed to Liantong "as anything except as a vehicle to advance its own interests; none is willing to jeopardize its relationship with the MPT."[49]

By the end of 1996, Liantong had further undercut its prospects by failing to follow through on a number of memorandums signed with potential foreign venture partners. This led to the widespread suspicion that Liantong was primarily interested in enriching itself rather than building a viable, competitive alternative to the MPT.

Bureaucratic Competition and Discontent

The struggle over the telecommunications market demonstrates the liabilities and limitations associated with the third major theme of this chapter: continued politicization of technology development. The telecommunications case shows clearly the limits of the "strategic weapons style" cooperative management institutions. It displays the marked differences between the weapons era and the 863 era; these are made especially clear by the dynamics of noncooperative technology development in an industry, such as telecommunications, that Chinese leaders—and 863 programmers—had decided was critical to China's future.

As late as January 1989, fiber-optic communications had yet to be industrialized for commercial use in China.[50] The MEI and several defense-technical institutes, such as the Tenth Academy, believed that they could leverage their special role in China's past technical transformation into present-day dominance. But political and bureaucratic adroitness ultimately won the day. The MPT proved to be a formidable competitor because the ministry had so many levers of bureaucratic power at its disposal.

Within the 863 Plan, meanwhile, telecommunications became an important focal area of the information technology field, and here the MPT accepted a more cooperative solution. Yet the MPT institutes and leading experts also took control of most of the major 863 steering committees under the plan. For "outsiders," who had ambitions to win 863 contracts, the

MPT's dominance of such structures proved a significant obstacle to entry. By 1994, MPT experts led most of the major groups involved in telecom planning under the program, and the MPT's chief engineer, Qian Zongjue, had been placed in charge of planning virtually all technology development related to China's information superhighway.[51]

For potential entrants and 863 hopefuls, this effectively built a wall around the MPT's domain. For example, at Institute 722 in Wuhan—a military industry facility under the old Seventh Academy that had developed the very low frequency (VLF) communications devices and shipboard myriametric-wave receivers for the nuclear ballistic missile submarine designed by Huang Xuhua—senior engineers had hoped to win national contracts for advanced fiber-optics development.[52] But during interviews in the fall of 1995, they dismissed this as "impossible" and "completely closed," primarily, they said, because MPT engineers on the relevant 863 expert committees and national contract-granting structures would incline to award support to applicants affiliated with their own system of MPT factories and institutes. This hit especially close to home, since the ultimate winner of the 863 contract to develop indigenous synchronous digital hierarchy technology—a major goal of telecommunications planning—was a local competitor of Institute 722, the MPT's Wuhan Institute of Telecommunications Sciences (Youdianbu Wuhan youdian kexue yanjiuyuan).[53]

Leadership ideologies, policy choices, and organizational solutions grounded in China's strategic weapons experience have continued to retain force and relevance to the present day. But their results have been mixed, at best. In military technology, China bought itself a limited—and highly circumscribed—strategic deterrent, with attendant trade-offs in the capabilities of its conventional forces and underlying microelectronics. More broadly, the results of programs such as 863 can be impressive, yet the underlying ideologies and organizational solutions remain self-limiting.

China must at last begin to break with this history if it seeks to join the front rank of international powers, both militarily and economically. What is required is a new industrial style, as well as a new political consensus that will forge a more symbiotic—and realistic—relationship between Chinese leaders' continuing commitment to self-reliance and the harsh reality of China's deep external dependence in an increasingly globalized world.

chapter seven

CHINA'S CHALLENGE: TO BREAK
WITH THE PAST

At the dawn of a new century, technology is the touchstone of China's rise to global power. China's defense planners have developed new, often lethal, capabilities that increasingly give it the capacity to coerce Taiwan and, perhaps, contemplate longer-distance force projection over time. Yet new weapons and information technologies advance so quickly—sometimes by a generation in just eighteen months—that PLA force planners have been dizzied. Ultimately, China's generals know, the PLA must upgrade its underlying capacity to absorb technology if it is to overcome the yawning gaps that have plagued force modernization for two decades.

Likewise, Chinese economic planners stress technology modernization as a means to strengthen national competitiveness and industrialists emphasize the modernization of production techniques. Import-export administrators routinely complain that international export controls undermine China's ambitions to forge a modern, competitive economy, and leading educators stress mathematics, the natural sciences, and engineering. Perhaps most significant, a new generation of entrepreneurs has become identified with a debate about how technology investment, if coupled to reform of the financial sector and a national competition policy, will promote greater innovation in industry across the board.

These are the technological dimensions of the rise of Chinese power, and they tie directly to a debate among strategists that increasingly pits those with faith in the transforming powers of commercial liberalism against skeptics of Chinese ambitions in East Asia, who anchor many of their arguments in technology issues. The way China organizes its quest for technology is central to the assumptions that all sides make in this debate.

Among those who view globalization as transformative, technology sectors have represented an important area of potential foreign penetration into China for more than two decades. Liberalization here was among the critical concessions facilitating China's entry into the WTO, and technology start-ups and cross-national strategic alliances lie at the heart of China's new private economy. Domestically, the private economy represents the most important alternative to five decades of state-led industrial policy. Externally, it has become one of the keypoints of foreign penetration into China's fastest growing and most profitable markets.

Meanwhile, those most skeptical of Chinese ambitions in East Asia readily concede that a China without the capability to project power will be unable to challenge American hegemony even if it wished to do so. China probably remains decades away from possessing the capability to challenge the forces of the United States and its allies on the open ocean. Despite a concerted drive to modernize and—most significantly—the likely deployment over the next ten years of sophisticated, capable new strategic missiles, such as the solid-fueled, road-mobile DF-31 and DF-41, China's strategic forces are, in some important areas, backward and vulnerable. PLA long-range naval projection capabilities remain negligible, although this may change in time. But a China fettered by across-the-board weakness can nonetheless challenge the United States through the acquisition of "asymmetric" capabilities—strengths targeted to counter specific American and allied weaknesses. This has particularly sensitized American defense planners to Chinese missile capabilities and key arms purchases from abroad, such as the 1996 purchase of the Russian Sovremenny-class destroyer *Yekaterinburg*, armed with eight nuclear-capable Sunburn (S-N-22) missiles, one of the most lethal antiship cruise missiles in existence. China has since purchased a second Sovremenny destroyer. And concern with China's growing arms purchases from abroad has led critics to take aim at the more open approach to technology trade with China that led many countries to remove some export controls in the 1990s and place commerce at the center of their policy toward the PRC.[1]

The evolution of Chinese technology policy intersects with this debate in complex ways. Breaking decisively with the past described in this book will more deeply embed China in the global economy than at any time in its modern history. But China would also need to shed many of the structural impediments that have hindered indigenous technical innovation. This would anchor it in the global economy and simultaneously gradually reduce its dependence on foreign technology transfers. It would also provide a far stronger foundation for defense modernization than currently exists.

By contrast, a China that clings to the core tenets of Mao-era technonationalism will remain burdened by a high-tech sector capable of impressive technical breakthroughs, but of limited competence in indigenous technology in general. This is precisely what has made the country so dependent on foreign technology transfers. But this would, in some ways, represent a China that continues to look askance at its trade partners and at globalization itself—viewing it largely as an instrument for acquiring from abroad what the country cannot provide for itself.

It is this set of contradictions that makes China's entry into the WTO so significant. For the first time in the history of the PRC, the government has committed itself to principles that are thoroughly inconsistent with many past technological, industrial, and political practices. These depend heavily on globalization and, thus, represent a sweeping change. But such policies must still overcome obstructionism from the entrenched industrial bureaucracies and political constituencies that have determined key aspects of China's technology transfer policy since the 1950s.

This ties technology issues more tightly than ever to the future of international relations and China's place in the emerging international system. It demonstrates the historic significance of China's entry into the WTO, and it says much about whether—and to what extent—China may be retaining the best of its historical experience, while shedding structural impediments that have hindered its modernization for nearly two centuries.

From the standpoint of the state, strategic technology efforts, such as the 863 Plan, have great promise. Through such programs, the central government guarantees core technical priorities and directly addresses the variety of market failures associated with long lead times from research to commercialization. It also supports laboratories and enterprises unwilling to invest scarce monies in risky R&D.

On balance, then, the transition from strategic weapons to the 863 Plan in critical technologies programming seems significant. There is little doubt that the program encompasses important defense technology goals that, to skeptical commentators on Chinese technology strategy, appear problematic. To some, the largely civilian, "national" high-tech focuses enshrined in 863 may be dubious, less a demilitarization of the country than a new way of organizing defense modernization—in short, a transition from the strategic weapons era model of spin-off to a subtle, if more technically broadranging, commercial-to-military "spin-on."

Yet this interpretation fails to capture important nuances in the 863 program. When Chinese strategic weaponeers accepted the vision first articulated to them by international counterparts in the 1970s, they also accepted that China's system of innovation required a dramatic overhaul reflecting new patterns of military-commercial interaction in a post-1960s industrialized world. With Silicon Valley as his point of reference, William Perry told his Chinese interlocutors that they were "doing it wrong" by placing military innovation in the driver's seat. But if one follows the logic of Perry's argument—were the Chinese instead to "do it right"—then it is clearly to be expected that their national R&D system should eventually come to resemble the pattern of commercially driven innovation (sometimes with direct government financial support) that has emerged in other nations since the mid-1960s. This is precisely what began to happen in China as a result of the 863 Plan. And that shift of focus is now supplemented by a broader emphasis on entrepreneurialism and venture finance, both of which are commercially oriented.

The 863 Plan thus reveals that Chinese technology programmers now understand defense requirements are thoroughly derivative of commercial developments. This is important because it represents a decisive shift of Chinese strategic technology goals, and at the same time, it makes it less likely than ever that U.S. export controls can be used to attenuate Chinese progress. Increasingly, the regionalization of international politics in the post–Cold War world has weakened attempts at multilateral control. Chinese technology planners have repeatedly demonstrated their ability to purchase key systems from other vendors when U.S. export laws prevent American firms from selling. Although it is unrealistic in view of current U.S. domestic politics—and symbolically undesirable—to remove controls on many dual-use products that the Chinese can, have, and will continue to purchase from others, such efforts to control the uncontrollable make little sense in purely technical terms.

For Americans, at least, the main brake on technology trade continues to be the presence of prominent defense goals even within ostensibly "commercial" aspects of programs such as 863. And yet this is probably unavoidable: it is simply unrealistic to expect a country of China's size, historical significance, pride, and economic potential to forgo a technological overhaul of a military that relies, in certain areas, on equipment of 1970s (and even 1960s) vintage. Analysts should be under no illusions about what motivates 863 and other programs. The mere fact of weakness makes Chinese planners uncomfortable. With a technology base that remains ten to twenty years behind international standards in most areas, strategists must hedge against uncertainties in an Asia whose international politics could change radically in just three to ten years. The pressure strategists put on industrial planners to fulfill the technical requirements of the hedge thereby intensifies, shaping the none-too-subtle dual-use character of programs such as 863. Clearly, the United States and Japan are being benchmarked, and quite explicitly. But given how problematic export controls have become, a response that invests heavily in the United States' own capabilities, rather than seeking to attenuate Chinese progress, except in areas that have unidimensional military significance, is perhaps the best strategy for maintaining America's edge. China's various defense goals must therefore be understood in the context of the dramatically changed sense in China of what makes and sustains a technology base.

CAN THE 863 MODEL SUSTAIN CHINA'S AMBITIONS?

In the event, the 863 model is also problematic for concerned Chinese who think systemically about modernizing their national industrial system. Chinese planners clearly recognize the limits and boundaries of targeted industrial policies. Thus the S&T reforms of the 1980s and 1990s have yielded programs similar to the 863 Plan: as in the 863 Plan, all involve significant institutional changes designed to introduce markets, promote entrepreneurialism, and use the hand of government to foster an environment conducive to innovation. Unlike the 863 program, however, they do not seek to target innovation directly. Planners clearly recognize just how far-reaching their S&T and industrial reforms must be. They also appear to recognize the inherent limits of focusing on key sectors and maintaining faith, even amid intraprogram competition, in top-down solutions to technical problems.

Such an approach, at least in its present form, will likely hinder China's struggle to join the ranks of international technology superpowers. It challenges much of what Chinese policy makers have learned over the past two decades about the difficulty of "managing" innovation from above. China remains weak in at least two of four areas that have proved critical to industrial success in Silicon Valley and elsewhere: private equity and government deregulation. In two others—entrepreneurship and strong university-led basic research—it has only just begun to make a breakthrough.[2]

Markets and Finance

China has only just begun to create the underpinnings of a genuine system of market mechanisms for technology research development: one in which consumer demand drives the decisions of the firm and noncentral government actors seek to innovate as an alternative to continuing reliance on state coffers. The record of innovation in the state sector is not at all promising. A recent study of China's place in the regional division of labor for electronics convincingly showed that all efforts to make the state sector more efficient and innovative have failed dramatically.[3] The "second-stage" spin-off sector may offer some promise, and top Chinese policy makers have also begun to stress venture finance as an alternative to public R&D investment. But output in the former category mostly consists of basic consumer products. In the latter, nongovernmental funds for risk investment have traditionally sat in banks as indirect public finance, and new venture-style finance involving an equity stake is still dwarfed ten to one by this type of capital (as opposed to a one-to-one or higher ratio in the United States).

Indeed, risk investment has virtually no history in China. And private equity scarcely has a toehold in China's expanding financial services sector. As the economist Nicholas Lardy has noted, China's central bank long set uniform lending rates for each loan category.[4] Although the bank periodically permitted slight adjustments above or below posted rates, lenders "were not encouraged to adjust from the posted rate on the basis of risk."[5] This imposed blinders on banks that precluded systematic risk assessments.

As Lardy has shown, this crushed Chinese banks under a mountain of bad debt. It also frightened off potential lenders to promising technology ventures. Even if the government were to encourage banks to take greater risks in loan decisions, small-scale start-ups remain too great a gamble for most banks in their current debt-ridden condition. For these ventures, foreign equity is the most viable source of capital. This accounts for the popularity among new Chinese technology firms of initial public offerings on markets in the United States or on Hong Kong's new Growth Enterprise Market (GEM). But when Minister Wu Jichuan reaffirmed the state's ban on foreign participation in Internet service providers in the fall of 1999, he undercut the fastest growing area of foreign equity capital in China.

Part of the problem for venture finance in China lies in the continued weakness of its capital markets, as well as a lack of legal and property rights guarantees. This is tied to the problem of unreformed corporate governance. But although the concept is new to Chinese financiers, they are clearly learning. In 1993, one finance center in Chengdu invested U.S.$24,920 in a pharmaceutical firm that now has net assets of over U.S.$2 million. San Francisco–based Hambrecht and Quist Group, a major source of Silicon Valley venture capital, launched a China dynamic growth fund in 1995 with total investment of U.S.$41 million and capital commitments of U.S.$85 million. In 1998, W. I. Harper of San Francisco established a U.S.$50 million fund for U.S.-based expatriate Chinese high-tech start-ups to form strategic alliances with partners in China.[6]

The Role of the State

The failure to introduce risk to lending decisions is compounded by continued regulation from above and a top-down approach to technology R&D investment. The larger Chinese system remains endemically non-innovative. From the standpoint of the central state, it is fine for 863 programmers to guarantee that strategic needs do not fall through cracks in the marketplace. But the 863 Plan alone cannot (and does not even seek to) promote long-range technological competitiveness or large-scale technological diffusion across the economy. Alternatives to the government as a basis for innovation must begin to emerge.

Status

The 863 Plan also reflects a continuing—and almost reflexive—fascination with the "latest" technology that ignores the huge gaps continuing to plague China's industrial base. In moments of candor, Chinese technology planners admit this. But such issues are still politicized in China, and although this can help keep politicians engaged with technological problems, it runs the risk of bogging down the system in the worst kind of political-scientific enterprise. As a U.S. biotechnology delegation argued as early as 1989, "Many Americans have been lulled into thinking that China is becoming progressively less ideological and political. In fact, today's idea of 'serving the economy' is no less rigorously pursued than was the idea of 'serving the people'" during the Mao era.[7] The process focus of 863, particularly in automation and computer modeling, is promising in this regard. But such promise can be realized only if better ways of diffusing technology are created within the economy and if bottom-up innovators, not merely 863 contractors, are able to exploit these opportunities.

Industry

Despite incorporating enterprises as contractors, the 863 Plan has few implications for the continuing problem of weak enterprise-level R&D investment. That enterprises, not merely laboratories, receive support under the 863 Plan is a positive development. And as described in Chapter 6, the government has worked assiduously to promote collaboration between research and production units (*lianheti*).[8] But the problem of divided research and production remains: in 1996 only 27 percent of R&D spending in China was done by industrial enterprises, in contrast to the 70 to 80 percent in the United States and other industrialized countries.[9]

The University

University-based innovation faces a variety of external pressures. In the 1950s and 1960s, academic scientists were critical to success in strategic weapons. But the transition from mobilization to the market has decreased official funding of university science and forced academics to go into business. At first glance, this is one of the most favorable trends in China's innovation system. It introduces competition, blends a healthy degree of market incentives into R&D, and compels university laboratories to think beyond socialist-style target setting. But top-quality basic research has suffered. And market pressure has left many university laboratory "spin-offs" producing cheaper versions of technologies that are widely available in the West. This is hardly the Silicon Valley paradigm that Chinese technology planners still dream of introducing into China.

Politics

The 863 program, like the strategic weapons efforts, assumes a committed leadership and some type of political-technical symbiosis. But one wonders whether fiber-optic telecommunications, for example, will have the same "pull" for political leaders plagued by a limited attention span as did nuclear weapons and strategic missiles in decades past. China's leaders are no longer soldiers; they are economic technicians. Yet weapons are profoundly politically appealing while protein-engineered vaccines and high-performance computers seem far less compelling as a basis for political engagement. For political reasons alone, this could direct even many commercial ventures toward systems with direct military significance. The result could be a scuttling of attempts to use the mobilizational powers embedded in programs such as 863 to modernize China's underlying industrial base.

To conceive strategic technology programs so narrowly might well aid a limited range of defense modernization, but it would stymie China's march toward parity with the great industrial powers. This provides a sense of how political pressures force those who set the policy agenda in China to think in terms of trade-offs. It also shows just how integrated commercial and military modernization have become in contemporary China. Clearly, foreign ideas have had a decisive impact on China's shift from weapons planning to more complex types of critical technologies planning; no one should underestimate outsiders' potentially profound influence on thinking in China. Yet neither can observers afford to misconstrue the commitment of China's leaders to redress their country's weakness. As with the strategic weapons effort, the 863 Plan proves once again that this commitment is total.

BREAKING WITH THE PAST

Ultimately, it is the growth of entrepreneurship on a smaller scale that will determine China's future prospects for becoming a leader in high technology. But this requires a clean break with China's historical approach to strategic technology, indigenization, and technology transfer. In 1999–2000, as in 1959–60, China's technology experts continued trying to seize the hen, not simply the egg.

But in a world of networked firms and networked people, Chinese entrepreneurs have forged links abroad that have redefined the meaning of "innovation" in a Chinese context. Small-scale start-ups have sprouted in great numbers. Most are poorly positioned either to absorb technology from abroad or to innovate themselves. Thus, of 1,000 prospective Chinese enterprises, expatriate venture capitalist Bo Feng funded just two—both of them Chinese-language Web portals—while managing U.S.-based equity funds. But some new private firms have extraordinary potential. They are networked to a borderless world that has given them strategic alliances to engineers—many of them expatriate Chinese—in Palo Alto, Sunnyvale, and Redwood Shores, California. They are tied to venture capital from American and Hong Kong investors and can collaborate in technical innovation from the ground up. This is a new development occurring almost entirely outside the state sector, beyond the scope of old-style technology planners and "target-setters." It lies at the very heart of China's new private economy.

Although this new economic system is the best hope for a new industrial style in China, Beijing's industrial bureaucrats may yet seek to regulate it to death. It represents, after all, a nearly complete break with China's past approach to technology planning and innovation. But so long as China looks to history as a model for future policy, it is unlikely to achieve its leaders' dreams of sweeping technological modernization.

THE STRATEGIC WEAPONEERS AND CHINA'S QUEST IN THE TWENTY-FIRST CENTURY

What might this teach us about the historical role of the military in China, and especially about the military's connection to the world of technology as a force for modernization?

Important precedents from history underpin the pervasive role of the Chinese military in national industrialization and technological modernization. Much of China's earliest modernization in the second half of the nineteenth century was driven by military imperatives. And much like the case of strategic weapons in the second half of the twentieth century, military modernization in the last decades of the Chinese empire quickly evolved from being a response to specific external threats into something larger and more encompassing.[10] Like the weapons programs of the 1950s–60s, the Self-Strengthening movement of the Qing dynasty offered alternative institutional and political models, and had powerful implications for China's subsequent political development and institution building.

By the end of the 1870s, defense industrialization and the development of a national technology base for military purposes had begun to offer China's leaders a genuine vision of the country's future course. This belied the narrowly military focus of the ordnance produced at the network of Qing-dynasty arsenals.[11] And as in the strategic weapons system nine decades later, the evolution of the Qing defense industry thus became intertwined with the political maneuverings of leading figures in the ruling elite on behalf of particular visions of a Chinese modernity.

Thomas Kennedy, the leading Western historian of the relationship between military development and technological change during the late Qing, has argued that "the Kiangnan [Jiangnan] Arsenal, China's premier national defense industry, was at the forefront of economic and technological change [in late imperial China] and was involved in the redistribution of governing power" within the dynasty.[12] Li Hongzhang, the Qing statesman and the motive force behind the Jiangnan Arsenal project, saw the arsenals as something greater than merely military industrialization. At the Jiangnan Arsenal, Kennedy writes, "Li confronted directly the technology on which China's survival depended."[13] It "was Li's vision of the development of a machine industry in China together with that of [his fellow statesman Zeng Guofan] that, in the 1860s, brought Kiangnan [Jiangnan] into existence."[14]

Just as China's strategic weapons industry in the second half of the twentieth century exerted an enduring influence on institutions in the PRC, these Qing arsenals had a long-range impact on institution-building in the last decades of imperial rule. Ironically, implementing the "Jiangnan vision" confronted Li and his fellow modernizers with issues that resonate across the century and would also preoccupy Marshal Nie and the strategic weapons community in the PRC. "It is widely acknowledged," Kennedy points out, that Li Hongzhang's "early interest in military industrial modernization led him to advocate the introduction of machine production in nonmilitary sectors of the economy in the late 1870s and 1880s and eventually to call for institutional reforms in education and armed forces organization. The record is clear. . . . Li advocated drastic reform of China's economic and educational institutions in the early 1860s as the vision of Kiangnan [Jiangnan] began to take shape in his mind."[15]

When the Chinese republic began to formulate the first large-scale development plans for Chinese industry in the 1930s, this connection between military industrialization and national goal-setting had become comparatively well institutionalized. "Chinese political leaders," William Kirby has written, "have periodically granted a degree of autonomy to specialists capable of enhancing national defense. The consensus of the 1930s between political and academic figures on the priority of a 'national defense economy' (*guofang jingji*) was particularly important, since it defined the economic priorities of the Guomindang Government and began an institutional process of historical consequence."[16]

Like the Qing arsenals, which arose in response to military humiliation at the hands of foreign powers, the planned, military-related development strategy associated with the Guomindang's National Resources Commission (NRC) during the years of the republic was also driven primarily by a foreign threat, in this case Japan. By skewing development priorities in much of Chinese industry, it ultimately had far-reaching consequences for the overall pattern of industrialization and development policy during the republic. In this respect, at least, the strategic weapons industry in the PRC is heir to a long and eventful history of military influence on development planning and institution building more generally.

In the PRC, the strategic weapons vision became more encompassing than the Qing and Republican precedents in two critical respects. First, it transcended the proximate external threats that seem to have propelled military-oriented development and industrialization throughout the history of modern China. Second, it provided the foundation for a larger pattern of development and institution building that would carry its proponents into national development debates even after objective external threats to the state had passed.

In its essentials, this is the story at the heart of this book. And the history of strategic weapons in Communist China inevitably departed from the Self-Strengthening and NRC precedents of the late Qing and the Republic because of it. As a result of this transformation of the Communist era strategic weapons elite and its vision, strategic weaponeers came to play a broader role in the economy and society than their military industrial predecessors of the Qing and Republican eras could even dream of. To be sure, their forebears struggled with similar issues of science and modern technology. At Jiangnan, Kennedy writes, Qing leaders wondered, "Could machine industry develop employing Chinese resources alone or would periodic transfusions of technology and personnel [from abroad] continue to be required?"[17] This was precisely the issue that preoccupied strategic weapons planners as they fought off opposition, skepticism, and occasionally out-and-out hostility to their core goals in the wake of the Sino-Soviet split.

But the diverse rationales the weaponeers developed to sustain the strategic weapons programs in the face of this opposition—as well as the unique managerial template they promoted as a national model once China's external and political environment began to change in the mid-1970s—gives them the distinction of having exerted a greater influence than any other technical elite in Chinese history.

They were not merely technical innovators, but institutional and organizational innovators. Their leaders ranked among China's greatest scientific pioneers, and also its most successful dispensers of patronage and practitioners of politics in Beijing and within the bureaucracy. Later, some of these men became leaders of the country by virtue of this combination of technical prestige and political connectedness and savvy. Song Jian did not merely have an "expert background" or a technical education. He is among the leading Chinese engineers of the last three decades of the twentieth century.

Above all, the structure of R&D in the Mao era placed the strategic weaponeers in the pivotal position among technology elites to appreciate the significance of global trends, and thus to act upon these when the Deng coalition began to dismantle the Maoist system. On the one hand, the weaponeers were a technology elite forged in military contexts and nurtured and protected by the PLA high command. But at the same time, they were the most experienced and cosmopolitan, possibly the most technically sophisticated, and certainly the best politically connected technology elite in China. This remained true even in 1986, well into the era of reform and readjustment.

These were important social and political traits with broadly systemic implications. The military scientific and engineering elite helped China's leaders, generals, and visionaries come to terms with the implications of technological change. In so doing, they shaped the distinctive process of innovation and change in the China that is emerging onto the international stage today—those aspects that have made China a nuclear power to be reckoned with, as well as the deep structural impediments that continue to hold China back.

Indeed, the role played by these scientists and engineers, and by their PLA patrons, shows just how profound and wide ranging is China's recent transformation. Globalization, common economic and environmental threats, the waning of the Cold War in Asia, and the rise of interdependence have removed the source of China's initial impetus to technological change. Yet the challenge itself remains as powerful as ever.

For the generation of Chinese scientists forged in the 1950s–60s, the drive to redress and overcome China's "backwardness" (*luohou*) was, first and foremost, a response to the threat posed by China's enemies. Three decades after the first thermonuclear test, China's borders are secure, its diplomats work to shape international regimes, and no enemy threatens China's troops or cities with a rain of nuclear ruin. The threats of yesterday have slipped into history. The enemy of today has become backwardness itself.

But backwardness, as Deng Xiaoping once argued, "must be recognized before it can be changed."[18] In Korea, it was China's professional warrior class that first confronted the terrible consequences of more than a century of technological weakness. By responding so forcefully to the challenges of a changed world, the men who inherited their legacy have shown that it is insufficient simply to adapt to change. It is possible, too, to shape and perhaps even alter its course. For China's strategic weapons pioneers—the alumni of the military science programs—and the generation they are now training, the challenge, even without the threats, remains today as it has been since the 1950s: to take up Mao Zedong's rallying cry to "apply the knowledge of the laws [of science] in order to change the world."[19]

APPENDICES

BIOGRAPHIES OF KEY PERSONALITIES

POLITICIANS AND COMMANDERS

BO YIBO 薄一波 (1908–)
China's second-ranking economic planner during the 1950s–60s under Li Fuchun. Minister in charge of the State Economic Commission, minister of finance, and, from 1957, vice premier. Returned to power in 1979, served as a state councillor and was a leading figure in economic restructuring.

CHEN YI 陈毅 (1901–1972)
Vice premier (1954–68), member of the Politburo (1956–68), minister of foreign affairs (1958–68), vice chairman of the Central Military Commission (1966–72). Marshal of the PLA. A strong supporter of strategic weapons priorities; appealed repeatedly to the Politburo to give special attention to weapons research and development.

DENG XIAOPING 邓小平 (1904–1997)
Vice premier (1954–66, 1973–76, 1977–80), member of the Standing Committee of the Politburo (1956–66, 1975–76, 1977–87), general secretary of the CCP Central Committee (1956–66), vice chairman of the CCP Central Committee (1975–76, 1977–82), chief of the general staff (1975–76, 1977–80), deputy director of the Central Special Commission (1977), vice chairman of the Central Military Commission (1975–76, 1977–81), and chairman of the commission (1981–89). Twice purged (1966, 1976) and rehabilitated (1973, 1977). In 1981, assumed China's supreme power with the final say in all Party and state affairs.

HE LONG 贺龙 (1896–1969)
Member of the Politburo (1956–67), vice chairman of the Central Military
Commission (1959–67), in charge of its daily affairs (1962–65), director of the
National Defense Industrial Commission (1959–63), vice premier (1954–67), mem-
ber of the Central Special Commission (1962–67). Marshal of the PLA. A key victim
of the Cultural Revolution, died after much physical and emotional abuse.

LI FUCHUN 李富春 (1900–1975)
China's leading economic administrator during the 1950s–60s. Joined the Politburo
in 1956. Played a major role in negotiating Sino-Soviet industrial cooperation, jour-
neying to Moscow in 1952 to help negotiate the return to Chinese sovereignty of
the Changchun Railway and an extension for the joint use of naval facilities at
Dalian. Later, served as lead negotiator of the agreement to extend Soviet aid to
nearly 150 industrial projects. Appointed chairman of the State Planning Commission and vice premier in 1954, charged with day-to-day management of the Chinese
economy. Served briefly as vice chairman of the central Science and Technology
Leading Group. Member of the Standing Committee of the Politburo of the
Central Committee of the CCP.

LI XIANNIAN 李先念 (1909–1993)
Vice premier (1954–80), minister of finance, member of the Politburo (1956–87)
and of its Standing Committee (1982–87), president of the PRC (1983–88). Assisted
Zhou Enlai in leadership of economic work (1966–76).

LIN BIAO 林彪 (1906–1971)
Vice chairman of the CCP Central Committee (1958–71), vice chairman in charge
of the daily affairs of the Central Military Commission (briefly lost this job to He
Long in 1962, and temporarily retired because of poor health in 1964), minister of
defense (1959–71), and officially designated successor to Mao Zedong. Marshal of
the PLA. Died while fleeing the country in 1971. Posthumously accused of plotting
to assassinate Mao Zedong and seize supreme state power.

LIU BOCHENG 刘伯承 (1892–1986)
President of the PLA Military Academy, vice chairman of the Central Military
Commission, and marshal of the PLA. Delivered important lectures on strategy
and tactics at the academy that stressed modernization and influenced a generation
of PLA officers.

LUO RUIQING 罗瑞卿 (1906–1978)
Chief of the general staff and secretary general of the Central Military Commission
(1959–66), director of the National Defense Industries Office (1961–66), member
of the Central Secretariat, director of the General Office in charge of the daily affairs of the Central Special Commission, and member of the commission. Was in
charge of coordinating research with production in the development of weapons

and equipment. A key victim of the Cultural Revolution, was officially removed from all offices in 1966. Senior general of the PLA.

MAO ZEDONG 毛泽东 (1893–1976)
Chairman of the CCP Central Committee and Central Military Commission. Until his death, was the supreme state and Party authority and had final say in all strategic weapons and high-priority technology decisions.

NIE RONGZHEN 聂荣臻 (1899–1992)
Director of National Defense Science and Technology Commission (1958–74) and of the State Science and Technology Commission, vice premier in charge of science and technology, director of the Central Science and Technology Leading Group, director of the Aviation Industrial Commission, member of the Central Special Commission, vice chairman of the Central Military Commission (1959–87), and acting chief of the general staff (1950–51). Marshal of the PLA. After 1958, headed the overall scientific component of the strategic weapons programs. Recruited most other top administrators in the strategic weapons programs. Nie is widely considered the founding father of China's programs in strategic weapons and strategic technology.

PENG DEHUAI 彭德怀 (1898–1974)
Commander of Chinese forces in the Korean War, vice chairman of the Central Military Commission in charge of its daily affairs, vice premier, and minister of defense. Marshal of the PLA. Criticized the Great Leap Forward at the CCP's 1959 Lushan Plenum, was accused by Mao Zedong of leading a counterrevolutionary clique. Stripped of most offices, he died in disgrace.

YE JIANYING 叶剑英 (1897–1986)
Chairman of the Guangdong provincial government and mayor of Guangzhou, president of the Academy of Military Sciences, and marshal of the PLA. Took over leadership of the Central Military Commission in 1971, serving as its vice chairman and general secretary and chairman of its Administrative Meeting. Defense minister and member of the Central Special Commission. Member of the Standing Committee of the Politburo. Played a crucial role in the reestablishment of Sino-American relations and, after the death of Mao Zedong, in the arrest of the Gang of Four and their radical supporters.

ZHOU ENLAI 周恩来 (1898–1976)
Member of the Politburo (1949–76), premier (1949–76), minister of foreign affairs (1949–57), member of the Standing Committee of the Politburo (1956–76), director of the Central Special Commission (1962–76). Participated in decision to develop strategic weapons in the mid-1950s and later, as commission director, had principal responsibility for implementing weapons policies and coordinating all strategic weapons organizations.

GENERALS AND BUREAUCRATS

CHEN GENG 陈庚 (1903–1961)
Deputy commander of Chinese forces in Korea, president of the Harbin College of Military Engineering, deputy chief of the PLA general staff, and deputy director of the National Defense Science and Technology Commission. Senior general of the PLA.

CHEN YOUMING 陈右铭 (1922–)
Director of the Project 09 (nuclear submarine) Office, director of Institute 701 of the Seventh Academy (warship design), deputy director of the academy, director of the Project 718 (instrumentation fleet) Office, and head of the navy's Naval Equipment and Technology Department.

DING HENGGAO 丁衡高 (1931–)
Assistant research fellow, Institute of Optics and Precision Mechanics, Chinese Academy of Sciences (1952–56); received candidate degree from Leningrad Institute of Precision Machinery and Optical Instruments in 1961. Deputy director of Institute 13 of the First Academy (general configuration and rocket engines) of the Seventh Ministry of Machine Building (missiles and space), deputy director of the Science and Technology Department of the Commission of Science, Technology, and Industry for National Defense, minister of the commission (1985–96), director of the General Office of the Central Special Commission in charge of daily affairs (1989–96), member of the 863 Plan Leading Group, and during 1996, a member of the new Science and Technology Leading Group of the State Council. An expert on optical and precision mechanics, helped to build the SLBM's inertial guidance platform. Son-in-law of Marshal Nie Rongzhen, husband of Nie Li.

GAN ZIYU 甘子玉 (1929–)
Vice minister of the State Planning Commission (1978–), with special responsibility for science and technology as well as import-export administration. Head of the defense conversion leading group under the State Council and board chairman of the China Association for the Peaceful Use of Military Industrial Technology. An electrical engineer, served as engineer and division chief in the First Ministry of Machine Building (civilian-oriented machinery) (1952–56), secretary in the office of Marshal Nie Rongzhen at the State Science and Technology Commission (1956–58), and secretary to Marshal Nie. After leaving Nie's service for civilian work, served as deputy chief of a planning group at the State Planning Commission (1975). Later, was deputy director of the General Office of the leading group on import-export administration of the State Council.

HONG XUEZHI 洪学智 (1913–)
Director of the General Logistics Department of the PLA, director of the National Defense Industries Office, and deputy secretary general of the Central Military

Commission. Commander of Chinese logistics headquarters in the Korean War, Hong was one of the founding fathers of the modern PLA logistics system. General of the PLA.

LIU HUAQING 刘华清 (1916–)
Director of the navy's Seventh Academy (warship design) (1961–65), vice minister of the Sixth Ministry of Machine Building (shipbuilding), deputy director of the National Defense Science and Technology Commission, and deputy chief of the general staff. Later, commander of the navy (1982–88), deputy secretary-general of the Central Military Commission, deputy director of the Central Military Commission, and vice chairman of the commission in charge of its daily affairs. Member of the Standing Committee of the Politburo of the Fourteenth Central Committee of the CCP.

LIU JIE 刘杰 (dates unknown)
A pre-1949 commissar under Nie Rongzhen, was recruited into military industry by Nie and played a critical role in the atomic and hydrogen bomb programs from their inception in the mid-1950s until the onset of the Cultural Revolution in 1966. Vice minister and later minister (1960–66) of the Second Ministry of Machine Building (nuclear industry), he oversaw the daily operations of both programs throughout this period. Also a member of the Central Special Commission.

LIU YALOU 刘亚楼 (1911–1965)
Commander of the PLA air force, deputy director of the National Defense Science and Technology Commission, member of the Aviation Industrial Commission, deputy director of the Fifth Academy, and deputy minister of defense. A leader in early aviation construction. General of the PLA.

LUO SHUNCHU 罗舜初 (1914–1981)
Chief of staff and second deputy commander of the PLA navy, director of the Tenth Academy (radio electronics) of the defense ministry, deputy director of the National Defense Science and Technology Commission, deputy director of the National Defense Industries Office, and deputy commander of the Shenyang Military Region. Pioneer in the development of the navy's technical education and R&D system.

SU YU 粟裕 (1907–1984)
Deputy chief and then chief of the general staff, deputy minister of defense, vice president and first political commissar of the Academy of Military Sciences, and member of the Central Military Commission. Su Yu was placed in charge of military control teams in the defense industry during the Cultural Revolution. A leading voice for the modernization of the PLA.

WANG ZHENG 王净 (1909–1978)
Director of the telecommunications division of the Central Military Commission, vice minister of the Ministry of Posts and Telecommunications, deputy director of

the Fifth Academy (missiles and space) of the defense ministry, minister of the Fourth Ministry of Machine Building (electronics), and deputy chief of the general staff. General of the PLA. Pioneering administrator of China's electronics and telecommunications industries.

XIAO JINGGUANG 肖劲光 (1903–1989)
Commander of the PLA navy, deputy minister of defense, and member of the Central Military Commission. A leading figure in the modernization of the navy, battled Li Zuopeng for control of the navy shortly before the Cultural Revolution. Senior general of the PLA.

ZHANG AIPING 张爱萍 (1910–)
Deputy chief of the general staff, deputy director and then director of the National Defense Science and Technology Commission, deputy director of the National Defense Industries Office, member of the Central Special Commission, director of the Science and Technology Equipment Committee of the Central Military Commission, and director of the General Office of the Central Special Commission in charge of its daily affairs. Minister of defense (1982–88). Director of the first atomic bomb test committee, and commander of the first atomic bomb test on-site headquarters. Oversaw all strategic organs involved in nuclear-powered submarine and missile work (1975–82). General of the PLA.

ZHAO ERLU 赵尔陆 (1905–1967)
The first PRC minister in charge of military industry, deputy director of the National Defense Industrial Commission under He Long, and executive vice chairman of the National Defense Industries Office. General of the PLA.

ZOU JIAHUA 邹家华 (1926–)
Vice premier, member of the Politburo, director of the State Planning Commission, state councillor, director of the State Council information industry leading group, director of the State Council telecommunications industry leading group, member of the 863 Plan Leading Group, minister of machine building and electronics, deputy director of the National Defense Science and Technology Commission (1982), deputy director of the National Defense Industries Office (1978–82), and minister of the Fifth Ministry of Machine Building (ordnance).

SCIENTISTS AND ENGINEERS

CHEN FANGYUN 陈芳允 (1916–)
Specialist in radioelectronics, graduate of the Department of Physics of Qinghua University, and worked in the research division of the Cossor Radio Factory in Great Britain (1945–48). Vice chairman of the Department of Technological Sciences of

the Chinese Academy of Sciences. Coauthor of the ground observation plan of the Dongfanghong satellite and chief designer of consolidated microwave measurement and control systems for satellite launch. Key contributor to the development of most measurement and control networks for Chinese satellites. Presided over the compilation of China's official satellite measurement technical handbook. One of the four scientists to propose the 863 Plan to Deng Xiaoping.

CI YUNGUI 慈云桂 (1917–1990)
Advisor to the Science and Technology Committee of the Commission of Science, Technology, and Industry for National Defense, member of the Department of Technological Sciences of the Chinese Academy of Sciences, and vice president of the National Defense Science and Technology University. Computer scientist and engineer, pioneered China's main supercomputer project, the Yinhe, and was chief designer of the project. Played a major role in introducing high-level computing to China for military and scientific purposes.

HUANG WEILU 黄纬禄 (1916–)
Director of Institute 12 of the First Academy (general configuration and rocket engines) of the Seventh Ministry of Machine Building (missiles and space). Later, deputy director of the ministry's Science and Technology Committee. Chief designer of the SLBM.

HUANG XUHUA 黄旭华 (1926–)
Deputy director and then director of Institute 719 of the Seventh Academy (warship design) of the Sixth Ministry of Machine Building (shipbuilding). As chief designer of the SSBN, was in charge of its comprehensive designs and made great contributions to China's first and second generations of nuclear-powered submarines.

LI XU'E 李绪鄂 (1928–)
Graduated from Qinghua University in aerospace engineering in 1952. Deputy chief designer of China's SLBM. Served under the principal deputy chief designer Song Jian, who would later be his superior at the State Science and Technology Commission. Worked in the miniaturization of warheads and related changes to missile configuration, as part of the modernization of China's strategic missile force. Deputy director of Institute 14 (warheads) of the First Academy (general configuration) of the Fifth Academy (missiles and space) (1962–71). Later director of the institute and director of the First Academy (1971–80). Vice minister and chief engineer of the Seventh Ministry of Machine Building (missiles and space), 1982–84. From 1988, deputy director of the State Science and Technology Commission and vice chairman of the commission's Standing Committee. Won a state prize in 1985 for his contributions to missile development. Played an important role at the SSTC in administering technology plans parallel to the 863 Plan, such as the Torch Plan.

LIANG SHOUPAN 梁守磐 (1916–)

Leading missile scientist; M.S. in aeronautical engineering from MIT in 1939. Onetime dean and chairman of the Department of Aeronautical Engineering at Zhejiang University, also taught at the Harbin College of Military Engineering. Chief designer of coastal defense antiship cruise missiles, and a major contributor to other missile programs. Leader of the Third (Sub-) Academy (coastal defense antiship cruise missiles) of the Seventh Ministry of Machine Building (missiles and space) and, in the start-up years of the missile programs, a leading figure in the Fifth Academy (missiles and space). Director of the rocket engines research section, and then director of the comprehensive design section, of the Fifth Academy. After 1982, was deputy director of the Science and Technology Committee of the Ministry of the Space Industry (former Seventh Ministry), and in 1990, became senior advisor to the ministry's successor organization.

LUO PEILIN 罗沛霖 (1913–)

Dormmate of Qian Xuesen at Shanghai's Jiaotong University, returned to China from Caltech in 1950, and emerged as one of China's leading electronics specialists. Technical advisor to Nie Rongzhen during the drafting in 1956 of the Twelve-Year Program for Science and Technology Development. Later, director of the telecommunication bureau of the Second Ministry of Machine Building (nuclear industry). Led national radar development (1958–66), and was director of the Science and Technology section of the Fourth Ministry of Machine Building (electronics) under Wang Zheng. During the 1970s, worked in computing. Joined Wang Daheng and Shi Changxu in the second 863 Plan proposal in 1992.

NIE LI 聂力 (1930–)

Graduated from Leningrad Institute of Precision Machinery and Optical Instruments in 1960. Leader of an engineering group in the Fifth Academy (missiles and space) of the defense ministry (1964–65), research section chief in the Seventh Ministry of Machine Building (missiles and space) (1965), deputy bureau director of the National Defense Science and Technology Commission (1978–82), deputy director of the Commission of Science, Technology, and Industry for National Defense (1982–85). Deputy director and secretary general of the commission's Science and Technology Committee (1985–92). Director of the electronics group of the commission, in charge of all military electronics work as well as coordination between military and civilian electronics projects. Played a crucial role in the administration of the Yinhe supercomputer project, in the coordination and building of the Yuanwang ("Distant Observer") survey instrumentation fleet, and in the launching of submarine-based missiles. One of China's few female generals, holds the rank of lieutenant general. Daughter of Marshal Nie Rongzhen, wife of Ding Henggao.

PENG SHILU 彭士禄 (1925–)

Acting director of Institute 715 of the navy's Seventh Academy (warship design), and later director of Institute 15 (successor to Institute 715) of the First Academy (reactor engineering) of the Second Ministry of Machine Building (nuclear industry), and vice minister of the Sixth Ministry of Machine Building (shipbuilding). As deputy chief designer of the SSBN, he contributed to the design of the its nuclear power plant.

QIAN SANQIANG 钱三强 (1913–)

Nuclear physicist with a French doctorate. Worked under Irene Joliot at the Nuclear Chemistry Laboratory of the French Academy, and under Frederic Curie at the Pierre Curie Laboratory of the Sorbonne's Radium Institute. Won the Parville Prize in physics from the French Academy (1946). With his wife, He Zehui, discovered tripartition and quarternary fission of uranium (1946–47). Returned to China in 1948 and played a key role in founding the Chinese Academy of Sciences and the Institute of Atomic Energy. Oversaw the scientific component of the atomic bomb project as the main technical administrator in Beijing. Qian became a key leader of the Second Ministry of Machine Building (nuclear industry), serving as its vice minister. Also served as deputy secretary-general of the CAS, and president of Zhejiang University.

QIAN XUESEN 钱学森 (1911–)

Rocket specialist considered to be the spiritual father of Chinese rocket development. Received Ph.D. in aerospace engineering from Caltech where he studied with Theodore von Kármán. Goddard Professor at Caltech, founding member of Caltech's Jet Propulsion Laboratory, and codeveloper of the Qian (Tsien)–Kármán formula for aerodynamic high subsonic aircraft design. U.S. army colonel, and member of U.S. missile survey team in Germany after World War II. Expelled from the United States in 1955, served as director of the Fifth Academy (missiles and space) of the defense ministry, vice minister of its successor, the Seventh Ministry of Machine Building (missiles and space), director of initial satellite and missile project leading groups, deputy director and senior adviser to the National Defense Science and Technology Commission, and deputy director of the Science and Technology Committee of the Commission of Science, Technology, and Industry for National Defense. Played a major role in missile administration and was a key advocate of missiles in the "missile-versus-bomber" debates of the 1950s–60s.

REN XINMIN 任新民 (1915–)

Chief designer of liquid propellant rocket engines, chief engineer of communication satellite programs, and a major contributor to most Chinese strategic missile programs. Received a Ph.D. from the University of Michigan and returned to China in 1949. Joined the Military Science Section of the Nanjing Military Region command within one month of his return. Joined the Fifth Academy (missiles) in 1956. Later was vice minister of its successor, the Seventh Ministry of Machine Building (missiles and space), and director of its Science and Technology Committee. Attended the April 1956 "missiles-versus-bombers" meeting with Qian Xuesen.

SHI CHANGXU 师昌绪 (dates unknown)

Aircraft engine designer and metallurgical scientist, joined Wang Daheng in the second 863 Plan proposal of 1992. As chairman of the Department of Technological Sciences of the Chinese Academy of Sciences, his support for the program ensured a continuing bureaucratic foundation in the academy. Task force leader on engine blades for the J-8 fighter plane. Won a state prize for his development of metal alloys for turbine discs, blades, and the combustion chamber of interceptor aircraft. Also pioneered development of specialized metals for Chinese military turboprop aircraft.

SONG JIAN 宋健 (1931–)

Deputy chief designer of the SLBM. Deputy director of the Second Academy (inertial guidance systems) of the Seventh Ministry of Machine Building (missiles and space) (1978–80), vice minister and chief engineer of the ministry (1981–82), vice minister of the ministry's successor, the Ministry of the Astronautics Industry (1982–84), and later director of the State Science and Technology Commission (1984–98), with the rank of vice premier, and state councillor. Chairman of the 863 Plan Leading Group. After March 1996, member of the Science and Technology Leading Group of the State Council. Lifetime Visiting Professor, Washington University, St. Louis.

TU SHOU'E 屠守锷 (dates unknown)

Chief designer of China's ICBM. Graduated from Qinghua University in 1940 and received his M.S. in aeronautical engineering from MIT. Worked at Curtis Aircraft in Buffalo (1943–45). Later served as a professor at Qinghua University, with a concurrent appointment at the Beijing Aeronautical Institute. Chief engineer of the Ministry of the Space Industry (the former Seventh Ministry of Machine Building) and director of its Science and Technology Committee. A deputy director of the Fifth Academy, also headed the academy's Department of Design.

WANG DAHENG 王大衡 (1915–)

Student in England during the 1940s, widely considered to be China's leading precision optics specialist. Director of the Changchun Optics and Precision Mechanics Institute under the Chinese Academy of Sciences, and chief engineer of Project 150 (missile telemetry, tracking, and control), key contributor to Project 160 (IRBM telemetry, tracking, and control). Nominal leader of the group of four scientists who proposed the 863 Plan to Deng Xiaoping. Played a major role in the 863 Plan's initial years, and was a member of the second group of scientists who proposed an expansion of the plan in 1992.

WANG GANCHANG 王淦昌 (1907–)

Nuclear physicist; Ph.D. from the University of Berlin. Deputy director, Joint Institute for Nuclear Research, Dubna, USSR (1956–60), deputy director of the Ninth Academy (1961–78), vice minister of the Second Ministry of Machine

Building (nuclear industry), and president of the Institute of Atomic Energy. Was in overall charge of developing and testing the explosive assembly and initiator for the atomic bomb. One of four scientists to propose the 863 Plan to Deng Xiaoping. Played a crucial role in the first years of the plan.

WANG SHIGUANG 王士光 (dates unknown)
Electronics pioneer. During the mid-1950s was a member of the Aviation Industrial Commission under Marshal Nie Rongzhen. Later, vice minister of the Fourth Ministry of Machine Building (electronics), chief engineer and chairman of the Science and Technology Committee of its successor, the Ministry of the Electronics Industry, and deputy chairman of the Advisory Committee to that ministry's successor, the Ministry of the Machine Building and Electronics Industries.

YANG JIACHI 杨嘉墀 (1920–)
Specialist in space technology; Ph.D. in electrical engineering from Harvard University. Returned to China in 1956. Under the Seventh Ministry of Machine Building (missiles and space), codesigned three-axis attitude control system for earth-observing satellites. Vice chairman of the Science and Technology Committee of the Chinese Academy of Space Technology, vice chairman of the China Automation Society, vice chairman of the China Instrumentation Society, and vice chairman of the Executive Bureau of the International Astronautical Federation. One of the four scientists to propose the 863 Plan to Deng Xiaoping.

ZHAO RENKAI 赵仁凯 (1923–)
Chief engineer of Institute 194 of the Second Ministry of Machine Building (nuclear industry), and later deputy director of Institute 15 of the ministry's First Academy (reactor engineering). As deputy chief designer of Project 09, the nuclear-powered ballistic missile submarine, played a key role in the development of the submarine's nuclear power plant.

ZHOU GUANGZHAO 周光召 (1929–)
President of the Chinese Academy of Sciences (1987–97), director of the Ninth Academy (nuclear weapons) of the Second Ministry of Machine Building (nuclear industry), director of the Institute of Theoretical Physics of the Chinese Academy of Sciences, and researcher at the Joint Institute for Nuclear Research, Dubna, USSR (1957–60). Performed theoretical design check for China's first atomic and hydrogen bombs.

ZHU GUANGYA 朱光亚 (1924–)
Nuclear physicist; Ph.D. from the University of Michigan. After transfer to the Ninth Academy, was assigned to supervise the organization of scientific research on the atomic bomb and later served as academy deputy director. Also served as deputy director of the National Defense Science and Technology Commission (1970–82), director of the Science and Technology Committee of the

Commission of Science, Technology, and Industry for National Defense (1985–), and president of the Chinese Academy of Engineering. From March 1996, served on the State Council Science and Technology Leading Group.

ZHU LILAN 朱丽兰 (1935–)
Civilian chemist, specializing in high polymer materials. Studied at Odessa University in the USSR and, while affiliated with the CAS, went to Germany as a visiting scholar at the High Polymer Chemistry Institute (1979–80). Spent twenty-five years as an associate research fellow and director of the Beijing Chemical Institute of the CAS (1961–86). In 1987, became executive vice minister of the State Science and Technology Commission, with daily responsibility for overseeing the 863 Plan, the Torch Plan, and other state guidance plans for science and technology. In 1998, when the SSTC was reorganized as the Ministry of Science and Technology, was appointed the first minister of the new ministry, serving until 2001.

HISTORICAL CODE NAMES OF MAJOR BUREAUCRATIC STRUCTURES IN CHINESE MILITARY INDUSTRY

This appendix is intended as a reference for readers confused by the use of code designations in the text of this study.

For details on code-named plants and institutes, see Lewis and Xue (1988a, 1994).

The main research academies were attached to relevant ministries in 1964 as part of Luo Ruiqing's effort to integrate research with production. These organizations were frequently absorbed into one another. Thus the Fifth Academy was one of three components merged into the Seventh Ministry of Machine Building when it was created as a new ministry of the State Council in 1965.

Code designations were often revised, as in the redesignation of the original nuclear ministry (called the Third Ministry, under Song Renqiong) as the Second Ministry of Machine Building. In 1982, these code-numbered ministries were redesignated with function-specific names. For example, the Seventh Ministry of Machine Building was redesignated the Ministry of the Space Industry, and the Third Ministry as the Ministry of the Aviation Industry.

Further consolidation took place in 1988 as some ministries were merged and others downgraded from constituent parts of the State Council and reorganized as state corporations, a process that has since continued, and led, for instance, to the merger of the Aviation and Space Ministries into a new Ministry of the Aerospace Industry, and to the redesignation of the former Second Ministry as the China National Nuclear Corporation. Later the Aerospace Ministry was corporatized and—again—subdivided into Aviation and Space Industry Corporations.

MINISTRY-LEVEL ADMINISTRATIVE STRUCTURES

First Ministry of Machine Building	Civilian Machinery[1]
Second Ministry of Machine Building	Nuclear Industry
Third Ministry of Machine Building	Aircraft Industry
Fourth Ministry of Machine Building	Electronics Industry
Fifth Ministry of Machine Building	Ordnance Industry
Sixth Ministry of Machine Building	Shipbuilding Industry
Seventh Ministry of Machine Building	Missiles and Space Industry
Eighth Ministry of Machine Building	Tactical Missiles[2]

SOME IMPORTANT R&D ACADEMIES

First (nuclear) Academy (Jiajiang, Sichuan) — Nuclear Reactor Engineering
  aka Southwest Reactor Research and Design Academy

Second (nuclear) Academy (Beijing) — Nuclear Weapons Design
  aka Beijing Nuclear Engineering Research and Design Academy

Third Academy (Tianjin) — Physical and Chemical Engineering
  aka Tianjin Physical and Engineering Academy

Fifth (missiles and space) Academy (Beijing) — Missiles and Jet Propulsion

  First (Sub-) Academy — General Configuration and Warheads

  Second (Sub-) Academy — Inertial Guidance Systems

  Third (Sub-) Academy — Antiship Cruise Missiles

  Fourth Academy[3] — Solid Rocket Propellants and Engines

Seventh (shipbuilding) Academy (Beijing) — Warship Design
  aka Warship Research and Design Academy

Ninth (nuclear) Academy   Nuclear Weapons Design
(Haiyan, Qinghai; Mianyang,
Sichuan)
aka Northwest Nuclear Weapons Research
and Design Academy (old name)
aka Chinese Academy of Engineering
Physics (new name)

Tenth (radioelectronics) Academy   Telemetry and Radio Electronics

585th (nuclear) Institute (Leshan, Sichuan)   Thermonuclear Experiments
aka Southwest Institute of Physics

728th (nuclear) Academy (Shanghai)   Nuclear Power Plants
aka Shanghai Reactor Engineering
Research and Design Academy

Eighth (nuclear) Institute (Shanghai)   Nuclear Materials

Ninth (nuclear) Institute (Beijing)   Nuclear Weapons
aka Beijing Institute of Applied Physics
and Computational Mathematics

Institute (nuclear) 21   Nuclear Technologies
(Malan and Xi'an, Shaanxi)
aka Northwest Nuclear Technology Institute

SOME WEAPONS TEST BASES

Base 20 (Shuangchengzi, Gansu)   Missile Test Base

Base 21 (Lop Nur, Xinjiang)   Nuclear Weapons Test Base

HIGHLIGHTS OF THE 863 PLAN

MAIN OBJECTIVES[1]

1. "Monitor the latest international high-tech developments, pursue innovation, narrow gaps between Chinese and foreign technologies, strive for breakthroughs in areas where China is strong."

2. "Train and cultivate a new-generation high-level S&T workforce in key disciplines connected to high technology industry."

3. "Commercialize and industrialize achievements in various phases of the plan so as to serve the reconstruction of traditional industries, lay a foundation for the formation of a new high-tech industry, economic development, and state security for around the year 2000."

4. "Play a leading role in the promotion of national high technology development, to create opportunities for China to form its own high technology base by the year 2000, and to prepare back-up support for the stable and continuous improvement of the national economy."

AUTOMATION TECHNOLOGY MANAGERIAL GROUP[2]

Staff Office: SSTC (after 1998, MOST) Headquarters

I. Computer Integrated Manufacturing Systems (CIMS) Expert Group

Administers the National CIMS Experimental Engineering
   Research Center.
Tracks developments in CIMS technology overseas.

Computer-aided design (CAD) and computer-aided manufacture
   (CAM) techniques.
Demonstration production lines for new-generation techniques for
   producing highly specialized high-quality, small-quantity, products. Runs extensive computer-aided exercises (CAX).

Targets and Objectives Have Included:

"Three categories of research: GH-CAD planar products developed by the
Beijing Gaohua Computer Co., Ltd; a GS-ICCC system jointly developed by
the Research Institute for Artificial Intelligence of Zhejiang University and the
CAD/CAM Center of the Ministry of the Space Industry; and other systems."

1. "Gaohua's CAD system consists of planar computer aided graph-making,
   together with designing functions and three dimensional geometric mould
   making. It has been widely applied in over ten industries in China, such as
   machinery, construction, textiles, automobiles, light industry etc. The
   system offers not only multiple and convenient graph-making functions
   to customers, but also is an open access system that makes standard DXF,
   IGES interfaces available to customers . . . Gaohua CAD had 300 customers in 2001, and the total number of installed CAD systems had
   surpassed 10,000 sets."
2. "GS-ICCC is set up under the universal UNIX system, and on the
   X-WINDOW/Motif platform. It can run on a variety of engineering
   workstations. The main functions of the system involve such phases as
   product design, technique planning, processing manufacturing, and
   engineering data management. GS-ICCC is international leading-edge
   technology in the following fields: feature design, based on parameters
   aimed at engineering, observing STEP standards; product data modeling
   aimed at integrated systems, centering on a customer's engineering
   database and an information integrated environment on the basis of STEP.
   Around 100 sets of the product had been sold to over 20 enterprises in
   China by 2001."
3. The 863-sponsored "Honeysuckle System has met the requirements of
   STEP standards and data sharing. Its goal is to design and manufacture
   machine products. The system's advanced functions come from three-
   dimensional substance modeling, feature design based on parameters,
   technique planning, and self-creating multi-coordinate and data control.
   All of these functions can be realized on workstations. By 2001, more than
   200 sales contracts had been sold for this system."

Concurrent engineering focused on the design and development of products
for China's space program, including Project 921.

1. "The key technology problems [in this field] were jointly tackled by
   Qinghua University, Institute 23 of the Changfeng Group, the Beijing

University of Aeronautics and Astronautics, the Central China Polytechnic University, and Jiaotong University. This was the first time that relevant technologies were systematically researched in China, and integral methods and technologies of concurrent engineering were developed. [The goals were to] reform the process of developing products, arrange groups of people to focus [collaboratively] on developing integrated products, and to realize the all-digital definition of relevant products. [The work of this group included] decision-making support based on QFD, concurrent design based on the PDM system, CAX/DFX integration based on STEP standards, and DFA/DFM-based design targeted at manufacturing and assembly." In December, 1997, this project was appraised by a group of experts designated jointly by the SSTC and the Ministry of Education. "The experts confirmed that the integral and partial key technologies had achieved advanced levels of world standard."

II. Intelligent Robotics Expert Group

Administers the National Research and Development Center
   for Intelligent Robotics.
Intelligent robots for precision assembly functions, especially
   in underwater or bioharzardous locales.

Targets and Objectives Have Included:

1. Underwater robot capable of operating at depths of 6,000 meters.

BIOTECHNOLOGY MANAGERIAL GROUP

Staff Office: SSTC (after 1998, MOST) Headquarters

I. Foodstuffs Expert Group

High-yield, high-quality animals and plant varieties.
Increases in grain, meat, fish, and milk yields.
Administers the National Research Center on Biological Products.

Targets and Objectives Have Included:

1. Create by the year 2000 a new hybrid double-harvest rice with a yield
    of over 15 tons per hectare.
2. Cultivate new varieties of high-protein wheat.
3. Develop disease and pest-resistant high-protein vegetables.
4. Develop drought-proof, saline/alkali-resistant high-protein pasture.
5. Increase the capability of corn, beans, and vegetables for symbiosis and
    joint azofication so as to decrease the amount of fertilizer required.

6. Create new varieties of disease and cold-resistant fish.
7. Master techniques for increasing the birth-rate of dairy cattle.

II. Medicine Expert Group

New medicines, vaccines, and genetic cures.
Administers the National Research Center on Genetically
 Engineered Vaccines.
Administers the National Research Center on Genetically
 Engineered Pharmaceuticals.

Targets and Objectives Have Included:

1. Develop new medicines and vaccines for preventing serious diseases that currently cannot be controlled effectively.
2. Develop new medicines and bioengineered products to combat cancers, cardiovascular disease, and major infectious diseases in humans and animals.
3. Develop techniques and uses for bioreactive engineering, and product separation and purification engineering.
4. Study the genetic diagnosis and treatment of hereditary diseases and cancers.

III. Protein Engineering Expert Group

Protein engineering techniques for use in the medical, chemical, foodstuff, and agricultural industries.

ENERGY MANAGERIAL GROUP

Staff Office: SSTC (after 1998, MOST) Headquarters

I. Coal Magnetic Technology Expert Group

Coal magnetic fluid power-generation technology to increase energy efficiency and preserve coal resources.
Finding cleaner ways of using the medium-grade and high-sulfur coal common to China.
Coal-powered transportation.

II. Nuclear Reactors Expert Group

Fast neutron breeder reactors.
High-temperature gas-cooled reactors.
Fission/fusion reactors based on existing technology to increase the fuel production ratio.

INFORMATION TECHNOLOGY MANAGERIAL GROUP[3]

Staff Office: SSTC (after 1998, MOST) Headquarters

I. Optical Electronics and System Integration Technology Expert Group

Optoelectronic devices and system integration technology for fiber-optic communication.
High-speed optical fiber applications.
Optical computing applications.
Optical sensing applications.
Administers the National Research Center for Optical Technology.

Targets and Objectives Have Included:

1. "Key optoelectronic devices and sub-system technologies for high capacity and high-speed fiber communication and advanced photonic switching systems," including "semiconductor laser diodes, photodetectors, optical amplifiers, optical modulators, optical isolators, optical switching matrices, optical frequency/wavelength multiplexing technologies, and photonic switching technologies."
2. "Optical interconnection and optical computing technologies," including "conceptual research, R&D of associative optoelectronic devices, module matrices, and non-linear materials."
3. "Optoelectronic integrated circuits (OEIC) and photonic integrated circuits (PIC) technologies," including "commercialized optical terminals using hybrid integrated circuitry, monolithic integrated optical transmitters/receivers, and application-specific PICs."
4. "Novell optoelectronic components and processing techniques," including "various quantum well/superlattice optoelectronic devices, symmetric self-electro-optical effect devices (S-SEED), vertical cavity surface emitting lasers (VCSEL), quantum line and quantum box materials and devices."
5. "Application-specific optoelectronic and system technologies."

II. Artificial Intelligence and Intelligent Computing Expert Group

Computer architecture.
Artificial intelligence technology in software engineering.
Intelligent interfaces.
Intelligent application systems.
Basic research.
Administers the National Center for Intelligent Computing (NCIC).

Targets and Objectives Have Included:

1. "Build several prototypes of intelligent computing systems in which the latest developments of high-performance computers will be fully utilized." Special focus on "areas of parallel computation, knowledge revision, integration of analog and digital processing and perception mechanisms."
2. "Build advanced intelligent computing systems scalable to MPP. These types of systems will be of high-speed and visualized computing capability, able to access and analyze huge amounts of complex information, be efficient and flexible in reasoning and learning, and able to interact with human users harmoniously via speech, text, image, and graphics interfaces. They can also be used in intelligent visualized computation, management information processing, information administration, information analysis and services, and so on. These systems will be distributed throughout China."
3. "Develop a number of intelligent application systems with economic benefits and a positive impact on society." To be achieved via "technology transfer and model systems distribution in High-Tech Zones" and the establishment of "high tech computer enterprises" within these zones.
4. In addition to R&D, "training programs for computer professionals" in the latest techniques.

III. Information Acquisition, Processing, and Automation Technology Expert Group

Earth-observation imagery.
Applications of information technology to space research.

Targets and Objectives Have Included:

1. "Technology for optoelectronic detection in high-resolution, three dimensional imaging."
2. "Corresponding technology for super high speed and real-time signal processing."
3. PtSi infrared focal-plane devices, as well as small InSb and HgCdTe array devices.
4. A "system integration laboratory for processing super high speed and real-time signals."
5. Super-high-speed microchips (FFT and DBF).

IV. Telecommunications Expert Group

(A) BIP-ISDN Networking Technology (B-ISDN System Engineering) Expert Group

"Broadband Intelligent and Personalized Integrated Services Digital Network (BIP-ISDN) concepts and corresponding architecture."

"Conceptual design of BIP-ISDN."
"System trials for BIP-ISDN."

(B) Fiber Optics Expert Group

"2.4 Gb/s optic fiber communications system technology."
"High Bit Rate Optical Fiber Amplifier and Wavelength Division
  Multiplex (WDM) technology."
"Technologies for Optical Frequency Division Multiplex (FDM)
  communication and coherent optic fiber communication."
"Antenna television (CATV) optical transmission technology" with a
  focus on its market potential.

(C) Communications Network and Switching Technology Expert Group

"Research and implementation of an experimental model of a
  single-node ATM switch with capacity no less than 8 × 8 input-
  output (I/O) ports and 155 megabit (Mb/s) data rate at
  each port."
"Applications [of this switch] in the current communications
  network."
Formulate a strategy and standards "for the development of an
  intelligent network in China."
"Implement five kinds of in-services in accordance with Consultative
  Committee on International Telegraphs and Telephones CS-1
  standards, based on the current network."

(D) Multimedia Expert Group

"Multimedia communication terminals and systems based on Public
  Switched Telephone Network (PSTN) and 64 kilobit (Kb/s)
  ISDN, and other projects."

(E) Personal Communications Networks Expert Group

"Research and implementation of the experimental PCN network
  (temporarily called China Digital Cordless Telephone Network—
  CDCT), which has capabilities for bi-directional calling and
  handover."
"Research on key technologies of Code Division Multiple Access
  (CDMA) and system design."
"Fulfill simulation study targets [set by the relevant 863 expert group]
  and system evaluations of satellite mobile telecommunications
  systems."

(F) Nodes and Switches Expert Group

(G) Information Superhighway Expert Group[4]

"Planning for the construction of a National Information
Infrastructure (NII) through the development of the 'China
National Super Information Infrastructure' (CNSII). CNSII
should be built on the basis of a 'unified open platform' atop the
national telecommunications infrastructure."
"Find ways to successfully combine cable television development with
telecommunications development."
"Complete a CNSII pilot project."
Begin "gradually implementing experimental systems in economically
developed areas to gain additional experience" for a more
widespread implementation. Ultimately, a "comprehensive CNSII
that covers major economic and social aspects of the country
should be completed before 2020."

LASERS MANAGERIAL GROUP

Staff Office: COSTIND (after 1998, PLA General Armaments
Department) Headquarters

I. Pulsed-Power Expert Group

II. Plasma Technology Expert Group

III. Laser Spectroscopy Expert Group

IV. New Materials Expert Group

NEW MATERIALS MANAGERIAL GROUP[5]

Staff Office: SSTC (after 1998, MOST) Headquarters, Department
of Industrial Technology

Administers the 863 Artificial Crystals Research and Development Center.

I. Photoelectric and Optolelectronic Materials Expert Groups

Photoelectric materials for communications, lasers,
computation, automation, aerospace, and a variety of military
industries. These include thin films, such as diamond film,
organic optical discs, organic photoconductor drums,
photoelectric film, superlattice, and super high frequency
transducers.

Targets and Objectives Have Included:

GaSb single crystal; high-power semiconductor quantum-well laser diode
material; GaInAsSb room-temperature infrared detector; polycrystal
germanium dioxide hollow-core fiber for transmitting carbon dioxide laser;
SCF optical sensors suitable for high-temperature environments; diamond film
tools; applications of diamond film heat sink; a new organic crystal used to
double the frequency of semiconductor lasers and to produce violet light;
organic photoconductor drums; display materials for color electroluminescent
thick films (ELTF); and multi-ion-beam reactive cosputtering apparatus and
related techniques for thick film fabrication.

II. High-Performance, Anticorrosion, and Light-Structural Materials Expert Group

"Intermetallic compounds that provide thermal structural materials
for use in aircraft, satellites, and rockets, as well as parts with
thermal- and wear-resistance properties." Such materials have
high melting points, low density, high resistance to oxidation,
low diffusion coefficients, yield strength, and high resistance to
elevated temperature creep.

Targets and Objectives Have Included:

Cast Ni_3Al base alloy; Ti_3Al alloy products; Fe_3Al corrosion-resistant alloys;
particle-reinforced aluminum matrix composites; boron filament; evaluating
thermal cycling damage to metal matrix composites; and fiber-enhanced
Mg-based composite materials.

III. Synthetic Crystals Expert Group

Artificial crystals applied to a variety of fields, e.g. generation and
frequency-tuning of lasers, light communications, light storage,
light calculations and laser processing, and surgery.

Targets and Objectives Have Included:

In the areas of laser crystals and NLO crystals, including frequency-tuning
and photorefractive crystals: superior-quality Ti-doped sapphire tunable laser
crystal ($Ti:Al_2O_3$); pulsed tunable Ti:sapphire lasers; new nonlinear optical
crystals CBO; new nonlinear optical crystals lithium triborate; and infrared
optical crystals ($AgGaSe_2$).

IV. High-Temperature-Resistant, Plastic, and Composite Materials Expert Group

Advanced plastics with the highest mechanical and thermal
properties among polymeric materials, relevant to energy, space,
aircraft, and machinery industries. Base resins, engineering
plastics, chopped fiber-reinforced plastics, and continuous

fiber-reinforced composites in the form of prepregs. These
materials are produced on pilot production lines, enabling
production according to the special requirements of customers.

Targets and Objectives Have Included:

CD-grade polycarbonate; thermosetting polyimide resins; micro-debonding
measurement techniques; production techniques for thermoplastic matrix
composites; and glass-mat reinforced thermoplastics.

V. Materials Surface Modification Techniques and Industrial Applications Expert Groups

Improvement of material surface properties, such as wear resistance,
lubrication, corrosion resistance, and fatigue resistance, in order
to prolong the life span of tools, automobile, and satellite parts.
Ion implantation; ion beam enhanced deposition; metal vapor
vacuum arc source ion implantation; plasma source ion
implantation; the synthesis of diamond and DLC films; and
double-glow plasma surface alloying and laser surface treatment.

Targets and Objectives Have Included:

Double-glow surface alloying technology; laser-induced chemical vapor
deposition; and ion beam assisted deposition techniques.

VI. New Energy-Storage Materials Expert Group

Administers a new National Center for Energy-Storage Materials.

Targets and Objectives Have Included:

A metal hydride compressor, coupled to a Joule-Thomson expander cryocooler.
Obtaining a 25 K low-temperature source for a system to include a compressor
group with gas and water cycling loops, a hydrogen expander cryocooler with
liquid nitrogen precooling capability, and microcomputer-based auto-control
and monitoring systems. Targeted cooling capacity is 0.4 W at 25 K. Main applications include aerospace cryogenic systems, infrared aerospace surveillance
apparatus in satellites and weapons that require low-temperature sources, and
various usages by liquid hydrogen engineering and chemical factories. Other
targets: nickel hydride batteries with sintering positive electrode, foaming positive electrode, bonding negative electrode, foaming negative electrode, and
starching negative electrode; sulfur batteries with specific energy of 130wh/kg,
energy density of 30Ah, and recycle life of 10000Ah; rechargeable lithium-ion
batteries; and high-energy rechargeable lithium-ion batteries, comparable to
AA cell types made by Japan's Sony Corporation.

VII. High Performance Ceramics Expert Groups

Functional and structural ceramics. In functional ceramics, emphases
include the development of a high-performance low-sintering

temperature mulitlayer ceramics capacitor, in cooperation with industrial enterprises. Structural ceramics projects include multiphase ceramics based on nonoxide ceramics such as silicon nitride and silicon carbide, as well as other oxide ceramics such as high performance mullite and microcrystalline Zirconia (ZrO_2). Also special inorganic composites, and X-ray systems for materials testing.

Targets and Objectives Have Included:

High-performance MLC with low-sintering temperature; high-performance whisker-reinforced and plastifying composite ceramics; a small system of continuous microwave sintering; pressureless sintering of mullite matrix multiphase ceramics; advanced electrostrictive ceramics and their multiplayer element fabrication process; a microfocal X-ray CT system for testing ceramic components; ultrasonic NDT of advanced structural ceramics; and continuous silicon carbide fiber containing Ti.

VIII. Synthesis and Processing Technologies Expert Groups

Super-high-temperature, high-pressure, and high-cooling-rate
conditions. Technologies and equipment for high production
capacity of silicon nitride, silicon carbide nanoscale powders
using laser and plasma methods.

Targets and Objectives Have Included:

Self-propagating high-temperature synthesis; microwave sintering of ceramics with pressure; laser synthesis technology and apparatus for ton/year nano silicon nitride powder production; bioreactive materials to substitute for human hard tissues; BMP-bone morphogenetic protein; and superplastic aluminum-lithium alloys.

SPACE TECHNOLOGY MANAGERIAL GROUP

Staff Office: COSTIND (after 1998, PLA General Armaments Department) 921 Office

I. Carrier Rockets Expert Group

Aeroengine technology, including some R&D funding for Project
921 (manned space program), initially administered by
COSTIND's 921 Office.

II. Payload Systems Expert Group

Monitoring and management technologies; ground integrated testing
technologies such as radio relays and data processing systems;
neural network technologies.

REFERENCE MATTER

NOTES

CHAPTER ONE

1. Qian Xuesen (1987a, p. 22).

2. The Soviet and Japanese cases are especially relevant to the emergence of a political-military nexus in China. On how militarism helped to forge the Soviet state, see Holloway (1980). On the state-economy nexus that emerged out of militarism in Meiji Japan, see Yamamura (1977). Eckstein (1977, p. 32) explored some of these themes in the context of the Chinese Communist state more than two decades ago. David Shambaugh (1997) has done so more recently.

3. Kargon, Leslie, and Schoenberger (1992, p. 339).

4. Quoted in Lewis and Xue (1988a, p. 107).

5. Quoted in Lewis and Xue (1994, p. 18).

6. Powell (1955, p. 6).

7. This theme has received widespread attention in the social sciences and political history, most notably in the work of Charles Tilly, Samuel Finer, Bruce Porter, and others. The intimate connection in China between militarization and late industrialization on the one hand and national security, economic development, and technology transfer on the other has antecedents. Historically, this bond derives both from mercantilist theory and later efforts to tie economic nationalism to defense and manufactures. In his 1791 "Report on Manufactures," Alexander Hamilton linked the concept of "infant" national industry to autarky. Several decades later, German economist Friedrich List identified national power as the primary concern of economic policy. Political and economic theorists, from Barrington Moore to Alexander Gerschenkron, have shown how the development of infant industries in latecomer societies, such as Germany and Russia, intertwined with hegemonic forms of state power and militarization. The same was true of China under Mao. But the immediacy of China's national security threat during the 1950s accentuated the military rationale for industrialization to a greater extent than in other late-developers, including China's Asian neighbors.

8. See Solinger (1993).

CHAPTER TWO

1. On the general tendency to squeeze the countryside to finance industrialization, see Selden (1993).

2. There is a voluminous literature on this subject; see especially, Lardy (1978a, 1978b), Donnithorne (1967), and Bachman (1991, pp. 96–132). Chinese planners

often gave even greater relative priority to heavy industry than did their Soviet counterparts, particularly during the two countries' respective first and second Five Year Plan periods. See, for example, Yeh (1967).

3. This approach emphasized less the sheer extractive capacity of the state than various financial mechanisms and price policies to control the economy and thus develop favored sectors. As with the Soviet-style approach, there is a voluminous literature on this subject. See all sources previously cited, as well as Solinger (1982, 1984), Sun Yefang (1979), and Bachman (1991, pp. 59–95). On Chen Yun, see Bachman (1985).

4. Social relations were central to this emphasis because, as Carl Riskin (1991) has argued, Maoist economics held that "'socialist transformation' of the relations of production would stimulate rapid economic development by mobilizing the population and promoting what Western economic theory calls 'x-efficiency'. . . . The conditions arousing greatest initiative were those that promised greatest success." See also Christine Wong (1991), and Riskin (1975).

5. See Bao Mingrong and Hu Guangzheng (1983, esp. pp. 39–40).

6. The Chinese People's Volunteers (Zhongguo renmin zhiyuanjun) was the official name of Chinese forces in Korea. In fact, these were regular units of the PLA. For Mao's order renaming the PLA units in question the "CPV," see Mao Zedong (1950).

7. Lewis and Xue (1988a, p. 8).

8. Hong Xuezhi (1990, p. 178).

9. Tan Jingqiao (1990, pp. 135–36); Hong Xuezhi (1990, p. 179).

10. Quoted in Lewis and Xue (1988a, p. 9).

11. Lewis and Xue (1988a, p. 9).

12. Ibid.

13. Goncharov, Lewis, and Xue (1993, p. 71). For more on this, see Shi Zhe (1988, p. 224). On Liu's secret visit, see Zhu Yuanshi (1991).

14. These included a misunderstanding over Soviet air support that came to a head during meetings between Stalin and Zhou Enlai in Crimea during 1950. When Zhou met Stalin on October 9, "Stalin withdrew his promise of air support for Chinese forces. He insisted that the Soviet Air Force needed more time to get ready. Zhou told Stalin that China might postpone the entry of its forces into Korea because it was not sure that the Chinese People's Volunteers could stop the UN forces without Soviet support. Stalin responded that he would be willing to speed up the training of Chinese pilots, and promised to provide equipment for twenty ground force divisions. . . . Zhou cabled a report to Mao on October 10" (Holloway, 1994, p. 281).

15. Lewis and Xue (1988a, p. 12).

16. Nie Rongzhen (1952).

17. Bo Yibo (1991, p. 477).

18. Xie Guang (1992, v. 1, pp. 26–27).

19. Lewis and Xue (1988a, p. 10).

20. This section is based on Li Mancun (1992), Li Pu and Shen Rong (1986), Ji Tingyu and Huo Dongyou (1989), Qi Shengping (1985), and some of Liu's talks, including Liu Bocheng (1956).

21. For an example of Peng's position, see Peng Dehuai (1958, esp. pp. 606–7).

22. The ten marshals (*yuanshuai*) of the PLA received their commissions on September 27, 1955. No one has since been appointed to this rank. Although Liu's lectures at the academy predated the adoption of a rank system, for the sake of clarity, I always refer to the marshals by their 1955 rank. For a discussion of the ten marshals, their backgrounds, and their differing positions on political and force structure issues, particularly regarding weapons and technology, see Feigenbaum (1997, part 2, pp. 31–287; 37–41).

23. On the important role played by high-level command colleges such as the Nanjing academy in PLA development during this period, see Zhang Zhenhua (1989).

24. Li Mancun (1992, p. 547).

25. See, for instance, Tao Hanzhang (1987).

26. Lewis and Xue (1994, p. 209).

27. Li Mancun (1992, p. 584).

28. Ibid.

29. Ibid. (p. 574).

30. Most students at the academy had at least divisional rank.

31. This paragraph is based on Li Mancun (1992, pp. 578–79).

32. Zhang Jiayu (1983). For more on these strategic shifts, see Lewis and Xue (1994, pp. 209–19).

33. Mao himself recognized the need for an indigenous deterrent as early as 1954, though the idea probably goes back to 1948–49. As noted above, Liu Shaoqi had asked specifically about the nature of the Soviet nuclear capability during his secret 1949 visit to the Soviet Union, before the October 1 establishment of the PRC. Just five years later, at a meeting in October 1954 with military leaders, Mao recognized that the advent of the nuclear era had raised the benchmark for Chinese modernization on *all* fronts: "Since the appearance of atomic weapons, military strategy, tactics, and weaponry have all changed dramatically. In this area, we haven't the faintest understanding" (Mao Zedong, 1954a, p. 358). This document is ostensibly from China's Central Party archive, which remains closed to foreigners. By October 23, Mao's decision for an indigenous program was firm. He told the visiting Indian Prime Minister Jawaharlal Nehru that China required an independent nuclear deterrent (Mao Zedong, 1954b, p. 171). Obviously, this flew square in the face of Mao's widely touted statements about nuclear weapons being "paper tigers" and "unable to decide wars." This contradiction between Mao's words and deeds has received extensive treatment in Lewis and Xue (1988a). On the "paper tiger" theme, see Hsieh (1962, p. 131). Mao's remark about nuclear weapons being "unable to decide wars" comes from a speech delivered just after the atomic bombings of Hiroshima and Nagasaki (Mao Zedong, 1945, p. 21).

34. Concern about the cost of developing sophisticated weapons began to weigh heavily on Chinese politicians and planners almost immediately after the establishment of the Communist state in October 1949. At issue was the matter of trade-offs: how much would the purely civilian system "lose" if army building and weapons development were to "win"? This question broadly paralleled a contemporaneous argument about the size of the armed forces, which led to a series of demobilizations throughout Mao's years in power. See, for example, Ai Lingyao (1990, pp. 74–78).

35. On the theme of weapons development in the absence of strategy, see Lewis and Xue (1994), and Lewis and Hua (1992, pp. 5–40).

36. On these issues and the dramatic effect of the post-Leap retrenchment on central government spending, see Lardy (1987, pp. 386–87).

37. John Gittings (1967, p. 203) has itemized the U.S. nuclear threats, including two issued during the Korean War (the first in January–February 1953, the second in May 1953), three related to Indochina (all delivered by John Foster Dulles, on September 2, 1953, December 29, 1953, and March 29, 1954), and two related to the offshore islands occupied by the Guomindang (March 8 [Dulles] and 16 [Eisenhower], 1955, and September 1958). If, as Gittings contends, the three Indochina threats were indeed taken seriously in Beijing, they nonetheless would seem in retrospect to have been rather less explicit than the other four. On nuclear coercion during the Korean War, see also Christensen (1992), Dingman (1988/89), Foot (1988/89), and Lewis and Xue (1988a).

38. In fact, the attempt to integrate the two spheres had some history, though it was Marshal Nie's struggle with the opposition that led to his most sophisticated proposals. As early as 1950, Mao began to urge his colleagues to think more comprehensively about the relationship between defense and civilian industrial construction, exhorting an unwavering emphasis upon the latter. Two years later, the government's Central Ordnance Commission urged military enterprises to begin producing civilian output even as they strove to meet their targets in weapons production. This concerted drive to integrate civilian with military work had a complex history in China during the 1950s. But the real watershed on the issue was the decision to pursue indigenous nuclear weapons delivery systems. These decisions increased the pressure on the central government to respond to the demands of competing constituencies. Mao made his remarks at the Third Plenum of the Seventh Central Committee, held from June 6 to 9, 1950. The 1952 report of the Central Ordnance Commission is discussed in Xie Guang (1992, v. 1, p. 174). On military-civilian integration during the 1950s, see Liao Guoliang (1991, pp. 507–11), Wang Li (1993, pp. 54–55), and Sun Zhenhuan (1991, pp. 175–76).

39. As Lewis and Xue have noted with respect to the nuclear submarine and its missile (SLBM), "building a[n] [SSBN] and an SLBM demands far greater technological-industrial knowledge and capacity than building nuclear weapons. From metallurgy to reactors, from solid rocket propellants to advanced guidance technology" the R&D problems for taking designs from drawing board to deployment are enormous, as is also the case with land-based strategic missile systems,

which similarly depend on complex inertial guidance technologies, including gyroscopes and accelerometers (Lewis and Xue, 1994, p. xviii).

40. Bo Yibo (1991, pp. 477–78).

41. Wang Yan (1993, pp. 492–570). See especially pp. 540–44 on the debate about how (and how much) to learn from the Soviet experience. See also Joffe (1965).

42. Zheng Wenhan (1988, p. 4).

43. There has been a relatively steady flow of biographical materials about Nie in recent years. Nie (1983, 1986) himself tells the story best in his three-volume memoir. See also Cai Renzhao (1994), and Wei Wei (1991). The latter volume explores Nie's relationship with Lin Biao (pp. 683–86), which was closer and more complex than that between Lin and the other marshals. Tian Xuan (1993) is less impressive, but includes vignettes by Generals Liu Huaqing and Yang Chengwu. On Nie's military thought, see Wei Wei and Zhou Junlun (1990); on his role in the civil war, see Liu Sheng (1993). An important collection of Nie's reports to the leadership, speeches, and other manuscripts are contained in *NRJW*.

44. Lewis and Xue (1988a, p. 197) note that "Beijing's foreign policy specialists and military planners understood that technological attainments—for example, the making of high-yield warheads or the mastery of missile engineering—could send important political messages to worst-case planners in Washington and Moscow. In the aggregate, such messages might serve in the place of declared new strategic doctrines; they could supersede people's war and paper tigers."

45. For more on this point, see Lewis and Xue (1994).

46. Nie Rongzhen (1986, pp. 818–19). A contemporary version of this argument, not one made retrospectively in a memoir account, is in a speech Nie made in April 1963. Nie Rongzhen (1963, pp. 496–518).

47. This quotation from a 1955 speech by Marshal Liu Bocheng was a plea for greater attention to defense expenditure. Cited in MacFarquhar (1974, p. 71).

48. Mao was a reflexive nationalist about what he thought to be China's destiny as a great power. Studies on this point include works by John Lewis and Xue Litai (1988, 1994), John Garver (1988), Shi Zhe (1998), Robert Ross (1995), and others. Mao justified a thoroughgoing modernization of high-tech weaponry in 1954, for example, on grounds of China's status as a "great power": "Our industry, agriculture, culture, and military [strength] are insufficient. Imperialists assess you in terms of these things and therefore bully us. They say, 'do you have the atomic bomb?' But they miscalculate in their assessment. China's latent capacity to develop its strength will astonish [them]" (Mao Zedong, 1954a, p. 359). Lewis and Xue (1994, pp. 10–18) vividly describe the Chairman's viscerally nationalistic reaction to perceived Soviet slights, a picture reinforced by transcripts of meetings between Mao and Soviet representatives. See also Mao's nationalistic tongue-lashing of the Soviet ambassador in 1958 over Soviet proposals for building a long-wave radio transmission station on Chinese territory to enable communication with the Soviet Pacific Fleet (Mao Zedong, 1958, pp. 322–33).

49. It is unclear whether Mao saw a copy of the actual Japanese report or whether it was summarized for him by Marshal Nie and his staff. The source of the report was a Japanese financial affairs research conference held in February 1960 that, judging from the wording of the editor's comments on the Chinese source, probably was sponsored by a defense office of the Japanese government. Apparently, the conference produced a document that was provided to Mao by Nie's staff either in full or as a summary. See Nie Rongzhen (1986, pp. 814–15), and the editor's footnote 2 on Mao Zedong (1961, pp. 530–31).

50. The Japanese term for the policy of indigenization, *kokusanka*, has been a key word in the Japanese debate since the 1950s over the importance of advanced defense production to industrial policy. See Green (1995, pp. 2–30), and Samuels (1994).

51. Nie Rongzhen (1986, p. 814).

52. Mao Zedong (1961, pp. 530–31).

53. Nie Rongzhen (1986, pp. 814–15).

54. Duan Zijun (1988).

55. Ibid. (p. 47).

56. On Qian Xuesen's background, see the biography by his longtime personal secretary, Wang Shouyun (1991). On Ren Xinmin's scientific background and work, see Tan Bangzhi (1991). See also Appendix 1 of this book.

57. Duan Zijun (1988, p. 47).

58. On metallurgy, see Lu Da (1989), and Du Chunshi (1989).

59. He Zuoxiu (1992).

60. For Qian's original argument for missile development after his return to China from the United States, see Qian Xuesen (1987b).

61. He Zuoxiu (1992).

62. This paragraph is based on Duan Zijun (1988, p. 169).

63. He Long (1960, p. 584).

64. Quoted in Lewis and Xue (1988a, pp. 128–29).

65. Nie Rongzhen (1961); Nie Rongzhen (1986, p. 816).

66. Nie Rongzhen (1986, p. 817). Italics are mine.

67. Ibid.

68. On this U-2 shootdown, see Fu Zhenguo (1990, pp. 25–32), Liu Shaoqiu (1988, pp. 43–44), and Liu Shaoqiu (1989, pp. 56–58). On the change in air defense policy, see Nie Rongzhen (1986, p. 817). All newly produced J-6 fighter planes (China's first supersonic fighter aircraft, a copy of the Soviet MiG-19) were grounded between 1959 and 1964 on account of technical problems. Xie Guang (1992, v. 2, pp. 181–82). In a personal communication, David Bachman has pointed out that this may well have made strategic weapons more compelling in light of the threats of 1962.

69. Reich (1987) coined the term "technonationalism." As Michael Green (1995, p. 11) points out, it is often used imprecisely and in many different ways. Generally, the term seeks to capture the idea that international relations—and especially

state-to-state competition—are affected by nationalistic ideas about technology. Suttmeier (1989) has explored some uses of the concept in a Chinese context.

70. McDougall (1985, p. 5).

71. Samuels (1994, p. 33). See also, Ostry and Nelson (1995), McDougall (1985), and Green (1995).

72. Samuels (1994, p. 34).

73. Quoted in ibid.

74. This is obviously quite different from classic "market failure" arguments for public technology investment; China, after all, did not have a true market during the Mao years. Both the market failure formulation and Chinese technonationalism recognize the inevitability of long lead-times and the incentive problems that this can cause. But this derives from different circumstances in each version. In market settings it can be traced to firms' need to earn profit on investments, thus introducing market pressure to earn a quick return on R&D expenditures. In the socialist setting, it reflects agents' tendency to maximize gross output. In this formulation, only the center (and technology programmers at the very apex of the planning system) are comparatively unburdened by the output problem—they seek output, of course, but many other things as well. This comprehensive approach is much more difficult for economic agents down the ladder, since they must maximize behaviors that can be easily observed (and hence rewarded) by superiors. This makes short-term output, not long-range R&D, the most likely priority for resource allocation at the firm level. On market failure in capitalist societies see Stoneman (1987); see also, Ostry and Nelson (1995, pp. 28–33), and Levin (1987).

75. China moved from reliance on advanced technologies and manufacturing techniques acquired from abroad, primarily from the Soviet Union, to building domestic industry via license, loans, or purchase and reverse engineering. The Soviet experience, in particular, convinced the Chinese that, even with maximum aid from abroad, indigenization in the shortest possible time was essential. In the nuclear program, for example, the Chinese believed that Soviet aid was not just slow in coming but given for the purpose of promoting Moscow's interests; Moscow, the Chinese came to believe, would readily have abandoned its Chinese "ally" as soon as it could no longer disproportionately benefit from its aid. Beijing voiced this frustration in an angry letter to the Soviet Central Committee in February 1964. It reminded Moscow that China had "furnished the Soviet Union with more than [1.4 billion] new rubles' worth of mineral products and metals. . . . Many of these mineral products," the Chinese reminded the Russians, "are raw materials which are indispensable . . . for the manufacture of rockets and nuclear weapons" ("Letter of the Central Committee," 1964, p. 25). By 1960, the sense of having been wronged in the nuclear aid arrangement had been exacerbated by Soviet refusals to aid in nuclear naval technology (Lewis and Xue, 1994, p. 12; Xiao Jingguang, 1988, p. 179), as well as with missile systems that the Chinese badly desired. At an enlarged meeting of the Politburo in Shanghai in January 1960,

Nie Rongzhen (1986) vented the frustrations of those who favored indigenization. The Soviets, Nie declared, were determined to "maintain their superior position" (*baochi lingxian diwei*). Key missile data and components would never be transferred because Moscow's goal was "always to keep [China] two or three steps behind" (*luohou tamen liang san bu*). In fact, Nie overstated his case since, as Lewis and Hua (1992, p. 13) have noted, it was standard practice of the USSR not to "allow the transfer of state-of-the-art weapons systems to allies before it had deployed at least two types of more advanced systems."

76. Even when it contradicted the antielitism of Maoist ideology, strategic weapons leaders allowed scientists and technicians considerable latitude to pursue innovative techniques and ideas.

77. As we shall see in later chapters, small-scale, private, and mixed-ownership R&D, particularly in the consumer electronics industry, has grown up during the past decade as an alternative source of innovation to state technology programming. Like the strategic weapons model described here, this, too, offers a flexible and open-ended model for managing innovation. But unlike the former, it discards the "command R&D" component in favor of a bottom-up approach to innovation much more in tune with the recent history of technology, including the start-up experience typical of the U.S. software industry.

78. Frieman (1989, p. 267).

79. Zhu Guangya (1987), Liu Shuqing and Zhang Jifu (1985), and Lewis and Xue (1988a, p. 145).

80. On the management of large projects, see the fascinating comparative history of four important U.S. projects (SAGE, Atlas, ARPANET, and Boston's Central Artery Tunnel) by Hughes (1998).

81. The importance of Wang Zheng, a key figure in the pre-1949 military elite attached to the Central Military Commission, stemmed from the special role played by communications technology in keeping scattered armies in touch with the party center. Wang headed the CMC's Third Bureau (communications) during the civil war, was a deputy chief of the PLA Operations Department, and had long been in charge of all military telecommunications. I will have more to say about Wang in later chapters. See *Zhongguo Renmin Jiefang jun Jiangshuai Minglu* (1986, v. 1, p. 160).

82. Initially located in Beijing, the academy's name was changed when it moved to Haiyan County, Qinghai Province. In the 1970s, the academy moved once again, this time to Mianyang City, Sichuan Province, and was renamed the Chinese Academy of Engineering Physics (Zhongguo gongcheng wuli yanjiusuo). In the years when the atomic bomb was in development, it was administered by Nie's NDSTC through Li Jue's Ninth Bureau, which reported to both the NDSTC and the Second Ministry. Li Jue served concurrently as director of both the Ninth Bureau and the Ninth Academy.

83. Lewis and Xue (1988a, p. 151).

84. I discuss Qian Sanqiang, Wang Ganchang, and Wang Shiguang in later chapters. On Li Siguang, see Ceng Wenqu (1991).

85. Lewis and Xue (1988a, pp. 116–17). The Communists launched the Hundred Regiments offensive in 1940, largely at the instigation of Peng Dehuai, who seems to have put it into motion before receiving approval from Yan'an, then the Communist capital. Between July and December 1940, the number of Communist regiments involved expanded to 104, but the results were mixed and the Japanese army responded with a massive counterattack in 1941. Since the enormous scale of the offensive directly contradicted the small-scale guerrilla tactics that Mao had advocated since 1937, some of Mao's subsequent enmity for Peng Dehuai, according to Teiwes (1986), can be traced to this period and the failures of the campaign.

86. Tu Shou'e (1989). For Tu's scientific background, see Shen Xincun (1991).

87. Lewis and Hua (1992, p. 8).

88. Tu Shou'e (1989, p. 267).

89. Lewis and Hua (1992, p. 14).

90. Frieman (1994).

91. See, for example, Song Wencong (1989). Song describes his work as chief designer of the J-7III fighter.

92. I discuss the CSC in greater detail below. On Zhou Enlai's role in this context, see, for example, Liu Xiyao (1987), Xie Linhuo (1986), and Zhu Guangya (1988).

93. Quotations in the next few paragraphs are from Nie Rongzhen (1986, pp. 827–28).

94. Nie's elite strategic weapons organs were by no means immune to the worst dysfunctions of the Leap, and this includes both the distortions in reporting and production and the hardships associated with the post-Leap famine. In October 1960, for example, Nie was forced to issue a special order to ensure priority access to supplies for his technicians (Nie Rongzhen, 1960a). He did so to guarantee a degree of creature comfort for his personnel amid national hardship, which certainly speaks to their privileged position. But he was also concerned to keep his programs operating smoothly.

95. See Nie's remarks to Fifth Academy scientists later that fall, in which he discusses political-technical symbiosis and the scientists' experiences. Nie Rongzhen (1960b).

96. On jurisdictional changes in the submarine program, see Lewis and Xue (1994).

97. Lewis and Xue (1988a, pp. 54–59). On the history of the Fuels Production Bureau, see Jiang Shengjie (1989).

98. Nie Rongzhen (1986, p. 820) comments in his memoir on his critical role in the reorganization of the metals and chemistry bureaucracies in the 1950s.

99. On why vertical compartmentalization has been such a problem in Chinese politics, see especially Barnett (1967), Lieberthal and Oksenberg (1988), and Lampton (1987).

100. On this first seminar, see Lewis and Xue (1988a, pp. 37–39), and Li Jue (1987, pp. 13–14).

101. Peng Shilu (1988, pp. 12–13).

102. Lewis and Xue (1994, p. 108). See also Peng Shilu and Zhao Renkai (1989, p. 207).

103. In a personal communication, Michel Oksenberg pointed out the application of this arrangement in the case of the Three Gorges Dam.

104. Chen Youming (1989).

105. A good discussion of the CSC is in Liu Boluo (1987, pp. 342–44), and Liu Boluo (1989, esp. p. 128). See also Lewis and Xue (1988a, 1994), Feigenbaum (1997, esp. pp. 170–75), and Xie Guang (1992, v. 1, pp. 47–51).

106. On the contest between Nie Rongzhen and He Long/Luo Ruiqing, see Lewis and Xue (1988a), and Feigenbaum (1997, chaps. 3–4).

107. Xie Guang (1992, v. 1, pp. 34–35).

108. Zhang Aiping (1989, p. 74).

109. Lewis and Xue (1994, p. 8).

110. Liu Yalou may be an exception since he was closely identified with a campaign to intensify the modernization of the air force and aviation. But Liu's relations with Marshal Nie extended at least back to when Nie led the NDSTC's forerunner agency, the Aviation Industrial Commission, in charge of both missiles and aircraft development. On Liu Yalou's role in promoting aviation construction, see Yang Wanqing (1992).

111. Xie Guang (1992, v. 1, pp. 46–47).

112. On this history, see Huang Yao and Zhang Mingzhe (1996, pp. 393–435).

113. Liu Boluo (1987, pp. 342–44). On the report, see Zhang Aiping (1961). On Liu Xiyao's participation in missile and weapons work, see Liu Xiyao (1987).

114. Nie Ronzghen (1986, p. 823).

115. On how the CSC worked, see Li Qi and Nie Li (1989).

116. Competition was adopted, in part, from the Soviet model, where it was utilized in the design of some weapons. On competition in Soviet weapons design, see Holloway (1982).

117. See Yuan Yaojun (1989) on Nie's promotion of an information system.

118. Xiao Jingguang (1988, pp. 174–79).

119. Liu Jingzhi (1989, pp. 12–13). These paragraphs are also based on Peng Shilu and Zhao Renkai (1989), Huang Xuhua (1989), Zhi Yin (1989), and Lewis and Xue (1994, pp. 30–32).

120. Holloway (1994, p. 361).

121. Lewis and Xue (1994, p. 112).

122. Nie Rongzhen (1986, pp. 767–68).

123. Holloway (1994, chap. 1).

124. Bethe (1979).

125. Chinese physics has been a male-dominated field. The two most prominent female physicists during the period of the PRC are He Zehui and Xie Xide. He Zehui was the wife of China's most famous nuclear physicist, Qian Sanqiang. She worked in Paris on the tripartite fission of uranium before returning to China with

Qian. Xie Xide is a surface physicist (*biaomian wuli*) who, together with her husband, played a major role in building physics at Shanghai's Fudan University.

126. On CAS membership, see "CAS Launches" (1995, p. 13).

127. Gu Yu (1989, p. 469). Gu Yu was highly placed in the political leadership as the wife of the late Hu Qiaomu, formerly a leading ideologue, secretary to Mao Zedong, and, during the Deng era, among the CCP's ten or fifteen top elders.

128. Nie Rongzhen (1986, p. 823).

129. Zhang Jingfu (1989, p. 79).

130. On the personnel of CAST, see Wang Shuntong (1994).

131. On the August 1955 transfers, see Xie Guang (1992, v. 1, p. 14). On the June 1956 transfers, see Nie Rongzhen (1986, p. 796).

132. Lewis and Xue (1988a, p. 42). See also, Lindbeck (1961, pp. 3–58).

133. On testing pools, see Huang Xuhua (1989), and Dong Shitang (1989). On shock tubes, see Tan Keming and Zhang Zi'an (1989).

134. Nie Rongzhen (1986, p. 823).

135. On strategic weapons programs and metallurgy, see Lian Jun (1992), Lu Da (1989), and Du Chunshi (1989). On the chemical industry, see Zhu Youdi (1990), and especially Tao Tao (1989). On Nie's role in establishing the metals and chemical industry bureaucracies, see Nie Rongzhen (1986, p. 820). On strategic weapons and the development of raw materials extraction industries and techniques, see Chen Zhaobo (1989). On the collaboration of the Ministry of Posts and Telecommunications (MPT) with the PLA on telemetry, tracking, and control networks for satellites and missiles, see Xie Guang (1992, v. 1, pp. 468–71). Although telecommunications became primarily a civilian sector in the 1950s, the military continued to play a major role in telecommunications development, controlling its own network and, later, China's entire network of 900 MHz frequencies. This subject is explored in Chapter 6.

136. On the Harbin college, see Luo Laiyong (1995), Nie Rongzhen (1986, p. 800), and Yin Jiamin (1988). On naval technical schools, see Lewis and Xue (1989). As Zhou Yiping (1989, p. 122) has noted, the entire network of PLA technical colleges grew out of the CMC decision to create the Zhangjiakou Engineering School in northeast China in 1949.

137. On the Moscow Aviation Institute agreement, see Nie's report to Premier Zhou Enlai (Nie Rongzhen, 1956, esp. p. 396). On Nie's push in electrical engineering, see Nie Rongzhen (1986, pp. 805–6).

CHAPTER THREE

1. For background to this shift, see Xiong Xianghui (1992).

2. See, for instance, the photograph of Deng inspecting the Jiuquan Atomic Energy Complex (Plant 404) in Gansu Province, in Lewis and Xue (1988a).

3. Fan Shuo (1990, p. 315).

4. Deng Xiaoping (1975a, p. 1).

5. Ibid.

6. Chen-ning Yang (C. N. Yang) won the Nobel Prize in physics for his contri-butions to a symmetry theory of fields. The son of a mathematician, he studied quantum mechanics in Kunming, Yunnan Province, where he became interested in gauge invariance in electromagnetic fields. After emigrating to the United States, Yang worked at the Brookhaven National Laboratory, and, together with his colleague Robert Mills, became a major contributor to the first gauge field theory beyond electromagnetism. This work earned him the Nobel Prize.

7. Deng Xiaoping (1975b, p. 2).

8. This section is based mainly on Xie Guang (1992, v. 1, pp. 148–54).

9. Ibid. (p. 125).

10. Ibid. (p. 148).

11. Ibid. (pp. 148–51).

12. The history of China's antiship cruise missiles is closely connected to the development of strategic weapons under Marshal Nie's missile and space adminis-tration. See especially, Liang Shoupan (1989), a memoir by the chief designer of Chinese cruise missiles. On Liang's background and technical bibliography, see Chen Encai (1991).

13. Xie Guang (1992, v. 1, p. 153).

14. Ibid. (pp. 151–52).

15. On the consequences of this discovery, see Feigenbaum (1997, pp. 237–43).

16. Xie Guang (1992, v. 1, p. 130).

17. The first Chinese ICBM flight test was in 1971, but the missile, which was then very rudimentary, was not ready for deployment until August 1981. When Tu Shou'e was appointed ICBM chief designer in 1977, his main charge was to redesign the missile in order to make it fully operational. I say more about Tu's appointment later in the chapter.

18. Li Runshan (1985, p. 373).

19. Xie Guang (1992, v. 1, p. 154).

20. Ibid.

21. Ibid.

22. Ibid. (p. 155).

23. On reporting relationships between the Dongfanghong-1 satellite pro-gram and the CSC, see Jing Cheng (1986, pp. 30–32). Luo Ruiqing, not Nie, was mainly responsible for supervising this program in 1965, the year Luo was purged. Jing Cheng (1986) cites verbatim Luo's April 28, 1965 report to Premier Zhou re-viewing technical meetings with Qian Xuesen, Luo Shunchu of the navy, Zhang Jingfu of the CAS, and Zhao Erlu, a longtime defense industrial administrator. The group called for a session of the CSC to review tentative proposals for the satellite program that emerged from these meetings. On what Luo's supervi-sion may have meant for the Nie-Luo power struggle, see Feigenbaum (1997, pp. 173–75).

24. Chen Liwei (1989, p. 440). Most of the pioneers in China's electronics in-dustry played seminal roles in the strategic weapons and the space program during

the Mao era. For example, Sun Junren, the editor-in-chief of China's electronics and computing encyclopedia (Sun Junren, 1986), as well as many of China's other major technical reference books on electronics, like Wang Shiguang, Chen Liwei, Ci Yungui, Wu Erzhen, and others, spent most of his career in weapons work and part of it as director of departments directly subordinate to the uniformed PLA Department of Communications Forces. On this history, see Wang Shiguang and Zhang Xuedong (1989).

25. Xie Guang (1992, v. 1, p. 156).

26. Ibid.

27. The Changsha academy is the forerunner of today's University of Defense Science and Technology (Guofang keji daxue).

28. Xie Guang (1992, v. 1, p. 156).

29. Ci Yungui (1989, p. 439).

30. This discussion of the Yinhe is based on Xie Guang (1992, v. 1, p. 156), and Ci Yungui (1989). For a scientific biography of and partial bibliography on Ci Yungui, see Liu Mingye and Wu Quanyuan (1991).

31. Nie Rongzhen played a role in launching the attack on rigid interpretations of Maoist thought. In September 1977 Nie "wrote an important article arguing that Mao Zedong Thought should be studied only in terms of its spirit, and not through isolated quotations that disregarded their spatial and temporal context" (Dittmer, 1987, p. 216).

32. Deng Xiaoping (1978b, p. 137).

33. Ibid. (p. 140).

34. Deng Xiaoping (1980).

35. Li Ping (1986).

36. Deng Xiaoping (1980, p. 204).

37. Ibid.

38. On the revival of certain aspects of Nie's view among some analysts in the early 1980s, see Han Jinteng (1988, p. 33).

39. Deng Xiaoping (1978a, p. 83).

40. Deng Xiaoping (1981, p. 350).

41. On the origin and meaning of this concept, see Cao Shixin (1994, pp. 33–49).

42. Godwin (1978).

43. Deng Xiaoping (1980, p. 204).

44. Ibid. (p. 213).

45. See "Deng Xiaoping zhonglun" (1985), Liu Huinian (1985), Liu Huinian and Yi Jianru (1985), Shi Wenting (1987), and Zhang Qinsheng and Zhang Chunting (1986).

46. Deng Xiaoping (1980, p. 205).

47. Ibid. (p. 204).

48. This visit, led by Under Secretary of Defense William Perry, is discussed in Chapter 4. For an excellent account of these early but difficult years of Sino-American military cooperation, see Pollack (1984).

49. Lewis, Hua, and Xue (1991, p. 90, n3). On the larger problem of assessing the size of the Chinese defense budget, see Gill (1999), Shambaugh (1994), Ding (1996), Wang Shaoguang (1996), Bitzinger and Lin (1994), Bitzinger (2000), and Harris (1991).

50. Bitzinger (2000).

51. The Third Line (*san xian*) policy aimed at building a "complete" and self-sufficient industrial base in China's strategic rear, partly through new construction and partly through the relocation of existing industry from the coast. Mao Zedong (1964) proclaimed the policy in 1964, although he had been concerned about one of the main "relationships" (*guanxi*)—that between coast and interior—at least since 1956 (Mao Zedong, 1956). For seven years after 1964, Chinese planning agencies allocated between one-half and two-thirds of all national investment to Third Line regions in the southwest and northwest. Mao also encouraged the creation of a network of local-level munitions plants to combat "revisionism" at the center (Wang Nianyi, 1989, p. 35). For an analysis in English of the Third Line, see Naughton (1988, 1991). For a good Chinese overview, see Yan Fangming (1987), Peng Min (1989), and Xie Guang (1992, v. 1, pp. 62–64). See Lewis and Xue (1994, pp. 88–99) on Third Line shipbuilding, and Chen Ping (1987) on aeronautics (pp. 61–67), electronics (pp. 93–98), and the nuclear weapons industry (pp. 164–66).

52. Folta (1992, p. 19).

53. Bitzinger and Lin (1994, p. 3).

54. Ibid.

55. The key concepts here are "People's War" doctrine, and especially the Third Line policy.

56. See, for example, Riskin (1991).

57. See, for example, Frieman (1989).

58. Xie Guang (1992, v. 1, p. 161).

59. Liu Luhong (1996, pp. 11–12).

60. Yao Yilin (1980), and Wang Bingqian (1980).

61. Cao Shixin (1994, p. 11). Chinese defense conversion has received sustained attention over the past decade. Superlative work by John Frankenstein has shown why it has been such an ambiguous process with many layers of meaning. The best account in English is Brömmelhörster and Frankenstein (1997). See also Frankenstein (1999), and Frankenstein and Gill (1996). In Chinese, see especially Cao Shixin (1994), as well as the numerous volumes published by the China Defense Science and Technology Information Center.

62. On the slogan, see Cao Shixin (1994, pp. 33–49). On *junmin jiehe,* see also Zhou Changqing (1985).

63. Cao Shixin (1994, p. 12).

64. On readjustment in Chinese industry during this period, see Solinger (1991), and Shirk (1985).

65. Sun Zhenhuan (1991, pp. 28–34).

66. Ibid. (p. 29).

67. Ibid. (p. 31).
68. Cao Shixin (1994, pp. 12–16).
69. Based on discussions with this official in the fall of 1995.
70. Sun Zhenhuan (1991, p. 31).
71. Liu Luhong (1996, p. 6).
72. This section is based in part on interviews conducted with managers and senior engineers from Chinese defense enterprises in 1995, as well as follow-up discussions from 1996 to 2001.
73. *Zhongguo Junzhuanmin Bao* (Apr. 2, 1993).
74. Frankenstein (1999, p. 211).
75. The next three chapters discuss fiber optics. On how the issue of dual use played out in the early 1990s in mineral metallurgy at four of the nuclear industry's mines in Jiangxi Province, see Liu Wenjun (1993).
76. Yan Shuheng (1994), Lu Yanxiao and Liu Xichen (1991, pp. 1–2).
77. Han Huaizhi and Tan Jingqiao (1989, pp. 81–83).
78. Ai Lingyao (1990).
79. Han Huaizhi and Tan Jingqiao (1989, p. 82).
80. Ibid. (p. 83). On the reduction of the PLA, see Yuan Houchun (1987), and Wu Hongye (1987).
81. Han Huaizhi and Tan Jingqiao (1989, p. 82).
82. Xie Guang (1992, v. 1, p. 126). On Tu Shou'e and Ren Xinmin, see Chapter 2. On Huang Weilu, see Liu Yadan, Liu Shaoqiu, and Lu Jing (1988).
83. Xie Guang (1992, v. 1, pp. 126–27).
84. Tu Shou'e (1989, p. 267).
85. Ibid. (pp. 268–69).
86. My account of the formation of COSTIND as a victory for strategic weaponeers, which differs substantially from Benjamin Ostrov's interpretation (1991), is based on more than eight years of discussion with PLA officers and Chinese military industry specialists and defense technicians.
87. On the creation of COSTIND, see, for instance, Xie Guang (1992, v. 1, pp. 133–34).
88. On Nie Li and the powerful role she has played in the development of China's military electronics industry, see Ma Jingsheng (1995).
89. In his 1956 speech (Zhou Enlai, 1956), the premier had signaled a major shift in CCP policy toward intellectuals, and thus the opening of the so-called Hundred Flowers campaign, yet it ran squarely against the deeply ingrained class biases of many cadres. Deng, too, sought to challenge these attitudes, especially in the wake of the Cultural Revolution. For context on this speech, see Goldman (1971, pp. 159–61). For its impact on the strategic weaponeers, see Dong Kegong, Song Guangming, and Zou Anshou (1982), "Nie Rongzhen tongzhi" (1982), and Feigenbaum (1997, pp. 77–81).
90. Deng Xiaoping (1978a, p. 93).
91. Ibid. (p. 95).

92. Deng Xiaoping (1977a).
93. Ibid. (p. 5).
94. Deng Xiaoping (1977b, p. 45).
95. Deng Xiaoping (1978a, p. 83).
96. Deng Xiaoping (1977b, pp. 45–46).
97. Deng Xiaoping (1978a, p. 84).
98. Hamrin (1990, p. 46).
99. For background, see Hamrin (1990, p. 46).
100. Gu Mainan (1987).
101. Hamrin (1990, p. 47).
102. Ibid.
103. Hamrin (1990, p. 61 n54) has written that Barney learned about one such example during his visit: T. C. Yang of Shanghai's Jiaotong University played a key role in introducing Western-style system modeling to China. "A 1930s Ph.D. from MIT, Yang reestablished old school ties and in 1980 translated into Chinese the book *Industrial Dynamics* by Jay W. Forrester of the MIT Sloan School of Management. In 1982–1983, Wang Qifan, a student of Yang, studied with the group working on Forrester's system dynamics national model, which was billed as an effective tool for policy analysts to balance short-run versus long-run goals, integrate forces of supply and demand, and interrelate human, financial, and natural resources."
104. Ibid. (p. 48).
105. Ibid. (p. 61 n54). For an example of Song Jian's work in demography, see Song Jian (1982).
106. The rise of scientific decision making in the social sciences and in economic policy is discussed in Halpern (1989).
107. Xie Guang (1992, v. 1, p. 166).

CHAPTER FOUR

1. Manion (1992, p. 9).
2. Ibid. (p. 10).
3. Quoted in Ibid. (pp. 10–11).
4. Wang Shouyun was secretary and personal assistant to Qian Xuesen. Before his death in a road accident in 1998, he was secretary general of COSTIND's S&T Committee. Shen Rongjun was trained as a telemetry, tracking, and control engineer. Together with Chen Fangyun, one of the 863 scientists, he served as coleader of the technical group in China's leading missile and satellite tracking R&D facility, the Luoyang Institute of Tracking and Telecommunications Technology under the NDSTC (Xie Guang, 1992, v. 1, p. 473). He later became a vice minister of COSTIND. Qian Shaojun is a physicist who trained at Qinghua University and the Sino-Soviet Joint Institute for Nuclear Research in Dubna, the USSR, as well as at the Institute of High Energy Physics (IHEP) of the CAS. A PLA major general, he was a department director, then deputy commander, and finally

commander of Base 21, the nuclear weapons test base at Lop Nur. By 1996, Qian was in charge of R&D for the entire Chinese nuclear weapons program.

5. This section is based primarily on interviews with specialists in the Chinese military.

6. On Ye's significance and the Administrative Meeting, see Fan Shuo (1995, pp. 605–8), and Xie Guang (1992, v. 1, pp. 93–95).

7. For background and details, see Lewis, Hua, and Xue (1991, p. 88–92), Zhi Shaozeng (1989), Yan Jingtang (1983), and Song Ke (1981).

8. Until a major reorganization in 1997–98, the main headquarters under the CMC were the General Staff Department (GSD), General Political Department (GPD), General Logistics Department (GLD), and COSTIND. Two smaller headquarters were the Academy of Military Sciences (AMS) and the National Defense University (NDU). Although COSTIND was autonomous in certain areas, it was highly specialized, weaker than the GSD, GPD, and GLD, and quite circumscribed in its broader authority vis-à-vis the other headquarters. Although the navy and air force commands sometimes function as essentially autonomous headquarters, the GSD's role is absolutely critical. It leads the services through its naval and air force bureaus, whose personnel often move back and forth between these bureaus and the service staff headquarters and occasional command assignments. Even though only the CMC can issue "leading" (*lingdao*) instructions to headquarters while the GSD can merely issue "guidance" (*zhidao*), the GSD speaks operationally for the CMC. Bureaucratic ranks are explicit in the Chinese system, and on interheadquarters leading committees, GSD representatives generally seem to rank first, with GPD representatives second, and GLD representatives a distant third. Thus, the GLD does not stand on an equal footing with the general staff and the political staff in the GPD. Likewise, since the GSD manages operations, it speaks with CMC authority on most important matters in which it would be charged with issuing instructions. The GSD acts as the CMC's day-to-day operational agent. COSTIND was split in 1998 into two structures, a PLA General Armaments Department (GAD) for weapons planning, R&D, and testing, and a new COSTIND that is entirely subordinated to the State Council, for weapons production in the defense industries. In the post-1998 system, the GSD, GPD, and GLD probably still rank ahead of the GAD.

9. Zhang Jingfu (1989, p. 80).

10. Zhang Aiping (1989, p. 74).

11. These sections are based on interviews with Chinese specialists.

12. Deng Xiaoping (1977b, p. 49).

13. For background on the SSTC, see Secretarial Division (1995, pp. 96–101), and General Office (1992).

14. Lieberthal and Oksenberg (1988, p. 78).

15. Yang Lizhong (1991, p. 226).

16. Wang Shouyun (1994, p. 105).

17. Chen Yisheng, Li Guogang, and Lu Rong'an (1991).

18. See State Science and Technology Commission (1986, p. 3).

19. Wang Shouyun (1994, p. 105).

20. Yang Lizhong (1991, pp. 248–49).

21. Zhang Aiping (1983, p. 21).

22. Ibid. (p. 22).

23. Suttmeier (1998).

24. The Sino-American exchanges resulted from agreements signed during a July 1978 visit to China by the heads of U.S. technical agencies, led by President Jimmy Carter's science adviser, Frank Press. This led to a trip in the fall of 1978 by Energy Secretary James Schlesinger and to important defense-technical meetings with Under Secretary of Defense William Perry, which I treat in detail below. For an account of the Press visit, as well as the overall importance of U.S.-China negotiations during this period, see ibid.

25. For example, on nuclear physics, see Bromley and Perrolle (1980); on solid state physics, see Fitzgerald and Slichter (1976); on high-energy physics, see Panofsky (1977). Panofsky was a founder of the Stanford Linear Accelerator Center and an important member of President Dwight Eisenhower's Scientific Advisory Committee.

26. Qian, indisputably China's most prominent nuclear physicist of the Mao era, acted as the group's official host in his role as vice president of the CAS and president of Zhejiang University. Qian had served as the political leadership's go-between to China's nuclear physicists in the early years of the atomic bomb program. He was also in charge of the program's theoretical division, procured China's first nuclear instruments in France, and carried a message to Mao from his mentor, the French physicist Frederic Joliot, encouraging China's nuclear ambitions. As noted in Chapter 2, Wang Ganchang, then serving as director of the Institute of Atomic Energy (IAE), had headed one of four main bomb design groups, played a key role in China's thermonuclear effort, and acted as an important administrator at the Sino-Soviet Joint Institute for Nuclear Research in Dubna. On the IAE (code-named "Institute 601," and later "401") in the Chinese nuclear weapons program, see Lewis and Xue (1988a).

27. See Bromley and Perrolle (1980, pp. 87–100).

28. Ibid. (p. 5).

29. Ibid.

30. Shen Rongjun (1988, p. 101).

31. Haas (1992).

32. The primary source for this history is personal communication with William Perry and interviews in China. An account that conflicts with some of Perry's recollections on the specifics of early U.S.-China defense technology cooperation is Mann (1998). On defense normalization more generally, see Pollack (1984).

33. Based on personal communication with Perry.

34. To truly understand the importance of Perry's visit and of his follow-up contacts with the Chinese after he left government, one must understand Perry's

importance in Chinese eyes, something that cannot be easily captured except by anecdotes. For instance, Perry's biography appeared in the main Chinese "dictionary" of military S&T before he entered the Clinton administration at the cabinet level, when he was merely a retired under secretary of defense teaching at Stanford University. The handful of other foreign names includes Oppenheimer, Teller, and Fermi. See Li Zhiqing (1993, p. 352).

35. Based on personal communication with Perry.

36. This has been a problem elsewhere, including the United States. See Alic et al. (1992, pp. 4–5).

37. Zhang Aiping (1983, pp. 23–24).

38. Zhang Aiping (1986, p. 568).

39. Me Wen (1989, pp. 20–21). Italics are mine.

40. Ibid. Intelligent robotics later became a key part of the 863 Plan. See Chapter 5.

41. Lin Yushu, Liu Yuren, and Zheng Wenyi (1992).

42. Ibid.

43. Chinese defense industrialists do not use the economist's term "market failure" to express this idea, but they do invoke the concept almost precisely (albeit descriptively) when they explain why they cannot bear long-term R&D risks. As a chief engineer of a major military industrial facility told me, "Pressure for immediate commercial return makes it impossible for us to invest our R&D resources in forward-looking (*yuanjian*) ways; this is the most important *technical* reason why we require state support." Despite hints of a coming reform from Premier Zhu Rongji, this situation is still compounded by the fact that firms must spend working capital on employee benefits, such as worker housing and clinics. This puts an even greater strain on capital that could conceivably be invested in R&D. In the face of these combined technical and political limitations, many interviewees told me, it is nearly impossible to behave in "future-oriented" ways.

CHAPTER FIVE

1. The concept of the "new technological revolution," a topic of wide-ranging discussion at high political levels throughout the 1980s, captivated many Chinese leaders, including the reformers Hu Yaobang and Zhao Ziyang. Marshal Nie Rongzhen is widely regarded as one of Hu Yaobang's political mentors. Indeed, when Hu was purged as CCP general secretary in 1987, Nie withdrew from politics. Some have suggested that this was to protest Hu's treatment by Nie's fellow party elders.

2. The term "chief" is often used in PLA circles to refer to the ten "old marshals" created in the years after the Communist revolution. No one has since been appointed to this rank, which is why the term "chief" has special resonance in the Chinese military.

3. Unspoken, but no doubt clear to Deng and other leaders, was that strategic weaponeers also hoped that they themselves would play the leading role in the formulation and implementation of S&T plans.

4. Yang Lizhong (1991, p. 226).

5. This assertion is based on a great many interviews in China. The importance of this type of coordination is reinforced in counterexamples cited by some interviewees where representatives of the defense and civilian S&T commissions that cooperated when former strategic weaponeers worked together did not do so when no such informal tie was in place to mediate the contentious formal relationship between these bureaucracies. In these cases, showdowns over the division of appropriations were routine.

6. Informality can eliminate ambiguity about who is responsible for a problem. See Chisholm (1989, p. 65). On China, against the backdrop of a shortage-based political economy, see Mayfair Yang (1994). On politics, see Pye (1981).

7. On how these groups normally function, see Lieberthal and Oksenberg (1988, chap. 4).

8. For Song's personal background, see Gu Mainan (1987). For his scientific and technical background, see Kong Deyong (1991).

9. The 40 percent figure, based on interviews, is rough. I believe this approximates the real figure. I return to these other plans in Chapter 6.

10. Gu Mainan (1987).

11. Ibid.

12. These assertions are based on interviews with Chinese missile specialists.

13. Sources on Li Xu'e include interviews with Chinese missileers, Liao Gailong and Fan Yuan (1989, p. 364), and Lewis and Xue (1994, p. 177 n33).

14. For background on Zhou Guangzhao, see Wang Jinghu (1989).

15. Wang Yougong (1990). For Zhou's view of the CAS's priorities in the late 1980s, see Guo Jinping (1988).

16. Biographical information on Zou Jiahua, as well as Gan Ziyu and Sheng Shuren (discussed below), is from Liao Gailong and Fan Yuan (1989), and interviews. On Zou's career, see also China Economic Information Network <http://ce.cei.gov.cn/G_body/a2/a2zpjbhb.htm>.

17. The best examples of Ye's role in strategic weapons development during this period come from the nuclear submarine program. Particularly noteworthy were Ye's battles on behalf of Project 718, an effort to develop and deploy an instrumentation fleet in support of the SSBN and its missile. See especially Peng Ziqiang (1986, pp. 3–4). See also Li Qi and Nie Li (1989). On the Special Commission meetings, see Xie Guang (1992, v. 1, p. 92), and Li Qi and Nie Li (1989, p. 393).

18. On the SPC, see He Jianzhang and Wang Zhiye (1984), and Secretarial Division (1995, p. 48–57). The latter source includes descriptions of internal departments and substructures. For surveys in English, see Lieberthal and Oksenberg (1988, pp. 64–72), and Wang Lixin and Fewsmith (1995).

19. On Gan's career, see China Economic Information Network <http://ce.cei.gov.cn/G_body/a2/a2gfziyu.htm>.

20. On Sheng's career, see Xinhuanet.com <http://202.84.17.13/english/htm/200001031/184158.htm>.

21. The history of surface physics in China is closely intertwined with that of Fudan. Madame Xie Xide (exclusively a civilian scientist), one of China's surface physics pioneers, was also a leader of the university and a key player in its post-1949 development. See Wang Zengfan (1991).

22. *Wenhuibao* (Dec. 25, 1992).

23. See especially Lieberthal and Oksenberg (1988), Lampton (1987), and Lieberthal and Lampton (1992).

24. Chisholm (1989, p. 65). On the peculiar strength of ties among acquaintances, see the classic treatment by the economic sociologist Mark Granovetter (1973).

25. In personal communication, Michel Oksenberg pointed out that this pattern among strategic weaponeers in the 1980s was very similar to efforts in the 1970s by leaders of China's petroleum industry—the so-called "petroleum faction"—to control the Chinese energy sector, and then leverage this into control of national economic planning.

26. Initially, the 863 Plan was a sensitive subject in China given its strategic implications for military and dual-use technologies, as well as its support at high political levels. These sections are based on interviews and sources published after 1989, when the plan became better defined. Early sources on the program include Yang Lizhong (1991, esp. pp. 225–50), Chen Jianping (1996), Yang Lianghua (1992), Hu Haitang (1989), Xie Guang (1992, v. 1, pp. 168–69), Huang Ma (1990), "Hewei" (1992), "Ba liu san" (1991), "Wanren toushen" (1991), Shang Mu (1989), and State Science and Technology Commission (1995, pp. 66–70). Today, the program has its own Internet website, which includes downloadable grant application forms. By January 1, 2001, the site had received over 100,000 hits. See <www.863.org.cn>.

27. Wang Daheng (1989).

28. A good Chinese technical biography of Wang, which includes parts of his English and Chinese language scientific bibliography, is Chen Xingdan (1991).

29. Wang Daheng (1989, p. 470).

30. Nie Rongzhen (1986, p. 822).

31. Wang Daheng (1989, p. 471), Xie Guang (1992, v. 1, p. 463).

32. Sources on Wang Ganchang include Shao Yihai (1989), Su Fangxue (1990), and Wang Ganchang's (1989) own short memoir.

33. Lewis and Xue (1988a, p. 248).

34. Shen Rongjun (1988, p. 48).

35. For background on Chen Fangyun's work on military technology, see Zou Jiahua (1985, p. 29), as well as Chen Fangyun's (1989) own reminiscences. For a scientific biography, with bibliographical references, see Sun Huaisu (1991). On Chen and the TT&C network, see Xie Guang (1992, v. 1, p. 426).

36. Chen Fangyun (1989).

37. For a detailed survey of China's TT&C network, see Yang Zhenming (1990). The Chinese support network is built around three satellite launch centers, in Jiuquan, Xichang, and Taiyuan. Each of these has responsibility for launching a different type of satellite; functional specialization is divided among the three.

TT&C for the system is supervised by the Xi'an Satellite Control Center, which relies upon data from five fixed and two mobile TT&C stations, several mobile recovery posts, and two Yuanwang instrumentation ships developed under the auspices of Project 718.

38. Shen Rongjun (1988, p. 132).
39. Xie Guang (1992, v. 1, p. 468).
40. Shen Rongjun (1988, p. 132).
41. Xie Guang (1992, v. 1, p. 473).
42. Ibid. (p. 397).
43. See Yang Jiachi (1990).
44. As two key military electronics specialists, Wang Shiguang and Zhang Xuedong (1989, p. 424), have pointed out, the guiding slogan of the electronics ministry shifted during the 1980s from "military work as the basis" (*yijun weizhu*) to "civilian work as the basis" (*yimin weizhu*).
45. These paragraphs on the report are based on Yang Lizhong (1991, pp. 227–28).
46. I cover this theme in greater detail in Chapter 6. While technonationalism always privileged indigenization, this did not mean that China would not rely on foreign partners. It could do both: rely on Soviet designs to build an indigenous military industrial base during the Mao era; import technology and then indigenize relevant knowledge and systems during the reform era. In discussing China's electron-positron collider, for example, Deng boasted that the project "was not merely copied from a foreign country; some of the equipment and technologies were developed by Chinese engineers." Deng Xiaoping (1986).
47. Deng Xiaoping (1988a, p. 290), and Shi Zhongquan and Chen Dengcai (1994, p. 89).
48. For background on the "productive force"/"number one productive force" argument, see Shi Zhongquan and Chen Dengcai (1994, pp. 84–96).
49. Deng Xiaoping (1988b, pp. 293–94). Italics are mine. For context on this speech, see "Wo jun lingdaoren" (1993). The completion of the Chinese collider made the PRC one of just four countries to possess such a facility, after the United States (Stanford Linear Accelerator), Switzerland (CERN), and Japan (Tsukuba). The Beijing center (BEPC) studies the movement and interaction of the smallest subatomic particles yet discovered, such as quarks and charms. BEPC operates on a power of 2.2-gev (billion-electron-volt). The linear accelerator is 200 meters long and complements a 240-meter perimeter storage ring, a 400-ton detector, a sychrotron radiation laboratory, and a computer facility.
50. Deng Xiaoping (1988a, p. 291).
51. Pollack (1992).
52. Zhu Lilan (1989).
53. Ibid. Zhu's career has been civilian, but she is widely acknowledged to have risen through the Chinese science administration system through the patronage of Song Jian, to whom she reported on matters concerning the 863 Plan before replacing Song at the top of China's S&T bureaucracy upon his retirement from

the position in 1998. As one of Song's vice ministers, Zhu was charged primarily with overseeing the 863 Plan.

54. Hamer and Kung (1989, p. 77).

55. In so doing, it has a complement in a national basic research plan, as well as regular basic science funding mechanisms of the CAS and of the National Natural Science Foundation of China (NNSFC). In the 863 Plan, funding for pure science follows a logic internal to the scientific disciplines. This makes it different from most other funding decisions in the plan, which follow the more applied logic of state goals. Nonetheless, basic research funding under the plan does assume, as did U.S. military funding of pure science after World War II, that theoretical debates can potentially yield applied technologies. See, for instance, Kevles (1992, p. 313). On NNSFC funding mechanisms, see U.S. Embassy Science and Technology Section (1999).

56. Lin Jin (1993a, 1993b). Lin and his colleagues obtained several sources of government funding to purchase nanosecond-accurate hydrogen clocks in the United States. Lin is a former Chinese missile and space scientist who, like Song Jian, worked on missile guidance. During the 1960s, Lin helped to pioneer first-generation guidance systems for the Long March–1 booster rocket. See Zhang Jun (1986, p. 165). Most recently, he has worked in the First Academy (general configuration and rocket engines) of the former missile ministry.

57. Zhu Lilan (1989).

58. These sections are based mainly on Xie Guang (1992, v. 1, pp. 168–69).

59. Hu Haitang (1989).

60. These were large grants by 1987 standards; today the numbers are larger still. In any case, although proportionally biotechnology is among the larger 863 fields, the size of single block grants in other areas (for instance, lasers, which have been administered by the military) is considerably larger; it appears to spread smaller amounts among a wider array of recipients. Substantive quantitative budget data have been hard to come by. The 1987 biotechnology figure is from Hamer and Kung (1989, p. 8).

61. Many Chinese, including some interviewed for this book, commonly use a popular expression to capture this idea: "Pavilions near the water receive the most moonlight."

62. See Francis (1996, pp. 839–59). I return to this theme in the next chapter. At least one state personal computer maker, Lianxiang (Legend) has learned how to outcompete multinationals through successful branding; in 1999, it had a 13 percent local market share, nearly double that of its nearest competitor, IBM. See Roberts (1999).

63. Hamer and Kung (1989).

64. Chen Zhangliang (1999).

65. Chinese Academy of Agricultural Sciences (2001).

66. On the scientific side, the program has been led by Zhang Heqi, an astronomer, who was chief scientist of 863 space-technology groups.

67. Based on interviews with Chinese bidders, including senior managers from Chengdu Aircraft.

68. Hamer and Kung (1989, p. 8).

69. Based on interviews with Chinese specialists. For published confirmation in open Chinese sources of the military orientation of the laser and aerospace fields, see Chen Jianping (1996, p. 4).

70. Stokes (1999, pp. 119–20).

71. On the interest in information technology, see the Chinese essays translated in Pillsbury (1996). See also Zhu Youwen, Feng Yi, and Xu Dechi (1994), and Liu Yichang (1993), a volume from the Academy of Military Sciences series on high-tech warfare.

72. State Science and Technology Commission (1995, p. 67). Italics are mine.

73. On the growing use of peer review since the late 1980s, see U.S. Embassy Science and Technology Section (1999).

74. See, for example, Shang Mu (1989, pp. 3–4).

75. See Suisheng Zhao (1995, p. 242).

76. Li is also a member of the Institute of Computing Technology under the CAS. His center is neither the only supercomputing facility in China nor the only recipient of 863 funding in this area. Moreover, its focus is not the extensive personal computer and software sector that now dominates the Chinese market. Rather, it serves as the clearinghouse and coordinator for government investment programs in parallel and symmetrical multiprocessing. See Li Guojie (1996).

77. Nie mentions artificial crystals in his memoir. Nie Rongzhen (1986, pp. 818–19).

78. State Science and Technology Commission (1995, p. 67).

79. Qian Zongjue (1994).

80. This section is based on interviews with recipients of 863 funds, as well as Hu Haitang (1989), and "Ba liu san" (1991).

81. Wang Yannian (1991).

82. For Chinese views of CAD, CAM, and CIMS processes, see Ren Gongyue (1986, p. 424).

83. See for example, Hu Haitang (1989).

84. Wang Yannian (1991).

85. "Ba liu san" (2001).

86. This section is based on Sandia National Laboratory (2001), and discussion with my Harvard colleagues in physics and engineering.

87. On some of these civilian applications, see University of Alaska (2001).

88. This section is based on "Ba liu san" (2001), "Ten Megawatt High Temperature Gas-Cooled Reactor" (2001), and "China Completes" (2001).

89. This section is based on "Ba liu san" (2001), Saint-Gobain Semiconductors (2001), "Diamond Films" (2000), and Gregory (2000).

90. Saint-Gobain Semiconductors (2001).

91. This section is based mainly on "Ba liu san" (2001), National Center for Intelligent Computing (undated), and Li Guojie (1996).

92. Hui Yongzheng (1998).

93. In 1995, the CAS launched a more formal strategic weapons–type mentoring program, dubbed the 321 Program. The decision to develop this program reflected the realities of an aging scientific workforce: in 1995, just 36 of 214 academicians of the CAS were under the age of 60. The 321 Program aims to train some 30,000 younger personnel, of whom 100 extremely talented younger scientists would comprise the core of the next generation. These 100 men and women would lead China's scientific institutes and R&D programs in the twenty-first century, assisted by some 2,000 less prominent younger scientists and approximately 28,000 research support personnel, most with master's degrees ("CAS Launches," 1995, p. 13).

94. This section is based mainly on "Ba liu san" (2001), and Hui Yongzheng (1998).

95. See Lewis and Xue (1994, p. 56), Dong Shitang (1989), and Huang Xuhua (1989).

96. Hui Yongzheng (1998).

97. For coverage in English of some of the debates over the manned space program, see Lawrence (2000).

98. Covault (1996, p. 22).

99. Ibid.

100. Zhang Jun (1986, p. 53).

101. See <www.863cims.net> or <www.cims.edu.cn>.

102. Based on company materials from its website, <www.spatial.com>, and undated materials from China on 863 CIMS automation.

103. See "Ba liu san" (2001).

104. See for example, U.S. Department of Agriculture (1994), which critiques a patent application for this type of hybrid rice technique.

105. Hui Yongzheng (1998).

106. Details in this section are primarily from Hui Yongzheng (1998), and "Ba liu san" (2001).

107. Details in this section are based primarily on Wei Long (2000).

108. Hui Yongzheng (1998).

CHAPTER SIX

1. Yang Lianghua (1992). The CAS Department of Technological Sciences evolved, in part, out of the 04 Bureau of the CAS (see Chapter 2), led by Gu Yu in the 1960s and established with support from Marshal Nie Rongzhen.

2. Two key members of this group were Shi Changxu and Luo Peilin, both of whom had backgrounds in weapons engineering. Shi had spent most of his career at the CAS Metals Research Institute in Shenyang where he had been the main designer of cast multiholed metallurgy for military aircraft (Shi Changxu, 1989) and a task force leader in the development of China's J-8 fighter plane. Chinese specialists consider Shi's contribution crucial to the development of the J-8 because his innovative design of hollow air-cooled blades for the engine proved more resilient than previous designs (Xie Guang, 1992, v. 2, p. 190). Shi also had won a state prize for

his development of metal alloys for turbine disks, blades, and the combustion chamber of military interceptor aircraft (Ibid., p. 420). Luo Peilin had been Qian Xuesen's dormmate at Jiaotong University in the 1930s. Luo and Qian became reacquainted at Caltech, in 1948 (Shi Zhu, 1986, p. 582). In 1956, Luo was a leading figure in drafting sessions for the Twelve-Year Plan for Science and Technology Development under Zhou Enlai, Chen Yi, and Nie Rongzhen. He became chief engineer of the Telecommunications Bureau (Dianxin gongye ju) of the nuclear weapons ministry, the Second Ministry of Machine Building. Reflecting Luo's high technical stature, he served simultaneously at the Fourth Ministry (electronics) as deputy director of its Science and Technology Committee. Between 1958 and 1966, Luo directed R&D of super-long-range radar systems (*chaoyuancheng leida*) (Shi Zhu, 1986, p. 582). In the 1970s, he turned his attention to military computing.

3. Yang Lianghua (1992).
4. Song Jian (1991, p. 2).
5. Quoted in Li Xu'e (1992, p. 53).
6. State Science and Technology Commission (1995, p. 72).
7. Ibid. (p. 74).
8. Ibid. (p. 77).
9. See, for instance, Li Xu'e (1989), Li Xu'e (1992), Yang Zhaobo (1991), Zhang Bingfu (1989), and State Science and Technology Commission (1995, pp. 70–72).
10. Li Xu'e (1992, p. 53)
11. Ibid. (p. 55).
12. Xiao Yuanzhen, Yang Bingxing, and Liu Jiaqing (1994, p. 1).
13. Li Xu'e (1992, p. 56).
14. Ibid. (pp. 53–54).
15. Ibid. (p. 54).
16. U.S. Embassy Science and Technology Section (1999).
17. Francis (1996, p. 265).
18. Ibid. (p. 266).
19. Ibid.
20. Ibid. (p. 263).
21. Chen Jianping (1996, p. 8).
22. Liu Jing (1995).
23. These sixteen special 863 companies were Shenzhen Kexing Biology Product Co. Ltd., Beijing Zhongzi Hanwang Science and Technology Co., Dongfang Software Co. Ltd., China Great Dragon Information Technology Co. Ltd., Langchao Information Industry Co. Ltd., Fenghuo Communications Science and Technology Co. Ltd., Datang Telecom Science and Technology Co. Ltd., Wuhan Huazhong Numerical Control System Co. Ltd., Shenyang Xinsong Machine Automation Co. Ltd., Zhong Liao San Pu Battery (Shenyang) Co. Ltd., Guangdong Fenghua High and New Science and Technology Group, Tianjin Heping Haiwan Real Estate Development Co., Shenzhen Leidi Science and Technology Enterprise Co. Ltd., Beijing San

Huan New Materials High-tech Inc. (of the CAS), Shandong Tian Da Medicine Co. Ltd., and Shandong Rong Cheng Xun Shan Aquaculture Group (*Keji Ribao,* Jan. 27, 2000).

24. "Scientists Pick" (1996). For some key projects in three 863 fields— biotechnology, information technology, and new materials—see "Zhongguo 'ba liu san'" (1996). For automation, see "Formulation of Strategic Objectives" (1989), and "Progress with Intelligent Automation" (1989).

25. Li Debin (1985). On China's early absorption of key facilities into Communist-controlled industry, prior to 1949, see Wang Zhaoquan (1991).

26. Goad and Holland (2000).

27. Lawrence (2000).

28. U.S. Embassy Science and Technology Section (2001).

29. Office of Technology Assessment (1987, p. 41).

30. Ibid., and Simon (1989, p. 299).

31. See Simon (1989, p. 300).

32. This squares with arguments by economic historians. Nathan Rosenberg (1982, p. 143) has argued, for example, that technological progress does not necessarily depend on inventiveness but may instead be founded on "the deployment of previously available information."

33. Grow (1989, pp. 319–21).

34. This resulted from a reflexive adoption of the Soviet-style system, in which research was separated from production. The Chinese tinkered with this many times under Mao's rule, but the weakness (and general lack) of enterprise-level R&D has been a pervasive problem. In many state-directed sectors, it remains so. This is one reason the development of private enterprise in high-tech areas has been so significant in the late 1990s.

35. Panofsky (1992, p. 132).

36. Chinese military researchers, especially at COSTIND and in the Academy of Military Sciences, have written a great deal about fiber optics and related matters. The most sophisticated and interesting treatment is Yang Lizhong (1991). See pp. 347–56 on fiber optics, and pp. 343–45 on satellite communications. Zhu Youwen, Feng Yi, and Xu Dechi (1994, pp. 177–80) concentrates on the military.

37. On the MPT's military roots, see Yang Taifang (1993, pp. 22–27).

38. Xie Guang (1992, v. 1, p. 492).

39. Hao Yunpeng (1996). For additional background on civilian telecommunications priorities, see Ke Gaochu (1989), as well as the voluminous material published by the MPT itself, especially the documents in Ministry of Posts and Telecommunications (1993).

40. Wang Chunyuan (1996, p. 7).

41. Ibid. (p. 18).

42. On Great Wall Mobile, see Sender (1997, p. 76).

43. "Guowuyuan" (1996).

44. Xie Guang (1992, v. 1, p. 492).

45. For background on this contest, see "Lian Tong" (1994), and Brauchli (1994). For a survey of MPT's preemptive attempts to discipline and reorganize itself, see "Breaking Up" (1994).

46. Quoted in Brauchli (1994).

47. Sender (1997, p. 75).

48. Ibid.

49. Ibid.

50. Ke Gaochu (1989, p. 3).

51. Qian Zongjue (1993a, 1993b, 1994).

52. On Institute 722's contributions to submarine communications, see Lewis and Xue (1994, pp. 118–19).

53. Discussion of Institute 722's perspectives is based on interviews with leading firm managers and engineers. On the contract won by MPT's local affiliate, for a 2.4 Gb/s SDH system, see "Ba liu san" (2001).

CHAPTER SEVEN

1. This was an important theme in the "Cox Committee" report of the U.S. Congress, "U.S. National Security and Military/Commercial Concerns with the People's Republic of China."

2. On these factors in Hong Kong, see Zerega (1999).

3. Naughton (1998), esp. chap. 8 by Huchet (1998).

4. Lardy (1998, pp. 207–8).

5. Ibid.

6. "Official Calls" (1998).

7. Hamer and Kung (1989, p. 77).

8. For a statement of policy to this effect, see Zhu Guangya (1998).

9. U.S. Embassy Science and Technology Section (1996).

10. Some of the parallels between the late Qing defense industry and the strategic weapons programs of the contemporary era are truly fascinating. A system, including a translation bureau, at the Jiangnan Arsenal for the absorption of foreign technical materials smacks of the Information Bureau in the Communist-era weapons programs. See, for example, Reardon-Anderson (1991, chap. 2). There are also interesting similarities between Li Hongzhang and Nie Rongzhen, although Li's career was, of course, considerably more encompassing than Nie's in national-level politics and included an important role in shaping foreign policy. Nie's rivalry with other leaders over the defense industry is perhaps mirrored in aspects of Li Hongzhang's political rivalry with Zhang Zhidong, who attempted to build the Hanyang Arsenal in Hubei as an alternative to the Jiangnan Arsenal, especially in the manufacture of smokeless powder, then among the highest priority national military technologies. The rivalry in China over smokeless powder was as important in its day as strategic weapons in the Communist era.

11. On the role of military technologies and challenges in the construction of a modern national chemical industry during the late Qing dynasty, see Reardon-Anderson (1991, pp. 153–57).

12. Kennedy (1994, p. 197). Kennedy's (1978) comprehensive history of the Jiangnan arsenal probes these issues more deeply.

13. Kennedy (1994, p. 197).

14. Ibid. (p. 210).

15. Ibid.

16. Kirby (1989, p. 27).

17. Kennedy (1994, p. 211).

18. Deng Xiaoping (1978a, p. 88).

19. The quotation is from Mao's essay "On Practice," quoted in the "Little Red Book" of sayings popular during the 1960s. For the complete essay, see Mao Zedong (1937).

APPENDIX TWO

1. The First Ministry was an exclusively civilian ministry, both administratively and functionally. It was occasionally called by this code name for reasons of standardization and convenience.

2. Originally, the designation "Eighth Ministry of Machine Building" referred to a structure involved with the production of agricultural machinery. However, when that structure was merged into other ministries during the mid-1960s, the code designation lapsed. It was later revived to refer to a subdivision of the Seventh Ministry. Known as the Eighth Bureau (Ba ju) of the Seventh Ministry of Machine Building, this bureau retained at least one crucial bureaucratic characteristic: though part of a ministry and therefore designated as a "bureau," the leader of the Eighth Bureau actually held the rank of vice-minister (*fubuzhang*) of the ministry and thus stood higher in the bureaucracy than an ordinary bureau chief (*juzhang*). The Eighth Bureau had originally been spun off from the ministry in part because Zhou Enlai believed that the chaos of the Cultural Revolution was making crucial work within the ministry difficult, as well because of its size: the Seventh Ministry had, by the early 1970s, become a behemoth, subsuming a variety of missile-related programs. The Eighth Bureau was therefore charged with the development of three types of missile systems: surface-to-air missiles with antiaircraft potential, cruise missiles, with both sea and ground-launch capability, and—most importantly— *tactical* ballistic missile systems (*zhanshu dandao daodan*), which received new emphasis after 1975. Sometime between Lin Biao's death in 1971 and the renewed emphasis on tactical programs in 1975, the Eighth Bureau seems to have mutated into the Eighth Ministry. By 1981, the Eighth Ministry was reabsorbed into the Seventh Ministry.

3. The Fourth Academy was founded after the 1965 merger of missile units into the new Seventh Ministry of Machine Building. Because the subacademies were renamed full "Academies," the Fourth Academy never had the "sub" or

"branch" (*fen*) designation that the First, Second, and Third Academies held prior to 1965.

APPENDIX THREE

1. All quotations are from untitled, undated materials published by the SSTC, including glossy brochures and introductory papers in Chinese and English on the information technology field of the 863 Plan. As indicated elsewhere in the Notes, readers wanting further information will find the 863 program's Chinese-language website especially useful. See <www.863.org.cn>.

2. Quotations are from Automation Technology Managerial Group (2001).

3. Quotations are from undated materials published by the 863 Information Technology Managerial Group.

4. Quotations in this section are from Qian Zongjue (1994).

5. Based on National Advanced Materials Committee (1998, 2001).

REFERENCES

The following abbreviations are used in this list:

BDS   *Bujin de Sinian* [Boundless Memories]. Beijing: Central Documents Press, 1987.

DXWX   *Deng Xiaoping Wenxuan, 1975–1982* [Selected Works of Deng Xiaoping, 1975–1982]. Beijing: People's Press, 1983.

HGYZW   Nie Li, and Huai Guomo, eds. *Huigu yu Zhanwang: Xin Zhongguo de Guofang Keji Gongye* [Retrospect and Prospect: New China's Defense Science and Technology Industry]. Beijing: Defense Industry Press, 1989.

JPRS-CST Joint Publications Research Service. China. Science and Technology Series. U.S. Department of Commerce.

NRJW   *Nie Rongzhen Junshi Wenxuan* [Selected Military Works of Nie Rongzhen]. Beijing: Liberation Army Press, 1992.

XSKJ   Central Documents Research Division of the Chinese Communist Party, ed. *Xin Shiqi Kexue Jishu Gongzuo Zhongyao Wenxian Xuanbian* [Selected Important Documents on Scientific and Technological Work in the New Era]. Beijing: Central Documents Press (CCP Central Committee), 1995.

ZXKZ   Lu Jiaxi, ed. *Zhongguo Xiandai Kexuejia Zhuanji* [Collected Biographies of Modern Chinese Scientists]. Beijing: Science Press, 1991.

Unless otherwise noted, all serials in Chinese are published in Beijing. Chinese volumes supervised by editorial boards have been cited according to the first name listed.

"A Guide to the Torch Plan." 1989. *Zhongguo Keji Luntan* [Forum on Science and Technology in China], no. 6 (Nov. 18): 7–10. Trans. and reprinted in JPRS-CST (Mar. 15, 1990): 5–10.

Ai Lingyao. 1990. "Zhongguo jundui de ba ci jingjian zhengbian" [The Chinese army's eight demobilization campaigns]. *Junshi Shijie* [Military World] 3, no. 1 (Jan./Feb.): 74–78.

Alic, John A., Lewis M. Branscomb, Harvey Brooks, Ashton B. Carter, and Gerald L. Epstein. 1992. *Beyond Spinoff: Military and Commercial Technologies in a Changing World.* Boston: Harvard Business School Press.

Allen, Kenneth, Glenn Krumel, and Jonathan D. Pollack. 1995. *China's Air Force Enters the Twenty-first Century.* Santa Monica, CA: RAND.

Automation Technology Managerial Group. 2001. 863 Program Priorities. Website accessed Feb. 28, 2001. <www.cims.edu.cn>.

"'Ba liu san': Zhongguo gao jishu fazhan de lantu" ["863": The blueprint for China's high technology development]. 1991. *Liaowang* [Outlook] (July 8): 11–13.

"Ba liu san jihua zhongda guanjian jishu xiangmu" [The major key technology projects of the 863 plan]. 2001. 863 program Chinese language website. Website accessed Jan. 25, 2001. <www.863.org.cn/policy/ply001.html>.

Bachman, David M. 1985. *Chen Yun and the Chinese Political System.* Center for Chinese Studies, China Research Monograph no. 29. Berkeley: Institute of East Asian Studies, University of California.

———. 1991. *Bureaucracy, Economy, and Leadership in China: The Institutional Origins of the Great Leap Forward.* Cambridge, UK: Cambridge University Press.

Bao Mingrong and Hu Guangzheng. 1983. "Qiantan Mao Zedong junshi sixiang zai kang Mei yuan Chao zhanzheng zhong de yunyong he fazhan de jige wenti" [Some problems in the application and development of Mao Zedong's military thought in the War to Resist America and Aid Korea]. *Dangshi Yanjiu* [Party History Research], no. 6: 32–41.

Barnett, A. Doak. 1967. *Cadres, Bureaucracy, and Political Power in Communist China.* New York: Columbia University Press.

Bethe, Hans A. 1979. "The Happy Thirties." In Roger H. Stuewer, ed., *Nuclear Physics in Retrospect: Proceedings of a Symposium on the 1930s,* 11–31. Minneapolis: University of Minnesota Press.

Bitzinger, Richard A. 2000. "A Lot of Explaining to Do: Assessing Chinese Defense Expenditures." Unpublished manuscript prepared for the Center for the Study of Chinese Military Affairs, Institute for National Strategic Studies, National Defense University, Washington, DC. Website accessed Feb. 26, 2001. <www.ndu.edu/inss/China_Center/paper9.htm>.

Bitzinger, Richard A., and Chong-pin Lin. 1994. "Off the Books: Analyzing and Understanding Chinese Defense Spending." Unpublished manuscript. Washington, DC: Defense Budget Project.

Bo Yibo. 1991. *Ruogan Zhongda Juece yu Shijian de Huigu* [Recollections of Certain Important Decisions and Events]. Vol. 1. Beijing: Central Party School Press.

Brauchli, Marcus W. 1994. "China Government Creates Second Telecom Network: In Win for Reformers, New Firm Introduces Competition to Sector." *Asian Wall Street Journal* (July), unidentified date (source is a newspaper clipping).

"Breaking Up." 1994. *Business China Supplement.* Telecoms. Newsletter published by the Economist Intelligence Unit, London (May).

Bromley, D. Allan, and Pierre M. Perrolle. 1980. *Nuclear Science in China.* Committee on Scholarly Communication with the People's Republic of China. CSCPRC Report no. 10. Washington, DC: National Academy of Sciences.

Brömmelhörster, Jörn, and John Frankenstein, eds. 1997. *Mixed Motives, Uncertain Outcomes: Chinese Defense Conversion.* Boulder, CO: Lynne Riener.

Cai Renzhao. 1994. *Zhongguo Yuanshuai Nie Rongzhen* [Nie Rongzhen: Chinese Marshal]. Beijing: Central Party School Press.

Cao Shixin, ed. 1994. *Zhongguo Junzhuanmin* [Defense Conversion in China]. Beijing: China Economic Press.

CAS Institute of Microbiology. 2001. "Constitution of R&D Funds in 1996." Website accessed Feb. 13, 2001. <www.im.ac.cn/impictures/gk1.jpg>.

"CAS Launches '321' Program to Foster 21st Century S&T Leaders." 1995. Trans. of article from *Guizhou Ribao* [Guizhou Daily] (May 25): 3. Reprinted in Foreign Broadcast Information Service Report. China. Science and Technology Series (Aug. 18): 13–14.

Ceng Wenqu. 1991. "Li Siguang." In *ZXKZ*, 299–314.

Chen Encai. 1991. "Liang Shoupan." In *ZXKZ*, 844–53.

Chen Fangyun. 1989. "Canjia wo guo weixing cekong xitong yanzhi de tihui" [Some personal experience with research and development on our country's satellite tracking system]. In *HGYZW*, 495–96.

Chen Jianping. 1996. "863 jihua: huihuang de shi nian" [The 863 plan: Ten glorious years]. *Xiandai Junshi* [Contemporary Military Affairs], no. 6 (June): 4–8.

Chen Liwei. 1989. "Guanyu fazhan junyong jisuanji jishu de jidian tihui" [A few words about the development of computer technology for military use]. In *HGYZW*, 440–41.

Chen Ping, ed. 1987. *Xin Zhongguo de Jiben Jianshe: Guofang Gongye Juan* [Capital Construction in New China: Military Industry]. Restricted circulation edition. Beijing: Defense Industry Press.

Chen Xingdan. 1991. "Wang Daheng." In *ZXKZ*, 138–45.

Chen Yisheng, Li Guoguang, and Lu Rong'an. 1991. "Exploring China's High Technology R&D Management System." *Zhongguo Keji Luntan* [Forum on China's Science and Technology], no. 5 (Sept. 18): 40–42. Trans. and reprinted in JPRS-CST.

Chen Youming. 1989. "Yingming de juece, jianju de gongcheng: ji Zhou Enlai deng laoyibei gemingjia guanhuai he qianting gongcheng" [Wise decision, arduous task: Recalling the concern of Zhou Enlai and other veteran revolutionaries for the nuclear-powered submarine project]. In *HGYZW*, 135–43.

Chen Zhangliang. 1999. "Unlimited Prospects for Biotechnology." *Zhishi Jingji* [Knowledge Economy] (Dec.): 22–28. Trans. and posted on-line by the U.S. Embassy Science and Technology Section, Beijing. Public Section Report

(Jan. 2000). Website accessed Mar. 12, 2001. <www.usembassy-china.org.cn/english/sandt/index.html>.

Chen Zhaobo. 1989. "Wo guo he gongye fazhan de yuanliao baozheng" [Supplying raw materials for the development of our country's nuclear industry]. In *HGYZW,* 216–19.

"China Completes Construction of New Type of Nuclear Reactor in Beijing." 2000. *Renmin Ribao* [People's Daily]. On-line edition in English (Dec. 23). Website accessed Feb. 13, 2001. <http://english.peopledaily.com.cn/200012/23/eng20001223_58648.html>.

Chinese Academy of Agricultural Sciences. 2001. Organizational Profile. Website accessed Feb. 13, 2001. <http://w3/itri.org.tw/k0000/apec/China/CHINA24.htm>.

Chisholm, Donald. 1989. *Coordination Without Hierarchy: Informal Structures in Multi-Organizational Systems.* Berkeley: University of California Press.

Christensen, Thomas J. 1992. "Threats, Assurances, and the Last Chance for Peace: The Lessons of Mao's Korean War Telegrams." *International Security* 17, no. 1: 122–54.

Ci Yungui. 1989. "Yishi yinhe luo jiutian: ji yinhe juxingji de dansheng" [Recalling the birth of the Yinhe supercomputer]. In *HGYZW,* 437–39.

Covault, Craig. 1996. "Chinese Manned Flight Set for 1999 Liftoff." *Aviation Week and Space Technology* 145, no. 17 (Oct. 21): 22–23.

Deng Xiaoping. 1975a. "Jundui yao zhengdun" [The army needs to be consolidated] (Jan. 25, 1975). In *DXWX,* 1–3.

———. 1975b. "Keyan gongzuo yao zou zai qianmian" [Research and development work should advance in front] (Sept. 26, 1975). In *XSKJ,* 1–3.

———. 1977a. "Zunzhong zhishi, zunzhong rencai" [Respect knowledge, respect talent] (May 24, 1977). In *XSKJ,* 4–5.

———. 1977b. "Guanyu kexue he jiaoyu gongzuo de jidian yijian" [Some opinions on work in science and education] (Aug. 8, 1977). In *DXWX,* 45–55.

———. 1978a. "Zai quanguo kexue dahui kaimoshi shang de jianghua" [Speech at the opening ceremony of the National Science Conference] (Mar. 18, 1978). In *DXWX,* 82–97.

———. 1978b. "Jiefang sixiang, shishi qiushi, tuanjie yizhi xiang qiankan" [Liberate the mind, seek truth from facts, and unite to look forward toward the future] (Dec. 13, 1978). In *DXWX,* 130–43.

———. 1980. "Muqian de xingshi he renwu" [The present situation and the tasks before us] (Jan. 16, 1980). In *DXWX,* 203–37.

———. 1981. "Jianshe qiangda de xiandaihua zhengguihua de geming jundui" [Build powerful, modern, and regularized revolutionary armed forces] (Sept. 19, 1981). In *DXWX,* 349–50.

———. 1986. "Zhongguo yao fazhan, libukai kexue" [China cannot develop without science] (Oct. 28, 1986). In *Deng Xiaoping Wenxuan, 1982–1992*

[Selected Works of Deng Xiaoping, 1982–1992], 183–84. Beijing: People's Press, 1994.

————. 1988a. "Kexue jishu shi diyi shengchanli" [Science and technology are the number one productive force] (Sept. 5, 12, 1988). In *XSKJ*, 290–92.

————. 1988b. "Zhongguo bixu zai shijie gao keji lingyu zhanyou yixi zhi di" [China must have a place in the realm of world high technology] (Oct. 24, 1988). In *XSKJ*, 293–94.

"Deng Xiaoping zhonglun guoneiwai xingshi" [Deng Xiaoping talks broadly about the situation at home and abroad]. 1985. *Liaowang* [Outlook] (Sept. 16): 9–12.

"Diamond Films for Electronic Packaging." 2001. Website maintained by the Electro-mechanical Systems Branch, Lewis Research Center, U.S. National Aeronautics and Space Administration (NASA). Website accessed Mar. 12, 2001. <http://powerweb.lerc.nasa.gov/psi/DOC/diamond.html>.

Ding, Arthur. 1996. "China's Defense Finance: Content, Process, and Administration." *China Quarterly*, no. 146 (June): 428–42.

Dingman, Roger. 1988/89. "Atomic Diplomacy during the Korean War." *International Security* 13, no. 3: 50–91.

Dittmer, Lowell. 1987. *China's Continuous Revolution.* Berkeley: University of California Press.

Dong Kegong, Song Guangming, and Zou Anshou. 1982. "Nie Rongzhen tongzhi yu zhishifenzi" [Comrade Nie Rongzhen and the intellectuals]. *Guangming Ribao* [Brightness Daily] (Oct. 4).

Dong Shitang. 1989. "Taihu zhi yan de yi xiang mingzhu" [A pearl on the bank of Lake Tai]. In *HGYZW*, 407–9.

Donnithorne, Audrey. 1967. *China's Economic System.* New York: Praeger.

Du Chunshi. 1989. "Lüge: ji youyexuejia Zhang Peilin" [Green song: A description of the uranium metallurgist Zhang Peilin]. In Shenjian ju, ed., 1989: 103–16.

Duan Zijun, ed. 1988. *Dangdai Zhongguo de Hangkong Gongye* [Contemporary China's Aviation Industry]. Beijing: Contemporary China Series Press (Chinese Academy of Social Sciences).

Eckstein, Alexander. 1977. *China's Economic Revolution.* Cambridge, UK: Cambridge University Press.

Fan Shuo. 1990. *Ye Jianying zai 1976* [Ye Jianying in 1976]. Beijing: Central Party School Press.

————, ed. 1995. *Ye Jianying Zhuan* [A Biography of Ye Jianying]. Beijing: Contemporary China Series Press (Chinese Academy of Social Sciences).

Feigenbaum, Evan A. 1997. "The Military Transforms China: The Politics of Strategic Technology from the Nuclear to the Information Age." Ph.D. diss. Stanford University.

Fitzgerald, Anne, and Charles P. Slichter, eds., 1976. *Solid State Physics in the People's Republic of China.* Committee on Scholarly Communication with the People's Republic of China. CSCPRC Report no. 1. Washington, DC: National Academy of Sciences.

Folta, Paul Humes. 1992. *From Swords to Plowshares: Defense Industry Reform in the PRC.* Boulder, CO: Westview.

Foot, Rosemary. 1988/89. "Nuclear Coercion and the Ending of the Korean Conflict." *International Security* 13, no. 3: 92–112.

"Formulation of Strategic Objectives in Automation Technology Completed." 1989. *Keji Ribao* [Science Daily] (Nov. 17): 1. Trans. and reprinted in JPRS-CST (Feb. 8, 1990): 4.

Francis, Corinna-Barbara. 1996. "Reproduction of *Danwei* Institutional Features in China's Market Economy: The Case of Haidian District's High-Tech Sector." *China Quarterly,* no. 147 (Sept.): 839–59.

Frankenstein, John. 1999. "China's Defense Industries: A New Course?" In James C. Mulvenon and Richard H. Yang, eds., *The People's Liberation Army in the Information Age,* 187–216. Santa Monica, CA: RAND.

Frankenstein, John, and Bates Gill. 1996. "Current and Future Challenges Facing China's Defense Industries." *China Quarterly,* no. 146 (June): 394–427.

Frieman, Wendy. 1989. "China's Military R&D System: Reform and Reorientation." In Simon and Goldman, eds., 1989: 251–86.

———. 1994. "People's Republic of China: Between Autarky and Interdependence." In Etel Solingen, ed., *Scientists and the State: Domestic Structures and the International Context,* 127–44. Ann Arbor: University of Michigan Press.

Fu Zhenguo. 1990. "Zhongguo 543 budui miwen" [The secret story of China's Unit 543]. *Junshi Shijie* [Military World] (Feb.): 25–32.

Galison, Peter, and Bruce Hevly, eds. 1992. *Big Science: The Growth of Large-Scale Research.* Stanford, CA: Stanford University Press.

Gao Chao. 1989. "He wuqi yanjiu zuzhi guanli gongzuo de jingyan he jiaoxun" [Experience and lessons of organizational and managerial work in nuclear weapons research]. In *HGYZW,* 220–22.

Garver, John. 1988. *Chinese-Soviet Relations, 1937–1945: The Diplomacy of Chinese Nationalism.* New York: Oxford University Press.

General Office of the State Science and Technology Commission. 1992. "Guojia kexue weiyuanhui" [The State Science and Technology Commission]. *Renmin Ribao* [People's Daily] (Dec. 27).

Gill, Bates. 1999. "Chinese Defense Procurement Spending: Determining Intentions and Capabilities." In James Lilley and David Shambaugh, eds., *China's Military Faces the Future,* 195–227. Washington, DC: American Enterprise Institute.

Gittings, John. 1974. *The World and China, 1922–1972.* London: Eyre Methuen.

Goad, G. Pierre, and Lorien Holland. 2000. "China Joins the Linux Bandwagon." *Far Eastern Economic Review* (Feb. 17, 2000): 8.

Godwin, Paul H. B. 1978. "China's Defense Dilemma: The Modernization Crisis of 1976 and 1977." *Contemporary China* 2, no. 3 (Dec.): 63–85.

Goldman, Merle. 1971. *Literary Dissent in Communist China.* New York: Atheneum.

Goncharov, Sergei N., John W. Lewis, and Xue Litai. 1993. *Uncertain Partners: Stalin, Mao, and the Korean War.* Stanford, CA: Stanford University Press.

Granovetter, Mark S. 1973. "The Strength of Weak Ties." *American Journal of Sociology* 78, no. 6: 1361–81.

Green, Michael J. 1995. *Arming Japan: Defense Production, Alliance Politics, and the Postwar Search for Autonomy.* New York: Columbia University Press.

Gregory, Ted. 2000. "Sparkling Discovery for Science." *Chicago Tribune.* On-line edition. Website accessed Feb. 13, 2001. <http://chicagotribune.com/news/local/article/0,1051, SAV-0009120250,00.html>.

Grow, Roy F. 1989. "Acquiring Foreign Technology: What Makes the Technology Transfer Process Work?" In Simon and Goldman, eds., 1989: 319–46.

Gu Mainan. 1987. "Cong xiao balu dao kexuejia" [From a little Eighth Route Armyman to a scientist]. *Liaowang* [Outlook] (Jan. 5): 13–16.

Gu Yu. 1989. "'Sanjia' ningcheng yi gu sheng xietong gongguan: yi wo guo guofang keyan de chuqi fazhan" ["Three families" pulling together the strands of a rope in a cooperative attack: Recalling the early years of our country's military research and development]. In *HGYZW,* 466–69.

Guo Jinping. 1988. "Da zhendong, da zhuanbian, da kaituo: fang Zhongguo kexueyuan yuanzhang Zhou Guangzhao" [Great shock, great shift, great opening: An interview with CAS president Zhou Guangzhao]. *Qiushi* [Seek Truth], no. 6: 21–27.

"Guowuyuan xinxihua gongzuo lingdao xiaozu chengli: zuzhang Zou Jiahua qiangdiao fazhan xinxi chanye bixu lizu guoqing" [The State Council Leading Group on "informationization" is formed: Group leader Zou Jiahua stresses that the development of the information industry must be based upon national conditions]. 1996. *Qiao Bao* [Overseas Chinese Daily] (May 28): 6.

Haas, Peter M. 1992. "Introduction: Epistemic Communities and International Policy Coordination." *International Organization* 46, no. 1 (Winter): 1–36.

Halpern, Nina P. 1989. "Scientific Decision Making: The Organization of Expert Advice in Post-Mao China." In Simon and Goldman, eds., 1989: 157–74.

Hamer, Dean H., and Shain-dow Kung. 1989. *Biotechnology in China.* Washington, DC: National Academy of Sciences Press.

Hamrin, Carol Lee. 1990. *China and the Challenge of the Future: Changing Political Patterns.* Boulder, CO: Westview.

Hamrin, Carol Lee, and Suisheng Zhao, eds. 1995. *Decision-Making in Deng's China: Perspectives from Insiders.* Armonk, NY: M. E. Sharpe.

Han Huaizhi, and Tan Jingqiao, eds. 1989. *Dangdai Zhongguo Jundui de Junshi Gongzuo* [Military Work of the Contemporary Chinese Armed Forces]. Vol. 1. Beijing: Contemporary China Series Press (Chinese Academy of Social Sciences).

Han Jinteng. 1988. "Guofang gao jishu dui junshi he jingji de yingxiang" [The influence of defense technology on military affairs and the economy]. *Junshi Shijie* [Military World] 1, no. 3 (Nov./Dec.): 32–33.

Hao Yunpeng. 1996. "China's Eighth Five Year Plan on Telecoms." Unpublished memorandum. Center for International Security and Arms Control, Stanford University.

Harris, James. 1991. "Interpreting Trends in Chinese Defense Spending." In *China's Economic Dilemmas in the 1990s: The Problems of Reforms, Modernization, and Independence,* 676–84. Study papers submitted to the Joint Economic Committee of the Congress of the United States. Vol. 2. Washington, DC: Government Printing Office.

He Jianzhang, and Wang Zhiye, eds. 1984. *Zhongguo Jihua Guanli Wenti* [Problems in the Management of China's State Plan]. Beijing: Chinese Academy of Social Sciences Press.

He Long. 1960. "Zai junwei kuoda huiyi shang de fayan (jielu)" [Speech at an enlarged meeting of the Central Military Commission (excerpt)] (Oct. 14, 1960). In *He Long Junshi Wenxuan* [Selected Military Works of He Long], 582–88. Beijing: Liberation Army Press.

He Zhengwen. 1989. "Caijun baiwan ji qi qianqian houhou" [On the eve and after the demobilization of one million troops]. In Yang Guoyu, ed., *Ershiba Nian Jian: Cong Shi Zhengwei dao Zongshuji* [Twenty-eight Years: From a Division Political Commissar to General Secretary], 246–55. Shanghai: Shanghai Literature and Art Press.

He Zuoxiu. 1992. "The Importance of Basic Research as Revealed in the Development of Missiles and the Atomic Bomb." *Keji Ribao* [Science and Technology Daily] (Dec. 4, 1992): 6. Trans. and reprinted in JPRS-CST (Mar. 2, 1993): 1–2.

Herring, Jan P. 1985. "U.S. Electronics Industry: Military-Civilian Interdependence." Unpublished manuscript. Motorola Company.

"Hewei '863' jihua?" [What is the "863" plan?]. 1992. *Zhongguo Junzhuanmin Bao* [China Defense Conversion News] (Jan. 21).

Holloway, David. 1980. "War, Militarism, and the Soviet State." *Alternatives,* no. 6 (Mar.): 59–92.

———. 1982. "Innovation in the Defence Sector." In Ronald Amann and Julian Cooper, eds., *Industrial Innovation in the Soviet Union,* 276–367. New Haven, CT: Yale University Press.

———. 1994. *Stalin and the Bomb: The Soviet Union and Atomic Energy, 1939–1956.* New Haven, CT: Yale University Press.

Hong Xuezhi. 1990. *Kang Mei Yuan Chao Zhanzheng Huiyilu* [Memoir of the War to Resist America and Aid Korea]. Beijing: Liberation Army Literature and Art Press.

Hsieh, Alice Langley. 1962. *Communist China's Strategy in the Nuclear Era.* Englewood Cliffs, NJ: Prentice-Hall.

Hu Haitang. 1989. "High Tech R&D Program (Project 863) Surges Ahead." *Zhongguo Keji Luntan* [Forum on China's Science and Technology], no. 5 (Sept. 18): 8–10. Trans. and reprinted in JPRS-CST (Jan. 4, 1990): 1–3.

Huang Ma. 1990. "Zhongguo shunli youxiao de tuijin ba liu san gao jishu jihua" [China smoothly and effectively implements the 863 high technology plan]. *Renmin Ribao* [People's Daily], overseas edition (Aug. 1).

Huang Xuhua. 1989. "Shuixia jujing: he qianting zongti yanjiu sheji" [The great underwater whale: The comprehensive design plan for the nuclear submarine]. In *HGYZW,* 396–98.

Huang Yao, and Yang Mingzhe, eds. 1996. *Luo Ruiqing Zhuan* [A Biography of Luo Ruiqing]. Beijing: Contemporary China Series Press (Chinese Academy of Social Sciences).

Huchet, Jean François. 1998. "The China Circle and Technological Development in the Chinese Electronics Industry." In Naughton, ed., 1998: 254–85.

Hughes, Thomas P. 1998. *Rescuing Prometheus.* New York: Pantheon.

Hui Yongzheng. 1998. "China's High-Tech Successes." *The Bridge* (U.S. National Academy of Engineering) 28, no. 2 (Summer).

Ji Tingyu, and Huo Youdong. 1989. "Liu Bocheng changdao de xunlingshi zhihuifa" [Liu Bocheng's proposed method for training in the task of command]. *Junshi Lishi* [Military History], no. 2: 39–43.

Jiang Shengjie. 1988. "Shenqie de huainian" [Cherished memories]. *Shenjian* [Magic Sword], no. 1 (Jan.): 8–10.

———. 1989. "Zili gengsheng de guanghui pianzhang: he ranliao hou chuli shiye de jianli he fazhan" [A glorious chapter in our efforts at self-reliance: The creation and development of nuclear fuel reprocessing]. In *HGYZW,* 210–12.

Jing Cheng. 1986. "Shou'ao cangqiong: wo guo diyi ke renzao weixing 'dongfanghong 1 hao' shang tian ji" [A first trip to the sky: The story of the ascent to the heavens of our country's first man-made satellite, the "East is Red-1"]. In Political Department of the Ministry of the Space Industry and Space Section of the Magic Sword Literature and Art Society, eds., *Hangtian Shiye Sanshi Nian* [Thirty Years of the Space Cause], 22–60. Beijing: Space Navigation Press (Ministry of the Space Industry).

Joffe, Ellis. 1965. *Party and Army: Professionalism and Political Control in the Chinese Officer Corps, 1949–1964.* Harvard East Asian Monographs. Cambridge, MA: East Asian Research Center, Harvard University.

Joseph, William A., Christine P. W. Wong, and David Zweig, eds. 1991. *New Perspectives on the Cultural Revolution.* Cambridge, MA: Harvard University Press.

Kargon, Robert, Stuart W. Leslie, and Erica Schoenberger. 1992. "Far Beyond Big Science: Science Regions and the Organization of Research and Development." In Galison and Hevly, eds., 1992: 334–54.

Ke Gaochu. 1989. "Plans, Achievements of High-Tech Development Areas Outlined." *Keyan Guanli* [Scientific Research Management], no. 1 (Jan.): 10, 11–15. Trans. and reprinted in JPRS-CST (Aug. 31, 1989): 1–5.

Kennedy, Thomas L. 1978. *The Arms of Kiangnan: Modernization in the Chinese Ordnance Industry, 1860–1895.* Boulder, CO: Westview.

———. 1994. "Li Hung-chang and the Kiangnan Arsenal, 1860–1895." In Samuel C. Chu and Kwang-Ching Liu, eds., *Li Hung-chang and China's Early Modernization,* 197–215. Armonk, NY: M. E. Sharpe.

Kevles, Daniel J. 1992. "K_1S_2: Korea, Science, and the State." In Galison and Hevly, eds., 1992: 312–33.

Kirby, William C. 1989. "Technocratic Organization and Technological Development in China: The Nationalist Experience and Legacy, 1928–1953." In Simon and Goldman, eds., 1989: 23–43.

Kong Deyong. 1991. "Song Jian." In *ZXKZ,* 899–910.

Lampton, David Michael. 1987. "Chinese Politics: The Bargaining Treadmill." *Issues and Studies* (Taipei) 23, no. 3 (Mar.): 11–41.

Lardy, Nicholas R. 1978a. *China's Economic Planning.* White Plains, NY: M. E. Sharpe.

———. 1978b. *Economic Growth and Distribution in China.* Cambridge, UK: Cambridge University Press.

———. 1987. "The Chinese Economy Under Stress, 1958–1965." In Roderick MacFarquhar and John K. Fairbank, eds., *The Cambridge History of China.* Vol. 14, *The People's Republic of China.* Part 1, *The Emergence of Revolutionary China, 1949–1965,* 360–97. Cambridge, UK: Cambridge University Press.

———. 1998. *China's Unfinished Economic Revolution.* Washington, DC: Brookings Institution Press.

Lawrence, Susan M. 2000. "Blasting Off." *Far Eastern Economic Review* (Aug. 3, 2000): 30.

"Letter of the Central Committee of the CPC [CCP] of February 29, 1964 to the Central Committee of the CPSU." 1964. In *Seven Letters Exchanged Between the Central Committees of the Communist Party of China and the Communist Party of the Soviet Union,* 21–41. Beijing: Foreign Languages Press.

Levin, Richard, et al. 1987. "Appropriating the Returns from Industrial R&D." *Brookings Papers on Economic Activity* 3: 783–831.

Lewis, John Wilson, and Hua Di. 1992. "China's Ballistic Missile Programs: Technologies, Strategies, Goals." *International Security* 17, no. 2 (Fall): 5–40.

Lewis, John Wilson, Hua Di, and Xue Litai. 1991. "China's Defense Establishment: Solving the Arms Export Enigma." *International Security* 15, no. 4 (Spring): 87–109.

Lewis, John Wilson, and Xue Litai. 1988a. *China Builds the Bomb.* Stanford, CA: Stanford University Press.

———. 1988b. "Chinese Strategic Weapons and the Plutonium Option." *Critical Technologies Newsletter* (Los Alamos National Laboratory) (Apr./May): 4–14.

————. 1989. *Military Readiness and the Training of China's Sailors*. Stanford, CA: Center for International Security and Arms Control, Stanford University.

————. 1994. *China's Strategic Seapower: The Politics of Force Modernization in the Nuclear Age*. Stanford, CA: Stanford University Press.

Li Debin. 1985. "Wushi niandai wo guo yinjin jishu shebei de wenti" [The issue of our country's importation of technology and equipment during the 1950s]. *Beijing Daxue Xuebao* [Beijing University Journal], Philosophy and Social Science Series (Apr.): 78–85.

Li Guojie. 1996. "Wo guo jisuanji chanye fazhan fangxiang yu shiming" [The development direction and mission of our country's computer industry]. *Renmin Ribao* [People's Daily] (May 7): 3.

Li Jue, ed. 1987. *Dangdai Zhongguo de He Gongye* [Contemporary China's Nuclear Industry]. Beijing: Contemporary China Series Press (Chinese Academy of Social Sciences).

Li Mancun, ed. 1992. *Liu Bocheng Zhuan* [A Biography of Liu Bocheng]. Beijing: Contemporary China Series Press (Chinese Academy of Social Sciences).

Li Ping. 1986. "Zhou Enlai he si ge xiandaihua" [Zhou Enlai and the Four Modernizations]. *Liaowang* [Outlook], overseas edition (Jan. 6): 6–7.

Li Pu, and Shen Rong. 1986. "Ta shi wo de hao laoshi: Xiao Ke jiangjun tan Liu shuai" [He was my good teacher: General Xiao Ke talks about Marshal Liu]. *Liaowang* [Outlook] (Nov. 10): 13–14.

Li Qi, and Nie Li. 1989. "Fazhan guofang jianduan jishu de yixiang zhongda juece: ji 'qi yi ba' yuanwang celiang chuandui de jiancheng" [An important decision to develop sophisticated defense technology: Recalling Project "718," the Yuanwang instrumentation fleet]. In *HGYZW*, 393–95.

Li Runshan. 1985. "Luo Ruiqing." In Zou Jiahua, ed., 1985: 373.

Li Xu'e. 1989. "Some Problems in the Development of China's High Technology Industry." *Zhongguo Keji Luntan* [Forum on Science and Technology in China], no. 6 (Nov. 18): 2–6, 14. Trans. and reprinted in JPRS-CST (Mar. 15, 1992): 1–5.

————. 1992. "Several Torch Plan Problems: A Speech Made on December 16, 1992 to the National-Level Conference of Torch Plan Project Evaluation Experts." *Keji Ribao* [Science and Technology Daily] (Feb. 20): 1. Trans. and reprinted in JPRS-CST (May 12, 1992): 53–56.

Li Zhiqing, ed. 1993. *Zui Xin Guofang Keji Cidian* [Newest Dictionary of Defense Science and Technology]. Beijing: Liberation Army Press.

Lian Jun. 1992. "There Is a Secret Arsenal Beneath Helan Shan." *Ningxia Ribao* [Ningxia Daily] (Sept. 12): 3. Trans. and reprinted in Foreign Broadcast Information Service. Daily Report. China. (Dec. 8): 12.

"Lian Tong Gets Its Call Through." 1994. *Business China*. Newsletter published by the Economist Intelligence Unit, London (Aug. 8).

Liang Shoupan. 1989. "Haifang daodan de fazhan" [The development of the coastal defense missile]. In *HGYZW*, 270–71.

Liao Gailong, and Fan Yuan, eds. 1989. *Who's Who in China: Current Leaders.* Bilingual edition. Beijing: Foreign Languages Press.

Liao Guoliang, ed. 1991. *Mao Zedong Junshi Sixiang Fazhan Shi* [A History of the Development of Mao Zedong's Military Thought]. Beijing: Liberation Army Press.

Lieberthal, Kenneth G., and David M. Lampton, eds. 1992. *Bureaucracy, Politics, and Decision Making in Post-Mao China.* Berkeley: University of California Press.

Lieberthal, Kenneth, and Michel Oksenberg. 1988. *Policy Making in China: Leaders, Structures, and Processes.* Princeton, NJ: Princeton University Press.

Lin Jin. 1993a. "Hangtian daohang dingwei lilun jichu: shijian he kongjian lilun zai cikao" [The theoretical foundations of navigation in space: A reexamination of the theory of space and time]. Unpublished manuscript. Institute 12 of the First Academy, Ministry of the Aerospace Industry.

————. 1993b. "Theoretical Foundations for Space Navigation and Reexamination of Theory of Space and Time." Paper presented at the Second William Fairbank Conference on Relativistic Gravitational Experiments in Space and Related Theoretical Topics (Dec. 12–16), Hong Kong.

Lin Yushu, Liu Yuren, and Zheng Wenyi. 1992. "Rely on Scientific and Technical Progress to Promote Defense Construction." Interview with CMC Vice Chairman Liu Huaqing, *Keji Ribao* [Science and Technology Daily] (Mar. 14): 1–2. Trans. and reprinted in JPRS-CST (June 29, 1992): 21–24.

Lindbeck, John M. H. 1961. "Organization and Development of Science." In Sidney H. Gould, ed., *Sciences in Communist China,* 3–58. Washington, DC: American Association for the Advancement of Science. Publication no. 68.

Liu Bocheng. 1956. "Guanyu peiyang kexue jiaoshi he kexue yanjiu gongzuo de wenti" [On the question of developing scientific training and scientific research]. In *Liu Bocheng Junshi Wenxuan* [Selected Military Works of Liu Bocheng], 546–48. Beijing: Liberation Army Press.

Liu Boluo. 1987. "Wo guo jianduan keji shiye ningju zhe Zhou zongli de xinxue" [Premier Zhou spent his heart and blood for the cause of our country's sophisticated science and technology]. In *BDS,* 341–56.

————. 1989. "Zhou zongli yu Zhonggong zhongyang zhuanmen weiyuanhui" [Premier Zhou and the Central Special Commission of the Chinese Communist Party]. In *HGYZW,* 128–34.

Liu Huinian. 1985. "Zhongda de zhanlüe juece: zhongyang junwei changwu fuzhuxi Yang Shangkun tan jundui gaige tizhi, jingjian zhengbian" [An important strategic decision: Executive vice-chairman of the Central Military Commission Yang Shangkun talks about how to reform the military system and streamline and reorganize the army]. *Liaowang* [Outlook] (July 8): 10–12.

Liu Huinian, and Yi Jianru. 1985. "Zhongguo jundui zai gaige zhengbian zhong qianjin: fang Zhongguo renmin jiefangjun zong canmouzhang Yang Dezhi" [China's army is advancing under reform and streamlining: An interview with the chief of the PLA General Staff Yang Dezhi]. *Liaowang* [Outlook] (July 29): 10–11.

Liu Jie. 1987. "Wo guo yuanzineng shiye de juecezhe he zuzhizhe" [The decision maker and organizer of our country's nuclear energy enterprise]. In *BDS,* 314–30.

Liu Jing. 1995. "'Golden' Character Project Series Sees Real Advances." *Jisuanji Shijie* [Computer World], no. 4 (Jan. 25): 1. Trans. and reprinted in JPRS-CST (Mar. 17, 1995): 12.

Liu Jingzhi. 1989. "Huichu he qianting lantu de ren: ji daodan he qianting zong shejishi Huang Xuhua" [The man who drew up the blueprint for the nuclear submarine: A description of Huang Xuhua, the chief designer of the nuclear-powered missile submarine]. *Junshi Shijie* [Military World] 2, no. 4 (June/July): 12–15.

Liu Luhong. 1996. "Challenge and Opportunity: Prospects for Sino-American Cooperation in Defense Industry Conversion." Unpublished manuscript. Center for International Security and Arms Control, Stanford University.

Liu Mingye, and Wu Quanyuan. 1991. "Ci Yungui." In *ZXKZ,* 854–64.

Liu Shaoqiu. 1988. "U-2 gaokong zhenchaji fumieji" [A record of the downing of the U-2 high-altitude reconnaissance aircraft]. Part 1. *Junshi Shijie* [Military World] 1, no. 1 (Aug.): 43–44.

———. 1989. "U-2 gaokong zhenchaji fumieji" [A record of the downing of the U-2 high-altitude reconnaissance aircraft]. Part 2. *Junshi Shijie* [Military World] 1, no. 2 (Sept./Oct.): 56–58.

Liu Sheng. 1993. *Nie Rongzhen zai Jin-Cha-Ji* [Nie Rongzhen in the Jin-Cha-Ji Border Area]. Beijing: Art Press.

Liu Shuqing, and Zhang Jifu. 1985. "Jinglei: wo guo di yi ke yuanzidan baozhaji" [A clap of thunder: Recalling our country's first detonation of an atomic bomb]. In Shenjian ju [Magic Sword Division], ed., *Mimi Licheng* [A Secret Course], 1–57. Beijing: Atomic Energy Press (Ministry of the Nuclear Industry).

Liu Wenjun. 1993. "Jiangxi hekuang jubu weinan" [Nuclear mining in Jiangxi]. *Zhongguo Junzhuanmin Bao* [China Defense Conversion News]. 2 parts. (Oct. 8): 3; (Oct. 12): 3.

Liu Xing. 1989. "Guti yunzai huojian yanzhi de 'san bu qu'" [A three-part account of the development of the solid-propellant carrier rocket]. Parts 1 and 2. *Junshi Shijie* [Military World] 2, no. 1 (Jan./Feb.): 65–68; 2, no. 2 (Mar./Apr.): 34–41.

Liu Xiyao. 1987. "Wo dang zongli lianluoyuan qianhou" [Around the time of my service as the premier's liaison]. In *BDS,* 331–40.

Liu Yadan, Liu Shaoqiu, and Lu Jing. 1988. "Weile hailang zhong tengqi julong: ji Zhongguo qianting yunzai huojian zong shejishi Huang Weilu" [A dragon emerges from the waves: A description of Huang Weilu, chief designer of China's submarine-launched carrier rocket]. *Junshi Shijie* [Military World] 1, no. 1 (Aug.): 47–48.

Liu Yichang, ed. 1993. *Gao Jishu Zhanzheng Lun* [On High Technology Warfare]. PLA Academy of Military Sciences multivolume series on high-tech warfare. Beijing: Military Sciences Press.

Liu Yin, ed. 1987. *Dangdai Zhongguo de Dianzi Gongye* [Contemporary China's Electronics Industry]. Beijing: Chinese Academy of Social Sciences Press.

Lu Da. 1989. "Gangtie yejin cailiao wei guofang fuwu sishi nian" [Metallurgical materials have served national defense for forty years]. In *HGYZW,* 476–77.

Lu Yanxiao, and Liu Xichen. 1991. "Zhongguo minyong he jishu kaifa de xianzhuang yu qianjin" [The present situation and the prospects for civilian use of nuclear technology]. Conference paper from a meeting on international cooperation in defense conversion (Oct. 22), Beijing.

Luo Laiyong. 1995. *Ha Jungong Hun: Zhongguo Guofang Keji Rencai Peiyang Jishi* [The Soul of the Harbin College of Military Engineering: A True Record of Personnel Training for China's Military Science and Technology]. Beijing: Central Party School Press.

Ma Jingsheng. 1995. "Cheng ru rongyi jianxin" [Ease becomes hardship]. In Cai Xianghua, ed., *Zhongguo Nü Jiangjun* [China's Female Generals], 37–81. Beijing: Liberation Army Art Press.

MacFarquhar, Roderick. 1974. *The Origins of the Cultural Revolution.* Vol. 1, *Contradictions Among the People, 1956–1957.* New York: Columbia University Press.

Manion, Melanie. 1992. "Politics and Policy in Post-Mao Cadre Retirement." *China Quarterly,* no. 129 (Mar.): 1–25.

Mann, James. 1998. *About Face: A History of America's Curious Relationship with China from Nixon to Clinton.* New York: Random House.

Mao Zedong. 1937. "Shijian lun" [On practice] (July 1937). In *Mao Zedong Xuanji* [Selected Works of Mao Zedong]. Vol. 1, 259–73. Beijing: People's Press, 1970 ed.

———. 1945. "Kang Ri zhanzheng shengli hou de shiju he women de fangzhen" [The situation and our policy after the victory in the War of Resistance Against Japan] (Aug. 13, 1945). In *Mao Zedong Xuanji* [Selected Works of Mao Zedong]. Vol. 4. Beijing: People's Press, 1969 ed.

———. 1950. "Guanyu zucheng Zhongguo renmin zhiyuanjun de mingling" [Order establishing the Chinese People's Volunteers] (Oct. 8, 1950). In *Jianguo Yilai Mao Zedong Wengao* [Selected Manuscripts of Mao Zedong since the Founding of the People's Republic]. Vol. 1, Sept. 1949–Dec. 1950, 543–44. Restricted circulation edition. Beijing: Central Documents Press (CCP Central Committee), 1987.

———. 1954a. "Zai guofang weiyuanhui diyi ci huiyi shang de jianghua" [Speech at the first meeting of the National Defense Commission] (Oct. 18, 1954). In *Mao Zedong Junshi Wenji* [Collected Military Works of Mao Zedong]. Vol. 6, 358–59. Beijing: Military Sciences Press (PLA Academy of Military Sciences) and Central Documents Press (CCP Central Committee), 1993.

―――. 1954b. "Women yinggai gongtong nuli lai fangzhi zhanzheng, zhengqu chijiu heping" [We should work together to end war and fight for an enduring peace] (Oct. 23, 1954), based on a transcript of a meeting with Jawaharlal Nehru. In Ministry of Foreign Affairs and Central Documents Research Section of the Chinese Communist Party, eds., *Mao Zedong Waijiao Wenxuan* [Selected Diplomatic Works of Mao Zedong], 168–74. Beijing: Central Documents Press (CCP Central Committee) and World Knowledge Press (Ministry of Foreign Affairs), 1994.

―――. 1956. "Lun shi da guanxi" [On the Ten Major Relationships], yuanshi wenxian quanwen [full text of the original document]. In "Mao Zedong 'Lun shi da guanxi' jianghua yuanwen yu gongbuwen zhi duizhao" [Mao Zedong's speech "On the Ten Major Relationships": A comparison of the original and official texts]. In *Feiqing Yuebao* [Enemy Information Monthly] (Taipei) 19, no. 8 (Feb. 5, 1977): 87–105.

―――. 1958. "Tong Sulian zhu Hua dashi Long Jin de tanhua" [A discussion with the Soviet ambassador to China, Yudin] (July 22, 1958), based on a meeting transcript. In Ministry of Foreign Affairs and Central Documents Research Section of the Chinese Communist Party, eds., *Mao Zedong Waijiao Wenxuan* [Selected Diplomatic Works of Mao Zedong], 322–33. Beijing: Central Documents Press (CCP Central Committee) and World Knowledge Press (Ministry of Foreign Affairs), 1994.

―――. 1961. "Zai guanyu Riben jingji zhengce he guofang gongye fazhan wenti de yifen cailiao shang de piyu" [Written comments on materials concerning Japanese economic policies and military industrial development] (July 13, 1961). In *Jianguo Yilai Mao Zedong Wengao* [Selected Manuscripts of Mao Zedong Since the Founding of the People's Republic]. Vol. 9, Jan. 1960–Dec. 1961, 530–31. Restricted circulation edition. Beijing: Central Documents Press (CCP Central Committee), 1996.

―――. 1964. "Talk on the Third Five Year Plan." In *Miscellany of Mao Tse-tung Thought (1949–1968)*. Joint Publications Research Service, no. 61269-2 (Feb. 20, 1974).

McDougall, Walter A. 1985. *The Heavens and the Earth: A Political History of the Space Age*. New York: Basic Books.

Me Wen. 1989. "Qian Xuesen boshi tan jianduan jishu" [Dr. Qian Xuesen talks about sophisticated technology]. *Junshi Shijie* [Military World], no. 7: 20–21.

Ministry of Posts and Telecommunications General Office, ed. 1993. *Jiushi Niandai Zhongguo Youdian Tongxin* [China's Posts and Telecommunications in the 1990s]. Beijing: People's Posts and Telecommunications Press.

National Advanced Materials Committee of China. 1998. Website accessed Jan. 12, 1998. <www.chimeb.edu.cn/e_863/S&PTAM.htm>.

―――. 2001. Website accessed Mar. 1, 2001. <www.chimeb.edu.cn/e_863/index.htm>.

National Center for Intelligent Computing (Beijing). n.d. "System Introduction," and background materials on the Shuguang 1 [Dawn 1] and
Shuguang 1000 [Dawn 1000] parallel multiprocessors, and NCIC Press
desktop publishing software.

Naughton, Barry. 1988. "The Third Front: Defence Industrialization in the
Chinese Interior." *China Quarterly*, no. 115 (Sept.): 351–86.

———. 1991. "Industrial Policy During the Cultural Revolution: Military
Preparation, Decentralization, and Leaps Forward." In Joseph, Wong, and
Zweig, eds., 1991: 153–81.

———, ed. 1998. *The China Circle: Economics and Electronics in the PRC,
Taiwan, and Hong Kong*. Washington, DC: Brookings Institution Press.

Nie Rongzhen. 1952. "Qin Chao Meijun jinxing xijunzhan ji wo caiqu cuoshi
qingkuang de baogao" [Report on bacteriological warfare by the U.S. Army
invaders of Korea and the steps we should take in response] (Feb. 28, 1952).
In *NRJW*, 365–66.

———. 1956. "Jiaqiang wo guo yanzhi daodan wenti de baogao" [Report on how
to strengthen our country's missile research and development] (Oct. 25, 1956).
In *NRJW*, 395–97.

———. 1960a. "Guanyu jianduan, jingmi shengchan he yanjiu gongzuo zhong
de qingjie he zhixu wenti" [On the questions of hygiene and order in sectors
concerned with sophisticated and precision production and research] (Oct. 4,
1960). In *NRJW*, 409–11.

———. 1960b. "Zai wuyuan gaoji zhishifenzi zuotanhui shang de jianghua"
[Speech at a discussion meeting of high-level intellectuals of the Fifth
Academy] (Oct. 9, 1960). In *NRJW*, 412–23.

———. 1961. "Guanyu daodan, yuanzidan ying jianchi gongguan de baogao"
[Report on our insistence on a concerted effort in the missile and atomic
bomb programs] (Aug. 20, 1961). In *NRJW*, 488–95.

———. 1963. "Zai jungong lingdao ganbu huiyi shang de jianghua" [Speech at a
meeting of leading cadres from the military industry] (Apr. 2, 1963). In *NRJW*,
496–518.

———. 1983. *Nie Rongzhen Huiyilu* [Memoirs of Nie Rongzhen]. Vol. 1. Beijing:
Soldier's Press (Liberation Army Press).

———. 1986. *Nie Rongzhen Huiyilu* [Memoirs of Nie Rongzhen]. Vol. 3. Beijing:
Liberation Army Press.

———. 1992. *Nie Rongzhen Junshi Wenxuan* [Selected Military Works of Nie
Rongzhen]. Beijing: Liberation Army Press.

"Nie Rongzhen tongzhi tan zhishifenzi wenti" [Comrade Nie Rongzhen talks
about the problem of intellectuals]. 1982. *Guangming Ribao* [Brightness Daily]
(Sept. 1).

Office of Technology Assessment. 1987. *Technology Transfer to China*. Washington,
DC: Government Printing Office.

"Official Calls for the Acceleration of Risk Investment." 1998. *Asia Pulse* (Oct. 1).

Ostrov, Benjamin C. 1991. *Conquering Resources: The Growth and Decline of the PLA's Science and Technology Commission for National Defense.* Studies in Contemporary China. Armonk, NY: M. E. Sharpe.

Ostry, Sylvia, and Richard R. Nelson. 1995. *Techno-nationalism and Techno-globalism.* Washington, DC: Brookings Institution Press.

Panofsky, Wolfgang K. H. 1977. *Observations on High Energy Physics in China: Report of a Visit to the People's Republic (October 5–22, 1976).* United States-China Relations Program Report no. 3. Stanford, CA: United States-China Relations Program, Stanford University.

———. 1992. "SLAC and Big Science: Stanford University." In Galison and Hevly, eds., 1992: 129–46.

Peng Dehuai. 1958. "Ba wo jun jianshe chengwei youliang de xiandaihua de geming jundui" [Build our military into first-rate and modern revolutionary armed forces]. In *Peng Dehuai Junshi Wenxuan* [Selected Military Works of Peng Dehuai], 602–19. Beijing: Central Documents Press.

Peng Min, ed. 1989. *Dangdai Zhongguo de Jiben Jianshe* [Contemporary China's Capital Construction]. Vol. 1. Beijing: Contemporary China Series Press (Chinese Academy of Social Sciences).

Peng Shilu. 1988. "Yanjin er cixiang de weiren: huiyi Zhou zongli dui yanzhi he qianting de guanhuan" [A rigorous but kindly great man: Recollections of Premier Zhou's concern for the nuclear submarine program]. *Shenjian* [Magic Sword], no. 1 (Jan.): 12–16.

Peng Shilu, and Zhao Renkai. 1989. "Canjia wo guo he qianting yanzhi gongzuo de tihui" [A few words about our participation in research and development on our country's nuclear submarine]. In *HGYZW,* 206–9.

Peng Ziqiang. 1986. "Yuanwang: wo guo di liu hangtian zonghe celiang chuandui de dansheng" [Yuanwang: The birth of our country's sixth comprehensive spaceflight measuring fleet]. *Shenjian* [Magic Sword], no. 6 (Dec.): 2–9.

Pillsbury, Michael, ed. 1996. *Chinese Views of Future Warfare.* Washington, DC: National Defense University.

Pollack, Jonathan D. 1984. *The Lessons of Coalition Politics: Sino-American Security Relations.* R-3133-RF. Santa Monica, CA: RAND.

———. 1992. "Structure and Process in the Chinese Military System." In Lieberthal and Lampton, eds., 1992: 151–80.

Powell, Ralph L. 1955. *The Rise of Chinese Military Power, 1875–1912.* Princeton, NJ: Princeton University Press.

"Progress with Intelligent Automation and Invigorate China's Manufacturing Industries." 1989. *Keji Ribao* [Science Daily] (Nov. 20): 1. Trans. and reprinted in JPRS-CST (Feb. 8, 1990): 7.

Pye, Lucian. 1981. *The Dynamics of Chinese Politics.* Cambridge, MA: Oelgeschlager, Gunn, and Hain.

Qi Shengping. 1985. "Jianfu qi shidai de shiming: ji junshi xueyuan de chuangjianren Liu Bocheng yuanshuai" [Shouldering the burden of the era's mission: Recalling the founder of the Military Academy Marshal Liu Bocheng]. *Xinghuo Liaoyuan* [A Single Spark Can Start a Prairie Fire], no. 2: 3–15.

Qian Haiyan, ed. 1994. *Restructuring the Military Industry: Conversion for the Development of the Civilian Economy.* Beijing: China Association for the Peaceful Use of Military Industrial Technology and United Nations Department of Development Support and Management Services.

Qian Xuesen. 1987a. "Scientific-Social Revolution and Reform." Part 2. Abridged English trans. of speech to senior Party and government cadres entitled "On Questions Related to the Understanding of the New Technological Revolution." *Beijing Review* 30, no. 12 (Mar. 23, 1987): 21–24.

———. 1987b. "Zhou zongli rang wo gao daodan" [Premier Zhou let me work on missiles]. In *BDS,* 287–304.

Qian Zongjue. 1993a. "Development Course of Nation's Fiber Optic Communications." *Zhongguo Dianzi Bao* [China Electronics News] (Nov. 29): 3. Trans. and reprinted in JPRS-CST (Jan. 24, 1994): 37.

———. 1993b. "Application, Development Directions for Domestic Fiber Optic Communications." *Zhongguo Dianzi Bao* [China Electronics News] (Dec. 6): 3. Trans. and reprinted in JPRS-CST (Jan. 24, 1994): 37–38.

———. 1994. "Information Superhighway, China National Super Information Infrastructure." *Keji Daobao* [Science and Technology Review], no. 11 (Nov.): 19–24. Trans., excerpted, and reprinted in JPRS-CST (Apr. 5, 1995): 67–69.

Reardon-Anderson, James. 1991. *The Study of Change: Chemistry in China, 1840–1949.* Cambridge, UK: Cambridge University Press.

Reich, Robert. 1987. "The Rise of Technonationalism." *Atlantic Monthly* (May): 62–71.

Ren Gongyue. 1986. "Jisuanji fuzhu zhizao" [Computer-aided manufacture]. In Sun Junren, ed., vol. 2, 1986: 424–25. Beijing: Chinese Encyclopedia Press.

Riskin, Carl. 1975. "Maoism and Motivation: Work Incentives in China." In Victor Nee and James Peck, eds., *China's Uninterrupted Revolution,* 415–61. New York: Pantheon.

———. 1991. "Neither Plan nor Market: Mao's Political Economy." In Joseph, Wong, and Zweig, eds., 1991: 133–52.

Roberts, Dexter. 1999. "How Legend Lives Up to Its Name." *Business Week* (Feb. 15): 75–78.

Rosenberg, Nathan. 1982. *Inside the Black Box: Technology and Economics.* Cambridge, UK: Cambridge University Press.

Ross, Robert. 1995. *Negotiating Cooperation: The United States and China, 1969–1989.* Stanford, CA: Stanford University Press.

Saint-Gobain Semiconductors. 2001. "Diamond Film." Technology capabilities, material properties, and applications information brochure. Company website. Website accessed Mar. 12, 2001. <www.saintgobainsemi.com/brochure/ Diamond%20Film/DIAMOND.html>.

Samuels, Richard J. 1994. *Rich Nation, Strong Army: National Security and the Technological Transformation of Japan.* Ithaca, NY: Cornell University Press.

Sandia National Laboratory. 2001. Synthetic Aperture Radar Research Description, Applications, and Laboratory Research Activities. Websites accessed Feb. 13, 2001. <www.sandia.gov/RADAR/whatis.html>; <www.sandia.gov/RADAR/sarapps.html>.

"Scientists Pick Top News Stories." 1996. *China Daily* (Beijing) (Dec. 25): 9.

Secretarial Division of the General Office of the State Council and Comprehensive Division of the General Office of the State Editorial Committee, eds. 1995. *Zhongyang Zhengfu Zuzhi Jigou* [Organizations and Structures of the Central Government]. Beijing: China Development Press.

Selden, Mark. 1993. *The Political Economy of Chinese Development.* Armonk, NY: M. E. Sharpe.

Sender, Henny. 1997. "Wrong Number." *Far Eastern Economic Review* (Hong Kong) 160, no. 2 (Jan. 9): 74–76.

Shambaugh, David. 1994. "Wealth in Search of Power: The Chinese Military Budget and Revenue Base." Paper delivered at the Conference on Chinese Economic Reform and Defense Policy (July), Hong Kong.

———. 1997. "Building the Party-State in China, 1949–1965: Bringing the Soldier Back In." In Timothy Cheek and Tony Saich, eds., *New Perspectives on State Socialism in China,* 125–50. Armonk, NY: M. E. Sharpe.

Shang Mu. 1989. "Progress in China's High Technology Research and Development Plan." *Keji Ribao* [Science Daily] (Nov. 17): 4. Trans. and reprinted in JPRS-CST (Feb. 8, 1990): 2–4.

Shao Yihai. 1989. "Zai he kexue jishu gaodi shang: ji he wulixuejia Wang Ganchang" [Atop the heights of nuclear science and technology: A description of the nuclear physicist Wang Ganchang]. In Shenjian ju, ed., 1989: 1–14

Shen Rongjun, ed. 1988. *Zhongguo Guofang Keji* [China Defense Research and Development]. Beijing: China Defense Science and Technology Information Center (COSTIND).

Shen Xincun. 1991. "Tu Shou'e." In *ZXKZ,* 865–71.

Shenjian ju [Magic Sword Division], ed. 1989. *He Kexuejia de Zujin* [Footprints of the Nuclear Scientists]. Beijing: Atomic Energy Press (Ministry of the Nuclear Industry).

Shi Changxu. 1989. "Wo guo diyi dai zhuzhao duokong wolun yepian de dansheng he tuiguang" [The birth of our country's first-generation cast multi-holed turboprop aircraft]. In *HGYZW,* 474–75.

Shi Wenting. 1987. "Gaige shi shixian wo jun xiandaihua de biyou zhi lu" [Reform is the indispensable path for realizing the modernization of our armed forces]. *Jiefangjun Bao* [Liberation Army Daily] (Sept. 18).

Shi Zhe. 1988. "Zai xin Zhongguo dansheng de qianye" [On the eve of new China's birth]. In *Mianhuai Liu Shaoqi* [Cherish the Memory of Liu Shaoqi], 214–26. Beijing: Central Documents Press.

———. 1998. *Zai Lishi Juren Shenbian: Shi Zhe Huiyilu* [At the Side of Historical Giants: Memoirs of Shi Zhe], rev. ed. Beijing: Central Party School Press.

Shi Zhongquan, and Chen Dengcai, eds. 1994. *Deng Xiaoping zai 1978: "Zhongguo di'er ci Geming" de Weida Kaituan* [Deng Xiaoping in 1978: The Great Beginning of "China's Second Revolution"]. Shenyang: Liaoning People's Press.

Shi Zhu. 1986. "Luo Peilin." In Sun Junren, ed., 1986: 582.

Shirk, Susan L. 1985. "The Politics of Industrial Reform." In Elizabeth J. Perry and Christine Wong, eds., *The Political Economy of Reform in Post-Mao China,* 195–221. Cambridge, MA: Harvard University Press.

Shu Deqi, and Ling Xiang. 1992. "Zhongguo he qianting dansheng ji" [A record of the birth of China's nuclear-powered submarine]. Part 1. *Zhongguo Junzhuanmin Bao* [China Defense Conversion News] (Aug. 11): 4.

Simon, Denis Fred. 1989. "Technology Transfer and China's Emerging Role in the World Economy." In Simon and Goldman, eds., 1989: 289–318.

Simon, Denis Fred, and Merle Goldman, eds. 1989. *Science and Technology in Post-Mao China.* Cambridge, MA: Harvard University Press.

Solinger, Dorothy J. 1982. "The Fifth National People's Congress and the Process of Policymaking: Reform, Readjustment, and the Opposition." *Asian Survey* 22, no. 12: 1238–75.

———. 1984. *Chinese Business Under Socialism: The Politics of Domestic Commerce in Contemporary China.* Berkeley: University of California Press.

———. 1991. *From Lathes to Looms: China's Industrial Policy in Comparative Perspective, 1979–1982.* Stanford, CA: Stanford University Press.

———. 1993. "Economic Reform via Reformulation: Where Do Rightist Ideas Come From?" *China's Transition From Socialism: Statist Legacies and Market Reforms, 1980–1990,* 13–26. Armonk, NY: M. E. Sharpe.

Song Jian. 1982. "Development in Mathematical Demography." *Theoretical Biology* 22, no. 3: 382–91.

———. 1991. "Fazhan keji zhenxing Zhonghua: Zhongguo keji shiye de huigu he zhanwang" [Expand science and technology to vigorously develop China: The past and future of China's science and technology cause]. *Keji Ribao* [Science and Technology Daily] (Dec. 16).

Song Ke. 1981. "Kangzhan qian zhongyang junwei zuzhi jiankuang" [An organizational introduction to the Central Military Commission before the war to resist Japan]. *Dangshi Yanjiu* [Party History Research], no. 4: 62–64.

Song Renqiong. 1994. *Song Renqiong Huiyilu* [Memoirs of Song Renqiong]. Beijing: Liberation Army Press.

Song Wencong. 1989. "Jian qi III feiji yanzhi zhong shejishi xitong" [The designer system in research and development of the J-7III fighter plane]. In *HGYZW,* 330–32.

State Science and Technology Commission. 1986. *Zhongguo Kexue Jishu Zhengce Zhinan* [A Guide to Chinese Science and Technology Policy]. *Baipishu* 1 [White Paper no. 1]. Beijing: Science and Technology Documents Press.

————. 1995. *A Guide to Chinese Science and Technology Policy*. White Paper no. 6. Trans. and reprinted in JPRS-CST (July 9, 1996).

Stokes, Mark A. 1999. *China's Strategic Modernization: Implications for the United States*. Carlisle Barracks, PA: Strategic Studies Institute, U.S. Army War College.

Stoneman, Paul. 1987. *The Economic Analysis of Technology Policy*. Oxford: Oxford University Press.

Su Fangxue. 1990. "Wang Ganchang jiaoshou: yi ge jiechu de Zhongguoren" [Professor Wang Ganchang: An outstanding Chinese]. *Zhongguo Zuojia* [Chinese Writers], no. 2: 5–24.

Sun Huaisu. 1991. "Chen Fangyun." In *ZXKZ*, 803–9.

Sun Junren, ed. 1986. *Zhongguo Dabaike Quanshu: Dianzi yu Jisuanji* [The Chinese Encyclopedia: Electronics and Computers]. Beijing: Chinese Encyclopedia Press.

Sun Yefang. 1979. *Shehuizhuyi Jingji de Ruogan Lilun Wenti* [Certain Theoretical Questions in Socialist Economics]. Beijing: People's Press.

Sun Zhenhuan. 1991. *Zhongguo Guofang Jingji Jianshe* [China's National Defense Economic Construction]. Beijing: Academy of Military Sciences Press.

Suttmeier, Richard P. 1989. "Science, Technology, and China's Political Future: A Framework for Analysis." In Simon and Goldman, eds., 1989: 375–96.

————. 1998. "Scientific Cooperation and International Conflict Management in U.S.-China Relations, 1978–Present." In Allison L. de Cerreno and Alexander Keynan, eds., *Scientific Cooperation, State Conflict: The Role of Scientists in Mitigating International Discord*. Vol. 866. New York: New York Academy of Sciences.

Tan Bangzhi. 1991. "Ren Xinmin." In *ZXKZ*, 834–43.

Tan Jingqiao, ed. 1990. *Kang Mei Yuan Chao Zhanzheng* [The War to Resist America and Aid Korea]. Beijing: Contemporary China Series Press (Chinese Academy of Social Sciences).

Tan Keming, and Zhang Zi'an. 1989. "Longmenshan xia you yi tiao 'long': huo guojia keji jinbu yi deng jiang de '1485' kangbao jibo guan ciji" [A "dragon" at the foot of Longmen Mountain: The story of the "1485" antidetonation shock tube]. *Junshi Shijie* [Military World] 2, no. 3 (May): 73–75.

Tao Hanzhang. 1987. "Ting Liu Bocheng tongzhi tan 'Sun Zi'" [Listening to Comrade Liu Bocheng discuss "Sun Zi"]. In Wu Zaowen, ed., *Liu Bocheng Huiyilu* [Recollections of Liu Bocheng]. Vol. 3, 325–33. Shanghai: Shanghai Art Press.

Tao Tao. 1989. "Huagong xin cailiao zai wei guofang keji gongzuo fuwu zhong cheng chang" [New chemical materials will grow to maturity through service to national defense science, technology, and industry]. In *HGYZW*, 478–80.

Teiwes, Frederick C. 1986. "Peng Dehuai and Mao Zedong." *Australian Journal of Chinese Affairs*, no. 16: 81–98.

"Ten Megawatt High Temperature Gas-Cooled Reactor (HTR-10)." 2001. System Description. Qinghua University Institute of Nuclear Technology Website.

Website accessed Feb. 13, 2001. <www.inet.tsinghua.edu.cn/English/project/htr10.htm>.

Tian Xuan, ed. 1993. *Nie Rongzhen.* Chengdu: Sichuan People's Press.

Tu Shou'e. 1989. "Zuohao xinghao zong shejishi gongzuo de jidian tihui" [A few words about how to be a good project chief designer]. In *HGYZW,* 267–69.

University of Alaska. 2001. Alaska Synthetic Aperture Radar Facility Website. Website accessed Feb. 13, 2001. <www.asf.alaska.edu/user_serv/sar_faq.html>.

U.S. Department of Agriculture. 1994. "PATN Patent Bibliographic Information, Hybrid Rice Production Utilizing Male Sterile Rice Plants, Applicant Li Qinxiu, Application Number 9066640, Patent Number 05304722, Series Code 7." Website accessed Feb. 20, 2001. <www.nal.usda.gov/bic/Biotech_Patents/1994patents/05304722.html>.

U.S. Embassy Science and Technology Section, Beijing. 1996. "Chinese Challenges in Absorbing and Producing New Technology." Public Section Report (Dec.).

———. 1999. "Breaking the PRC Iron Test Tube: Peer Review and the National Natural Science Foundation of China." Public Section Report (May).

———. 2001. "Academy Report: China Should Look to World Market for Raw Materials." On-line Public Section Report, "EST Update" (Feb. 2). Website accessed Feb. 8, 2001. <www.usembassy-china.org.cn/english/sandt/estnews0202.htm>.

U.S. National Security and Military/Commercial Concerns with the People's Republic of China. 1999. <www.house.gov./coxreport>.

Wang Bingqian. 1980. "Report on the Final State Accounts for 1979, the Draft State Budget for 1980, and the Financial Estimates for 1981." In *Main Documents of the Third Session of the Fifth National People's Congress of the People's Republic of China,* 48–85. Beijing: Foreign Languages Press.

Wang Chunyuan. 1996. *China's Space Industry and Its Strategy of International Cooperation.* Stanford, CA: Center for International Security and Arms Control, Stanford University.

Wang Daheng. 1989. "Guangxue lao you xin qiancheng duansijin" [Optics, old and new: A bright future]. In *HGYZW,* 470–73.

Wang Ganchang. 1989. "Wo guo he kexue jishu de fazhan" [The development of our country's nuclear science and technology]. In *HGYZW,* 196–98.

Wang Jinghu. 1989. "Wo zhi shi shiwan fen zhiyi: ji he wulixuejia Zhou Guangzhao" [I am but one among a hundred thousand: A description of the nuclear physicist Zhou Guangzhao]. In Shenjian ju, ed., 1989: 257–78.

Wang Li, ed. 1993. *Dangdai Zhongguo de Bingqi Gongye* [Contemporary China's Ordnance Industry]. Beijing: Contemporary China Series Press (Chinese Academy of Social Sciences).

Wang Lixin, and Joseph Fewsmith. 1995. "Bulwark of the Planned Economy: The Structure and Role of the State Planning Commission." In Hamrin and Zhao, eds., 1995: 51–65.

Wang Nianyi. 1989. "Mao Zedong fadong 'wenhua da geming' shi dui xingshi de gujia" [Mao Zedong's appraisal of the situation when he unleashed the "Cultural Revolution"]. In Xiao Yanzhong, ed., *Wannian Mao Zedong* [The Late Years of Mao Zedong], 32. Beijing: Spring and Autumn Press.

Wang Shaoguang. 1996. "Estimating China's Defense Expenditure: Some Evidence from Chinese Sources." *China Quarterly,* no. 147 (Sept.): 889–911.

Wang Shiguang, and Zhang Xuedong. 1989. "Fazhan junshi dianzi cujin guofang xiandaihua" [Develop military electronics to promote defense modernization]. In *HGYZW,* 420–25.

Wang Shouyun. 1991. "Qian Xuesen." In *ZXKZ,* 767–802.

———. 1994. "Conversion, Dual Use, and Transfer of Technology." In Qian Haiyan, ed., 1994: 105–7.

Wang Shuntong, ed. 1994. *Zhongguo Kexue Jishu Xiehui* [The China Association for Science and Technology]. Beijing: Contemporary China Series Press. (Chinese Academy of Social Sciences).

Wang Yan, ed. 1993. *Peng Dehuai Zhuan* [A Biography of Peng Dehuai]. Beijing: Contemporary China Series Press (Chinese Academy of Social Sciences).

Wang Yannian. 1991. "Management of Keypoint S&T Projects Discussed." *Zhongguo Keji Luntan* [Forum on Science and Technology in China], no. 6 (Nov.): 7–9. Trans. and reprinted in JPRS-CST (May 12, 1992): 3–5.

Wang Yougong. 1990. "Zhongguo kexuejia de guangrong shiming: Zhou Guangzhao yuanzhang tan weilai shinian keji fazhan" [The glorious mission of China's scientists: CAS president Zhou Guangzhao talks about the next ten years of scientific development]. *Renmin Ribao* [People's Daily], overseas edition (Jan. 4).

Wang Zengfan. 1991. "Xie Xide." In *ZXKZ,* 171–77.

Wang Zhaoquan. 1991. "Dalian Jianxin gongsi de chuangjian ji qi dui Huaihai zhanyi de zhiyuan" [The creation of the Dalian Jianxin corporation and its contribution to the Huaihai campaign]. *Junshi Lishi* [Military History], no. 1: 48–49.

Wang Zhenxian. 1987. "Guofang buzhang de shouzhang" [The defense minister's stick]. In *Shenjian Zhulian Qu* [The Melody of Casting a Magic Sword]. Beijing: Liberation Army Art Press.

"Wanren toushen 'ba liu san' jihua, wo gao jishu yanjiu chengguo fengshuo" [Ten thousand throw themselves into the work of the "863" Plan; our country scores great successes in high technology research and development]. 1991. *Renmin Ribao* [People's Daily], overseas edition (Apr. 23).

Wei Long. 2000. "China Expands Space Breeding Program Using Recoverable Satellites." Space Daily.com. (May 29). Website accessed Feb. 18, 2001. <www.spacedaily.com>.

Wei Wei, ed. 1991. *Nie Rongzhen Zhuan* [A Biography of Nie Rongzhen]. Beijing: Contemporary China Series Press (Chinese Academy of Social Sciences).

Wei Wei, and Zhou Junlun. 1990. "Nie Rongzhen de junshi lilun gaisu" [A quick survey of Nie Rongzhen's military thought]. *Junshi Lishi* [Military History], no. 4: 14–18.

"Wo jun lingdaoren tan gao jishu yu zhanzheng" [The leader of our armed forces talks about high technology and war]. 1993. *Zhongguo Junzhuanmin Bao* [China Defense Conversion News] (Nov. 30).

Wong, Christine P. W. 1991. "The Maoist 'Model' Reconsidered: Local Self-Reliance and the Financing of Rural Industrialization." In Joseph, Wong, and Zweig, eds., 1991: 183–96.

Wu Hongye. 1987. "Shixian caijun yibaiwan" [Realizing the reduction of the armed forces by one million]. *Renmin Ribao* [People's Daily] (Aug. 5).

Xiao Jingguang. 1988. *Xiao Jingguang Huiyilu* [Memoirs of Xiao Jingguang]. *Xuji* [Sequel]. Beijing: Liberation Army Press.

Xiao Yuanzhen, Yang Bingxing, and Liu Jiaqing. 1994. "Discussion of Key Elements and Strategic Goals of China's High and New Technology Development Zones." *Jishu Jingji yu Guanli Yanjiu* [Research in Technical Economics and Management], no. 6 (Nov.-Dec.): 46–47. Trans. and reprinted in JPRS-CST (May 3, 1995): 1–2.

Xie Guang, ed. 1992. *Dangdai Zhongguo de Guofang Keji Shiye* [Contemporary China's National Defense Science and Technology Cause]. 2 vol. Beijing: Contemporary China Series Press (Chinese Academy of Social Sciences).

Xie Linhuo. 1986. "Zhou zongli zai yuanzidan baozha yihou gei women de zhibiao" [The instructions given to us by Premier Zhou after the explosion of the atomic bomb]. *Shenjian* [Magic Sword], no. 4 (Aug.): 17–18.

Xing Qiuheng. 1989. "Zili gengsheng fazhan wo guo de guti huojian shiye [Develop our country's solid rocketry cause through self-reliance]. In *HGYZW,* 281–82.

Xiong Xianghui. 1992. "Dakai Zhong Mei guanxi de qianzou: 1969 nian si wei laoshuai dui guoji xingshi yanjiu he jianyi de qianqian houhou" [Prelude to the opening of Sino-American relations: The prelude and aftermath of research and proposals made by four veteran marshals in 1969]. *Zhongguo Dangshi Ziliao* [Materials on the History of the Chinese Communist Party], no. 42: 56–96.

Yamamura, Kozo. 1977. "The Role of Meiji Militarism in Japan's Technical Progress." *Journal of Economic History* 37, no. 1 (Mar.): 113–35.

Yan Fangming. 1987. "San xian jianshe shuping" [A review of Third Line construction]. *Dangshi Yanjiu* [Party History Research], no. 4: 70–73.

Yan Jingtang. 1983. "Zhongyang junwei yan'ge gaikuang" [A survey of the evolution of the Central Military Commission]. *Dangshi Yanjiu* [Party History Research], no. 2: 50–59.

Yan Shuheng. 1994. "China's Nuclear Science Technology Applied to the National Economy." In Qian Haiyan, ed., 1994: 267–69.

Yang Jiachi. 1990. "Zhongguo kongjian jishu de erci kaifa yu yingyong" [The development and uses of space technology spin-offs in China].

Shijie Daodan yu Hangtian [World Missiles and Spacecraft] (Ministry of the Aerospace Industry), no. 5 (May): 3–6.

Yang Lianghua. 1992. "Shi Changxu, Wang Daheng deng xuebu weiyuan tichu zhongyao jianyi zhiding zhanlüe cuoshi cujin gao jishu chanyehua" [Shi Changxu, Wang Daheng, and other members of the Academy of Sciences submit an important suggestion to draw up strategic measures for speeding up high technology industrialization]. *Renmin Ribao* [People's Daily], overseas edition (Apr. 25).

Yang Lizhong, ed. 1991. *Gao Jishu Zhanlüe: Kua Shiji de Tiaozhan yu Jiyu* [High Technology Strategy: Challenges and Opportunities at the Turn of the Century]. Beijing: Military Sciences Press (Academy of Military Sciences).

Yang, Mayfair Mei-hui. 1994. *Gifts, Favors, and Banquets: The Art of Social Relationships in China.* Ithaca, NY: Cornell University Press.

Yang Taifang, ed. 1993. *Dangdai Zhongguo de Youdian Shiye* [Contemporary China's Posts and Telecommunications]. Beijing: Contemporary China Series Press (Chinese Academy of Social Sciences).

Yang Wanqing. 1992. "Renmin kongjun de shouren silingyuan, Liu Yalou" [The first commander of the People's Air Force, Liu Yalou]. In CCP Central Party History Institution, eds., *Zhonggong Dangshi Ziliao* [Materials on the History of the Chinese Communist Party], 215–58. Beijing: CCP Party History Press.

Yang Zhaobo. 1991. "'Ba wu' qijian 'huoju jihua' jiang zhongdian zhuahao 10 xiang gongzuo" [The "Torch Plan" will emphasize 10 tasks during the Eighth Five-Year Plan]. *Keji Ribao* [Science and Technology Daily] (Dec. 16).

Yang Zhenming. 1990. "Zhongguo hangtian cekongwang" [China's space tracking network]. *Shijie Daodan yu Hangtian* [World Missiles and Spacecraft] (Ministry of the Aerospace Industry), no. 11. (Nov.): 18–22.

Yao Yilin. 1980. "Report on the Arrangements for the National Economic Plans for 1980 and 1981." In *Main Documents of the Third Session of the Fifth National People's Congress of the People's Republic of China,* 5–47. Beijing: Foreign Languages Press.

Yeh, K. C. 1967. "Soviet and Chinese Industrialization Strategies." In Donald W. Treadgold, ed., *Soviet and Chinese Communism,* 326–63. Seattle: University of Washington Press.

Yin Jiamin. 1988. "Chen Geng dajiang chuangjian Ha jungong" [General Chen Geng created the Harbin College of Military Engineering]. *Yanhuang Zisun* [The Chinese], no. 4: 28–31.

Yuan Houchun. 1987. "Baiwan da cai jun" [The great one-million-man reduction of the armed forces]. *Kunlun* [Kunlun], no. 2: 4–8.

Yuan Yaojun. 1989. "Guofang keji qingbao shiye de huigu yu zhanwang" [The past and future of China's defense science and technology information cause]. In *HGYZW,* 514–16.

Zerega, Blaise. 1999. "Hong Kong Fooey: Can the Former British Colony Become the Silicon Valley of Asia Even as It Assimilates into Greater China?" *Red Herring* (Nov.): 134.

Zhang Aiping. 1961. "Yuanzineng gongye jianshe de jiben qingkuang he jidai jiejue de ji ge wenti" [The basic situation and outstanding issues in the construction of the atomic energy industry] (Nov. 14, 1961). In *Zhang Aiping Junshi Wenxuan* [Selected Military Works of Zhang Aiping], 218–45. Beijing: Long March Press (PLA General Political Department).

———. 1983. "Guanyu guofang xiandaihua de ruogan wenti" [On certain issues in the modernization of national defense]. *Hongqi* [Red Flag], no. 5: 21–24.

———. 1986. "Guofang keji gongye zhanxian de zhanlüe zhuanbian" [A strategic shift on the defense science and technology industry front] (June 11, 1986). Speech at a discussion conference on defense science and technology industry. In *Zhang Aiping Junshi Wenxuan* [Selected Military Works of Zhang Aiping], 568–72. Beijing: Long March Press (PLA General Political Department).

———. 1989. "Huigu yu jiyu" [A look to the past and future]. In *HGYZW*, 74–78.

———, ed. 1994. *Zhongguo Renmin Jiefang Jun* [The People's Liberation Army]. 2 vols. Beijing: Contemporary China Series Press (Chinese Academy of Social Sciences).

Zhang Bingfu. 1989. "An Excellent Start in Implementing the Torch Plan." *Zhongguo Keji Luntan* [Forum on Science and Technology in China], no. 6 (Nov. 18): 11–14. Trans. and reprinted in JPRS-CST (Mar. 15, 1990): 10–14.

Zhang Chunting. 1987. "Zhongguo heneng zhuanjia, Jiang Shengjie" [The Chinese nuclear expert, Jiang Shengjie]. In *Liaowang* [Outlook], overseas edition (July 20): 5–6.

Zhang Jiayu. 1983. "Renmin zhanzheng sixiang de fazhan" [The development of People's War ideology]. *Mao Zedong Sixiang Yanjiu* [Research on Mao Zedong Thought], no. 3: 25–30.

Zhang Jingfu. 1989. "Zhongguo kexueyuan yu guofang kexue jishu" [The Chinese Academy of Sciences and defense science and technology]. In *HGYZW*, 79–81.

Zhang Jun, ed. 1986. *Dangdai Zhongguo de Hangtian Shiye* [Contemporary China's Space Cause]. Beijing: Contemporary China Series Press (Chinese Academy of Social Sciences).

Zhang Qinsheng, and Zhang Chunting. 1986. "Gaige yu kaifang gei Zhongguo jundui dailai shenke bianhua" [Reform and opening to the outside world have produced thoroughgoing changes in the Chinese army]. *Liaowang* [Outlook], overseas edition (Apr. 21): 19.

Zhang Zhenhua. 1989. "Jianguo chuqi wo jun yuanxiao de zhengguihua jianshe" [The standardization of our army's academies and schools in the early years of the People's Republic]. *Junshi Lishi* [Military History], no. 4: 14–18.

Zhao, Suisheng. 1995. "The Structure of Authority and Decision-Making." In Hamrin and Zhao, eds., 1995: 233–45.

Zheng Wenhan. 1988. "Peng zong zai 50 niandai dui wo jun jianshe de zhongda gongxian" [Chief Peng's important contributions to our army's construction during the 1950s]. *Junshi Lishi* [Military History], no. 6: 3–7.

Zhi Shaozeng. 1989. "Zhongyang junshi weiyuanhui fazhan gaiyao" [A summary of the development of the Central Military Commission]. *Junshi Lishi* [Military History], no. 6: 50–54.

Zhi Yin. 1989. "Zhongguo he qianting de jiemi" [The secret of China's nuclear submarine]. *Junshi Shijie* [Military World] 2, no. 6: 15–21.

Zhong Yixin, and Wang Baiyi. 1994. "Communications High Tech Research Plan." *Keji Ribao* [Science and Technology Daily] (Nov. 16): 7. Trans. and reprinted in JPRS-CST (Feb. 13, 1995): 11.

"Zhongguo 'ba liu san' jihua dui san da xinxing chanye gongxian" [Some contributions of China's "863" Plan to three newly emerging key industries]. 1996. *Renmin Ribao* [People's Daily] (Apr. 25): 3.

"Zhongguo gongcheng wuli yanjiuyuan" [The Chinese Academy of Engineering Physics] (Mianyang, Sichuan). n.d. Introductory materials published by the Ninth Academy.

Zhongguo Junzhuanmin Bao [China Defense Conversion News], 1993 (Apr. 2).

Zhongguo Renmin Jiefangjun Jiangshuai Minglu [Biographical Dictionary of Generals and Marshals of the Chinese People's Liberation Army]. 1986. 3 vols. Beijing: Liberation Army Press.

Zhou Changqing. 1985. "Jianchi gaige, cujin junmin jiehe" [Persist in reform, promote military-civilian integration]. *Jingji Guanli* [Economic Management], no. 4: 15–21.

Zhou Enlai. 1956. "Guanyu zhishifenzi de baogao" [Report on intellectuals]. In *Zhou Enlai Xuanji* [Selected Works of Zhou Enlai]. Vol. 2, 158–89. Beijing: People's Press.

Zhou Yiping. 1989. "Ba rencai peiyang tidao zhanlüe diwei shanglai" [Build a pool of technical talent as a matter of national strategy]. In *HGYZW,* 121–24.

Zhu Guangya. 1987. "Wo guo baozha diyi ke yuanzidan qianhou" [Around the time of our country's first detonation of an atomic bomb]. In *BDS,* 305–13.

————. 1988. "Dui Zhou Enlai zongli lingdao jianduan kexue jishu de pianduan huiyi" [Fragmentary recollections of Premier Zhou Enlai's leadership of sophisticated science and technology]. *Shenjian* [Magic Sword], no. 1 (Jan.): 4–7.

————. 1998. "Engineering in China (Editorial)." *The Bridge* (U.S. National Academy of Engineering) 28, no. 2 (Summer).

Zhu Lilan. 1989. "Development of High Tech, Basic Research Explored." *Zhongguo Keji Luntan* [Forum on Science and Technology in China], no. 3 (May): 4–5, 7. Trans. and reprinted in JPRS-CST (Sept. 26, 1989): 1–2.

Zhu Youdi. 1990. "Guofang huaxue gongye xingcheng xin tixi" [The formation of a new national defense chemical industrial system]. *Jiefangjun Bao* [Liberation Army Daily] (Dec. 7).

Zhu Youwen, Feng Yi, and Xu Dechi. 1994. *Gao Jishu Tiaojian Xia de Xinxi Zhan* [Information Warfare Under High Technology Conditions]. Beijing: Military Sciences Press (Academy of Military Sciences).

Zhu Yuanshi. 1991. "Liu Shaoqi yi jiu si jiu nian mimi fang Su" [Liu Shaoqi's secret visit to the Soviet Union in 1949]. *Dang de Wenxian* [Party Documents], no. 3: 74–80.

Zou Jiahua, ed. 1985. *Zhongguo Dabaike Quanshu: Hangkong Hangtian* [The Chinese Encyclopedia: Aviation and Space]. Beijing: Chinese Encyclopedia Press.

INDEX

3M Corporation, 206
04 Bureau (New Technologies Bureau of CAS), 62
09 Office (Lingjiuban), 52–53, 81, 124
321 Program, 285n93
585th Institute (thermonuclear experiments), 247
728th Academy (Shanghai Reactor Engineering Research and Design Academy), 247
863 Plan, 8, 141–43, 193, 218–24.
  see also specific sector topics; allocation of funds, competitive bidding system for, 165–69; basics of original proposal, 157–58; biographies of sponsoring scientists, 154–57; cross-system horizontal collaboration, 169–73, 182; decision-making authority, 171–72; Deng Xiaoping's acceptance of, 141–42, 157, 158–62; economic development, national security, and technology, 157–58, 190; expansion proposals, 189, 198; expert and topic groups, 165, 169, 174–79, 199, 248–58; flattened hierarchies, 174–76; formal program, meeting establishing, 164–65; formation of, 141–43, 153; funding and budget, 166–69; goals and objectives, 162–64, 248–58; Golden Projects, 198–200; implementation to recipients, 176–78; indigenization of technology, 179, 188; innovation changes, 219–21; limitations of, 191, 220–21; "national research centers," 173; Nie Rongzhen, influence of, 142, 153, 161–62, 171, 173; organization and management, 157, 165, 169–76, 208–10, 248–58; political

support and involvement, 141–43, 161–73, 178, 188, 224; projects, 178–87; seven sectors, 157; strategic nature of, 163; Super-863 or S-863 (*chaoji 863 jihua*), 198; support for program, obtaining, 141–43, 151; symbiotic technology systems as theme of, 170; Torch Plan and, 195
921 Project, 169, 181, 183–84

abbreviations and acronyms, xi–xiii, 291
academies, *see* research and development (R&D); individual academies and institutions
ACIS, 185
Administrative Meeting (*bangong huiyi*), CMC, 122, 149
Agricultural Institute of Heilongjiang Province, 187
agriculture: breeding seeds in space, 186–87; Bumper Harvest Plan, 194; Central China Agricultural University, 186; Chinese Academy of Agricultural Sciences, 166, 186–87; pest-resistant crops, 187; state-led technological development plans, 193; two-line hybrid rice technology (*liangxi fazhi jiaodao jishu*), 185–86
air force and aircraft industry: air traffic management, 205; aircraft production *vs.* missile systems, 31–37, 84; Aviation Industrial Commission of the Ministry of National Defense, 54; Beijing University of Aeronautics and Astronautics, 184; China Aerospace Industry Corporation, 187; civilianization, 103; emphasis on conventional weaponry for, 81–82, 98;

319

Ma Hong, 114
Machine Building, Ministries
of, 42, 49–50, 245, 246.
see also individual ministries
macroeconomic policy, parametric data
in support of, 200
male-dominated field, Chinese physics
as, 270n125
"man over weapons," 18, 22
management styles, *see* bureaucratic
structures; strategic weapons public
management style
Manhattan Project, 61
Mann, James, 133
manned space program, 169, 181,
183–84, 203
Mao Zedong: biographical information,
235; change in economic policy,
consideration of, 78; death of, 38, 73,
77, 79, 90, 119; era of, 13 et seq., 71–72;
great power, China's destiny as, 265n48;
indigenous nuclear deterrent, need for,
263n33, 264n38; leadership seminars
between technical personnel and
scientists, 51; Nie Rongzhen's
interpretation of, 273n31; Nie's
contacts with, 120; nuclear weapons,
need for, 4; opposition, overruling of,
159; science, challenge to apply, 229;
Spark Plan inspired by dictum of, 194;
technonationalism argument,
conversion to, 22, 29–31, 36, 71, 116
map of China, ii
"market failure," 267n74, 279n43
market principles, 203, 207, 216–17
marshals, conferral of ranks on, 263n22
Marxist theory and S&T, 112
massively parallel processors (MPP), 181
McDougall, Walter, 37
measurement and control (*cekong*), 86
medical research, 186
medium-altitude high-speed fighter
planes (zhonggao kongsu jianjiji), 81
MEI (Ministry of the Electronics
Industry), 208, 211–14
Meitner, Lise, 61
mentoring, 67–68, 155, 182, 285n93

metallurgy development, 29, 33,
66, 271n135
Microbiology, Institute of (CAS), 167, 168
microchip technology, 189, 200
microelectronics, 83–86, 116, 117, 181
Microsoft Windows, 203
military budget and
expenditures, 95–97, 100
military industry enterprises, effect of
Deng Xiaoping policies on, 98–104
military organizational chart,
1982–1997, 123
military's role in Chinese life, 5–6,
13–14, 225–29
military's role in technological
development, xv–xvi, xix, 1–9, 13–14,
216–29; decision-making authority,
40–48, 78; demilitarization under
Deng Xiaoping (*see* demilitarization);
education and training, 66–68;
General Staff Department (GSD), 121,
123–24, 277n8; historical background,
225–29; infrastructure, 65–66;
innovation relationships, changes in,
117–18; Korean War, influence of,
16–24; modernizing visions,
competing, 21–37; organizations
and networks, 121–25; personnel,
scientific and technical, 60–65;
political support and involvement,
2–8, 46, 59, 116–21; retirement of
senior strategic weapons
patrons, 118–20; space and laser
technologies, 863 Plan, 166, 169–70;
telecommunications, 208–15
Millikan, Robert, 154
ministries, 42, 49–50, 245, 246.
see also individual ministries
Ministry of National Defense, Aviation
Industrial Commission, 54
Ministry of Posts and
Telecommunications (MPT),
208–15
Ministry of the Electronics Industry
(MEI), 208, 211–14
Ministry of the Information
Industry, 213